The Collected Works of John Dewey, 1882–1953

JOHN DEWEY

THE MIDDLE WORKS, 1899–1924

Volume 11: 1918–1919

Edited by Jo Ann Boydston
Textual Editor, Harriet Furst Simon
With an Introduction by Oscar and Lilian Handlin

Carbondale
SOUTHERN ILLINOIS UNIVERSITY PRESS

Printed in the United States of America
Designed by George Lenox

The Collected Works of John Dewey

CENTER FOR EDITIONS OF
AMERICAN AUTHORS
AN APPROVED TEXT
MODERN LANGUAGE
ASSOCIATION OF AMERICA

Editorial expenses for this edition have been met in part by grants from the National Endowment for the Humanities. Publication expenses have been met in part by grants from the John Dewey Foundation and from Mr. Corliss Lamont.

ISBN-10: 0-8093-1003-1 (cloth: alk. paper)
ISBN-13: 978-0-8093-1003-6 (cloth: alk. paper)
ISBN-10: 0-8093-2806-2 (pbk.: alk. paper)
ISBN-13: 978-0-8093-2806-2 (pbk.: alk. paper)

The Library of Congress has cataloged the original issue of this book as follows:
Dewey, John, 1859–1952.
The middle works, 1899–1924.
Vol. 11 has introd. by Oscar and Lilian Handlin.
Includes bibliographies and indexes.
1. Dewey, John, 1859–1952. 2. Education—Philosophy. I. Title.
LB875.D34 1976 370'.1'0924 76-7231
ISBN 0-8093-1003-1 (v. 11)

The paper used in this publication meets the minimum requirements of American National Standard for Information Sciences—Permanence of Paper for Printed Library Materials, ANSI Z39.48-1992. ♾

CONTENTS

INTRODUCTION

By Oscar and Lilian Handlin

In 1918, John Dewey approached his sixtieth year. His *Democracy and Education: An Introduction to the Philosophy of Education* had appeared in 1916; and he would publish *Reconstruction in Philosophy* in 1920. He had long since established his position in the fields of psychology, education and philosophy, and the professorship at Columbia gave him a vantage point from which to regard national and international affairs and from which to make his opinions known on a broad range of matters. He had easy access to the pages of scholarly and educational journals as well as to the broader audiences of the *Dial*, the *Nation*, the *New Republic* and the *Independent*. Secure in reputation, the beneficiary of intimate contacts with numerous figures in public life and in cultural affairs, Dewey could explore the full range of earlier interests and expand into entirely new areas.

The two years encompassed within this volume were relatively uneventful in his personal life. But for his country and for the world they were momentous indeed. The First World War slowly ground to its costly conclusion; and the immensely more difficult task of making peace got painfully under way. The armistice that some expected would permit a return to normalcy opened instead upon a period of turbulence that agitated further a society already unsettled by preparations for battle and by the debilitating conflict overseas.

More disturbing still was the inability to achieve stability in Europe or Asia. The failure of the colonial system that the great powers had attempted to impose upon the rest of the world in the half century before 1918 created immense problems in distant lands where traditional patterns of life had collapsed, where their replacements had scarcely begun to take form. Japan and China had participated in the war on the allied side; they both attempted to profit from the defeat of Germany and the revolution in Russia, but took different courses in the effort to do so; and the results of their efforts were as yet unclear. These unfamiliar features of the kaleidoscopic landscape about him challenged the perceptive observer.

Dewey's vigor had by no means slackened, and he regarded events at home and abroad with intense interest. He continued to express his views on the philosophy of knowledge, refining positions long since taken rather than striking out in new directions. The problems of war and peace also held his attention, as they had since 1914. And he now looked curiously out at the entirely different world of the Far East where fresh experiences awaited him.

Instrumentalism had by now attained a defined position; and admiring followers, in his own country and elsewhere, made Dewey, in effect, the founder of a school. He did not alter, modify or reformulate his basic ideas in 1918 and 1919 but continued actively to explore their implications in essays, speeches and reviews. He responded sharply to criticism and found occasion to comment on the implications of the war and of the long-term development of technology and of science. His central argument stressed the value of knowledge-based intelligence in solving all problems. The philosopher's role was to stimulate the process and to urge the imposition of adequate force and controls to make it effective.

Hence Dewey's sympathy for Hobbes who, he believed, sought to free morals and politics from divinity and, by secularizing philosophy, to give it "a strict scientific or rational form." Dewey viewed Hobbes as the forerunner of Bentham and of utilitarianism; both thinkers were protagonists in the development of a science of human nature operating through social controls in behalf of the common good.

Dewey envisioned the same role for himself, though it sometimes carried him in strange directions. Espousal of F. Matthias Alexander's call for conscious controls to resolve the conflict between the functions of the brain and those of the body provoked an attack by a one-time disciple. Randolph Bourne, who had other reasons for querulousness, criticized the rosy aspect of this conscious and manipulative view of evolution. The times were inappropriate for a philosophy of conscious control, for the war revealed how irrational, incompetent and blind man was.

But for Dewey the time was appropriate. It was precisely in the midst of the great conflict that the burden fell upon science to apply intelligence to the solution of human problems.

The urgency of the crisis left Dewey impatient with the lagging pace of the social sciences and critical of the obtuseness of scholars in those fields. The crying need for knowledge during the war exposed the deficiencies of existing formulations and formulators. The slowness of academic sociology and economics to respond to current challenges dismayed Dewey. Adherence to abstraction and impracticality and disregard of realism characteristic of those disciplines and of political science and law attached them to myths and prevented them from deploying the information by which to set up the techniques of social control. The war had shown that society was amenable to intelligent controls. But it had also revealed that the weakness of a democracy in the face of reactionary conservatism could be offset only by the organization of labor into a balancing force to the concentration of capital. Yet the social scientists had done little to further the transformation. Incapable of explaining change, they tried to fit new phenomena into old explanatory frameworks and, in effect, denied the utility of social controls in a universe they considered bound by eternal laws, in the face of which man was impotent.

On the issues of war and peace, some of the younger generation of writers had already disagreed with Dewey. Those who had expected to make his philosophy the foundation stone of a thoroughgoing social and cultural revolution painfully discovered that he would not lead where they wished to go. He had supported American entry into the war, while Randolph Bourne, among others, held to a pacifist position out of fear lest the techniques employed unleash forces unamenable to social control. Pragmatism, Dewey's critics argued, had failed to pose a valid counter-ideal. The war, they pointed out, subverted to unintended ends his much vaunted creative intelligence and demonstrated the emptiness of his assumptions about a store of human rationality. Winning the war rather than social reconstruction had become a goal of the instrumentalists he had trained. Endorsement of the Allies had placed him on the side of the old powers, still engaged in quarrels of no concern to the United States, or, indeed, to any of the people led into conflict after 1914. Furthermore, he had launched an unequivocal frontal attack on war resisters and pacifists.

For Dewey, however, the issue had all along taken a different form and he regarded his position on it as totally consistent with his earlier beliefs. Peace was not an absolute. War, although an evil, was sometimes a necessary evil to be exploited for socially beneficial goals. Between 1914 and 1917, the choice had ceased to be between peace and war. It had, rather, become one of whether the central powers or the allied countries would win. Faced with those alternatives, Dewey did not hesitate to strike the balance clearly on the side of the Allies. American participation to help them win became the only acceptable course, one followed also by Walter Lippmann and a few other younger commentators.

In fact, Dewey believed, the war gave Americans at home a welcome opportunity to expose and correct the deficiencies of the prevailing social and economic order. At last, universal recognition of the common good would transcend private greed. Unemployment, a parasitical leisure class, inefficient production and distribution, drift and lack of organization, no longer accepted as inevitable features of man's social existence, now would be liquidated as by-products of the past, alterable with the application of sufficient will, determination and force.

Dewey's eminence and national reputation drew him into novel activities concerning the coming shape of the peace. In article after article, between 1918 and 1919, he outlined his vision of the post-war world. He foresaw science applied to communal purposes, national boundaries obliterated by air navigation and world unity strengthened by recognition of the economic interdependence of all countries. A federated global government was the ultimate goal. A new politics would parallel the new diplomacy. Purely personal relationships under the old aristocratic code of honor and dignity would give way to the management of international affairs along lines similar to those in industry and modern commerce.

Within that roseate context Dewey considered the future fate of enemy territories. The problems of the Austro-Hungarian empire had earliest attracted the attention of his fellow citizens. Well before 1914, strong nationalist movements had taken root in central and eastern Europe. President Wilson unhesitatingly supported the right of self-determination, a position that won widespread approval among Americans, ready to draw parallels between the struggling new nations and their own situation a century and a half earlier. This seemed the appropriate way for the mother of republics to help spread liberty and free institutions to the Old World.

The problem was, of course, far from simple. The South Slavs, Czechs, Slovaks, Ruthenians, and Poles all were making claims to statehood, claims by no means compatible with one another. Eastern Europe was actually home to a hodgepodge of peoples. The alignments were complex, for many minorities enfolded smaller minorities—Rumanians in Hungary, Sudetens in Bohemia, Ruthenians in Polish Galicia, and Jews almost everywhere. Moreover, nationality was often defined by intellectuals remote from the mass of peasants and proletarians; and the intellectuals themselves divided further over ideological, social and religious issues.

In addition, Britain, France and Italy had their own stakes in the outcome, and the United States was not quite prepared to trust them. In fact, it was not clear what those stakes were. Hesitations on this account were among the elements that kept it from becoming a full ally; it fought the war and attempted to make the peace as "an associated power." With regard to these somewhat unfamiliar parts of Europe, the American government remained warily on guard lest the European great powers draw it along a course it did not wish to follow.

The presence in the United States of substantial populations which had migrated from the areas in dispute further complicated the situation. Americans who had thought vaguely, and disparagingly, of the new immigrants as Slavs or "hunkies" now discovered that sizeable communities of Poles, Slovaks, Czechs, Serbians and Croatians lived among them. The newcomers, strangers though they were, had participated in the war effort. Yet their cultural and family ties reached beyond the enemy lines, so that they must have known about the developing movements in the regions about to be liberated. Certainly they had more information than any citizen of older stock, in the government or outside it. But what they knew, where they stood, and what their interests were remained unclear.

The Polish Americans were the largest of these groups. Recent immigrants, mostly laborers, widely scattered in the great cities and industrial towns from the Atlantic to the Middle West, they spoke and read a language few natives understood. Sharp internal divisions complicated the problem of communicating with the Poles in the United States; local lines of division only imperfectly matched those of the old homeland. As authority collapsed in the region across which rival armies had fought for years, two prospective governments took form. Poland had been divided since the eighteenth century among Prussia, Austria and Russia; none of those countries was in a position to assert control in 1918. The vacuum was potentially dangerous and became immediately noticeable on the occasion of the tour of the United States by Ignace Paderewski, the famous pianist but also a politician of somewhat conservative leanings and prospectively the first president of the new Polish republic. Americans found it hard to make judgments about what was going on. Everyone agreed on self-determination as a principle. But how were benevolent outsiders to decide: who spoke for Poland?

That question intrigued Albert C. Barnes, a Philadelphia physician and chemist grown rich by the invention of Argyrol, and owner of a great collection of French paintings. Eager to put art to some educational use, Barnes had enrolled in Dewey's seminar at Columbia; and thus began a life-long association between the two men.

Barnes wished to discover, scientifically, the forces which operated in opposition to the development of free and democratic life among such groups as the Poles. "The idea would be to work out a practical plan, based upon first-hand knowledge, to eliminate forces alien to democratic internationalism and to promote American ideals in accordance with the principles announced by President Wilson. . . ." Barnes asked Dewey to recommend a number of Columbia students willing to study an immigrant community during the summer months; and the Polish group in Philadelphia became the subject of inquiry. It was significant that Barnes turned not to any available sociologists, or to the nearby scholars at the University of Pennsylvania, but to the man whose preeminent reputation commanded confidence. Dewey had read widely in anthropology and knew some of the sociological literature; but the subject attracted him mostly for the opportunity to test general propositions about the quality of American life.

The issues under investigation involved, from Dewey's point of view, some of the basic questions of national identity. He hoped to reach useful conclusions about the immigrants' contributions to their adopted country, about their willingness to take the road to assimilation, about the reasons for exploitation by selfish leaders callous with regard to the welfare of ordinary men and women. The attributes of nationality that furthered segregation rather than integration and the impact of all these problems on American foreign policy also puzzled him.

The outcome of the Philadelphia study confirmed what Dewey had come to suspect by 1918. Immigrants at one and the same time contributed to, and were victims of, a basic contradiction in American life. The open, welcoming and hospitable country also isolated the newcomers and prevented them from getting their fair share of its rewards, while their prejudices and ignorance exposed them to exploitation by alien interests and complicated the process of adaptation. The Detroit convention that aimed to unite the Poles behind the Paderewski faction actually was organized by self-seeking leaders, who hardly represented the constituency for which they claimed to speak.

The Philadelphia study led to a wider assignment on behalf of the United States government. Assistants did most of the work; Dewey coordinated their efforts and wrote up the results. He gave the Military Intelligence Branch first a preliminary report on the Detroit convention and then a lengthy analysis of the Polish community in the United States. An account of the tortuous course of Polish history after the third partition in 1795 led to an examination of the causes for the current divisions among the Poles in America. The tedious survey was necessary, Dewey pointed out, because much of the disarray had roots in European problems unrelated to American conditions. Reactionary Catholic priests, a National Council openly opposed to Americanization, a conservative faction which once saw Poland's salvation in the Tsar, assorted enemies of socialism, pro-German agents, and a domineering Mme. Paderewski all combined further to confuse the issues.

These fratricidal struggles increased industrial unrest in the United States, hampered the war effort, and deprived the American government of valuable sources of information and of active aid in the Liberty Loan and Red Cross drives. Only outside pressure, such as officials in Washington could exert, would restore unity.

Dewey's study was not particularly enlightening and had little measurable influence on the outcome at Versailles or, later, in Poland. But it may have injected an element of discouragement into his thinking about the war and its results. He was less disillusioned than the younger writers and critics of the 1920s would be. His disappointment arose not from any sense that failure had been inevitable, but rather from a perception of inadequate strength in the United States and the lack of will to stand behind its commitments.

America's participation in the war had failed to yield results in accord with its announced expectations. Bluntly put, the people had been "played for suckers." Childish, naïve, sentimental and trusting, they failed to understand the world in which they lived. They had defeated Germany militarily, but had not used the force applied intelligently. The war had not discredited idealism but rather American sentimentalism and complacent, emotional pacifism. Common sense had failed at the moment it was most crucially needed. Instead, the United States had "revelled in emotionalism and grovelled in sacrifice" and the war, welcomed initially for the opportunity to break old customs and habits, became instead just another missed opportunity to buttress morals with intelligence, to apply force to ideals. In these comments, as elsewhere, he may have articulated, unknowingly, elements of that heritage from Vermont and from his earlier life which threaded a sense of moral purpose and humanitarian concern through his cold talk about instrumentalism and scientific method.

The United States remained the fortunate laboratory of the modern world; its national mission was still intact, its people still rational and amenable to intelligent manipulation. The war merely proved that it had chosen inadequate means for the worldwide institutionalization of its experience and knowledge. The United States had to find new methods to overcome the obstacles history placed in the path of mankind's progress. Most important, the war experience was not to be misinterpreted. The future alone mattered. "Remember Lot's wife," Dewey wrote in a letter from China in 1919; she looked back and, "looking back, was fixed into a motionless pillar."

Thoughts such as these passed through his mind when the Deweys, on a sabbatical in Berkeley, California, decided to visit Japan. They were closer to the Orient than in New York, and Dewey believed it was "now or never." Former students—two of them bankers—arranged lectures that defrayed the costs and otherwise eased his journey. The Imperial University in Tokyo became the forum in which Dewey delivered, in February and March of 1919, his talks on the present position of philosophy. Therein he intended to challenge Japanese intellectuals and reformers to continue their country's adaptation to the modern, that is, the Western, world.

The lectures, later revised and published as *Reconstruction in Philosophy*, defended positions articulated in the past. With the war experience fresh in his mind, Dewey reaffirmed his belief in the role of the philosopher as the bearer of necessary and welcome innovations. The very concern with the old against the new in philosophy, with the relationship between social conflicts and fundamental issues, with past experience and future transformation, further revealed the impact of recent difficulties. Trying to understand his own experience, Dewey traced, against a historical background, the development of an active philosophy that tested ideal meanings by their consequences. He once more emphasized education as the harbinger of social progress, no doubt because he realized that his ideas had taken hold in Japan as well as in China through this channel.

Having hailed the United States as the model for world reconstruction, Dewey had no difficulty in perceiving about him the effects of its influence. Articles in the *Dial* and the *New Republic* reported every trace of liberalism and democracy in Japanese society. What the war had been unable to accomplish until then in the United States, Japan had achieved. The defeat of Germany had there discredited Prussian philosophy and militarism. Industrial expansion had allied economic interests and the administration of the state, thus introducing modern ways of thought and action into the social mechanism. Rice riots and an epidemic of strikes revealed the beginnings of labor and class consciousness. Radical ideas imbued the younger generation. A small middle class rebelled against authority and the extension of universal suffrage was a democratic and liberal sign. Luckily for Japan, a solid historical base, in the form of a tradition of social democracy embodied in manners and customs, eased the birth of a new order. Dewey assumed that his American readers knew what democracy and liberalism stood for, and had no doubt that the Japanese understood the terms in the same way.

Dewey was fully aware of the difficulties involved in the changes through which Japan was passing. Meetings with students, teachers, government officials and friends exposed him to a wide array of opinions and to diverse sources of information. These optimistic judgments set the tone for his journey of exploration into the Asian mainland.

Hu Shih and some former students of Dewey, with the aid of five progressive educational associations, organized the tour of China. The first month's itinerary took the travelers to Shanghai, Hangchow and Nanking, where they visited schools, local colleges, mills and factories, before arriving in Peking. There, as one of the first foreigners invited to lecture at a Chinese university, Dewey delivered his lectures, beginning in June 1919. He spoke also at the Tsing Hua College, outside Peking, an institution established with money donated by the United States from its Boxer Indemnity Fund.

A month after his arrival, Dewey's first article appeared in the *New Republic*. These expressions of initial impressions reflected Dewey's exuberance. With little or no preparation, simply on the basis of casual encounters, he proceeded to dissect the psychological makeup of the Chinese, which he contrasted with that of the Japanese. Neither the vastness of the country nor the enormous crowds of people on the streets, who impressed him in their capacity for coexistence, dampened his enthusiastic generalizations. A man who laid claim to a scientific outlook that cautiously formulated statements on the basis of factual knowledge might have been more circumspect. Dewey was not. He compiled a list of commonly held Western views of China. He judged its people talkers, not doers, their highly rational self-criticism a substitute for action. One could almost hear Dewey sighing for a Chinese Teddy Roosevelt who would act when necessary.

Dewey's life-long fascination with the past as an obstacle to be surmounted and with history as an experimental laboratory accounted for his continuing interest in the way change worked itself out in time. China was another field in which to test his philosophical hypotheses. How did Western ways accommodate to an inhospitable setting? That was the guiding question.

No state could long adopt Western technological knowledge and at the same time cling to socially and politically antiquated traditions, as Japan and China at first tried to do. True, historical circumstances precluded facile generalizations and easy analogies but Dewey was certain that human nature was uniform, even though the past had produced the unique civilization of China. China could easily acquire the techniques involved in the introduction of railroads, but actual construction required an intellectual change that would permit the disregard for ancestral graves, respect for which obstructed the efforts of builders to acquire a clear right of way. An alteration of modes of thought had preceded industrialization in Britain, Germany and the United States. A similar change in the Chinese mind was essential.

The hope lay in its innately democratic habits of life and thought. In fact, Dewey saw the Chinese village as the focal point of the democracy of the future. In the absence of classes, it enjoyed social and civil equality, and controlled its members by moral rather than physical force. Only the white picket fences and the town greens were missing. National institutions, developing against this background, would forge China into a coherent and a democratic political entity.

The alternative was a continuation of the tradition of autocratic government. But there were enough indicators to promise a favorable outcome. Dewey even interpreted the current idealization of the United States as a projection of China's hopes. He could always point to the inarticulate masses who knew, really knew, that democracy alone was compatible with the "historic spirit of the Chinese race"—loaded terms Dewey failed to examine.

That signs of change appeared sooner than he had expected pleased Dewey no end. Student unrest, which coincided with his arrival in China, he promptly construed as the necessary response to an untenable situation. Here was a younger generation which determined its own goals, applied intelligence and know-how in the effort to attain them, and was ready to act—unlike American reformers shackled by moral scruples and by concern with inner purity of conscience.

In response to the national weakness and widespread corruption of their pro-Japanese government, the younger Chinese intellectuals had called for a general boycott of Japanese goods and for a purge of officials. Dewey hailed the May 4th Movement, as it eventually was known, as the correct rebellion against an oppressive past, once and for all dissolving typical national apathy and bringing the fruits of activism to China. Students everywhere mobilized, from the university level down to the high schools; they spoke in every part of the country and even won the merchants over to their side. The Chinese were learning the lessons of self-reliance, as the movement for home industry showed, and were realizing that the salvation of their country lay in their hands only. It was all, to Dewey, a glorious example of what moral and intellectual force, backed by will and determination, could accomplish and he heartily welcomed it.

At the end of his tour, he thus remained ever the optimistic and innocent American observer. The perception of instrumentalism in practice, of the controlled intelligent manipulation of social forces in China, was a revealing commentary on the society which crowned him its leading philosopher. The man who so easily made his peace with the outcome of the war was not about to be deterred by other historical obstacles that hampered progress in a different setting.

Essays

THE OBJECTS OF VALUATION

In an earlier number of the *Journal of Philosophy, Psychology and Scientific Methods*,[1] I presented a theory about valuation-judgments. In so doing, I intentionally put to one side the question of the nature of value. I did not wish to add further complication by introducing a subject about which so much difference of opinion already existed. It seemed to me that it was theoretically possible to distinguish the logical or formal aspect of valuation from the nature of value in the same way in which it is possible to distinguish the logical form of, say, a descriptive judgment from the particular subject-matter described, or an asymmetrical transitive relation from the question as to whether the relation concerns a spatial, temporal or numerical series. I still think this distinction of problems is logically sound, but intervening discussions have changed my mind about its availability at the present time. Consequently, I hope at a later time to take up a discussion of the nature of value itself. Just now I want, however, to take advantage of some of the recent discussions to show wherein I failed to make clear the primary point of my theory. I shall use selections from the articles of Mr. Perry[2] and Mr. Bush as texts upon which to hang certain comments.

Mr. Perry says: "Suppose a situation in which I suffer from ill-health and hope to recover through the agency of a physician. There are several items in this situation which must be distinguished. I suffer from ill-health, and am aware that I dislike it. I desire recovery and am aware that I desire it. I believe that con-

1. Vol. XII, pp. 512–23, since reprinted with some additions in my *Essays in Experimental Logic*, pp. 349–89. [*The Middle Works of John Dewey, 1899–1924*, ed. Jo Ann Boydston (Carbondale: Southern Illinois University Press, 1979), 8:23–49.]
2. *Journal of Philosophy, Psychology and Scientific Methods*, Vol. XIV, No. 7, "Dewey and Urban on Value Judgments," the quotation being from pp. 173–74. [See this volume, p. 366.]

[First published in *Journal of Philosophy, Psychology and Scientific Methods* 15 (1918): 253–58. For articles to which this is a reply, see this volume, Appendixes 2 and 3.]

sulting a physician conduces to recovery. I adopt the course of consulting a physician, as a course conducive to my recovery. . . . Subsequently, because of what I dislike, desire and believe, I do consult the physician, and, thereupon, in consequence of having consulted the physician, I recover. . . . But there is no case of a value's being constituted by a judgment of it."

Now on the basis of the particular situation described by Mr. Perry I quite agree. According to the terms of the illustration, there is already in determinate existence a negative value, ill-health, there is also a determinate positive value, recovery (which, of course, is none the less determined for knowledge because it does not as yet physically exist). In addition to these intrinsic, immediate, or independent values, as they are variously termed by different writers, there is also a determined instrumental, or dependent, value: seeing the physician is serviceable, useful, valuable, *for* the positive value of health. Nothing could be clearer or more satisfactory. The most that a deliberative judgment could effect under such circumstances would be to assist in bringing into *physical* existence a value already, as value, given. And only an extreme bungler could confuse the assistance given by judgment in bringing a value into existence with that given by judgment in determining a value as such.

Of that particular bungling performance I plead not guilty. It might be a purely verbal matter to say that I do not conceive that propositions *about* values already given *as* values are valuation-judgments at all, whether they are about value as immediate or about value in the sense of useful, any more than I should wish to term a judgment about a pin a pin-judgment. In such a case as that stated above,there is nothing whatever to mark off any distinctive logical type of judgment. If we call such judgments valuation-judgments, they are on precisely the same logical level as any propositions about matters of established fact. I can not make it too emphatic that I started out, so far *as respects cases of this kind*, from precisely the point of view maintained by Mr. Perry.

But there remains a question of fact, a question which is not concerned with the proper linguistic use of the term valuation or value-judgment. Are there not situations in which, while a man dislikes ill-health, it is not, *under the specific circumstances*, the object of his supreme dislike, and where, moreover, he does not know *what* he should supremely dislike and supremely desire?

Are there not situations wherein the adequate data for settling a determinate like and dislike *can not* be had until after an act which issues from a preliminary estimate or valuation as to what the good *will* be? This does not mean that health has not been a good in the past, or that it is not a good "in general." It means that there may be a case in which an agent is genuinely uncertain whether to desire—or like—the recovery of health or to desire making a medical discovery at the cost of his own health. In such cases there is no good or value given to judgment; whether the good be recovery of health or loss-of-health-along-with-increase-of-reputation-and-a-medical-discovery-to-aid-others is genuinely unsettled. Now it was of this sort of situation and of this only that I contended that valuations aid in determining a new good; and contended that *such* valuations possess a distinctive logical character which the orthodox logics have passed over too lightly. Now either or both of these convictions may be wrong, but their error can hardly be shown until the prior question has been raised: Are there situations such that it is objectively uncertain what *their* good, value or end is—it being understood that their good *if* determinately given would be an intrinsic and immediate good? After this question has been dealt with, the question of the nature of the judgment of valuation (estimation or appraisal) involved in them will naturally follow.[3]

The passage from Mr. Bush is as follows: "The city of Syracuse has a very beautiful institution. The state fair is held there every autumn, and on the evening of the last day there is a parade

3. It is possible, though I am not sure, that I might make my point in terms of Mr. Perry's own thinking by reference to his theory of the "objective" of judgments involving belief or committal. See the *Journal of Philosophy, Psychology and Scientific Methods*, Vol. XIII, pp. 569–73. It seems reasonable to suppose that there are cases of genuine doubt as to what the "objective" *should* be, as to what the purport or deliverance of an entertained belief *better* be. In such a case, if we employ reflection, if we make a judgment to decide upon an "objective" as a precondition of applying that "objective" in a further judgment, there is found, I fancy, a kind of judgment logically similar to that with which I was dealing. When Mr. Perry in the same connection says that the "pragmatic theory is correct in emphasizing the formative, creative action of mind, and in likening the cognitive situation to the desiderative or volitional situation" (p. 572), and yet in a later article takes such pains to deny any formative action on the part of thought in constituting the object of a desiderative situation, I confess myself perplexed. I get the feeling that he has left his older opinion about the nature of valuation-judgment untouched by his revision of his theory of belief-judgment, and that if he applied his latter theory to the former topic it would inevitably result in a view of valuation not incompatible with that which I set forth.

of all the city's children. The people of Syracuse regard this parade with an almost passionate affection. It seems natural to say that they value it supremely. Does value really attach to things like this or to the means used to bring them about? Of course, it is a verbal question, but it is a question that takes us to considerations where instrumentalism is no longer a sufficient point of view."[4]

As in the case of the former quotation, I can only express my unqualified agreement—except that instrumentalism is not so much insufficient as grossly impertinent, irrelevant. It would be, as Mr. Bush intimates, a purely verbal matter to say that in such cases no valuing at all occurs. Yet such a verbal approach might be one way of getting at a fact, namely, that no valuing occurs in the sense of reflective comparison, an inquiry which involves deliberating, weighing one consideration against another. This might be a rhetorical way of getting at the fact that to the citizens the object is in-valuable, that is to say one whose worth is not subjected to critical questioning. The citizens value it "supremely" not in the sense that after considering and comparing any number of things they have arrived at a definitive scale in which the procession outweighs all other goods, but in the sense that they unreservedly, without any questioning, prize and cherish the institution.

So far there is, I take it, no difference of opinion between Mr. Bush and myself; he recognizes as explicitly as any one could desire that I expressly drew a distinction between the non-cognitive act of prizing, finding good or dear, and the cognitive act of valuation. But he goes on to ask whether in making this distinction "the word value does not become synonymous, in the instrumentalist presentation, with the word use." And if such be the case, why not, as Mr. Bush pertinently asks, drop the word value and confine one's self to the term use or valuable? And he goes on to interpret my position as meaning "value occurs when we face the question, What things or methods have the value of utility under the circumstances?"

Just here is where I entirely failed to make myself comprehensible to Mr. Bush. Just how far the obscurity of my exposition is the cause I can not well judge; if my exposition as a whole gave

4. *Journal of Philosophy, Psychology and Scientific Methods*, Vol. XV, No. 4, pp. 95–96. [See this volume, p. 387.]

Mr. Bush this impression, I express my appreciation of his tenderness in dealing with an account which is complicated and prolix to no other end than to arrive at a result which can be stated in a few sentences and with which, as he says, no one would disagree. Possibly the term "instrumentalism" itself suggests that judgments are held to be about instruments or means; possibly calling a judgment of valuation a practical judgment suggests, in the current implications of the word practical, the same idea. If so, both suggestions are quite misleading. The instrumental theory of judgment does not mean that judgment is about instruments; it refers to the *function* of all judgment *qua* judgment, not to the subject-matter of some judgments. In any case, the emphasis was put not upon the instrumental, but upon the *experimental* character of valuations. It may well be that the primary linguistic connotation of the term "practical" is useful; unfortunately we have no unambiguous words in this connection. But I tried to make it clear that by "practical" I meant *what* is to be done, rather than *how* to accomplish something already given as a satisfactory end. Judgments about means, so far as they do not themselves enter into judgment about the constitution of an end or good,[5] are, I should say, technical rather than practical; by which I mean that our important practical inquiries concern ends and goods.

This brings me, of course, to exactly the point which I made in discussing the passage from Mr. Perry. Sometimes every immediate or intrinsic good goes back on us. We do not confront any indubitable good. We are in the dark as to what we *should* regard with passionate esteem; we are beginning to suspect that something which we prized unquestioningly and directly in the past is no longer worth our while, because of some growth on our part or some change in conditions. Now in such a state of affairs we may of course trust to luck; we may wait for something to turn up which will afford a new unquestioned object to cherish and hold to. But sometimes we attempt to further by means of deliberation the production of such a good. We search in order to form an estimate of what would be the good of the situation if we could attain it. Add to these conditions the further condition that we

5. See *Essays in Experimental Logic*, pp. 340–44, and pp. 358–62 for cases in which valuation of means and of ends, respectively, are two ways of getting at the same thing. [*Middle Works* 8:17–20, 29–32.]

can not be *sure* that we shall prize or like the thing in question until it has been brought into existence by an act following upon a judgment, and we have before us the kind of situation with which I was concerned. It frequently happens that, being in uncertainty, I conclude after consideration that the best thing that I can do is so and so—in short, that if I act so as to bring certain consequences into existence I *shall* like them or find them good. But when I act and the consequences follow, I do not relish them at all. Now this, I submit, is a very different sort of thing from discovering that I have made a mistake in my judgment as to the useful means of accomplishing something. It means that I have made a mistake in my valuation of an immediate good—that is of what, *when it is brought into existence*, will be an immediate good—or bad.

Let us return to the illustration of Mr. Bush. It is conceivable that some citizen of Syracuse who had habitually regarded the procession with passionate regard, might be led to question its worth. He might learn that a number of children had been made ill, or become seriously over-excited, or were becoming over-fond of display for sake of attracting attention to themselves. This would not alter what was past, his former liking, the fact that he *had* experienced an immediate, independent good. But it would lead him to a new act of valuation; he would seriously question whether he is henceforth to regard the parade with liking, hesitation or repugnance. He might attempt to use his judgment to come to a reasoned conclusion in the matter, and might then try to arrange so that the next parade would not involve these obnoxious features. Or he might attempt to arrange some other function giving the opportunity for an immediate realization of the beauty of congregated child-life. In any case, the result when it occurs will be an immediate good or bad—a matter of direct liking or the reverse. But, none the less, it will have been constituted, in part,[6] by the prior valuation—the prior reflective estimate of a non-instrumental good.

I should be glad to think that this explanation, if I have succeeded in making anything plain, would evoke an opinion that if this is what is meant, nobody will disagree. But I am not sanguine

6. I have never said that judgment is the *sole* determinant of a new object, but only that it serves to *re*construct or *re*organize, which implies another and independent variable.

that such will be the case. For my view goes contrary to the classic view not only as to the logic of all judgments, but of moral and political conceptions. For the prevailing view is that goods, ends, "values" are all given, given in the sense of being completely there for knowledge, provided only we could get at them. Disputes in ethical and social theory have concerned themselves for the most part only with the question of *where* and *how* the goods are given: whether in experience, feeling, sensation, or in thought, intuition, reason; whether in the subject or in the object; whether in nature or in some transcendental realm. The important fact (provided it be a fact) that serious inquiries into conduct, individual and collective, must be concerned with an hypothetical and experimental effort to bring *new* goods into existence, an attempt made necessary by the slipping away of all given determinate goods, fails to secure recognition. I console with a belief that while my own inexpertness in statement is largely responsible for my failure to make myself understood, some of the difficulty lies with the immensely difficult transformation in methods of thinking about all social matters which the theory implies.

CONCERNING ALLEGED IMMEDIATE KNOWLEDGE OF MIND

In his suggestive book entitled *The Problem of Conduct*, Professor Taylor discusses mistakes as to one's own motives. He says, "It is a commonplace of ethics that the human heart is so utterly deceitful that we are constantly being deluded not only as to the motives of our fellows, but even as to our own. What more common, for instance, than the discovery that an action we believed ourselves to have performed from motives of magnanimity was really prompted by a desire to make ourselves a reputation?" In such cases "we have at first sight a puzzling psychological problem. . . . Surely, it may be argued, there can be no such thing as an unconscious motive; an emotion is, from the very nature of the case, just what it is at the time felt to be, nothing more and nothing less." In short, accepting the idea that motives are states of consciousness or feelings which are just what they are as states of consciousness, how is error possible as to what they are?

Professor Taylor imagines a case in which the influence of an emotion prompts a person to confer a benefit upon a fellow at some cost to himself, which he takes for an act of generosity. Later on, the same person finds himself *not* strongly prompted to perform a similar act under circumstances such that there is no chance for the beneficence being known. If the man is frank with himself, he will admit that his motive on the first occasion was not the feeling of pure generosity which he had supposed it to be. But how was error possible, the emotion being "just what it was felt as being; an unfelt emotion being a *contradictio in adjecto*"? The solution is that the "mistake came not in estimating the emotion, but in apprehending the circumstances necessary for its production."[1]

Students of ethical theory ought to be grateful to Professor

1. See Taylor, *Problem of Conduct*, pp. 98–99.

[First published in *Journal of Philosophy, Psychology and Scientific Methods* 15 (1918): 29–35.]

Taylor for raising so definitely a question usually slurred over. I think his proposed solution makes the best of a bad job if one accepts his psychological premises, which are not so much his as the truisms of an introspective psychology; for ethical theory as to the nature of motives has been profoundly affected—in common with most other branches of ethical theorizing—by the terminology and notions of introspectionist psychology with its assumption of ideas, feelings, as just states of consciousness, whose nature is identical with their happening. We all recognize that meaning or nature is not all one with occurrence in the case of physical happenings, that it is something to be searched out with exceeding pains, utilizing all the knowledge we command. No one expects that the nature of infantile paralysis or of fire or gold will be open to the most careful *direct* inspection. One has, however, only to read Descartes to see that at the same time when this notion was first gaining ground as to physical existences, it was insisted that mental events, especially facts of something called consciousness, carry their whole character in their bare face or presence, so that about them immediate certainty remains not only possible, but inevitable. Clearly Mr. Taylor's difficulty is due to a translation of this doctrine into the ethical doctrine of motives. That motives are feelings (emotions, sentiments) and that feelings are of such a sort that they are known to be just as and what they are in their occurrence is of the essence of this translation.

Does not the conflict of this ethical rendering with the fact of difficulty in ascertaining one's own motive give good ground for questioning the psychological assumption on which it rests? Is Professor Taylor's solution successful? Just what does it imply? Its apparent implication is that we were not wrong in thinking we were animated by a motive or feeling of generosity. Our mistake was only in supposing that this emotion would be aroused by certain conditions, those of distress of another, when as matter of fact it is aroused by distress plus opportunity for the act to secure the attention of others. This, I say, is the apparent implication. For otherwise the feeling was not one of generosity at all, but only of love of notice or of praise. Then there was a mistake about the feeling itself—which is said to be a contradiction in terms.

But in escaping one difficulty is not a greater one raised? Can the feeling be said to be generosity when it can be excited only if the act it prompts is an object of favorable regard on the part of others? Is not this the most extreme ethical subjectivism, equaled, if equaled at all in history, only by the doctrine ascribed to Protagoras in the Platonic *Theaetetus*? Is it not the same as saying that if a man "feels" that his motive in committing what others would describe as an act of malicious revenge is one of lofty justice, all debate is closed? Such was his motive. The other alternative is that the "feeling as barely felt" has *no* character or nature; that to conceive it *as* generosity (or *as* love of praise) is identical with referring it to conditions of production and to the consequences which follow from it, a reference which is as difficult and as exposed to error as in the case of physical events.

I am questioning in short whether the distinction upon which Mr. Taylor relies, between "estimating an emotion" and "apprehending the circumstances necessary for its origin," is anything more than verbal. I do not see how any emotion can be estimated *except* in terms of its objective conditions or its objective consequences, preferably both. Is not to "feel" a feeling *as* generosity or greed or fear or anger all one with ascribing to it certain conditions of origin and of outcome? Before we raise the question as to whether I can be wrong about my own attitude, we must then consider the question as to whether we can be *either* right or wrong about it unless we view it in connection with the circumstances which evoke it and the consequences which flow from it.

For my own part, then, I can see no meaning in "estimating" an attitude of my own to be anger excepting that it is an attitude produced by an insult or an unexpected injury, and which leads, if unchecked, to certain violently destructive acts. (This, of course, is a very gross identification, quite too gross to be of scientific value, and is used only for purposes of illustration.) Unless this position can be successfully denied, there is a dangerous ambiguity in saying "an emotion is from the very nature of the case what it is at the time felt to be." It may mean the tautology that the *event* is just what it is, irrespective of whether or not we know or characterize it. Then it stands on exactly the level as any natural occurrence of which no notice is taken. Or it may mean that as matter of fact we take it—judge it, class it—to be such and such, whether it *is* so or not, just exactly as we take a certain moving twig to be a snake in spite of the fact that it *is* a twig.

Only by compounding into one these two different facts—both facts, but different facts—does, I am persuaded, the notion arise that there states of consciousness or feelings exist which wear their hearts on their sleeves, so much so that the sleeve is the heart, and *vice versa*.

In other words, we come to exactly the position taken by Dr. Singer in criticizing a current assumption. "Did we start with an immediate fact of consciousness and construct a world? Then let us now begin with the world and construct a fact of consciousness." And again, "It takes all the science in the world to make out whether *A* is in love or whether *B* sees red."[2] And the context makes it clear that this holds even when *A* or *B* is one's self.

One has, of course, only to extend this line of reasoning to be in the middle of the discussion of introspectionist *versus* behaviorist psychology. Says Watson, "One must believe that two hundred years from now, unless the introspection method is discarded, psychology will be still divided on the question as to whether auditory sensations have the quality of 'extension,' whether intensity is an attribute which can be applied to color, whether there is a difference in 'texture' between image and sensation; and upon many hundreds of others of like character."[3] And why not, if the meaning which any one of these questions may have is really a matter of the *connection* of one event with certain other events, events which either constitute the circumstances of its production or which are its results? To decide upon these connections is a matter of observation, but of observation of exactly the same sort as is used in arriving at a conclusion as to the nature of, say, typhoid fever, an observation which, instead of staring at what is directly present with the hope that the stare, if sufficiently intent, will disembowel the object, uses all the resources of what is already known about other things to uncover a specific connection between events. I am quite sure that some of the objections to behaviorism, at least in its general sense, would disappear if it were recognized by its critics that behavior is not an isolated thing—a muscle twitching—but concerns the connection of an organic event with circumstances necessary to its production and with other events which follow from it. It would then be clear, I think, that we do not first have a certain feeling

2. *Journal of Philosophy, Psychology and Scientific Methods*, Vol. IX, pp. 16, 17.
3. *Behavior*, p. 8.

or state of mind or consciousness complete in itself, generosity, fear, anger, or whatever, but that there is a certain (instinctive) reactive attitude which *when viewed* in its connections, in its relation to the situation in which it occurs and the specific consequences which flow from it, may be called emotion or sentiment or feeling of, say, generosity. I have employed the word "viewed" which might be thought to imply "consciousness," and I have admitted that a certain complex reference of an attitude to other things may properly be called a feeling or sentiment. This probably appears like a surrender of behaviorism. But I would point out that nothing more is here involved than is stated by Watson when he says: "The separate observation of 'states of consciousness' is, on this assumption, no more a part of the task of the psychologist than of the physicist. We might call this the return to a non-reflective and naïve use of consciousness. In this sense consciousness may be said to be the instrument or tool with which all scientists work."[4] That is to say, I am merely assuming that an *observation* takes place, and that its aim is to *understand*. When (or if) the psychologist wishes to observe and understand observation and understanding, he must take for his object a certain event studied in its context of other events—its specific stimulus and specific consequences. It may well be true that at present there are no methods by which one can determine at what points in the animal scale observation (in the sense defined) and understanding take place,[5] but the query as to their first manifestation would not be an inherently impossible, a meaningless one. "One can assume either the presence or absence of consciousness anywhere in the phylogenetic scale without affecting the problems of behavior one jot or one tittle." This is certainly true if we start with the introspectionist's conception of "consciousness." But if we start with observation and understanding as they are *used* in daily life and by the scientist, then of course the case stands differently. The problem is when and where a specific or differential type of behavior presents itself.

Now I take it that the observations of daily life differ from those of the laboratory chiefly in the coarseness or grossness of the former, due to lack of control of detailed conditions. This is not a reason for discarding the former; it is an argument for mak-

4. *Ibid.*, p. 27.
5. Watson, *ibid.*, p. 4.

ing them, as rapidly as possible, more refined and accurate. But men would never have arrived at a minute anatomy of man or of the nervous system if they had not started from the gross observation of these things. In fact, the objects of gross observation always persist as limiting conditions which give point and meaning to specific determinations. Just so I think the coarser observations of the non-laboratory psychologist about, say, observation and understanding as they display themselves in human life, may set very important problems to future experimentalists, suggest hypotheses and even determine the limits within which experiments may be fruitfully carried on. To be more specific, I take the recent discussion of "consciousness" by Bode.[6] I am not concerned about names. It makes little difference if such a discussion be called philosophy and the name psychology be reserved for laboratory findings. (I use the word "laboratory" loosely to mean all findings under conditions of great artificial control.) But it makes a good deal of difference whether the inquiry is intellectually legitimate, that is, whether it deals with genuine subject-matter. It may make a real scientific difference, in other words, whether the things called observation and understanding are identifiable with a type of behavior which contrasts with merely impulsive and routine human behavior in that future things, things not yet having happened, operate as part of the stimulus in a present response: Bode's hypothesis roughly stated. For in time this identification may define the limits of an inquiry into behavior carried on under conditions of refined control. Meantime, the coarser observations into human conduct may serve to keep alive the sense that the naïve sense of "consciousness," that in which it is a tool of layman, physicist, and psychologist alike, is itself capable of being understood from a behavioristic point of view. And this also is a matter of scientific import. For it protects experimental behaviorists from a charge of wilfully denying the existence of certain facts (facts like those of observation and understanding as used by all scientific men) merely because their technique is not yet developed to the point of dealing with them. To recognize that the behavioristic principle can make a place for them is important. For science is, after all, carried on by men, and a seeming denial that such facts do exist and do come under

6. In the volume entitled *Creative Intelligence*.

the behavioristic principle is sure to keep alive in the minds of some a futile introspectionist method, by setting to one side a realm of facts to which (so it is thought) it *must* be applied since the behavioristic method confessedly does not apply.

However, this may not seem to justify the use of the words "feeling" and "sentiment," or the recognition of any distinctively *conscious* attitude. This may appear like a relapse into the "state of consciousness," psychology proving that one's behaviorism is hardly, after all, skin deep. So I conclude with pointing out in what sense such a term as sentiment may be applied to a specific type of angry behavior. Obviously *not* in the sense in which Taylor—in common with the usual tradition—uses the word, to indicate something which is, *per se* in its original self-enclosure, generosity or anger or whatever. In their *first* sense, such terms must denote strictly a way of reacting to particular stimuli, not anything which may be called a "feeling." But suppose that one of these behavioristic attitudes is connected with what precedes and issues from it in the way of behavior. Then a new fact may come into existence, or the old fact gain a new quality. To tell a child who is quite innocent of any feeling or sentiment, who is merely grabbing for something to put in his mouth, that he is selfish or greedy is to requalify a mode of response in this way. It is a way of telling him that he is *going* to act in a certain way and that his action when complete is *going* to call out a certain unfavorable attitude on the part of others. Now suppose the child carries over this way of observing and understanding his immediate attitude into his own attitude—that is to say, next time as soon as he begins to react in this way he also acts to observe his act in its context of origin and consequence. Now this supervening of a new attitude toward a more primary attitude may constitute the old attitude into a motive or spring of action which in current terminology is an impulse or sentiment or feeling.

My suggestions or theses are, then, threefold. Negatively, there is no more reason for supposing that personal events have a nature or meaning which is one with their happening, and hence open to immediate infallible inspection, than is the case with impersonal events. In each case the event only sets a problem to knowledge, namely, the discovery of its connections. Secondly, it is desirable and possible that we should observe and understand observation and understanding and allied phenomena themselves. Such a study would be a study of "consciousness" in the naïve sense mentioned. Thirdly, such a study, with a recognition of "consciousness" in this sense, is quite compatible with a behavioristic standpoint, whether or no the technique exists at a given time for its successful accomplishment.

THE MOTIVATION OF HOBBES'S POLITICAL PHILOSOPHY

It is the object of this essay to place the political philosophy of Hobbes in its own historic context. The history of thought is peculiarly exposed to an illusion of perspective. Earlier doctrines are always getting shoved, as it were, nearer our own day. We are familiar with the intellectual struggles of our own time and are interested in them. It is accordingly natural to envisage earlier thought as part of the same movement or as its forerunner. We then forget that that earlier period had its own specific problems, and we proceed to assimilate its discussions to our present interest. Hobbes has been especially subject to this temporal displacement. For over a century the chief question in social philosophy has centered about the conflict between individual freedom and public and institutional control. The central position of the theory of sovereignty in Hobbes's thought has made it easy to translate his political philosophy into terms of this debate; the issue which was really acute in his day—the conflict of church and state—now lacks actuality for English and American writers at least.

I

To prove this statement as to the central issue of Hobbes's day would require more than the space allotted to this paper. In general, I can only refer to the voluminous political discussions of the seventeenth century and to the overt history of England during the time of the civil wars. Specifically, let me note the admirable studies of Mr. Figgis.[1] They are enough to relieve my statement from any charge of exaggeration. Some quotations from Mr. Figgis will, then, be used to introduce the discussion. He points

1. *The Divine Right of Kings* and *From Gerson to Grotius*.

[First published in *Studies in the History of Ideas*, edited by the Department of Philosophy, Columbia University (New York: Columbia University Press, 1918), 1:88–115.]

out that the controversy regarding the divine right of kings belongs to a day when politics, by common consent, was a branch of theology, and goes on to say, "All men demanded some form of Divine authority for any theory of government. . . . Until the close of the seventeenth century, the atmosphere of the supporters of popular rights is as theological as that of the upholders of the Divine Right of Kings."[2] And again, "There is no more universal characteristic of the political thought of the seventeenth century than the notion of non-resistance to authority. 'To bring the people to obedience' is the object of writers of all schools. When resistance is preached, it is resistance to some authority regarded as subordinate. Nor is the resistance permitted at the pleasure or judgment of private individuals. It is allowed only as a form of obedience, as executing the commands of some superior and ultimate authority, God, or the Pope, and the Law."[3]

In other words, everybody worked upon an assumption of a supreme authority, of law as command by this authority, and duty as ultimately obedience. Not these conceptions, but rather the special content given them, mark off Hobbes. There was, of course, a party which opposed such centralization as Hobbes argued for, but the opposition was not in the name of the individual, but of something very different, the People.

So far as I can discover, the term people still had its meaning fixed by the traditional significance of *Populus*—a meaning very different from that of *plebs* or the French *peuple*. This notion, as defined, say, by Cicero, was a commonplace among the "civilians" and those trained in scholastic philosophy. In Cicero's words, the people is "not every gathering of men, assembled in any way whatsoever, but is the multitude associated by a common sense of justice and by a common interest." It is a *universitas*, not a *societas*, much less a mere aggregate of individuals. And the appeal of the upholders of popular against royal government was to the *authority* of this organized body, of which the Commons was frequently (but not always) taken to be the representative. The following words from Lawson, taken from *An Examination of the*

2. *Divine Right of Kings*, p. 11.
3. *Ibid.*, pp. 221–22. Technically, discussions centered about the nature of *Jus*. The ambiguity of Jus, meaning both command and law on one side, and right, on the other side, has been frequently noted. At this time, it was not so much ambiguity which existed as two sides of one notion. Jus is primarily *authority*, and secondarily *authorization*, depending, of course, upon authority.

Political Part of Mr. Hobbs, his Leviathan (1657) are worth quoting: "The liberty which the English have challenged and obtained with so much expence of blood is . . . that which is due unto us by the constitution of the State, Magna Charta, the Laws, and the Petition of Right. It is but the liberty of subjects, not Soveraigns; when he hath said all he can, we are not willing to be slaves or subject our selves to Kings as absolute Lords. . . . By liberty Aristotle meant such a privilege as every subject might have in a free-State . . . where it is to be noted that one and the same person who is a subject, and at the best but a Magistrate, hath a share in the Soveraign power. Yet this he hath not as a single person, but as one person joyntly with the whole body or major part at least of the people" (pp. 67–68). This correlativity of three things: the people, a society organized through laws and especially through the fundamental law, or constitution, and liberty is in marked opposition to Locke's conceptions of a natural right or authority found in the individual himself. It is not, I think, paradoxical to say that Locke derived this conception of a natural right belonging to the individual as such from Hobbes rather than from Hobbes's popular opponents.

It is noteworthy that Cumberland, the chief systematic opponent of Hobbes on rationalistic grounds, objects to the latter's political philosophy because "Hobbes's principles overthrow the Foundations of all Government";—they would not suffer any man to enter into civil society; they excite subjects to rebellion. In short, it is Hobbes's psychological and moral individualism rather than his theory of sovereignty to which objection is taken. The same is true of a much less effective writer, Tenison, in his *Creed of Mr. Hobbes Examined* (1671). He says that since Hobbes identifies the law of nature with the counsels of self-interest "the Fundamentals of your Policy are Hay and Stubble, and apter to set all things into blaze than to support Government" (p. 156); and again, "Wo to all the Princes on earth, if this Doctrine be true and becometh popular; if the multitude believe this, the Prince . . . can never be safe from the Spears and Barbed irons which their ambition and presumed interest will provide." Hobbes's principles, in their appeal to self-interest, are but "Seeds of sedition" (pp. 170–71). That Hobbes himself was aware that, as matter of fact, a government is not likely to retain enough strength to secure obedience unless it has regard to the common weal, will appear in the sequel—though naturally he never made this moral explicit.

Let us hear from Mr. Figgis again. "It is true that with the possible exception of Hobbes, all the political theorists up to the end of the seventeenth century either have religion as the basis of their system, or regard the defence or supremacy of some form of faith as their main object."[4] Now Hobbes is precisely the exception which proves the rule. He is theological in motive and context in the sense that he is deliberately anti-theological. Along with his exclusive self-interest doctrine, it was his theory of a secular basis for sovereignty, not the doctrine of a supreme authority, which brought him into disrepute.[5] His familiar title was atheist, so that even the royalists who might be supposed, on purely political grounds to welcome his support, found it necessary to disclaim him. Compare the following from a contemporary letter: "All honest men who are lovers of monarchy, are very glad that the King hath at last banisht his court that father of atheists Mr. Hobbes, who it is said hath rendered all the Queen's court, and very many of the Duke of York's family, atheists."[6] In the apologetic dedication of his *Seven Philosophical Problems* to the King after the Restoration in 1662, Hobbes in defending himself against this charge says of his *Leviathan*, "There is nothing in it against episcopacy. I cannot therefore imagine what reason any episcopal man can have to speak of me, as I hear some of them do, as of an atheist or man of no religion, *unless it be for making the authority of the Church depend wholly upon the regal power.*" In the words which I have italicized Hobbes flaunts his ground of offense.

II

Postponing, for the moment, the important point in Hobbes, his attempt to secularize morals and politics, I take up his own sayings regarding the immediate occasion of his political writings. Croom Robertson and Toennies have made it clear that the

4. *Ibid.*, p. 219.
5. See, for example, the quotations from royalist writers, Falkner and Filmer, in Figgis, *ibid.*, pp. 388–89.
6. Quoted by Toennies in *Archiv fuer Geschichte der Philosophie*, Vol. III, p. 223.

first of his writings[7] dates from 1640 and is substantially what we have in his *Human Nature* and *De Corpore Politico*. In his *Considerations upon the Reputation of T. Hobbes* (1662) Hobbes says this little treatise "did set forth and demonstrate that the said power and rights were inseparably annexed to the sovereignty," and that the treatise was so much talked of, although it was not printed, that if the King had not dissolved Parliament, it would have brought him into danger of his life.[8] There is here, indeed, no reference to just what the points were in the quarrel about the regal power, but his *Behemoth or the Long Parliament* leaves no doubt. There he says that the Parliament of 1640 "desired the whole and absolute sovereignty. . . . For this was the design of the Presbyterian ministers, who taking themselves to be, by divine right, the only lawful governors of the Church, endeavoured to bring the same form of Government into the civil state. And as the spiritual laws were to be made by their synods, so the civil laws should be made by the House of Commons."[9] And at the beginning of this work, in stating the causes of the corruption of the people which made the civil wars possible, he puts first the Presbyterians, second the Papists, and third the Independents.[10]

In the *Considerations* already referred to he says he "wrote and published his book *De Cive*, to the end that all nations which should hear what you and your Con-Covenanters were doing in England, might detest you." Not less significant is his letter, from Paris, in 1641 to the Earl of Devonshire. He says, "I am of the opinion that ministers ought to minister rather than governe; at least, that all Church government depends on the state, and authority of the Kingdome, without which there can be no unity in ye church. Your Lordship may thinke this but a Fancy of Philosophy, but I am sure that Experience teaches thus much, that the dispute for (the word is variously read preference and precedence) betweene the spirituall and civill power, has of late more than any other thing in the world bene the cause of civill warre."[11] Of the *Leviathan*, he says: "The cause of my writing that book

7. Now published (from mss.) by Toennies under the title of *The Elements of Law, Natural and Politic*, London, 1889.
8. Molesworth, *English Works of Hobbes*, Vol. IV, p. 414.
9. I quote from Toennies's edition, p. 75. See also pp. 63, 57, 49, 95, 172, *etc.*
10. *Ibid.*, pp. 2–3.
11. Quoted by Toennies, in *Archiv*, Vol. XVII, p. 302. See also Molesworth, Vol. IV, p. 407.

was the consideration of what the ministers before, and in the beginning of the civil war, by their preaching and writing did contribute thereunto."[12] And it may be worth noting that considerably over one-half of the *Leviathan* is explicitly devoted to the bearing of religious and scriptural matters upon politics as they touch upon the relation of church and the civil power.

In his controversy with "the egregious professors of the mathematics in the University of Oxford" he remarks of the *De Cive*: "You know that the doctrine therein taught is generally received by all but the clergy, who think their interest concerned in being made subordinate to the civil power."[13] Again he expresses his surprise that some even of the episcopal clergy have attacked him, and thinks it can be explained only as a "relic still remaining of popish ambition, lurking in that seditious division and distinction between the power spiritual and civil."[14] Most significant of all, perhaps, are his remarks in the Preface of the *Philosophical Rudiments*, where after saying that he does not "dispute the position of divines, except in those points which strip subjects of their obedience, and shake the foundations of civil government," he goes on to say, "These things I found most bitterly excepted against: That I made the civil powers too large, but this by ecclesiastical persons. That I had utterly taken away liberty of conscience, but this by sectaries. That I had set the princes above the laws, but this by lawyers."[15] In no enumeration of the criticisms brought against his teachings does he mention the principle of absolute sovereignty, nor does he set his doctrine of sovereignty in antithesis to any doctrine except that of divided sovereignty—divided, that is, between the spiritual and temporal power. Locke's doctrine of a sovereignty limited by prior natural rights of those who were its subjects had neither provocation nor justification till after the revolution of 1688 called for some theoretical explanation.

One can hardly, of course, accept Hobbes as an unbiased witness to the way in which his doctrine was received. But Eachard's *Mr. Hobbs's State of Nature Considered* (1696) (a genuinely witty work) gives corroborative evidence that it was not the doctrine of

12. Molesworth, Vol. VII, p. 335.
13. *Ibid.*, Vol. VII, p. 333.
14. *Ibid.*, Vol. IV, p. 432.
15. *Ibid.*, Vol. II, pp. xxii–xxiii.

sovereignty which aroused dissent, for he repeatedly states that that was old matter dressed in new form. "Your Book called *Dominion* chiefly consists of such things as have been said these thousands of years." And again, "it might easily be shewn how all the rest (so much as is true) is the very same with the old plain Dunstable stuff which commonly occurs in those who treated of Policy and Morality." Aside from the aspersion on human nature contained in Hobbes's doctrine of self-interest, what Eachard objects to is Hobbes's "affected Garbs of Speech, starch'd Mathematical Method, Counterfeit Appearances of Novelty and Singularity."[16] How habitually the ideas of the evils of divided sovereignty were in Hobbes's mind appears from a note in the *Rudiments*: "There are certain doctrines wherewith subjects being tainted, they verily believe that obedience may be refused to the city, and that by right they may, nay, ought, to oppose and fight against chief princes and dignitaries. Such are those which, whether directly and openly, or more obscurely and by consequence, require obedience to be given to others besides them to whom the supreme authority is committed. I deny not but this reflects on that power which many, living under other government, ascribe to the chief head of the Church of Rome, and also on that which elsewhere, out of that Church, bishops require in their's to be given to them; and last of all, on that liberty which the lower sort of citizens, under pretence of religion, do challenge to themselves. For what civil war was there ever in the Christian world, which did not either grow from, or was nourished by this root?"[17]

As an *argumentum ad hominem* in his own time, it is impossible to overestimate the force of his argument. All Protestants united in declaiming against the claim of the Roman Church to interfere in matters temporal. Yet some of the episcopalian bishops declared that in matters of religious actions, such as rites, appointments, preferments, the Church represented God, not man, and had a superior right to obedience. The Presbyterians in general were committed to a dual theory of authority and obedience. Yet all of these ecclesiastical institutions united in repri-

16. Harrington, on the contrary, who was a genuinely democratic writer with an interest which was modern, economic, and secular, in differing radically from Hobbes as to respective merits of royal and popular government, says, "in most other things I believe Mr. Hobbs is, and in future Ages will be, accounted the best Writer in this day in the world."

17. Molesworth, Vol. II, p. 79, note.

manding the fifth monarchy men, Anabaptists, Levelers, *etc.*, who claimed that their personal conscience as enlightened by the indwelling presence of the Holy Spirit was the ultimate source of knowledge of divine law, and hence the rule for obedience. Luther, Calvin, English bishop, and Scotch presbyter alike attacked this doctrine as anarchic and immoral. Hobbes, in effect, points out that all churches are in the same anarchic class, for they all appeal to something other than publicly instituted and proclaimed law.

In connection with the sectaries, it is interesting to note that they expressly cried out for "natural rights derived from Adam and right reason." According to this view, "all men are by nature the sons of Adam, and from him have derived a natural propriety (property), right, and freedom. . . . By natural birth all men are equally and alike born to like propriety, liberty, and freedom; and as we are delivered of God by the hand of nature into this world, every one with a natural innate freedom and propriety, even so we are to live, every one equally and alike, to enjoy his birthright and privilege."[18] That this anarchic doctrine of the Levelers was wrought by Locke into a stable foundation for a reasonably conservative Whig doctrine, testifies to his altered background and outlook. There is no evidence that Hobbes was influenced by the doctrine, but it is more than a coincidence that he makes a precisely similar notion of natural rights the origin of the war of all upon all, and the basis of demand for absolute sovereignty. If he had this notion in mind in his picture of the state of nature, it adds a piquant irony to his sketch, as well as to his repeated assertions that there was no difference of principle between the sectaries' appeal to the court of private judgment and the doctrines of Papist, Presbyterian, and of such Episcopalians as did not recognize that the authority of the Established Church was by grace of the political sovereign and not by divine right.

Lawson was one of the better tempered and more moderate opponents of royal sovereignty, an episcopalian rector with obvious sympathies with Cromwell. He admits as a "certain truth" that sovereignty is above all civil law, but asserts the supreme legislator "is subject to the superiour will of God"—which, of course, was Hobbes's own doctrine. "All the sovereignty's power

18. Quoted from Ritchie, *Natural Rights*, p. 9. He quotes from the preface of Firth to the *Clarke Papers*.

of making Laws, Judgements, *&c.*, are from God. . . . Men may give their consent that such a man or such a company of men shall raign, but the power is from God, not them." From this doctrine, it is not a long step to his statement that the true believer in God "may, must within himself, even of laws, so far as they are a rule, and bind him, enquire, examine, and determine whether they are good or evil. Otherwise, he can perform only a blind obedience even to the best; and if he conform unto the unjust, he in obeying man disobeys God, which no good man will do. Romans, xii, 14–15." Subsequently he adds, "Nor doth this doctrine any waies prejudice the civil power, nor encourage any man to disobedience and violation of the civil Laws, if they be just and good as they ought to be; and the subject hath not only liberty, but a command to examine the Laws of his Soveraign, and judge within himself and for himself, whether they be not contrary to the Laws of God."[19] Yet Lawson joins in the common animadversions upon the leveling sectaries. Moreover, Lawson deplores the disorder and divisions of the time. "Our form of Government is confounded by the different opinions of common Lawyers, Civilians, and Divines who agree neither with one another, nor amongst themselves." Nor can the history of England be appealed to as an umpire—as many were doing, for as Lawson, clearer-headed than most, perceived, it shows "only as matter of fact how sometimes the King, sometimes the Barons, sometimes the Commons were predominant and ascendant." And he concludes, "yet for all this, a free Parliament of just, wise, and good men might rectifie all this, and *unite the supreme power so miserably divided to the hazard of the State*."[20] In a situation where a writer sees that the great need is for a unified authority or sovereignty, and yet argues in support of that very principle of private judging of laws which had been a large factor in bringing about the situation he deplores, Hobbes's case almost states itself.

III

A few words are now to be said about another motif in Hobbes's ardent assertion of a unified sovereignty. The part of his

19. Lawson, *An Examination of the Political Part of Mr. Hobbs*, pp. 96, 123, 127. When one considers the prevalence of this idea of the duty of private judgment, one is almost inclined to align Hobbes's criticism of it with that passed by Auguste Comte upon Protestantism.
20. *Ibid.*, pp. 133–34. Italics mine.

doctrine which was not directed against the claim of the Churches to obedience was aimed at the claim of the authority of Law set up by the lawyers. To go fully into this matter would require a summary of certain phases of parliamentary history in England, beginning in the time of Elizabeth and becoming highly acute in the reign of James. On the one side were the lawyers and judges, and on the other were the claims of the legislature representing statute law, and of the Chancellor representing equity. The king then largely dominated parliament, and this made the party of the judges against parliament essentially the popular party of later controversy. In the earlier words of Aristotle, and the later words of the Constitution of Massachusetts, they proclaimed a government "which was a government of laws, not of men."[21]

Consider, for example, such a statement as this of John Milton, arguing against Salmasius: "Power was therefore given to a king by the people, that he might see by the authority committed to him that nothing be done against law, and that he keep our laws and not impose upon us his own. Therefore, there is no regal power but in the courts of the kingdom and by them." And Harrington's constant contention is that only a commonwealth is a government of laws, since law must proceed from will, and will be moved by interest; and only in a commonwealth is the whole will and the whole interest expressed. In a monarchy or oligarchy, the laws are made in the interest of a few, so that what exists is a government of men. Harrington, however, is an innovator in connecting law with legislation rather than with the courts. "Your Lawyers, advising you to fit your Governments to their Laws, are no more to be regarded than your Taylor if he should desire you to fit your body to his doublet"—another point of sympathy between him and Hobbes.

It was lawyer's law then which was usually meant—the law of courts, not of legislation. As Figgis says, speaking of the reliance of the popular party upon government by law, "Nor is it of statute law that men are thinking; but of the Common Law, which, . . . possesses that mysterious sanctity of prescription which no legislator can bestow. The Common Law is pictured

21. As Hobbes saw, this doctrine is either a negation of sovereignty or works out practically (as it has done so largely in this country) in placing the judges in the seat of sovereignty—a "government of lawyers, not of men," to paraphrase the old saying. Locke comes close to this legal position, and historically is half way between Hobbes's location of sovereignty and Rousseau's ascription of sovereignty to the legislative body alone.

invested with a halo of dignity, peculiar to the embodiment of deepest principles and to the highest expression of human reason and of the law of nature implanted by God in the heart of man. As yet men are not clear that an Act of Parliament can do more than declare the Common Law."[22] It is with this doctrine in mind that Hobbes is so insistent that the sovereign is absolved from all law save the moral law—which, as we shall see later, is for him the law of an enlightened hedonism. But Hobbes is not just begging the question. Bacon before him had pointed out many of the defects of common law and the need of codification and systematized revision. The demand for legislative activity was constantly increasing; the Long Parliament in effect restated the common law. Courts of equity had been obliged to assume an extensive activity, and it is not unimportant that the Chancellor's court was essentially a royal court and followed the law "of reason," the law "of nature," the law of conscience and of God. Hobbes's essential rationalism was shocked at calling anything law which expressed, as did the common law, merely custom and precedent.[23]

Hobbes does away at one sweep with any alleged distinction between written and unwritten law. All law is written, for written *means* published. And as published, it proceeds only from him (or them) who has authority—power to require obedience. And that, of course, is the sovereign. "Custom of itself maketh no laws. Nevertheless, when a sentence hath once been given, by them that judge by their natural reason, . . . it may attain to the vigour of a law . . . because the sovereign power is supposed tacitly to have approved such sentence for right. . . . In like manner those laws that go under the title of *responsa prudentum*, the opinions of lawyers, are not, therefore, laws because *responsa prudentum*, but because they are admitted by the sovereign."[24]

But Hobbes is most explicit in a work, too infrequently made use of by historians of philosophy, entitled *A Dialogue between a Philosopher and a Student of the Common Laws of England*.[25] This dialogue opens with an attempt to prove that it is the king's reason which is the soul even of the common law. He quotes

22. Figgis, *Divine Right of Kings*, pp. 228–29. See his note for references in support of the text.
23. See Molesworth, Vol. III, p. 91.
24. *Ibid.*, Vol. IV, p. 227. See also Vol. VI, pp. 194–95.
25. *Ibid.*, Vol. VI.

Coke's saying (and it is to be recalled that Coke had been on the lawyers' side against King James) that law is reason, although an artificial reason, got by long study and observation; such a perfection of reason, however, that "if all the reason that is dispersed into so many several heads were united into one, yet could he not make such a law as the law of England is, because by many successions of ages it hath been fined and refined by an infinite number of grave and learned men." As against this view, Hobbes inserts his usual caveat; it was not the succession of lawyers or judges that made the law, but the succession of kings who created the judges and who enforced the decisions. "The King's reason, when it is publicly upon advice and deliberation declared, is that *anima legis*, and that *summa ratio*, and that equity which . . . is all that is the law of England." And even more emphatically: "There is not amongst men a universal reason agreed upon in any nation, besides the reason of him that hath the sovereign power. Yet though his reason be but the reason of one man, yet it is set up to supply the place of that universal reason which is expounded to us by our Saviour in the Gospel; and consequently our King is to us the legislator both of statute-law and of common-law."[26] Later he suggests that common law and its lawyers are the chief source of excessive litigation on account of "the variety and repugnancy of judgments of common-law," and because "lawyers seek not for their judgments in their own breasts, but in the precedents of former judgments," and also in the liberty they have to scan verbal technicalities.[27] Still later his aversion to reference to mere custom and precedent becomes more marked, and he even goes so far as to say that all courts are courts of equity in principle if not in name[28]—than which it would be hard to find a doctrine more obnoxious to lawyers:—all of which throws light upon the opening sentence of his book, that the study of law is less rational than the study of mathematics, and possibly suggests a slight irony in his reference to the reason of kings as the source of the supreme rationality of common law claimed for it by such a writer as Coke.

26. *Ibid.*, Vol. VI, pp. 14, 15, and 22. In the *Leviathan* (Vol. III, p. 256), he criticizes this definition of Coke's on the ground that long study only increases error unless the foundations are true and agreed upon.
27. *Ibid.*, Vol. VI, p. 45.
28. *Ibid.*, Vol. VI, p. 63.

IV

When I first became aware of these specific empirical sources for Hobbes's political philosophy, I was inclined to suppose that he had made the latter a necessary part of a deductive system from that inordinate love of formal system to which philosophers are given. And the closing words of the *Leviathan* seem to bear out the impression, when, as if in a relieved tone, he says that having brought to an end his discourse on Civil and Ecclesiastical Government "occasioned by the disorders of the present time," he is now free to "return to my interrupted speculation of bodies natural." Croom Robertson, no mean judge where Hobbes is in question, says "the whole of his political doctrine . . . has little appearance of having been thought out from the fundamental principles of his philosophy. Though connected with an express doctrine of human nature, it doubtless had its main lines fixed when he was still an observer of men and nature, and not yet a mechanical philosopher. In other words, his political theory is explicable mainly from his personal disposition, timorous and worldly, out of sympathy with all the aspirations of his time."[29]

Further study led me, however, to a different position, to the position that Hobbes was satisfied that (even if his ideas had arisen in his own experience) he had given them a strict scientific or rational form. And while this point is of no great importance as merely an item in Hobbes's biography, it is, I think, of fundamental importance in the theme that Hobbes's great work was in freeing, once for all, morals and politics from subservience to divinity and making them a branch of natural science. So I offer no apology for setting forth the evidence that Hobbes himself believed in the scientific status of his politics.

As a point of departure, take the following passage from the preface to his *Rudiments* (the original *De Cive*). "I was studying philosophy for my mind's sake and I had gathered together its first elements in all kinds, and having digested them into three sections by degrees, I had thought to have written them, so as in the first I would have treated of body . . . ; in the second of man . . . ; in the third of civil government and the duties of subjects. . . . It so happened in the interim, that my country, some few years

29. Robertson, *Hobbes*, London, 1886, p. 57.

before the civil war did rage, was boiling hot with questions regarding the rights of dominion and the obedience due from subjects; and was the cause which, all those other matters deferred, ripened and plucked from me this third part."[30] And in a letter written in 1646 to Mersenne, speaking of his delay in completing his first part, namely, that on Body, he says that laziness is in part the cause, but chiefly because he has not yet been able to satisfy himself in the parts relating to the senses, and adds, "for that which I hope I have done in moral doctrine, that I am anxious to do in First Philosophy and in Physics."[31]

More specifically we have the claims he puts forth for his *De Cive* (claims which he continued to put forth even after he was aware that they exposed him to the accusation of actuation by egregious vanity), that it was the first treatise to put morals and politics on a scientific basis. Molesworth quotes from an unpublished manuscript on *Optics* the following concluding paragraph. "If it bee found to bee true doctrine, I shall deserve the reputation of having beene ye first to lay the grounds of two sciences: this of *Optiques*, ye most curious, and the other of Natural Justice, which I have done in my booke *De Cive*, ye most profitable of all other." In the epistle dedicatory to his *Elements of Philosophy*, in which he executed his plan to give a systematic treatment of his entire philosophy, he says that geometrical science dates from antiquity; natural philosophy from Galileo, while "Civil Philosophy is much younger, being no older (I say it provoked, and that my detractors may know how little they have wrought upon me) than my own book *De Cive*."[32]

The matter becomes one of more than biographical importance when we recall Hobbes's conception of science or demonstrative knowledge and the importance attached by him to science. Science is reasoning from cause to effect, and hence universal and certain, while empirical knowledge, or prudence, reasons from effect to cause, and is but probable and hypothetical. The end or object of science is power, control, for if we know the generation or cause of things, we have it in our power to deter-

30. Molesworth, Vol. II, pp. xix–xx. See also p. xxii, in which he says that there is only one point not *demonstrated* in the whole book—namely, the superior commodiousness of monarchy; for, as we must remember, Hobbes always means mathematical method by demonstration.
31. Toennies, *Archiv*, Vol. III, p. 69.
32. Molesworth, Vol. I, p. ix.

mine them. The question of the scientific character of morals and politics is, then, a question of the possibility of enduring social security and safety—"peace." Unless men attained to first principles from which any one could proceed, as by mathematical reasoning, to determinate conclusions, politics would remain still a matter of opinion, uncertainty, controversy, in short, of war. It is in this light that we have to understand his assertion that geometry, physics, and morals form one science, as the "British, the Atlantic, and the Indian seas . . . do all together make up the ocean."[33] Strictly speaking, moreover, *natural* philosophy can not be a science, for in it we must, perforce, reason from effects to causes, and thus arrive only at what "may be." "The science of every subject is derived from a precognition of the causes, generation, and construction of the same; and consequently where the causes are known, there is place for demonstration. . . . Geometry, therefore, is demonstrable, for the lines and figures from which we reason are drawn and described by ourselves; and civil philosophy is demonstrable, because we make the commonwealth ourselves."[34]

Moreover, the situation of the times made Hobbes's belief, whether it were rightly grounded or not, of more than academic import. We have already seen the extent to which private and variable opinion was to him the source of the ills from which the state suffered. Scientific demonstration is the sole alternative to the continuation of the troubled regime of opinion. Hobbes is in the somewhat paradoxical opinion of holding that while all order proceeds from the unquestioned authority of the sovereign, the permanent and settled institution of sovereignty itself depends upon a recognition of the scientific truths of morals and politics as set forth by him. While his controversies with Wallis and Ward doubtless gave asperity to his attacks on the universities, there is no questioning the fact that they were sincerely actuated by the belief that the doctrines of morals and politics therein taught were largely responsible for the evils of the time. They are to England as the Wooden Horse to Troy; the core of rebellions; the source of

33. *Ibid.*, Vol. II, p. iv.
34. *Ibid.*, Vol. VII, p. 184. I think that there is more than a shadowy reminiscence of Hobbes in Locke's contention that morals and mathematics are the two demonstrative subjects. What we "make ourselves" and general notions which, being the "workmanship of the understanding," are their own archetypes, are not, after all, far apart.

opinions contrary to the peace of mankind; the shops and operatories of the clergy; the fountains of civil and moral doctrine.[35] Hobbes was equally sincere in believing that the new science of morals and politics ought to be taught in the universities, and that such inculcation was a precondition of lasting social security.[36] If this nation was "very lately an anarchy and a dissolute multitude of men, doing every one what his own reason or imprinted light suggested,"[37] a considerable part of the remedy is to be found in the control, in the future, of instruction by the civil authority. "Because opinions, which are gotten by education and in length of time are made habitual, cannot be taken away by force and upon the sudden; they must, therefore, be taken away also by time and education." And then he goes on, as usual, to charge the universities with having been the corrupters of opinion, and to add that if the true doctrine of a body politic and of law were taught to young men "whose minds are as white paper," they would teach it to the people even more sedulously than false doctrine is now taught.[38] It is in this context, then, that we have to take Hobbes's famous contention that the practical utility of moral science is to be found more in what men have suffered from its absence than in what they have gained by its presence, and his contention that he is the first in morals to "reduce the doctrine to the rules and infallibility of reason."[39]

V

Such are some of the grounds for thinking that the final importance of Hobbes's political philosophy is found in its attempt to make the subject secular and scientific. Not merely in external matters was he motivated by the conflict of civil and ecclesiastic

35. *Ibid.*, Vol. VI, p. 213; Vol. VI, p. 236; Vol. III, p. 330; Vol. VII, p. 345; Vol. III, p. 713. See also Vol. IV, p. 204.
36. See *ibid.*, Vol. III, p. 713 for his suggestion to Cromwell to have his doctrines taught in the universities; see Vol. VII, pp. 343–52 for a defence of the proposal.
37. *Ibid.*, Vol. IV, p. 287.
38. *Ibid.*, Vol. IV, p. 219.
39. In his dedication to the Earl of Newcastle, dated in 1640, where men's agreement in mathematics, due to dependence on reason, is contrasted with their controversies and contradictions in policy and justice, due to their following passion.

power, but even more in intellectual aim and method. We fail to get the full force of Hobbes's conception of sovereignty until we see that to Hobbes the logical alternative is setting up the private opinions of individuals and groups of individuals as the rule of public acts—a method whose logical inconsistency has division and war for its practical counterpart.

There exists, indeed, a paradox in Hobbes. On one hand, we have the doctrine of the sovereign's arbitrary institution of duties, and right and wrong. On the other, we have his doctrine of the strictly scientific character of morals and politics. In view of the seeming contradiction it is little wonder that his opponents—notably Cudworth and his school—passed over the latter strain and assumed that the whole content of Hobbes consisted in an assertion of the purely arbitrary character of all moral distinctions. Nevertheless Cudworth's view is thoroughly one-sided. Cumberland, not Cudworth, was Hobbes's most intelligent opponent, and in his *De Legibus Naturae* we find an attempt to meet Hobbes on his own ground in a way which reveals the positive influence of Hobbes's conception of morals as a branch of natural science. In speaking of the natural light and innate ideas of the Platonizers, he remarks scornfully, "I have not been so happy as to learn the laws of nature in so short a way." He argues for an order of logical precedence in moral laws from the analogy of the laws of motion in natural science. He expressly points out that other writers, in reasoning from approved sentiments and the common consent of mankind (*e.g.*, Grotius and his followers), had reasoned from effects to causes only, and in his search for laws of nature commits himself to the essentially Hobbesian conception that they are "the foundations of all moral and civil knowledge" in such a way as to compel the use of a deductive method. He differs radically as to substance of the fundamental axioms, but agrees as to the form of morals as a science. He "abstains" from theological matters, because he will prove the laws of nature only from reason and experience. He believes that "the foundations of piety and moral philosophy are not shaken, but strengthened by Mathematics and the Natural Philosophy" that depends thereon. In making benevolence, or regard for the happiness of all, his fundamental principle, instead of egoistic regard for private happiness, the influence of Hobbes may be seen in the fact that he, too, starts from

Power, but argues that the effective power of man in willing his own happiness is limited to willing it *along with* the happiness of others. And since Hobbes had held that the desire for purely personal good contradicts itself when acted upon, the transformation upon the basis of Power of Hobbes's axiom of self-love into one of benevolence was not difficult.

VI

I do not mean, however, that Hobbes is free from the paradox mentioned. On the contrary, his position is precisely the paradox of attempting to derive by mathematical reasoning the authority of the sovereign to settle arbitrarily all matters of right and wrong, justice and injury, from rational, universal axioms regarding the nature of good and evil. His method of dealing with the paradox takes us to the meaning given by him to natural law, and to his conception of the aim and purpose, or "offices" of sovereignty. Both sides of the matter are worth attention because they reveal a thoroughgoing utilitarianism.

The mistake of so many of Hobbes's critics in thinking that he identified morals with the commands of the sovereign because he identified justice and injustice, right and wrong, with the latter, arises from overlooking the fundamental distinctions which Hobbes draws between *good* and *right*, and between intention and act—or *forum internum* and *forum externum*. Good is simply, to Hobbes, that which pleaseth a man; that which is agreeable to him—which, in turn, means "whatsoever is the object of any man's appetite or desire." It follows, of course, that since men differ in constitution and circumstance from one another, conflict or the state of war ensues; from difference of constitution, because what one man calls good another man finds evil; from circumstance, because when two men find the same object good it ofttimes can not be shared or mutually possessed. But besides the good of passion or desire of appetite, which is immediately determined by the momentary desire, whatever that may be, there is the good of reason, or rational good. To Hobbes, of course, the rational good does not differ from the sensible good in kind or quality; it is as much the pleasing as is the good of appetite. But it differs in being the object of a survey which includes *time*, instead of being a momentary estimate. For since finding good in present appetite brings a man into conflict with others, it puts his life and possessions in jeopardy; in seeking present pleasure he exposes himself to future evils "which by strict consequence do adhere to the present good," or even to destruction of life. Hence, when a man is in a "quiet mind" he sees the good of present passion to be evil, and is capable of perceiving that his true good lies in a condition of concord or agreement with others—in peace which preserves his body and institutes secure property. "They, therefore, who could not agree concerning a present, do agree concerning a future good; which indeed is a work of reason; for things present are obvious to the sense, things to come to our reason only."[40]

Moral laws,[41] laws of nature, are then equivalent to the counsels or precepts of prudence, that is to say, of judgment as to the proper means for attaining the end of a future enduring happiness. The rules of good and evil are the procedures which any man, not perturbed by immediate passion, would perceive to be conducive to his future happiness. Let it be remembered that according to Hobbes all reason (in matters natural as well as moral) is simply a sequence of thoughts directed toward an end which regulates the sequence. Hobbes, then, really believes in laws (or at least counsels) of morality which in their origin are wholly independent of the commands of the sovereign. He ascribes to these all the eulogistic predicates which were scholastically current regarding the laws of nature: they are eternal, immutable, divine, *etc*. Right reason is the "act of reasoning, that is, the true and peculiar ratiocination of every man concerning those actions of his which may redound to the damage or benefit of his neighbours. . . . I call it true, that is, concluding from true principles rightly framed, because that the whole breach of the laws of nature consists in the false reasoning, or rather folly of those men

40. Molesworth, Vol. II, pp. 44, 47–48. Compare with this the following from the *Leviathan*: "For all men are by nature provided with notable multiplying glasses, that is, their passions and self-love, through which, every little payment appeareth a great grievance; but are destitute of those prospective glasses, namely, moral and civil science, to see afar off the miseries that hang over them, and cannot without such payments be avoided." Vol. III, p. 170.

41. They are called laws only metaphorically, since only a command is a law. But in the sense in which the faculty of reason is a gift of God, and God may be said to command us to act rationally, they are true laws or commands.

who see not those duties they are necessarily to perform towards others in order to their own conservation."[42]

It is not easy to estimate just how sincerely meant were all of Hobbes's professions of piety. I think it may safely be assumed, however, that whether or no he believed in a theological God, he did believe that reasoning was divine, and that there is a sincere piety toward reason in his regarding rational precepts as divine; and that accordingly he believed in some genuine sense that God was reason. There is something besides accommodation in the following language: "Finally, there is no law of natural reason that can be against the law divine: for God Almighty hath given reason to man to be a light unto him. And I hope it is no impiety to think that God Almighty will require a strict account thereof at the day of judgment, as of the instructions which we were to follow in our peregrinations here, notwithstanding the opposition and affronts of supernaturalists now a-days to rational and moral conversation."[43]

One of the necessary conclusions of such ratiocination on future well-being and conservation is the conclusion that it is not safe for any individual to *act* upon the moral law—which in effect is not to do anything to another which one would not have him do unto us—until he has some guarantee that others will do likewise. A person so acting renders himself exposed to evil from others. Hence suspicion and mistrust, even on the part of one disposed to regard the happiness of others, are inevitable where there is no power or authority which can threaten the evilly minded with such future pains as to give assurance as to their conduct. Hence, it is one of the laws of sound reasoning to enter into a civil state, or to institute a sovereign authority with power to threaten evil doers with evils in return, to such extent as to influence their conduct.[44]

42. *Ibid.*, Vol. II, p. 16, note. In his own day, Hobbes had logically the benefit of the fact that "self-preservation" was laid down by practically all writers as the first article of the law of nature. Moral laws are "eternal" to Hobbes in exactly the same way as are geometrical propositions. They flow from original definitions whose subjects include their predicates in such a way that the latter can not be denied without falling, at some point, into formal self-contradiction. The absolute "obligation" which the subject is under not to withdraw from the compact by which he entered the State is the obligation not to contradict his own premises.

43. *Ibid.*, Vol. IV, p. 116.

44. Hobbes never attributes physical omnipotence to the sovereign, but only a power to threaten and to enforce threats which arouses enough fear to influ-

Hence it follows in Hobbes, quite as much as with any of the upholders of the popular theory, that the end or purpose of the state is the "common good." He but insists upon the correlativity of this good with implicit obedience to the commands of a protecting power. To set up any private judgment about the *acts* by which the common good is to be attained is to weaken the protective power, and thereby to introduce insecurity, mutual fear and discord—all negations to the attaining of that happiness for whose sake the state was instituted. No matter how arbitrary the sovereign's acts, the state is at least better than the anarchy where private judgments as to good (that is to say, immediate appetite and passion) reign.

But there are other checks. The sovereign is himself under the law of nature: that is to say, he is subject to the "sanctions" of utility. As a reasoning creature, he will perceive that his interests as sovereign coincide with the prosperity of the subjects. "The profit of the sovereign and the subject goeth always together."[45] Hobbes uniformly lays down certain precepts which bind the sovereign's conscience. In his *Leviathan* he develops at length the "Offices of the sovereign." They include equality of taxes, public charity, prevention of idleness, sumptuary laws, equality of justice to all, and the care of instruction. In his earliest writing he mentions all these, and also lays emphasis upon the duty of the civil authority to foster husbandry, fishing, navigation, and the mechanical arts.[46] In his discussion of the need that the state take charge of education, he clearly recognizes the limitations placed upon power to control action through positive commands appealing to fear. *Allegiance to the state is not a matter of positive command, but of moral obligation.* "A civil law that shall forbid rebellion (and such is all resistance to the essential rights of the sovereignty) is not, as a civil law, any obligation but by virtue only of the law of nature that forbiddeth the violation of faith." Hence,

ence men's outer conduct. His whole position very closely resembles that of Kant regarding the relation of the moral and the legal, much as the two differ in their conception of the moral.

45. Molesworth, Vol. IV, p. 162.

46. *Ibid.*, Vol. III, *Leviathan*, Part Two, Ch. 30; and Vol. II, Ch. 13, "Concerning the Duties of Them Who Bear Rule." See also Vol. IV, *De Corpore Politico*, Ch. 9, which sets out from the proposition, "This is the general law for sovereigns, That they procure, to the uttermost of their endeavour, the good of the people."

its ground has to be diligently and truly taught; it can not "be maintained by any civil law, or terror of legal punishment."[47]

Moreover, there are natural, or utilitarian, checks to the exercise of the power of sovereignty. In the first place, it can not affect, and (except through education) is not intended to affect inner inclinations or desires, but only acts—which are external. There is always a distinction between the just *man* and a just *act*; the former is one who means to obey the law or to act justly to others, even if by infirmity of power or by reason of circumstance he fail to do so. Even more significant is the check upon despotic action on the part of sovereignty in the mere fact that all acts *can not* be commanded. "It is necessary that there be infinite cases which are neither commanded nor prohibited, but every man may either do or not do them as he lists himself. . . . As water, inclosed on all hands with banks, stands still and corrupts; having no bounds it spreads too largely, and the more passages it finds the more freely it takes its current; so subjects, if they might do nothing without the commands of the law, would grow dull and unwieldy; if all, they would be dispersed; and the more that is left undetermined by the laws, the more liberty they enjoy. Both extremes are faulty; for laws were not invented to take away, but to direct men's actions; even as nature ordained the banks not to stay, but to guide the course of the stream."[48] The sovereign who attempts too much dictation will provoke rebellion.

This summary account should make it clear that Hobbes deduces the need, the purpose, and the limits of sovereign power from his rationalistic, or utilitarian, premises. Undoubtedly a certain arbitrariness of action on the part of the sovereign is made possible. It is part of the price paid, the cost assumed, in behalf of an infinitely greater return of good. Right and wrong are nothing but what the sovereign commands, but these commands are the means indispensable to procuring good, and hence have a moral or rational sanction and object. To use Hobbes's own words: "In sum all actions and habits are to be esteemed good or evil by their

47. *Ibid.*, Vol. III, pp. 323–24. It is in the same vein when Hobbes says that rebellion is not an offence against the civil law, but against the moral or natural law, for they violate the obligation to obedience which is before all civil law—since the institution of civil law depends upon it (Vol. II, pp. 200–201).

48. *Ibid.*, Vol. II, p. 178. Compare the *Leviathan*, Vol. III, p. 335.

causes and usefulness in reference to the commonwealth."[49] No franker or more thoroughgoing social utilitarianism could be found.

When we seek for Hobbes's natural historical associates, we should turn not to the upholders of political absolutism for its own sake, but to Jeremy Bentham. They are one in opposition to private opinion, intuition, and *ipse dixitism* as sources of the rules of moral action; they are one in desire to place morals and politics upon a scientific basis; they are one in emphasis upon control of present and private good by reference to future and general good, good being understood by both as pleasure. Their unlikenesses flow from the divergent historic settings in which their ideas were generated. To Hobbes the foe was ecclesiastic interests, the source of divided allegiance and of the assumption of a right of private judgment over against a public law of right and wrong. His remedy was a centralized administrative state. Bentham found the foe in vested economic interests which set private or class happiness above the general good, and which manipulated the machinery of the state in behalf of private advantage. His remedy was a democratizing of government to be obtained by a mass participation in it of individuals, accompanied by a widening of personal initiative in the choice and pursuit of happiness to the maximum possible limit. To both, however, moral science was one with political science, and was not a theoretical luxury, but a social necessity. It was the common fate of both to suffer from a false psychology, from an inadequate conception of human nature. But both are protagonists of a science of a human nature operating through an art of social control in behalf of a common good. Progress beyond them comes not from a hostile attitude to these conceptions, but from an improved knowledge of human nature.

49. *Ibid.*, Vol. VI, p. 220.

PHILOSOPHY AND DEMOCRACY

Why such a title as Philosophy and Democracy? Why Philosophy and Democracy, any more than Chemistry and Oligarchy, Mathematics and Aristocracy, Astronomy and Monarchy? Is not the concern of philosophy with truth, and can truth vary with political and social institutions any more than with degrees of latitude and meridians of longitude? Is there one ultimate reality for men who live where suffrage is universal and another and different reality where limited suffrage prevails? If we should become a socialistic republic next week would that modify the nature of the ultimates and absolutes with which philosophy deals any more than it would affect the principles of arithmetic or the laws of physics?

Such questions, I fancy, lurk in your minds when they are confronted by a title like that which is chosen for this evening. It is well that these questions should not be allowed to lurk in subconscious recesses, but should be brought out into the open. For they have to do with what is the first and last problem for a student of philosophy: The problem of what after all is the business and province of philosophy itself. What is it about? What is it after? What would it have to be possessed of in order to be satisfied? To such questions as these must the remarks of the evening be chiefly addressed, leaving the nominal and explicit subject of the relation of democracy to philosophy to figure for the most part as a corollary or even as a postscript.

If then we return to the imaginary interrogations with which we set out we shall find that a certain assumption underlies them—or rather two assumptions. One is that philosophy ranks as a science, that its business is with a certain body of fixed and finished facts and principles. Philosophy is viewed not as its ety-

[First published in *University* [of California] *Chronicle* 21 (1919): 39–54, from an address to the Philosophical Union of the University of California, 29 November 1918. Republished in *Characters and Events*, ed. Joseph Ratner (New York: Henry Holt and Co., 1929), 2:841–55.]

mology would lead us to expect as a form of love or desire, but as a form of knowledge, of apprehension and acknowledgment of a system of truths comparable in its independence of human wish and effort with the truths of physics. Such, I take it, is the first assumption. The second is that since the realities or truths to be known must be marked off from those of physics and mathematics in order that philosophy may be itself a distinctive form of knowledge, philosophy somehow knows reality more *ultimately* than do the other sciences. It approaches truth with an effort at a more comprehensive, a more completely total vision, and takes reality at a deeper and more fundamental level than do those subjects which orthodox philosophers have loved to call the *special* sciences. What they take piecemeal and therefore more or less erroneously (since a fragment arbitrarily torn from the organic whole is not truly a truth) philosophy takes *teres et rotundus*. What they take superficially, in, so to say, its appearance, philosophy takes at that deeper level where connections and relations within the whole are found.

Some such suppositions as these have, I think, been fostered by many philosophers. They are in the back of the minds of many students when they come to the study of philosophy. They are equally in the minds of many foes of philosophy who also compare philosophy with science, but only to contrast them—at the expense of philosophy. Philosophy, they say, is circular and disputatious; it settles nothing, for its schools are still divided much as they were in the times of the Greeks, engaged in arguing the same questions. Science is progressive; it settles some things and moves on to others. Philosophy moreover is sterile. Where are its works? Where are its concrete applications and living fruits? Hence they conclude that while philosophy is a form of knowledge or science, it is a pretentious and pseudo-form, an effort at a kind of knowledge which is impossible—impossible at all events to human minds.

Yet every generation, no matter how great the advance of positive knowledge, nor how great the triumphs of the special sciences, shows in its day discontent with all these proved and ascertained results and turns afresh and with infinite hope to philosophy, as to a deeper, more complete and more final revelation. Something is lacking in even the most demonstrated of scientific truths which breeds dissatisfaction, and a yearning for something more conclusive and more mind-filling.

In the face of such perplexities as these there is, I think, another alternative, another way out. Put baldly, it is to deny that philosophy is in any sense whatever a form of knowledge. It is to say that we should return to the original and etymological sense of the word, and recognize that philosophy is a form of desire, of effort at action—a love, namely, of wisdom; but with the thorough proviso, not attached to the Platonic use of the word, that wisdom, whatever it is, is not a mode of science or knowledge. A philosophy which was conscious of its own business and province would then perceive that it is an intellectualized wish, an aspiration subjected to rational discriminations and tests, a social hope reduced to a working program of action, a prophecy of the future, but one disciplined by serious thought and knowledge.

These are statements at once sweeping and vague. Let us recur to the question of whether there is such a thing as a philosophy which is distinctively that of a social order, a distinctive type appropriate to a democracy or to a feudalism. Let us consider the matter not theoretically but historically. In point of fact, nobody would deny that there has been a German, a French, an English philosophy in a sense in which there have not been national chemistries or astronomies. Even in science there is not the complete impersonal detachment which some views of it would lead us to expect. There is difference in color and temper, in emphasis and preferred method characteristic of each people. But these differences are inconsiderable in comparison with those which we find in philosophy. There the differences have been differences in standpoint, outlook and ideal. They manifest not diversities of intellectual emphasis so much as incompatibilities of temperament and expectation. They are different ways of construing life. They indicate different practical ethics of life, not mere variations of intellectual assent. In reading Bacon, Locke, Descartes, Comte, Hegel, Schopenhauer, one says to oneself this could have proceeded only from England, or France, or Germany, as the case may be. The parallelisms with political history and social needs are obvious and explicit.

Take the larger divisions of thought. The conventional main division of philosophy is into ancient, medieval and modern. We may make a similar division in the history of science. But there the meaning is very different. We either mean merely to refer to the stage of ignorance and of knowledge found in certain periods, or we mean not science at all but certain phases of philosophy. When we take science proper, astronomy or geometry, we do not find Euclid especially Greek in his demonstrations. No, ancient, medieval, modern, express in philosophy differences of interest and of purpose characteristic of great civilizations, great social epochs, differences of religious and social desire and belief. They are applicable to philosophy only because economic, political and religious differences manifest themselves in philosophy in fundamentally the same ways that they are shown in other institutions. The philosophies embodied not colorless intellectual readings of reality, but men's most passionate desires and hopes, their basic beliefs about the sort of life to be lived. They started not from science, not from ascertained knowledge, but from moral convictions, and then resorted to the best knowledge and the best intellectual methods available in their day to give the form of demonstration to what was essentially an attitude of will, or a moral resolution to prize one mode of life more highly than another, and the wish to persuade other men that this was the wise way of living.

And this explains what is meant by saying that love of wisdom is not after all the same thing as eagerness for scientific knowledge. By wisdom we mean not systematic and proved knowledge of fact and truth, but a conviction about moral values, a sense for the better kind of life to be led. Wisdom is a moral term, and like every moral term refers not to the constitution of things already in existence, not even if that constitution be magnified into eternity and absoluteness. As a moral term it refers to a choice about something to be done, a preference for living this sort of life rather than that. It refers not to accomplished reality but to a desired future which our desires, when translated into articulate conviction, may help bring into existence.

There are those who think that such statements give away the whole case for philosophy. Many critics and foes of philosophy coming from the camp of science would doubtless claim they were admissions of the claims that philosophy has always been a false light, a pretentious ambition; and that the lesson is that philosophers should sit down in humility and accept the ascertainments of the special sciences, and not go beyond the task of weaving these statements into a more coherent fabric of expression. Others would go further and find in such statements a virtual confession of the futility of all philosophizing.

But there is another way of taking the matter. One might rather say that the fact that the collective purpose and desire of a given generation and people dominates its philosophy is evidence of the sincerity and vitality of that philosophy; that failure to employ the known facts of the period in support of a certain estimate of the proper life to lead would show lack of any holding and directing force in the current social ideal. Even wresting facts to a purpose, obnoxious as it is, testifies to a certain ardency in the vigor with which a belief about the right life to be led is held. It argues moral debility if the slave Epictetus and the Emperor Aurelius entertain just the same philosophy of life, even though both belong to the same Stoic school. "A community devoted to industrial pursuits, active in business and commerce, is not likely to see the needs and possibilities of life in the same way as a country with high aesthetic culture and little enterprise in turning the energies of nature to mechanical account. A social group with a fairly continuous history will respond mentally to a crisis in a very different way from one which has felt the shock of distinct breaks." Different hues of philosophic thought are bound to result. Women have as yet made little contribution to philosophy. But when women who are not mere students of other persons' philosophy set out to write it, we cannot conceive that it will be the same in viewpoint or tenor as that composed from the standpoint of the different masculine experience of things. Institutions, customs of life, breed certain systematized predilections and aversions. The wise man reads historic philosophies to detect in them intellectual formulations of men's habitual purposes and cultivated wants, not to gain insight into the ultimate nature of things or information about the make-up of reality. As far as what is loosely called reality figures in philosophies, we may be sure that it signifies those selected aspects of the world which are chosen because they lend themselves to the support of men's judgment of the worth-while life, and hence are most highly prized. In philosophy, "reality" is a term of value or choice.

To deny however that philosophy is in any essential sense a form of science or of knowledge, is not to say that philosophy is a mere arbitrary expression of wish or feeling or a vague suspiration after something, nobody knows what. All philosophy bears an intellectual impress because it is an effort to convince some one, perhaps the writer himself, of the reasonableness of some course of life which has been adopted from custom or instinct. Since it is addressed to man's intelligence, it must employ knowledge and established beliefs, and it must proceed in an orderly way, logically. The art of literature catches men unaware and employs a charm to bring them to a spot whence they see vividly and intimately some picture which embodies life in a meaning. But magic and immediate vision are denied the philosopher. He proceeds prosaically along the highway, pointing out recognizable landmarks, mapping the course, and labeling with explicit logic the stations reached. This means of course that philosophy must depend upon the best science of its day. It can intellectually recommend its judgments of value only as it can select relevant material from that which is recognized to be established truth, and can persuasively use current knowledge to drive home the reasonableness of its conception of life. It is this dependence upon the method of logical presentation and upon scientific subject matter which confers upon philosophy the garb, though not the form, of knowledge.

Scientific form is a vehicle for conveying a non-scientific conviction, but the carriage is necessary, for philosophy is not mere passion but a passion that would exhibit itself as a reasonable persuasion. Philosophy is therefore always in a delicate position, and gives the heathen and Philistine an opportunity to rage. It is always balancing between sophistry, or pretended and illegitimate knowledge, and vague, incoherent mysticism—not of necessity mysticism in its technical definition, but in that sense of the mysterious and misty which affects the popular meaning of the word. When the stress is too much on intellectual form, when the original moral purpose has lost its vitality, philosophy becomes learned and dialectical. When there is cloudy desire, unclarified and unsustained by the logical exhibition of attained science, philosophy becomes hortatory, edifying, sentimental, or fantastic and semimagical. The perfect balance may hardly be attained by man, and there are few indeed who can even like Plato rhythmically alternate with artistic grace from one emphasis to the other. But what makes philosophy hard work and also makes its cultivation worth while, is precisely the fact that it assumes the responsibility for setting forth some ideal of a collective good life by the methods which the best science of the day employs in its quite different task, and with the use of the characteristic knowledge of its day. The philosopher fails when he avoids sophistry, or the conceit of knowledge, only to pose as a prophet of miraculous intuition or mystic revelation or a preacher of pious nobilities of sentiment.

Perhaps we can now see why it is that philosophers have so often been led astray into making claims for philosophy which when taken literally are practically insane in their inordinate scope, such as the claim that philosophy deals with some supreme and total reality beyond that with which the special sciences and arts have to do. Stated sincerely and moderately, the claim would take the form of pointing out that no knowledge as long as it remains just knowledge, just apprehension of fact and truth, is complete or satisfying. Human nature is such that it is impossible that merely finding out that things are thus and so can long content it. There is an instinctive uneasiness which forces men to go beyond any intellectual grasp or recognition, no matter how extensive. Even if a man had seen the whole existent world and gained insight into its hidden and complicated structure, he would after a few moments of ecstacy at the marvel thus revealed to him become dissatisfied to remain at that point. He would begin to ask himself what of it? What is it all about? What does it all mean? And by these questions he would not signify the absurd search for a knowledge greater than all knowledge, but would indicate the need for projecting even the completest knowledge upon a realm of another dimension—namely, the dimension of action. He would mean: What am I to do about it? What course of activity does this state of things require of me? What possibilities to be achieved by my own thought turned over into deed does it open up to me? What new responsibilities does this knowledge impose? To what new adventures does it invite? All knowledge in short makes a difference. It opens new perspectives and releases energy to new tasks. This happens anyway and continuously, philosophy or no philosophy. But philosophy tries to gather up the threads into a central stream of tendency, to inquire what more fundamental and general attitudes of response the trend of knowledge exacts of us, to what new fields of action it calls us. It is in this sense, a practical and moral sense, that philosophy can lay claim to the epithets of universal, basic and superior. Knowledge *is* partial and incomplete, any and all knowledge, till we have placed it in the context of a future which cannot be known, but only speculated about and resolved upon. It is, to use in another sense a favorite philosophical term, a matter of *appearance*, for it is not self-enclosed, but an indication of something to be done.

As was intimated at the outset, considerable has been said about philosophy, but nothing as yet about democracy. Yet, I hope, certain implications are fairly obvious. There has been, roughly speaking, a coincidence in the development of modern experimental science and of democracy. Philosophy has no more important question than a consideration of how far this may be mere coincidence, and how far it marks a genuine correspondence. Is democracy a comparatively superficial human expedient, a device of petty manipulation, or does nature itself, as that is uncovered and understood by our best contemporaneous knowledge, sustain and support our democratic hopes and aspirations? Or, if we choose to begin arbitrarily at the other end, if to construct democratic institutions is our aim, how then shall we construe and interpret the natural environment and natural history of humanity in order to get an intellectual warrant for our endeavors, a reasonable persuasion that our undertaking is not contradicted by what science authorizes us to say about the structure of the world? How shall we read what we call reality (that is to say the world of existence accessible to verifiable inquiry) so that we may essay our deepest political and social problems with a conviction that they are to a reasonable extent sanctioned and sustained by the nature of things? Is the world as an object of knowledge at odds with our purposes and efforts? Is it merely neutral and indifferent? Does it lend itself equally to all our social ideals, which means that it gives itself to none, but stays aloof, ridiculing as it were the ardor and earnestness with which we take our trivial and transitory hopes and plans? Or is its nature such that it is at least willing to cooperate, that it not only does not say us nay, but gives us an encouraging nod?

Is not this, you may ask, taking democracy too seriously? Why not ask the question about say presbyterianism or free verse? Well, I would not wholly deny the pertinency of similar questions about such movements. All deliberate action of mind is in a way an experiment with the world to see what it will stand for, what it will promote and what frustrate. The world is tolerant and fairly hospitable. It permits and even encourages all sorts of experiments. But in the long run some are more welcomed and assimilated than others. Hence there can be no difference save one of depth and scope between the questions of the relation of the world to a scheme of conduct in the form of church government or a form of art and that of its relation to democracy. If there be a difference, it is only because democracy is a form of desire and endeavor which reaches further and condenses into itself more issues.

This statement implies a matter of definition. What is meant by democracy? It can certainly be defined in a way which limits the issue to matters which if they bear upon philosophy at all affect it only in limited and technical aspects. Anything that can be said in the way of definition in the remaining moments must be, and confessedly is, arbitrary. The arbitrariness may however, be mitigated by linking up the conception with the historic formula of the greatest liberal movement of history—the formula of liberty, equality and fraternity. In referring to this, we only exchange arbitrariness for vagueness. It would be hard indeed to arrive at any consensus of judgment about the meaning of any one of the three terms inscribed on the democratic banner. Men did not agree in the eighteenth century and subsequent events have done much to accentuate their differences. Do they apply purely politically, or do they have an economic meaning?—to refer to one great cleavage which in the nineteenth century broke the liberal movement into two factions, now opposed to one another as liberal and conservative were once opposed.

Let us then take frank advantage of the vagueness and employ the terms with a certain generosity and breadth. What does the demand for liberty imply for philosophy, when we take the idea of liberty as conveying something of decided moral significance? Roughly speaking, there are two typical ideas of liberty. One of them says that freedom is action in accord with the consciousness of fixed law; that men are free when they are rational, and they are rational when they recognize and consciously conform to the necessities which the universe exemplified. As Tolstoi says, even the ox would be free if it recognized the yoke about its neck and took the yoke for the law of its own action instead of engaging in a vain task of revolt which escapes no necessity but only turns it in the direction of misery and destruction. This is a noble idea of freedom embodied, both openly and disguisedly, in classic philosophies. It is the only view consistent with any form of absolutism whether materialistic or idealistic, whether it considers the necessary relations which form the universe to be physical in character or spiritual. It holds of any view which says that reality exists under the form of eternity, that it is, to use a technical term, a *simul totum*, an all at once and forever affair, no matter whether the all at once be of mathematical-physical laws and structures, or a comprehensive and exhaustive divine consciousness. Of such a conception one can only say that however noble, it is not one which is spontaneously congenial to the idea of liberty in a society which has set its heart on democracy.

A philosophy animated, be it unconsciously or consciously, by the strivings of men to achieve democracy will construe liberty as meaning a universe in which there is real uncertainty and contingency, a world which is not all in, and never will be, a world which in some respect is incomplete and in the making, and which in these respects may be made this way or that according as men judge, prize, love and labor. To such a philosophy any notion of a perfect or complete reality, finished, existing always the same without regard to the vicissitudes of time, will be abhorrent. It will think of time not as that part of reality which for some strange reason has not yet been traversed, but as a genuine field of novelty, of real and unpredictable increments to existence, a field for experimentation and invention. It will indeed recognize that there is in things a grain against which we cannot successfully go, but it will also insist that we cannot even discover what that grain is except as we make this new experiment and that fresh effort, and that consequently the mistake, the effort which is frustrated in direct execution, is as true a constituent of the world as is the act which most carefully observes law. For it is the grain which is rubbed the wrong way which more clearly stands out. It will recognize that in a world where discovery is genuine, error is an inevitable ingredient of reality, and that man's business is not to avoid it—or to cultivate the illusion that it is mere appearance—but to turn it to account, to make it fruitful. Nor will such a philosophy be mealy-mouthed in admitting that where contingency is real and experiment is required, good fortune and bad fortune are facts. It will not construe all accomplishment in terms of merit and virtue, and all loss and frustration in terms of demerit and just punishment. Because it recognizes that contingency cooperates with intelligence in the realization of every plan, even the one most carefully and wisely thought out, it will avoid conceit and intellectual arrogance. It will not fall into the delusion that consciousness is or can be everything as a determiner of events. Hence it will be humbly grateful that a world in which the most extensive and accurate thought and reason can only take advantage of events is also a world which gives room to move about in, and which offers the delights of consummations that are new revelations, as well as those defeats that are admonishments to conceit.

The evident contrast of equality is inequality. Perhaps it is not so evident that inequality means practically inferiority and superiority. And that this relation works out practically in support of a regime of authority or feudal hierarchy in which each lower or inferior element depends upon, holds from, one superior from which it gets direction and to which it is responsible. Let one bear this idea fully in mind and he will see how largely philosophy has been committed to a metaphysics of feudalism. By this I mean it has thought of things in the world as occupying certain grades of value, or as having fixed degrees of truth, ranks of reality. The traditional conception of philosophy to which I referred at the outset, which identifies it with insight into supreme reality or ultimate and comprehensive truth, shows how thoroughly philosophy has been committed to a notion that inherently some realities are superior to others, are better than others. Now any such philosophy inevitably works in behalf of a regime of authority, for it is only right that the superior should lord it over the inferior. The result is that much of philosophy has gone to justifying the particular scheme of authority in religion or social order which happened to exist at a given time. It has become unconsciously an apologetic for the established order, because it has tried to show the rationality of this or that existent hierarchical grading of values and schemes of life. Or when it has questioned the established order it has been a revolutionary search for some rival principle of authority. How largely indeed has historic philosophy been a search for an indefeasible seat of authority. Greek philosophy began when men doubted the authority of custom as a regulator of life; it sought in universal reason or in the immediate particular, in being or in flux, a rival source of authority, but one which as a rival was to be as certain and definite as ever custom had been. Medieval philosophy was frankly an attempt to reconcile authority with reason, and modern philosophy began when man doubting the authority of revelation began a search for some authority which should have all the weight, certainty and inerrancy previously ascribed to the will of God embodied in the divinely instituted church.

Thus for the most part the democratic practice of life has been at an immense intellectual disadvantage. Prevailing philosophies have unconsciously discountenanced it. They have failed to furnish it with articulation, with reasonableness, for they have at bottom been committed to the principle of a single, final and unalterable authority from which all lesser authorities are derived. The men who questioned the divine right of kings did so in the name of another absolute. The voice of the people was mythologized into the voice of God. Now a halo may be preserved about the monarch. Because of his distance, he can be rendered transcendentally without easy detection. But the people are too close at hand, too obviously empirical, to be lent to deification. Hence democracy has ranked for the most part as an intellectual anomaly, lacking philosophical basis and logical coherency, but upon the whole to be accepted because somehow or other it works better than other schemes and seems to develop a more kindly and humane set of social institutions. For when it has tried to achieve a philosophy it has clothed itself in an atomistic individualism, as full of defects and inconsistencies in theory as it was charged with obnoxious consequences when an attempt was made to act upon it.

Now whatever the idea of equality means for democracy, it means, I take it, that the world is not to be construed as a fixed order of species, grades or degrees. It means that every existence deserving the name of existence has something unique and irreplaceable about it, that it does not exist to illustrate a principle, to realize a universal or to embody a kind or class. As philosophy it denies the basic principle of atomistic individualism as truly as that of rigid feudalism. For the individualism traditionally associated with democracy makes equality quantitative, and hence individuality something external and mechanical rather than qualitative and unique. In social and moral matters, equality does not mean mathematical equivalence. It means rather the inapplicability of considerations of greater and less, superior and inferior. It means that no matter how great the quantitative differences of ability, strength, position, wealth, such differences are negligible in comparison with something else—the fact of individuality, the manifestation of something irreplaceable. It means, in short, a world in which an existence must be reckoned with on its own account, not as something capable of equation with and transformation into something else. It implies, so to speak, a metaphysical mathematics of the incommensurable in which each speaks for itself and demands consideration on its own behalf.

If democratic equality may be construed as individuality, there is nothing forced in understanding fraternity as continuity, that is to say, as association and interaction without limit. Equality, individuality, tends to isolation and independence. It is centrifugal. To say that what is specific and unique can be exhibited and become forceful or actual only in relationship with other like beings is merely, I take it, to give a metaphysical version to the fact that democracy is concerned not with freaks or geniuses or heroes or divine leaders but with associated individuals in which each by intercourse with others somehow makes the life of each more distinctive.

All this, of course, is but by way of intimation. In spite of its form it is not really a plea for a certain kind of philosophizing. For if democracy be a serious, important choice and predilection it must in time justify itself by generating its own child of wisdom, to be justified in turn by its children, better institutions of life. It is not so much a question as to whether there will be a philosophy of this kind as it is of just who will be the philosophers associated with it. And I cannot conclude without mentioning the name of one through whom this vision of a new mode of life has already spoken with beauty and power—William James.

EDUCATION AND SOCIAL DIRECTION

It is not surprising that many persons in the United States who are accustomed to think of themselves as belonging to the "upper" and therefore rightfully ruling class, and who are impressed by the endurance and resistance of Germany in the war, should look with envious admiration upon the Prussian system of authoritarian education. To suppose however that they desire a direct importation of the German system of autocratic power and willing submissiveness in order to secure the discipline and massive order of Germany, is to make a blunder. They see America retaining its familiar traditions; for the most part they would be sincerely shocked at a suggestion of surrender of democratic habits. What they see in their fancy is an America essentially devoted to democratic ideals and rising to the service of these ideals with a thoroughness, a unanimity, an efficiency and ordered discipline which they imagine would be secured by a judicious adoption of German methods. Since they do not perceive the interdependence of ends and means, or of purposes and methods, their error is intellectual rather than perversely immoral. They are stupid rather than deliberately disloyal.

It is one of the many merits of Veblen's most enlightening book on Imperial Germany that he makes clear the high human cost of the envied German habit. Under modern conditions social automatism is not automatically self-sustaining. It represents a delicate and complicated piece of machinery which can be kept in proper working order only by immense pains. The obedient mind is not a thing which can be achieved by the segregated means of school discipline alone. All the resources of all social institutions have to be centred upon it without let-up. "It can be maintained only by unremitting habituation, discipline sagaciously and relentlessly directed to this end." Successful warfare, the effects of warlike preparation, and indoctrination with warlike

[First published in *Dial* 64 (1918): 333–35. Republished in *Education Today*, ed. Joseph Ratner (New York: G. P. Putnam's Sons, 1940), pp. 139–43.]

arrogance are more necessary than the technique of the class room. Only "bureaucratic surveillance and unremitting interference in the private life" of subjects can, in the face of the disintegrating tendencies of contemporary industry and trade, develop that "passionate aspiration for subservience" which is a marked feature of the Prussian diathesis. If we look these facts in the face, we shall quickly see the romanticism of any proposal to secure the German type of disciplined efficiency and of patient and persistent "industry" by borrowing a few features of the personal relation of teacher and pupil and installing them in the school. Only an occasional pedagogical Dogberry can rise to the level of a New York school administrator who would secure permanent good loyal citizenship by "teaching [sic] instinctive obedience" in the schools.

Taken in this crude form, the desire to Prussianize the disciplinary methods of American schools is too incoherent and spasmodic to constitute a serious danger. A serious danger there is, however, and it lies in the confused thinking which such efforts stimulate and strengthen. The danger lies not in any likelihood of success. Save here and there and for a brief period, the attempts run hopelessly counter to the trend of countless social forces. The danger is that the vague desire and confused thought embodied in them will cover up the real problems involved in securing an effectively loyal democratic citizenship, and distract attention from the constructive measures required to develop the kind of social unity and social control required in a democracy. For the whole tendency of current lamentations over the failure of American education to secure social integration and effective cohesion, is to put emphasis upon the futile and irritating relations of personal authority and personal subjection, or else upon the regulative power of blind engrained habits, whose currency presupposes an authoritative deus ex machina behind the scenes to supply the ends for which the habits are to work. And anybody who hasn't put his soul to sleep with the apologetics of soporific "idealism" knows that at the present time the power which would fix the ends to which the masses would be habituated is the economic class which has a selfish interest in the exercise of control. To cater to this class by much talk of the importance of discipline, obedience, habituation, and by depreciation of initiative and creative thought as socially dangerous, may be a quick path to favor.

But it represents an ignobility of spirit which is peculiarly out of place in an educator, who above all others is called upon to keep his supreme interest sensitively human.

Unfortunately there is much in the tradition of what is regarded as scientific sociology which lends itself, unwittingly, to such base uses. Sociological science inherited a basic error from the older political science, and has too often devoted itself to a pompous dressing-out of solutions of a problem resting upon a "fact" which isn't a fact. It has taken as its chief problem how individuals who are (supposedly) non-social become socialized, how social control becomes effective among individuals who are naturally hostile to it. The basic supposition is, of course, mythological. Docility, desire for direction, love for protective control are stronger original traits of human nature than is insubordination or originality. The scales are always weighted in favor of habituation and against reflective thought. Routine is so easy as to be "natural," and initiative is so difficult as to require the severe discipline of art. But the sociological antithesis of the individual and the social has invaded educational thought and is employed by the pedagogue to defend unintelligent convention, unexamined tradition, and to feed the irritable vanity of that petty tyrant, the educational administrator, who learns by study of the new sociological pedagogy that the exercise of his personal authority is in reality an exemplar of the great problem of sociology—the "social control" of the unregenerate, unsocialized individual.

This thoughtless sociology does something, however, even more harmful than the rationalization of mere personal authority. It serves to justify the laziness, the intellectual inertia, of the educational routineer. The latter finds it easier, say, to rely upon books than to make himself a well informed man at first hand. He is solemnly told that textbooks socialize the pupil, for they embody the intellectual heritage of the race. He then puts to one side the onerous task of achieving any personal originality in the subjects he teaches, lest he might fire his students with "individualism" having socially disastrous consequences. An uneasy intellectual conscience tells a teacher that in his methods he is following the lines of least resistance furnished by school customs which he has unreflectively picked up. But he is consoled by being told that thinking merely develops individualism, that custom is the great social balance wheel. And far be it from him to undermine the sanctities of institutionalized habit by a little adventure in personal reflection. He has a sense that his ways of dealing with pupils are external and perfunctory. He feels that if he took pains to acquaint himself with the scientific methods of gaining insight into human nature and applied himself with sympathy to understanding it in its immense diversity, he might be able to work from the inside to release potentialities instead of from the outside to impose conventionalities. But then the solemn guardian of "social control" comes along and warns him of the "social" value of respect for authority as such, and the dangers of "catering" to individuality. A scientific excuse for natural laziness and ignorance can go a long way.

The worst of all this, I repeat, is that it leaves problems which are pressing untouched and ignores the urgent need for the particular kind of social direction fitted to a democratic society—the direction which comes from heightened emotional appreciation of common interests and from an understanding of social responsibilities, an understanding to be secured only by experimental and personal participation in the conduct of common affairs. At this point the antithesis between individual and social ceases to be merely silly. It becomes dangerous. For the unsolved problem of democracy is the construction of an education which will develop that kind of individuality which is intelligently alive to the common life and sensitively loyal to its common maintenance. It is not an antithesis of social control and individual development which our education requires. We want that type of education which will discover and form the kind of individual who is the intelligent carrier of a social democracy—social indeed, but still a democracy.

VOCATIONAL EDUCATION IN THE LIGHT OF THE WORLD WAR

For several hundred years every great war has been followed by a very general educational readjustment that has been one of the valuable by-products of war. The religious wars of the seventeenth century were the precursors of the organization of general education of youth throughout Europe. The defeat of Germany by Napoleon and the efforts of the Germans to get ready for their war of liberation is the basis of the national general educational scheme of Germany. The older ones among us will remember that in 1870 the common saying was that France had been defeated not so much by the armies of Germany as by the German schoolmasters, and the educational reorganization of France, the foundation of the present system of general national education, dates from that particular time; and one of the most interesting books coming around from France that I saw since the war, has been one which claims that the spirit which has animated the French people and army during this war is the product of the public primary school, which made for civic training: education, as it says, in the duties of the citizen and the rights of humanity. England would seem to be the exception to this statement which I have made, but it is one of those exceptions—they do exist—which prove the rule. The lack of a national system of education in England, Great Britain, for so long a time was probably the product of the religious controversies of the sixteenth and seventeenth centuries, the civil war resulting, and the condition of toleration that came after that civil war when each of the church factors was afraid of a national or state system of education, for fear that it would become an instrument in the hands of the most powerful church body. So the result was that it scattered and to our minds disorganized the system of education which is characteristic of Great Britain, or England at least.

[First published as *Bulletin No. 4* (Chicago, 1918), 9 pp., of the Vocational Education Association of the Middle West, from an address to the Association, Chicago, 25 January 1918.]

It was right after the Napoleonic wars, however, that Lord Brougham made the first proposal for universal compulsory and public education in England, and anyone who has followed the discussions in England at the present time knows that the war has given a very great stimulus to the movement towards national education in Great Britain. In fact, there is a bill now prepared by the present minister of education himself, the first practical school man that has ever held a cabinet position, which sets forth a very large, comprehensive scheme of education; in fact it carries, in spite of their heavy taxes, an appropriation of many thousand pounds—more than the government has ever donated, or devoted, in England, to public education before. It also contains a provision for the continuation of education up to the age of eighteen, which will reduce the hours of labor for wages on the part of thousands under eighteen up to an average of about four hours per day through the week, in order to make sure that this continuation of education becomes a business necessity and a significant thing. Of course, we cannot tell just what forms this demand for educational readjustment will take in this country, but I wish to call attention to what seems to me the basic fact to be borne in mind, that all attempts at an educational reconstruction on the surface are futile. The war looks like a war of physical resources, a war of material, a war of ammunition, munitions, with the factories behind them, a war of foods, a war of transportation, a war generally of the effective organizations and mobilizations of the physical and material resources of the various nations at war, a struggle of ships and railways, of farms and factories; but just in the degree in which the war has become more and more a war of the organization of materials, munitions, food and transportation, it has been made clear that effective production and mobilization of all of these things is absolutely dependent upon the underlying human capacity, upon inventive, organizable, energetic human resources.

"The man behind the gun" has always been a significant phrase, and the present war has simply shown that "the man behind the gun" includes the women in our homes, the men on the farms and in the factories; and that this strain on the material side comes back after all to a question of human morale and of our capacity and training. It is significant that an English newspaper whose sub-title is "a journal of practical trade and finance," has been led by the emergencies of the war to say that the true wealth of England consists not in capital but in the labor, industry, skill, intelligence and experience of man. If this lesson of the war is fully learned, it is the lesson upon which educational reconstruction and reorganization after the war must go on—it must go on with a view of greater liberation of human power.

Now, I am speaking particularly of the bearing of this possible and necessary educational reconstruction upon vocational education. I wish to confine myself particularly to the older years—the years which in the present scheme are covered by what are ordinarily called the continuation schools, or the continuation educational work. In the light of the emergencies, the stress and the strain, revealed by the war, it sometimes seems to me that there are bolder plans, and that some more comprehensive and fundamental realignment is demanded. Mr. Arthur Dean has recently truly remarked that educational conscription is the only form of conscription to which, as a permanent policy, the American public is committed, and that it committed itself to the universal educational conscription quite early in its career. He also pointed out that those who have been urging both before and during the war the adoption of universal military training for the male youth of our country between the ages of eighteen and twenty, have put the primary emphasis upon the general educational values—educational values for physical training, for moral and civic training as a fundamental thing—and it was asked that if such be the case why not make the movement frankly and fundamentally an educational movement? And it is from that point of view of those two suggestions that I would approach this problem. Even the military aspects of the war have shown that the most fundamental training which is necessary for the successful military achievement must be found in the development of industrial efficiency, of industrial resourcefulness, and the adaptability of social cooperation in those national aims where enduring and enthusiastic loyalty is necessary.

Is it not, then, absurd to go on thinking of a universal training for a universal service—as if it could be exclusively or even primarily a military training for war service? The only really universal training which we could adopt for the war would be the training for a social service, because the only universal service is social service and the only possible war plan for the realignment of our vocational education must then, it seems to me, start along this line, a general national plan for the reconstruction of the conventional European plan of general training of youth into a training for social service.

The plans which have been advanced in the past for universal training are in substance, with a slight modification, stereotyped, imitation systems which have been built up under alien European conditions. These schemes which refer to our own conditions do not exhibit imagination, courage, nor an understanding of the peculiar needs and the peculiarities of American life. It is interesting to see the number of persons, many of them themselves educators, who, having been impressed with the military efficiency of Germany, seem to be intent upon Germanizing our own system of education, calling for methods of discipline and of teaching which will produce docility; a kind of fixed arrangement of superior and inferior skill in giving orders and in taking them. Technical specialization is a characteristic of the German educational system both in and out of the army, developing what in a recent school trouble in New York City has been called training for instinctive obedience and respect for authority as authority, irrespective of the ends and aims for which it is exercised. I say this is interesting not simply because these traits are the moral bases of what we call the obnoxious Prussianization of Germany, not simply because of the absurdity of the claim that we are struggling for the elimination of Prussianization when at the same time we are secretly admiring and envying it, but even more because it is possible to secure a social organization in our own country only along the lines that are in harmony with our own tradition and our own distinctive purposes. It is our own life, in other words, that we must organize efficiently, and not that of some other people. What we want, then, is an American system of universal service which the rest of the world may emulate so far as it becomes pervaded by a democratic spirit instead of our imitating the European standards.

Approaching the post-war problem, what I have to say has to do, then, with preparing for the reorganization after the war. I would bear it out that the war has brought us a large physical plant which may be and which ought to be used, after the war is over, for constructive and educational purposes. The existence of these large cantonments and buildings and various resources will certainly be employed after the war as an argument, and a strong argument, for forcing upon the reluctant but practical minded people some system of military training unless it can be shown to be still more usefully employed, more usefully available, in other directions.

Our cantonments, the equipment of physical and mechanical facilities which the war has been creating, furnish, then, a considerable part of the background of the scheme of vocational education which I have sketched. It is meant to include the youth of the country of the same ages. It ought to be truly universal, applying to young women as well as young men. Now upon this physical basis that we have spent millions of dollars securing, an education should be built which comprises the four essentials of preparation for a vocation, namely: Physique, economic efficiency, social competency and a trained capacity for the consumption and for the employment of labor. A thorough-going solution of the economic and industrial problem from the labor point of view in this country is a national scheme of socialized education applying to the youth between the older ages, just as we have already made our more elementary system universal and conscriptive.

It is not necessary to speak of the first of these elements—the need of a sound physique. The war enforces that as it does so many other things. A sound physique in a population is not merely an element designed for the success and happiness of an individual, but it is the fundamental basic social asset. If the war had not made it clear that no nation can afford to neglect systematic attention to the physical condition of its citizens, the same lesson has been impressed in a score of other ways. We have realized that one very significant aspect of our slum problem is the extent to which it is undermining national health and national efficiency on a broad scale. Our housing and recreation problem has brought us face to face with the same question of the social and national necessity of good health, as have the campaigns against consumption, against contagious sexual diseases, while the rapid spread of the movement against the drink evil has centered in a recognition again of the undermining of health from a social point of view. Consequently we have learned to see from a variety of points of view the very close connection which exists between physical deficiencies on the one side and civic delinquencies and the various forms of degeneration which require great waste of money and energy in the mitigating forms of private and public charitable relief. At the same time, although we are beginning to recognize this need, the problem involved in the production of a citizenship of a thoroughly sound physique has never been systematically presented, and one of the strongest factors in the claims which are put up for the universal military training, apart from the exigencies of war, is precisely along this line. While, however, all of the lessons of methods of training which the war has produced should be utilized, as well as all other expert knowledge in physical training and culture, it must be noted that the military system not only neglects the future mothers of the nation but is fatally defective in that it begins by rejecting and eliminating precisely that portion of the male population—from forty to fifty per cent—which is already most imperatively in need of the training that will furnish a remedy for the defects, and, I am sure, a better physique.

While this more universal training for social service would include instead of eliminating just this element which is in particular need of physical training, this side of the training would of course not consist simply of gymnastics, of organized games and athletics, and instruction in the various forms of personal hygiene, but would involve the large association of human beings. It must include definite instruction in the elements of public sanitation, thus making for increased standards regarding all the features of public hygiene and sanitation in our civic life as the youths, systematically trained, go to their home conditions.

By the second element, economic efficiency, I mean industrial training in its stricter sense. The plan that we already have, can, if imaginatively and wisely used, be made the basis for instruction in agriculture, various kinds of farming, various forms of productive industry, manufacturing distribution, household management of different forms. The aims should not, of course, be immediate, highly-specialized efficiency that is so immediate and so specialized as to limit future growth or to predestine individuals to occupy simply a particular niche. It should be aimed, rather, at a discovery of personal aptitude to practice familiarly with the fundamental processes of industry and should be devoted to the development of as much initiative, as much variety, as is possible. Moreover, the industries and the education that goes with them should be organized from the beginning on a productive—socially productive—basis, not merely to reduce the expense but even more than that, to cultivate the self-respect which comes to individuals when they know that they are doing work which is of actual practical use, financially measured; to introduce, for example, precisely the same facts towards which Mrs. Talbot in her very interesting address has already shown you it is capable of modifying the vocational training in our schools at present. It should be used, but on a productive basis, so as to avoid that deadening influence which comes from the mechanical exercises and the doing of pieces of work which have been devised simply for purposes of teaching and education as they are found in several of our best schools, and which so readily impair the training given in many of these schools, for a very considerable part of the school population. What we need in this industry, organized on a productive basis, would be to have the education devised so as to meet actual social needs, productively measured instead of being based on exercises which have been invented to be repeated simply in the hope of sooner or later getting a certain amount of education.

By social competency I mean the necessity for a certain surrounding atmosphere and spirit in connection with the industrial and physical training; the necessity for methods of training; the necessity for methods of industrial management and operation which will promote civic efficiency and the cooperative spirit. The industry should be run as far as possible on a democratic basis. Cooperation in respect to sharing in products or in profits is not nearly so important as the cooperation in the method of management. The aim should be to secure training of persons in and for groups. This should apply, of course, to the physical work, athletics, etc., and as much as is possible, to the industry; training them for self-government, the capacity to take part in managing their own affairs. This means, of course, putting individuals in positions of responsibility as rapidly as they are prepared to take it, to give them the experience of directing, of leading as well as of being led, so as to initiate the individuals into what at the present time are so largely the mysterious secrets of trade management and of the marketing of goods; taking men out from the haphazard industrial education which individuals now get, whether in school or in labor itself, which leaves so many of them totally unfitted for anything beyond routine labor under the direction of others.

The demand for the socialization of industry, for the subordination of production and manufacturing to the social need, instead of their being carried on for private profit, to which the war has already given so much stimulus, which we see being realized about us in the government—taking over railroads and control of fuel, etc.—I say, that demand for such a socialization of industries as will see to it that industry is carried on primarily to meet actual needs of society, rather than being carried on primarily for private profit, is bound to increase very rapidly after the war because of the stimulus given to it by the war as well as by the stimulus to the imagination, and the general change of conditions. It is bound to accrue when these millions of men now in the camps are finally demobilized. Now this demand, these experiments and struggles for a greater industrial self-government, the democratization of industry, are going to break down because of the absence of previous education and training to make them a success, or are going to lead simply to a substitution of governmental capitalization and a subordination of individuals to governmental bureaucracy instead of to private owners, unless this change of our industrial methods rests upon a fundamental sub-structure of human beings that have already been trained to work cooperatively with each other.

No mere schemes of governmental action will ever make a success without this educational reconstruction. Education for leisure and for the purposes of sensible, well-ordered and aesthetic recreation covers what we already call, I take it, the rudiments of a general education. In other words, they should be inspiring and releasing rather than disciplinary and scholastic. Just as music has been found to be a practical human necessity in our camps at present, and just as provision for various kinds of social aesthetic recreation seems to be a practical human necessity, so of course these same things continued and extended would constitute a large part of the type of a vocational education preparing for the leisure time of the laborer after the war. The reading of books should be stimulated upon the highest plane possible, but not upon such a high plane as to discourage the general feeling for reading altogether. The condition of community life in the playgrounds and in the factory should, as I said, be employed in order to detect and discover personal aptitude, and these great national schools or popular schools for the youth of the country which we can see in our imagination would also have every laboratory resource of science and art necessary to carry further the development of the special aptitudes.

Probably the greatest social waste which exists at present is our failure to detect tastes, capacity and ability, and find for them the channels in which they can operate with advantage to their possessors and with usefulness to others. We either put all individuals through an undifferentiated training, a required uniform training, in the pious hope that it will catch some of them, unspecified, at some point—also unspecified; or else, under the name of an elective system, we permit individuals to drift along according to their own untrained and unenlightened wishes from moment to moment. We have as yet, I think, absolutely no conception of the possibilities of an education, its possibilities both with respect to personal happiness and social usefulness, which should engage youths in activities sufficiently varied and sufficiently productive to detect their capacity, needs and powers; and then, after that has been done, to concentrate our specialized resources upon a full training of these selected capacities.

In mentioning these four points, I have been attempting to paint an outline in very broad features on a very broad canvas, and not to outline details of practical procedure. I want to add two more considerations. When it became necessary to give military training to the hundreds and thousands of the youths whom the necessities of war have called to the colors, the first step was to prepare the officers who later on would take charge of training the soldiers. As we all know, these officers come very largely from our colleges and higher institutions, and the appeal that was made draws, as all of us know who are in close connection with these colleges, upon the young men who have superior energy, who have large intelligence and who have genuine social devotion. Never, I think, were men selected more definitely on the basis of intelligent social loyalty than this appeal called out. Now, a similar appeal conducted upon similar lines for teachers in this newer type of post-war social training would call out, would have a wonderful response in calling out, the young man and woman of precisely the same equipment of social idealism.

The social idealism of the young people of our country has

not been genuinely touched and called upon in times of peace, and we have, I think, to admit that one of the features of the war system has been that hundreds of thousands of young men have been brought to view their training and their capacity in the light of social needs and demands, in a way in which their college and technical education before that was not calling them out. At present our young people simply do not know how to see clearly the opportunities and the channels, so that their native social idealism gradually flickers and sinks for lack of a field for exercise; or is diverted into fields of business ambition where their energies get an outlet or, still worse, become dissipated in the trivial channels of society pursuits. The younger citizens of our country who have not learned the full meaning of a release from the smaller things, that release which comes from a chance to take part in directing larger social activities, will respond with eagerness to any further appeal and all the more so because it is in line with the traditions and occupations of our reconstructed social relation. It would be, it seems to me, hardly short of a crime if we permit this newly stirred idealism of our youth to dissipate itself, after the war, in the colleges and beaten channels.

My other suggestion is of the same nature, but applies not so much to the young of human beings as to the branches of learning and science which have gone into the conscious service of the nation. We all know how large the organization is—we all know how large are the organized resources of the sciences of physiology, hygiene, medicine, political economy, psychology, how these sciences have been organized and mobilized on a large scale for national use. Now, through this fact, hundreds and thousands of scientific and technical men have learned in an intense way, and a direct way, in which they have not learned before, the lesson of the social importance of their particular branch of knowledge and skill. There are, for example, over two hundred youths of our country who have been trained in our schools in the science of psychology who are immediately going to have their activities put to actual national use. That is one illustration with which I happen to be personally familiar, but it merely indicates what is going on in all lines on account of the war throughout this country. They have been given a chance to translate specialized knowledge into some direct public and national service. I don't think that if many of the men have a chance to use their specialized learning, their scientific knowledge or their artistic skill after the war in some constructive form of national service, they will be compelled to withdraw into their former aloof seclusion and continue to carry on their work in the remote over-specialized, over-technical way in which most of us were carrying it on before. There is the opportunity, one might say, of the censor to gather together the resources of men of science, of art in various lines, and concentrate them upon the plan of first working out this scheme and then of putting it into actual execution. Surely the needs of health and happiness, of efficiency, of artistic creation, of the enjoyment of leisure in times of peace, cannot be less important than securing and calling out the mobilization of these resources under the necessities of the war situation.

There is one answer, not exactly a reply, but a rejoinder to some such project as I have endeavored here to paint in its large outline, and that is the old answer: It is impracticable, for it has never been done. With respect to its practicability, I should like to ask one question: Is it practicable to continue our present scheme of social disorder and confusion and conflict? Is that practicable, and again is it practicable to expect a more ordered and a more harmonious and peaceful type of social life in the future except upon the foundation and sub-structure of an educational system which has been framed on a large scale for this particular purpose? The nations of the world have found the capital and resources, the money by the billion, for the maintenance of the social values and standards of these countries when they were threatened with disintegration by an enemy from without. Is it not absurd to say that the resources and the money may not be made available nationally for a positive and constructive development, and ordering of the social values in time of peace?

The nations which have been called upon to make the sacrifices of billions of dollars and of human lives will not, I think, long remain content without demanding the expenditure of public funds on a large scale for making a more secure and a more satisfactory basis of national life. What is needed is the will, the imagination and the trained intelligence to plan and, to execute the plan. And with whatever mistakes or blunders and defects there have been in our preparation in the last few months, I think it has been demonstrated that it is possible to organize and mobilize the intellectual and moral resources as well as the financial resources of the nation in a period of national stress. Certainly we Americans have prided ourselves upon being an inventive people, an adaptable people, a people that easily and readily meets new emergencies and new inventions. Are we going to fall down when it comes to the final test of invention, the invention of social methods and of social machinery? Now is the time to begin to consider this question and now is the time to begin the planning of the campaign for our after-war educational activities. Now is the time indeed in which to make out our detailed plans and specifications for this large educational reorganization. If the educators will take upon themselves the primary responsibility for settling down to a consummation and elaboration of the scheme, I am sure that they will find among the men in science and the men in art, painting, music, and so on, among the statesmen of the country and among the larger-visioned captains of industry, a kind of cooperative assistance which will enable a plan to be worked out so that when the days of demobilization and facing the post-war problems come, we shall not be caught inert, unprepared, going on with a policy of patching up and of muddling through till some other social catastrophe, if possible even greater than the present one, shall overwhelm us.

AMERICA IN THE WORLD

There seems to be a little irony in the fact that upon Washington's Birthday the topic most apt for discussion is connected with the participation of America in a world war. Instead of a little strip of territory sparsely populated, able to maintain its own with the great nations of the world chiefly because of the advantage of remoteness, we are now a continental state, able to confer with the nations of the world on equal terms. While once there was enough to do in conquering a wilderness, we have now come to the end of the pioneer period, and have a margin of energy to draw upon.

The change has, of course, been brought about by that same development of industry and commerce which has annihilated distance, drawn all peoples into closer relations, and made the affairs and interests of one nation the concern of all, for weal or for woe. The fact that the interdependence which the new industry and the new methods of transportation and intercommunication have brought about should first reveal itself in strains and alignments for conflict does not alter the essential fact that the world for the first time now finds itself a round world, politically and economically as well as astronomically. That nations from every continent on the globe are engaged in the war is the outer sign of the new world struggling to be delivered.

It is a commonplace that whatever else the war means, it signifies for our own country the end of its period of isolation. Whether for better or for worse, America is no longer a people unto itself. America is now in the world. Unless this change of position is to mean that we are to be affected by the jealousies, the intrigues, and hostilities which have marked other nations longer in the world, we must see to it that those other nations

[First published in *Nation* 106 (1918): 287, from an address at Smith College, 22 February 1918. Republished in *Characters and Events*, ed. Joseph Ratner (New York: Henry Holt and Co., 1929), 2:642–44, with the title "America and the World."]

accept and are influenced by the American idea rather than ourselves by the European idea. Of late we have been afflicted with national bashfulness, with a shy self-consciousness as to noting even that there is an American idea, lest we be guilty of spread-eagleism. We have assumed a self-depreciatory, almost apologetic, attitude towards the rest of the world. But unless our contribution to the present world struggle is to be confined to military and economic force, it must be that we have an idea to contribute, an idea to be taken into account in the world reconstruction after the war. What are the important aspects of this idea?

Politically, federation; *e pluribus unum*, where the unity does not destroy the many, but maintains each constituent factor in full vigor. It is not accident that the conceptions of a world federation, a concert of nations, a supreme tribunal, a league of nations to enforce peace, are peculiarly American contributions. They are conceptions which spring directly out of our own experience, which we have already worked out and tested on a smaller scale in our own political life. Leaders of other nations may regard them as iridescent dreams; we know better, for we have actually tried them.

One of the greatest problems which is troubling the Old World is that of the rights of nationalities which are included within larger political units—the Poles, the Irish, the Bohemians, the Jugo-Slavs, the Jews. Here, too, the American contribution is radical. We have solved the problem by a complete separation of nationality from citizenship. Not only have we separated the church from the state, but we have separated language, cultural traditions, all that is called race, from the state—that is, from problems of political organization and power. To us language, literature, creed, group ways, national culture, are social rather than political, human rather than national, interests. Let this idea fly abroad; it bears healing in its wings.

Federation, and release of cultural interests from political dictation and control, are the two great positive achievements of America. From them spring the other qualities which give distinction and inspiration to the American idea. We are truly interracial and international in our own internal constitution. The very peoples and races who are taught in the Old World that they have an instinctive and ineradicable antipathy to one another live here side by side, in comity, often in hearty amity. We have become a peace-loving nation both because there are no strong Powers close to our borders and because the diversified elements of our people have meant hope, opportunity, release of virile powers from subjection to dread, for use in companionship and unconstrained rivalries. Our uncoerced life has been at liberty to direct itself into channels of toleration, a general spirit of live and let live. Since our minds have not been constantly impressed with the idea that the growth of another power means the decay of our own, we have been emancipated to enjoy sharing in the struggles which exist wherever there is life, and to take its incidental defeats in good humor.

In working out to realization the ideas of federation and of the liberation of human interests from political domination we have been, as it were, a laboratory set aside from the rest of the world in which to make, for its benefit, a great social experiment. The war, the removal of the curtain of isolation, means that this period of experimentation is over. We are now called to declare to all the world the nature and fruits of this experiment, to declare it not by words or books, but by exhibiting the two primary conditions under which the world may achieve the happiness of a peace which is not the mere absence of war, but which is fruit-bearing concord. That we should have lost something of our spirit of boasting about our material greatness is a fine thing. But we need to recover something of the militant faith of our forefathers that America is a great idea, and add to it an ardent faith in our capacity to lead the world to see what this idea means as a model for its own future well-being.

INTERNAL SOCIAL REORGANIZATION AFTER THE WAR

Many of you have doubtless read that remarkable pronunciamento which the English Labor party, or at least a committee of it, has issued regarding its policy in the social and industrial reorganization for the period immediately following the war. One of the striking sentences that introduces that document is that war is consuming the very basis of the peculiar social order in which it has arisen; that the war, in short, is consuming not merely munitions and steel and ships and human lives, but the social order out of which it arose. The same document refers to a statement by a Japanese statesman that the present war represents the collapse of European civilization. And they go on to say that it does mark, if not the death, in Europe, of civilization, at any rate the culmination and collapse of a distinctive industrial civilization which the workers will not seek to reconstruct.

These, perhaps, are extreme statements. But they come, at all events, from an influential section. They represent the opinions of the organized wage earners of Great Britain, the best organized laborers as laborers, probably, in the world. But we have all of us seen statements, which if not so extreme, would have seemed extreme to the point of exaggeration only a few years ago—statements coming from such very different quarters as Mr. Schwab, the steel magnate, in this country, Cardinal Bourne, of the Roman Catholic Church in England, Mr. Ralph Adams Cram, the architect. Coming from men of very unlike antecedents and outlook, they agree that, in all human probability, the world faces, as an indirect consequence of the war, serious and profound internal changes, internal reorganization; and they all agree that these changes have to be met and forestalled with sympathy and intelligence on the part of the community as a whole, unless we are to drift into a time of serious internal disorder and unrest.

[First published in *Journal of Race Development* 8 (1918): 385–400, from an address at Clark College, Worcester, Mass., 5 March 1918. Republished in *Characters and Events*, ed. Joseph Ratner (New York: Henry Holt and Co., 1929), 2:745–59, with the title "Elements of Social Reorganization."]

An English journal of trade and finance, a class journal of finance, remarked a little while ago that the war had revealed that the true wealth of England consists not in its capital, but in its human resources, in the enterprise, the initiative, the enduring, organizing power, the skill and industry of the men and the women. It is that point, perhaps, which the war has made to stand out, that though we are living in a mechanical civilization, and living in a war which is a mechanical war beyond anything known in the past, yet, after all, it is not the gun so much as the man behind the gun, and not so much the man behind the gun as the man in the field and in the factory, and the women in the home and in the shop and in the kitchen, that are really determining the outcome of this war. All other wars have been, to a large extent, wars of armies, wars of those who have been expressly mobilized for military service; but it is the commonest of commonplaces about the present war that the men on the front, the men in the trenches, the men in uniform, represent merely the first line of that larger army which includes practically the entire organization of all of the people. Now, it is because this war has thrown such a strain upon the entire economic, industrial and social organization, that it is so fraught with symptoms of change. We need to ask ourselves what are the chief weaknesses in the existing order which have been brought to light by the excessive stress and strain of war. In general, of course, those weaknesses are all of the same sort. War, whatever else its qualities and traits, at all events represents a necessity of unity of action, of organized, cooperative action, for a public, general, and common purpose and end; and the weaknesses that have been revealed exhibit the extent to which that life which we call social has been organized and arranged for private and conflicting purposes, rather than for a common and public end. They show that because of disposition of our affairs upon this private, particular and conflicting basis, we have failed to secure that stability of organization, that efficiency of conjoined action, which the modern world demands.

Now, some of these weaknesses (I rather should say all of them) most people had been conscious of before the war. There have been, in one sense, no absolutely new revelations regarding the weak points in our social fabric, but the war has been nevertheless a tremendous education. It has thrown into relief upon a large scale, has projected on a map as it were, a picture which he who runs may read. It has taken the discussion of these weaknesses and defects out of the region of academic discussion and made them a matter of general knowledge and of public interest.

The first of the deficiencies which I will mention as having to be cared for in any effective reorganization which may take place after the war is the failure of our social order in the past to secure to its members steady and useful employment. It would be difficult to bring any more severe indictment against anything that calls itself a civilization, than the fact that it is not able to utilize the energy, physical, intellectual and moral, of the members who are desirous and anxious of rendering some kind of service, the production of some kind of needed and useful commodity; that it has not been able systematically to give all of its members a chance to do something. The evil, and the unnecessary character of the evil of unemployment is, then, the thing which I would put first, because it represents, in anything that professes to be civilization, the most obvious and definite point of weakness.

Now, this is serious, not merely from the standpoint of the enormous poverty and misery which insecure and precarious employment entails upon a large part of the population, but, if possible, even more serious because of the undermining of morale, of character, which comes with such a situation as this. We all know how demoralizing charity is. Every society of organized charity is teaching and constantly preaching the evils of indiscriminate charity, how it destroys the character of those who become its recipients. Cannot we generalize this lesson and apply it to the whole industrial situation? What is the effect upon the self-respect of the large classes of men and women who periodically, once in so often, find themselves in large numbers thrown out of employment, and find that they have to beg, not for charity, but for even a chance to do work in turning out commodities or in rendering services which society actually needs? The undermining of confidence in oneself, of respect for oneself, the undermining of faith or belief in the world and in others that comes because of precarious and insecure tenure of employment is I think impossible to overestimate. When people find that they cannot do things that they are capable of doing, the attitude that comes toward the world is either one of impotence and enfeeblement, or else one of bitterness and hostility. Now, these things are, perhaps, sufficiently obvious. They are not new. There was plenty of discussion of the problem of unemployment and the remedies for it, before the war, but the war in its conduct has made the consciousness of it more acute and more general, and it has shown that the problem is not inevitable, that it is capable of human administration and handling. It has proved that it is possible for men, pooling and organizing their intelligence and experience, and having the authority of the government behind them, to take hold of the industrial and economic processes and see to it, even in a period of such great stress as during the war, that no man or woman who is capable of work shall lack useful, steady, and reasonably remunerative employment.

Another phase of the unemployment problem is that of the leisure class, so called. You may have heard the anecdote of the foreign critic who said to an American young woman that the great lack of American life was the absence of a professional leisure class; and she said, "Oh, no; we have them, only we call them tramps!" But unfortunately not even in this country does the professional leisure class consist entirely of tramps. We have the unemployed not only at the lower end of the social and industrial scale, but we have them at the upper end, also, of the industrial and economic scale—the parasites, the persons who live for display and luxury, instead of from the fruits of social service actually rendered.

Now, the war has made emphatic, self-conscious, the term "slacker." Is there anything worse, anything more contemptible or obnoxious, in social slackers in times of war than in times of peace? Will not the pressure on everybody today for what he can do in this time of stress remain after the war in an increased social contempt directed at all persons and all classes who persistently remain slackers, parasites, from the standpoint of engaging in occupations which perform a work useful to society?

The second evil that I would mention is the degraded and inhuman standard, or scale, of living which is found on the part of so many of the industrial population—of course, partly as a consequence of chronic unemployment or, at least, insecure employment, but partly because of the low rate of return for employment. We are accustomed, of course, to connect low wages and lack of work with poverty and suffering, but we too often fail to translate poverty and the misery that goes with it into terms of the general vitiation, the general deterioration of the scale of life on the part of a large element of the population. We fail to note what an unhuman lowering it means of the standard of physical health—though here again was a point that was being agitated more and more, even before the war, involving a consideration of the question of the socially unnecessary deaths, illnesses, accidents and incapacitations that come from the bad economic conditions under which so much of modern industry is carried on. You may have seen the statistics which were collected some time ago—not very long ago—by the department of Child Welfare in Washington, showing the relative chances of life for children born in the well-to-do portions of the population, as compared with the similar chances on the part of children of the wage-earning class. The loss there is merely one symptom of this lowered, this almost inhuman, standard of living under which a considerable part of the population exists. It affects not merely the bodily health, nutrition, nourishment, physical vigor, et cetera, but it enters also the aesthetic and the intellectual scale. We are too apt to pride ourselves upon our public and universal system of education without knowing that the great majority of the population get the benefit only of the more rudimentary and elementary phase of our educational system, and that by far the larger percentage of children leave the public schools before they have an education which any one of us—any member of the well-to-do and cultivated portions of society—would regard as any education at all. They leave us with the ability to read and write, to figure, with a little geographical and historical knowledge, and a miscellaneous acquaintance with trivial literature, but at an age so early that it is not possible for them to have reached, under the influences of education, a matured, trained intelligence. If they rise then, if they have the ability to rise, it is rather because of the native superiority which they retain than because of the training which they have received under our educational system. I need not dwell upon this. We need only to think of the conditions under which masses of our populations live, not merely in the slums, but wherever there is a congested industrial population, to realize how low, as compared with the attained standards of the well-to-do element of the population, their plane of living really is.

In the third place, the war has revealed the serious weaknesses and defects which exist with respect to efficiency of production and distribution. Now, this is the particular phase of the matter upon which our existing old social order most prided itself. It might have admitted that it had not done so well with the human side of the problem, but it has been contended that, so far as efficiency in the invention, organization and utilization of the machinery of production and distribution is concerned, the present age is almost infinitely in advance of any that has preceded. Of course, in a certain sense, as compared with older civilizations—those that came before the great industrial revolution—this is true enough; for these mechanical inventions are, of course, the product of scientific discovery. They are the product of the release of men's minds in the study of nature and the mystery of natural forces. It is a great mistake to suppose that our mechanical inventions of machines and implements—the steam engine, the telegraph, the telephone, the motor car, and the other agencies of production and distribution—are the actual fruit of the present industrial order. On the contrary, they are the fruit of the discoveries of a comparatively small number of scientific men who have not labored for recognition and who have never got it, very much—at least, in the way of pecuniary recognition. It simply happened that conditions were such that the men of means, men possessed of the financial and pecuniary resources, could utilize these fruits of natural science.

Furthermore, efficiency is not an absolute thing; but, of course, as every engineer tells us, it is a matter of ratio. Efficiency is a matter of the ratio which the actual output bears to the available resources; and looked at from that standpoint, not in comparison with the output of past ages, but as a matter of ratio which exists now between the present output and the resources now available, we cannot pride ourselves on having attained any great amount of even industrial efficiency in production. I need hardly remind you of the fact that when greater efficiency was required in England and in this country, the government had to take charge of the distributing agencies, the railroads. I need not remind you of the breakdown in the production and distribution of coal, from which we suffered a little while ago; and however much or however little the blame for that is to be laid at the doors of any particular individuals, the real difficulty, of course, goes much further back. It goes back to the fact that we have had production and distribution organized on a non-social basis—a basis of pecuniary profit. And when they suddenly had to be switched over to the basis of public need and public service, they naturally broke down. The great inefficiency here is, however, the failure to utilize human power. The great advance has, of course, been in the utilizing of natural power—steam and electricity, the machines, implements, and so on; but we have not succeeded in engaging, enlisting and releasing available human energy. Even before the war, the great employers of labor and those who were compelled to make a study of the labor problem were coming to realize that the problem was increasingly a psychological problem due to the failure of work, under present conditions, to enlist the interest and the attention of the great masses of the wage earners. What is called the "turn over" of labor, the fact that so many men have to be hired and then fired in order to keep a certain average number at work, is simply one symptom of the breakdown of our industrial system on the human side. I heard the other day of one of our new shipyards on the New Jersey coast where, in order to keep a thousand men steadily at work a week, they had to hire 1200 men a week—that is to say, they had to hire 50,000 men a year to keep 1000 men at work a year. Now, that, of course, is a very large average, fifty to one, but I saw, as you may have seen in today's paper, in the report of the Pennsylvania Railroad, that in order to keep 250,000 men steadily at work, they had to engage, during the past year, 250,000 more—and the Pennsylvania Railroad has the reputation of being, on the whole, if not *the* best, one of the very best organized industrial enterprises in the United States. Now, that is simply a symptom of the fact that men's minds, hearts, thoughts, interests, are not engaged, under the present system, in the work which they are doing, and that there is, consequently, an enormous waste and inefficiency. It is said that in many industries in England, the average output since the war is higher than the highest estimate of the industrial expert, the industrial labor engineer, before the war: in other words, the average laboring person, under the increased stimulus, the interest which he takes in his work because of the war, is doing more now beyond the limit that the labor expert thought was possible for the most skilled laborer before the war. In this country, many persons have estimated that the average efficiency of the average workman, under ordinary conditions, is about 40 per cent as compared with what the individual might do if he took anything like a personal, not to say vital, interest in his work.

Now, this is serious not merely because of the relative failure of production and the waste of energy, but because of the intellectual and moral deterioration which inevitably occurs when large bodies of people are doing things for which they do not care, to which they have an aversion, and which do not in any way appeal to them. The rapid growth of migratory labor, vagrant and tramp labor, is another evidence of the intellectual and moral deterioration that comes. I suppose almost every adult person who has a job in life which interests him, which appeals to him intellectually and morally, would say that his occupation, together with his personal relations to his family and friends, is the great, steadying influence in his life, the axis about which his activities are organized, that which gives his conduct stability, that which gives his thoughts, his emotions and interests direction. Now, when a person is separated or divorced from interest in his work, you have a psychological and moral phenomenon of almost incalculable significance.

Another failure on the side of human efficiency is the failure to detect and utilize the great variety of abilities which actually exist in the population. A colleague of mine made a study of the distribution of men of science in this country, taking those who now have a reasonable standing as men of science. He traced back their childhood education and early environment. He found that these New England states produced, in proportion to the population, a number of scientific men which is out of all ratio to the corresponding number produced in the southern states. Now, I do not think those of us who are New England born ought to pride ourselves that there is superior hereditary native ability on the part of the Yankee. It is simply an illustration of the compelling power and the stimulating, selective power of environment, including education, social prestige, demand, and all the other factors. When you get a figure of, say, twenty-five to one, it gives a definite picture of the amount of talent, the amount of ability and capacity, which is left dormant, latent, unutilized under our present social system. When we consider that the mass of the population are wage earners, and, as I have already said, that the great mass of the population leave school and systematic, educational opportunities cease, somewhere between the age of twelve and fourteen, when they have got along to the fifth or sixth grade of the elementary school, we may apprehend that the amount of waste which comes from unutilized capacity in the present social order is literally incalculable. The abilities which are stimulated by the present order in industry are great, but they are very one-sided. What is especially stimulated, because it is especially demanded and rewarded, of course, in our present system, is a highly specialized form of ability—pecuniary and financial ability. Even the technological ability, the scientific and engineering ability, is nowhere nearly as highly stimulated or rewarded as is the particular kind of financial and pecuniary ability that goes with capacity to command a market and secure a sale in the market for goods. The artistic capacities and abilities, a large part of the scientific capacity, a considerable portion, as I intimated, of technological ability, and many, if not most, forms of social capacity, ability to inspire and to lead others remain only partially stimulated.

Now, in such a situation as this, we are not, I think, entitled to unthinking optimism about the certainty of great progress or about the particular direction which social reorganization will take after the war. There is going to be, of course, a very great demand and a very great pressure, especially from the side of labor, as is indicated in this British document to which I have referred; but there will also be a very great inertia, very great obstacles and difficulties to contend with. We are not entitled to assume that automatically there is going to be a desirable reorganization and reconstruction after the war. We may, possibly—it is conceivable—go through a long period of social drifting and social unrest. The question is whether society, because of the experience of the war, will learn to utilize the available intelligence, the insight and foresight which are available, in order to take hold of the problem and to go at it, step by step, on the basis of an intelligent program—a program which is not too rigid, which is not a program in the sense of having every item definitely scheduled in advance, but which represents an outlook upon the future of the things which most immediately require doing, trusting to the experience which is got in doing them to reveal the next things needed and the next steps to be taken. Now, the one great thing that the war has accomplished, it seems to me, of a permanent sort, is the enforcement of a psychological and educational lesson. Before the war, most persons would have said, who recognized these evils: Well, they are very great. We all recognize them. We deplore them, but the whole situation is so big and so complicated that it is not possible to do anything about it. We have got to wait for the slow process of evolution. We have got to wait for the working out of unconscious, natural law to accomplish anything serious and important in the way of reorganization. Well, I think the war has absolutely put an end to the right to the claim of anybody to say things of that sort. It is proved now that it is possible for human beings to take hold of human affairs and manage them, to see an end which has to be gained, a purpose which must be fulfilled, and deliberately and intelligently to go to work to organize the means, the resources and the methods of accomplishing those results. There was a saying, made famous by the Boer War, and largely through the writings of Mr. Wells the novelist, about "muddling through somehow." Now you might call it muddling through, or trusting to evolution: it does not make much difference in the practical effect. That was the general attitude, I think, even of well-intentioned people—people who recognized before the war these evils of which I have been speaking and who hoped for a better world, but under the stress of war it has been found possible to get hold, if not of all the brains of the nation, of at least a considerable part of them and of its executive and administrative ability, and to systematize and mobilize them as well as the physical and natural forces, to do a certain job, to realize a definite end and aim—the job which had to be done, and the end which had to be secured.

Now, in view of this situation, it seems to me that we cannot in any good conscience return, after the war, to the old period of drifting, so-called evolution, as a necessary method of procedure. The real question with us will be one of effectively discerning whether the intelligent men of the community really want to bring about a better reorganized social order. If the desire, the will and the purpose are strong enough, it has been demonstrated that, under conditions of very great strain—abnormal strain and pressure—human beings can get together cooperatively and bring their physical resources and their intellectual resources to bear upon the problem of managing society, instead of letting society drift along more or less at the mercy of accident.

That is the great psychological lesson, it seems to me, of the war, with reference to social re-ordering after the war. The lines of action—intelligent, organized and cooperative action—must, of course, be determined from a consideration of these points of weakness which I have pointed out; and I have spent so much time on the negative side of the question because until we know where the weak points are, the deficiencies, the ills, and the diseases, we can have, of course, no clear cue as to where to direct our intelligent efforts.

The first great demand of a better social order, I should say, then, is the guarantee of the right, to every individual who is capable of it, to work—not the mere legal right, but a right which is enforceable so that the individual will always have the opportunity to engage in some form of useful activity; and if the ordinary economic machinery breaks down through a crisis of some sort, then it is the duty of the state to come to the rescue and see that individuals have something to do that is worth while—not breaking stone in a stone yard, or something else to get a soup ticket with, but some kind of productive work which a self-respecting person may engage in with interest and with more than mere pecuniary profit. Whatever may be said about the fortunes of what has technically been called socialism, it would seem to be simply the part of ordinary common sense that society should reorganize itself to make sure that individuals can make a living and be kept going, not by charity, but by having productive work to do.

In the second place, war has revealed the possibilities (this is simply repeating what I have already said) of intelligent administration—administration which will raise and maintain on a higher level the general standard and scale of living. The minimum wage is not one of the visions of the nations that have been longer in the war than we have; it is not, with them, a dream, an uplift notion: it is an accomplished fact. Great Britain is already spending an immense amount of money for the housing of its laborers, and, as we have found out in connection with our shipping program, we can not do what we have got to do, unless we first see to it that there are decent, comfortable and sanitary housing facilities for the population. One of the demands which has already been made in England, which would help, also, to take care of the unemployment problem after the war, is that this great work of housing, conducted under national social auspices, shall go on until the slums, with their bad sanitary, moral, and bad aesthetic influence, have disappeared and every individual has a home to live in and surroundings to live in which observe the ordinary amenities of human life. The movements for insurance against accident, insurance against illness, insurance against the contingencies of old age, which were already active before the war, have also, of course, been given a tremendous acceleration.

Now these are all phases of keeping up the standard of livelihood—not merely of economic livelihood, but of physical, moral, intellectual, and aesthetic livelihood on the part of the great wage earning masses of the population; and as I have already said, the war has shown that even with the extraordinary demand upon the thought and the attention and the energy upon the battlefield, there is still left over, in time of war, enough ability and energy to deal much more effectively with these questions than they were being dealt with before the war. That means that there can be no excuse for any delay when there comes a time of greater leisure. Upon the cessation of the stress of the war, society can take hold of these problems in a much more vigorous, intellectual and systematic way than ever before.

The third phase that I mention is the need of securing greater industrial autonomy, that is to say, greater ability on the part of the workers in any particular trade or occupation to control that industry, instead of working under these conditions of external control where they have no interest, no insight into what they are doing, and no social outlook upon the consequences and meaning of what they are doing. It is often said that the war has given an enormous stimulus, temporarily, at least, to state socialism. But if any one notes what is actually going on in Great Britain and in this country, he will conclude, I think, that it is not so much unmitigated state socialism, as what we might call industrial socialism that is being promulgated. Great Britain, for example, has not taken the ownership of the railways, nor the coal mines and other great industries. It would be very difficult to say who does own them any more. What has happened is that the government now insists upon having its representative—that is to say, a representative of the interests of the community as a whole, of the state and nation, on every controlling board. The investors, the owners of the stocks, et cetera, have also a representative; but it has also been found that in order to maintain complete efficiency, the laborers themselves have to have a representative.

That, in the main, has been the direction which economic

and industrial reorganization is taking during the war, first in Great Britain, where they have had a longer experience, and it seems to have pretty well marked the path upon which we are entering. This does not involve absolute state ownership and absolute state control, but rather a kind of conjoined supervision and regulation, with supervisors and arbiters, as it were, to look after the public interests, the interests of the consumer, the interests of the population as a whole, others to represent those who have their capital immediately invested, and others to represent those who have their lives (in the form of work) immediately invested. And just because, under the stress of war, things so naturally and almost inevitably take that direction, it seems to me that that is the line of future social reorganization, if it goes on in a continuous, orderly way. But this means an increasing share given to the laborer, to the wage earner, in controlling the conditions of his own activity. It is so common now to point out the absurdity of conducting a war for political democracy which leaves industrial and economic autocracy practically untouched, that I think we are absolutely bound to see, after the war, either a period of very great unrest, disorder, drifting, strife—I would not say actual civil war, but all kinds of irregular strife and disorder, or a movement to install the principle of self-government within industries.

These three things, then, seem to me the essential minimum elements of an intelligent program of social reorganization:

First, the securing for all of steady occupation or employment;

Second, through administration under state and municipal auspices, the raising and maintaining at a higher level of the general standard of living; and,

Third, the continuous, steady, even if slow, promotion of industrial democracy, industrial self-government in the various chief lines of economic activity of society.

In closing, then, I may refer to the words of President Sanford. It does seem to me altogether probable that, if we project ourselves into the future and take the standpoint of a historian looking back, while emphasis may be put upon certain lines of international reorganization and general political and dynastic changes which have resulted, it is altogether probable that the chief emphasis will be put rather upon this phase of the matter, that in order to become efficient in waging war under modern conditions, where the whole population has to be largely organized and mobilized, the most permanent and significant and far-reaching changes have come from this reorganization of the social forces; that is, the means that had to be used in order to wage the war effectively and to win the war, changed the way in which human forces were handled and organized. And this will produce effects which, in the long run, will be the most significant of any. And it will be seen, as we are dimly, vaguely realizing today, that the social order in which we are living is not the product of anything that can rightfully be called natural law, that it is not the product of intelligent insight, intelligent foresight and control, but that it is rather the historical accident due to the converging, at a certain period of history, of a large number of forces which happened to come together; the future historian may say, if the issue of the present event is as happy and fortunate as we would like to have it, that this war represents the period when mankind realized how largely its forces had been left to drift at the mercy of accident, and so decided to bring to bear upon the conduct of public affairs, upon the conduct of the common interests of mankind the same kind of intelligence, the same kind of forethought, the same kind of organized control that up to the time of the war had been devoted to private affairs.

A NEW SOCIAL SCIENCE

The pronunciamento of the committee of the English Labor party says the war is consuming the peculiar social order in which it arose; that if it is not the end of civilization it is at least the end of an industrial civilization which the workers will not willingly resuscitate. Mr. Schwab, according to newspaper statements, has gone considerably further. He foresees a social renaissance in which the man without property, the workman who labors with his hands, is going to be the man who will dominate the world. I doubt if those who fear and dislike any serious change in the constitution of society could be better served than by the development of a lazy automatism which assumes that as a matter of course tremendous social changes, all tending to improve the condition of wage-earners, are bound to occur after the war. If the change is left to either miscellaneous evolution or miscellaneous revolution to accomplish, the magician will probably disappear at a critical moment and leave things much as before, plus increased unrest and disorder on one side and increased stringency of control on the other. The English manifesto is too wise to indulge in optimistic infantilisms. It recognizes that there is a job ahead which requires an extraordinary union of energy, emotional warmth and intellectual light.

With respect to England, Mr. Hobson in his *Democracy After the War* has clearly set forth the coalition of forces which will prevent if it can a democratic reorganization of industrial society. This country will be in worse plight in many respects. The employment problem with demobilization of soldiers and munition workers will be immense. The pressure in any case for reduction of high wages will be great; already many employers and large investors want an importation of Oriental labor and would publicly work for it if they thought there was any chance of success.

[First published in *New Republic* 14 (1918): 292–94. Republished in *Characters and Events*, ed. Joseph Ratner (New York: Henry Holt and Co., 1929), 2:733–38, with the title "The New Social Science."]

The industrial dislocations effected by the war will affect labor rather than capital, because the effect of war is amalgamation of industries and integration of capital. This relatively fluid and impersonal character will keep capital in the concentrated reservoirs into which the war has gathered it. Powerful financial interests are largely in control of credit and hence of the value of money, and they will have under their management a huge accumulation of evidences of debt bought in conditions of expanding credit or cheap money. Through the contraction of credits which will follow the inflations of war they will be in a position to demand payment with an "honest dollar," that is, dear money. Up to the present there is little evidence in this country of any corresponding organized concentration of power on the part of labor. Its centralization is hampered by a fixed habit of thinking and acting in terms of immediate wages and hours of labor instead of in terms of control of economic conditions. The public shows little signs of intervening to alter the guerilla warfare going on between employers and employed—of which every daily paper gives the evidence. At the best the problem of effective concentration of labor power has all the difficulties of a human problem as against the mainly technical problem of solidifying financial power. In addition to these considerations, effective political action will meet an obstacle which does not exist in Great Britain. Our Constitution will presumably be again in force after the war. To see the property-less man in the saddle under such conditions requires a peculiarly exuberant imagination.

Set over against these difficulties and obstructions there is as yet just one large accomplishment sure to become more salient with every month which the war continues: An awakened and altered sense for human affairs. Up to the present the advance is almost exclusively psychological and educational. Fixed beliefs have been shocked into disintegration. Complacent convictions which were thought to be based on reason have been pried loose and the rock of prejudice exposed. Imagination has got used to seeing "impossible" things done in a large way, and the achievement has rendered us docile, more receptive alike to the lessons of experience and to entertainment of strange ideas, of new possibilities. Certain factors in society, especially labor on one side and scientific competency or intellectualized skill on the other, have been quickened by the strains of great social emergency to a sense of their pivotal place. Above all, it has been discovered that intelligence and training are available for the conduct of great public affairs in the public interest when occasion generates the will to employ them for that end. The feeling is subtly spreading that after such a demonstration of power in behalf of public concerns, only absence of effective desire, or the power of contrary desire to serve private interests, will permit the restoration of the older order. We have gained a presentiment that what the public wants there is the intelligence and skill to make good; that sinister wants rather than lack of capacity stand in the way. This education, this change in social psychology, is what has occurred. An altered state of imagination and desire will not of itself go far. But it is a condition without which other changes will not go anywhere. A changed outlook due to facing the world from another attitude is a precondition of a permanent invasion of new fields. A clarification of the outlook through definition of the altered attitude is itself a practical undertaking. It signifies something to realize in just what respects the intellectual supports of reactionary conservatism have been weakened. To note that supposed "scientific" foundations are turning into a bundle of myths is to aid in defining what had to be done next. When the cheeks of the augurs so bulge that their speech ceases to be understandable, it is time for a new articulation. The exposed myth is that the existing social order is a product of natural laws which are expounded in a rational, a scientific, way in the traditional sciences of society. A "science" of any subject-matter implies a rational order in that subject-matter. The accepted social sciences do not, indeed, hold that any comprehensive directive intelligence is so much at the base of the existent social order as perforce to justify its being what it is. But political and legal science rest upon the assumption of certain general and fixed conceptions which in the main the present static order exemplifies. Economic science regards the dynamic order of society as the result of the cumulative intelligence of an indefinitely large number of beings, each devoting his own intelligence to the things to which it is peculiarly adapted, namely, the pursuit of interests which lie within personal control. The net result in the existent social order is supposed to be resolvable into an immense assemblage of minute and wonderfully interwoven acts of intelligent adaptation. While sociology has been uneasy under the domination of these sciences, it has largely devoted itself to discovering other "laws," especially those of evolution, which determine society to be what it is and in so far justify it, or which at least throw the burden of change upon the future workings of evolution, that Providence of the modern enlightened man, piously credulous in spite of all his professed scepticisms.

If the war has revealed that our existing social situation is in effect the result of the convergence of a large number of independently generated historic incidents, it has shown that our ordinary rationalizing and justifying ideas constitute an essential mythology in their attributions of phenomena to basic principles and intelligently directed forces. When it is seen that intelligence has for the most part been confined to working within the sphere of these various incidental happenings to glean from each some local usufruct, it becomes apparent that the net result is something irrational, something unplanned and unintended, in short a historic accident. And in turn it appears that any science which pretends to be more than a description of the particular forces which are at work and a descriptive tracing of the particular consequences which they produce, which pretends to discover basic principles to which social things conform, and inherent laws which "explain" them, is, I repeat, sheer mythology. This is the negative side of the education enforced by the war. The need of radical modification of aims and methods in the face of a serious social crisis, which makes clear the extent to which the present order rests upon habit, intrigue, private deflections of social forces to personal uses, love of barbaric luxury and display, secret business and secret diplomacy, reveals how little affairs have been effects of intelligent desire and direction. In so doing, they give a blow in the end certain to be fatal to the "sciences" which assume intelligence and rational law in their explanations and systematizations. One may doubt whether William James foresaw how soon events would confirm his presentiment that a substitution of pragmatic experimentalism for the reign of rationalistic sciences involves an "alteration in the seat of authority."

The exigencies have shown that intelligence exists as an operative power. They have revealed the capacity of organized intelligence to take hold of affairs and direct the movement of massed details. The response of affairs has proved them amenable to such management. A centralized intellectual policy has been demonstrated to be feasible as well as imperatively needed. Empirical description of forces is not, then, the whole of the social science which should replace our rationalized mythology. What is required is large working hypotheses concerning the uses to which these forces are to be put. Legislation, administration and education must be regarded as having the role of an experimentation which tests and perfects ideas rather than as a program which merely executes them. There is, of course, an immense amount of empirical subject-matter contained within the confines of existing social sciences. The only trouble is that it has been "framed up" and betrayed by its mythical and apologetic setting. When released from this context it is available for defining present tendencies and obstacles, and hence is relevant to the development of plans of social reordering and a technique of social control. Only by becoming instruments of projected action and responsible to consequences effected by action can the social sciences escape from archaic theological designs and from methods framed on the model of a mathematical rationalism which is extinct outside of morals and politics.

The social situation creates a demand for such a science if the intelligence to be brought to bear on social reconstruction is not to be lamed and confused. A happy presentiment is displayed in the fact that the English Labor program terminates with a demand for science and yet more science, and in the fact that the hand worker and brain worker are everywhere coupled. But the outcome will be as happy as the instinct only if it be acknowledged that a new social order cannot be built with the help of a science inherited from an old social order. The war ought to give a final blow to that myth still current in Marxian circles that a new era will be ushered in by the breakdown of the present regime of capitalism due to the completed evolution of the latter, a breakdown in which it remains only for the proletariat to step in and take complete possession. The doctrine smacks, of course, of the Hegelian dialectic of opposites. But that is only its formal aspect. Its subject-matter is the belief in a catastrophe, an end of the world, to be followed by a millennial period. This recurrent doctrine always testifies to the existence of a desire which is not capable of translation into specific means and ends through intelligent action. Its adoption into "scientific socialism" is merely a confession of the absence of science, of the absence of that spirit of projecting, reasoning and experimenting in terms of detail which is the mark of every science that has achieved itself. The war has shown, I repeat, that it takes detailed intelligence, not mere desire, however praiseworthy, to manage society in an emergency. It has thereby cleared the way for a science of ideas in action which will trust not to negative forces, to bankruptcy, to bring about what is desired, but to positive energy, to intellectual competency, to competency of inquiry, discussion, reflection and invention organized to take effect in action in directing affairs. The result will not be sudden and millennial. But it will be steady; and, as in all experimental science, a mistake will be a source of enlightenment and not a cause of reaction.

POLITICAL SCIENCE AS A RECLUSE

The conquest of the rude and disorderly phenomena of physical nature by science had a peculiar unforeseeable reflex upon man's attitude toward social institutions and occurrences. That it should suggest that they also are neither the manifestations of inscrutable supernatural forces nor the sport of chance was natural. There was nothing peculiar or unexpected in the conception that social phenomena, like physical, come under "the reign of law." This is explicable enough. But chance, arbitrary free will and supernatural intervention were not the only rival causal powers with which the notion of a science of collective human affairs had to contend. The radical foes of the existent social order in the eighteenth century taught almost unanimously that institutions were the product of accidents due to human ignorance, plus fraud and the despotic will of a few men to use the many. They taught that the new social order was to be a product of the voluntary arrangements among men who substituted knowledge for ignorance, and freedom for political and ecclesiastic enslavement. The conception of "the reign of law" in human affairs cut across this humanism of the French Enlightenment, and as a consequence the project of a social science turned into a rationalizing of social phenomena by showing that they are necessary, not accidental; the effect of universal, and hence rational, laws, not of the play of human beliefs and choices, wise or unwise.

Social science thus became in substance an organized justification of the main structures of society as they exist: it operated to strengthen the sentiment of human impotency and futility. To intervene is to interfere; to interfere is to invite the disaster that comes from any attempt to "violate" natural law. This is the uniform intellectual background of the laissez-faire philosophy of society. And, the reaction against laissez-faire as a practical policy

[First published in *New Republic* 14 (1918): 383–84. Republished in *Characters and Events*, ed. Joseph Ratner (New York: Henry Holt and Co., 1929), 2:728–32.]

has not come into the possession of *ideas* with which to arm itself, by which to define and justify itself. It has presented rather a fusion of philanthropic sentiment, of the practical feeling that something had to be done whether there was any scientific warrant for it or not, of the working of an underlying traditional empiricism which had not been seriously affected by pretensions to a science, and of a vague belief that the new science of evolution gave philosophic support to attempts to accelerate social evolution even though nothing could be done to alter or direct its course.

While the conception that the economic phenomena of society are the necessary products of natural laws was essentially a contribution of English thinkers, the "sciences" of history, institutions and the state were constructed in Germany. Typically German philosophy is all of it primarily a defensive reaction against French revolutionary philosophy. Since the latter had exaggerated the effect of human ignorance, deliberate imposture and deliberate despotism in behalf of consciously entertained self-interest, German science revelled in a philosophy of inner necessity, a higher reason transcending human reasoning, an intrinsic absoluteness of law. The fact that Germany alone of modern nations underwent no political revolution and was imbued with the doctrine of the hopelessness of a revolution rendered such a justifying science a compensatory necessity. The great and successful German propaganda of the nineteenth century consisted in the spread of its distinctive scientific rationalization of history and institutions, especially of the state.

This accounts for the obvious scholastic flavor which hangs about the orthodox treatise of political science. Universal and necessary laws and principles mean something rational, and reason as distinct from experience means—vide Kant—concepts. There must be then an essential nature of the state, from which its significant attributes must flow; all the general notions must then hold together in logical order. Otherwise there would be no "science," but only a collection of empirical facts lacking the credentials of an authenticated science. Such an incident as the lobby at Albany would stand on the intellectual level of state sovereignty, Tammany Hall be as important as the bicameral system, and the methods by which big corporations influence legislation rank with the eternal truth of the proper distribution of governmental powers. In a true "science," mere empirical facts cannot figure except as they are framed within a concept or trimmed down to be an illustration of a law, in either, dislocated from their everyday context.

Every rationalistic science, that is to say every science whose aim is to explain by reference to general notions, is bound down to static principles, just as every experimental science is held to description of what is going on. The former "explains" the necessity of things as they exist by showing their connection with eternal truths; the latter sees how things are changing into something else so as by seeing to facilitate prediction and control. Classic political science thus becomes a recluse from the world of affairs and alternates between a pedantic conservatism and a complacent acceptance of any brute change which happens, if only a decent time be allowed to elapse. To label anything "truth" is indeed to use a powerful preventive. But social phenomena do not congeal simply because they are covered over with static conceptions; classic social science is no Joshua. When physical science consisted of classifying and explanatory concepts, the world of nature presented facts which conformed to them, and also anomalies and accidents. There was nothing to *do* about either of these things, once they had been squared up with the concepts duly provided. Since change is the primary social fact as surely as motion is the primary physical fact, a science which despises change as empirical is impotent before the facts. Thus it is that the dominion of static ideas over men's minds makes for ill-considered revolution as truly as for reactionary conservatism.

A genuine conservatism is an attitude of will or endeavor; it marks a union of thought with effort. It is compelled to take account of actual changes, to select and to adapt in order to conserve. The static standards of the classic science of nature did not indicate an affectionate clinging to things as they had been in opposition to things as they might become. They rather expressed the intense inclination of the imagination to take them as they never had been and never would be. Much of what arrogates to itself the high name of social conservatism is also nothing but the lazy indulgence of a secluded and self-involved imagination.

There is something humorous in the way in which the classicist detects personal wilfulness, romantic fancy and undisciplined impulse in the projects and experiments of the reformer or radical in politics and art. His own standards (called rational because they consist in a circle of logically ordered concepts) express in effect only one of his emotions—a personal aversion to change. Lacking the intellectual and moral force to face change and to assume the onerous task of directing it, rendered uncomfortable and irritable when the facts of a moving world are forced upon him, he recovers his disturbed calm by holding some innovating subversive group, some Bolsheviki, responsible for the change, and seeks again the soothing contentment of his own well ordered intellectual drawing room. In these smoothed out and becalmed precincts, he becomes the romantic expounder of truths "eternal" enough, he hopes, to last out his life time of undisturbed complacencies.

Meantime the serious work, the work of observing the multitudinous changes which are going on, of detecting their quality and movement, of forecasting their probable consequences, and inventing mechanisms to turn them to account, gets poorly done. Social control becomes a matter of luck. The dull fellowship of legitimate and allowable truths is confronted by an onrush of social forces which work their will upon us. We oscillate between eulogizing the established order as though there were any order except that of change and eulogizing all change—after it has happened—as an illustration of some mysterious law of evolution. We argue as if stability and alteration, order and innovation, were to be discussed as possible alternatives. We talk as if it were a question of putting the matured wisdom of the fathers over against the irresponsible whims of youngsters, or of letting loose the vital spirit of youth to do battle with a musty and decrepit antiquity. But all this is romantic and secluded; it does not get beyond the confines of the imagination. If the unescapable fact is that changes are going on anyway and incessantly, effective intelligence has no point of contact with such fantasies. Its concern is to find out what particular changes are going on, how their consequences may be forecast, and through what further changes within our command they may be directed to the better of two possible results. In the world of natural change, men learned control by means of the systematic invention of effective tools only when they gave up preoccupation with lofty principles logically arranged, and occupied themselves seriously with the turmoil of concrete observable changes. Till we accomplish a like revolution in social and moral affairs, our politics will continue to be an idle spectator of an alternation of social comedies and tragedies, compensating for its impotency by reducing its applause and hisses to a scheme of fixed canons which the show is then imagined to exemplify.

WHAT ARE WE FIGHTING FOR?

Severally and collectively mankind always builds better or worse than it knows. Even in the most successful enterprises aims and results do not wholly coincide. In executing our immediate purpose we have to use forces which are outside our intent. Once released, however, they continue to operate, and they bring with them consequences which are unexpected and which in the end may quite submerge the objects consciously struggled for. Such an immense undertaking as the present war is no exception. The will to conquer describes the immediate aim. But in order to realize that end all sorts of activities are set going, arrangements made, organizations instituted, as incidental means. After they have been called into being they cannot be whisked out of existence merely because the war has come to an end. They have acquired an independent being and in the long run may effect consequences more significant than those consciously desired. If, for example, one takes a cross section through the warring countries at present, one finds a striking rise in power of the wage-earning classes. Through the necessities of war, their strategic position in modern social organization has been made clear, and the Russian Revolution has brought the fact to dramatic self-consciousness. Is it not conceivable that some future historian may find this consequence outweighing any for which the war was originally fought?

If it is the unintended which happens, a forecast of the consequences of the war seems doubly futile, for it is hard enough to disentangle even the professed aims in such a manner as to make them precise and definite. Yet it is possible to see some of the forces which have been released by the war. Through fixing attention upon them, we make some guess about the future in its larger outlines. The first result which I see is the more conscious

[First published in *Independent* 94 (1918): 474, 480–83. Republished in *Characters and Events*, ed. Joseph Ratner (New York: Henry Holt and Co., 1929), 2:551–60, with the title "The Social Possibilities of War."]

and extensive use of science for communal purposes after the war. Changes which are effected by embodying scientific discoveries in mechanical inventions and appliances endure. The transformations brought about first in industry and then in general social and political life by the stationary steam-engine, the locomotive, the internal combustion engine, etc., have stayed put, while matters which absorbed in their day much more of conscious attention and made much more of a stir in the realm of thought, have sunk beneath waves of oblivion. Mechanically speaking, the greatest achievements of the year have been, of course, the submarine and airplane, the mastery of the undersea and the air. Is it not likely that the combined effects of the two will do more to displace war than all the moralizing in existence? Anticipations of the future are too readily couched in terms of the fantastic rather than of the commonplace; or rather the miraculous, once established, becomes commonplace. But considering the social revolution wrought by steam and electric transportation on land and water in abolishing parochial and provincial boundaries, it seems probable that air navigation will round out their work in obliterating nationalistic frontiers. The war has, in addition to specific inventions, made it customary to utilize the collective knowledge and skill of scientific experts in all lines, organizing them for community ends. It is unlikely that we shall ever return wholly to the old divorce of knowledge from the conduct of social affairs—a separation which made knowledge abstract and abstruse, and left public affairs controlled by routine, vested interest and skilled manipulation. The one phase of Prussianism, borrowed under the stress of war from the enemy, which is likely permanently to remain, is systematic utilization of the scientific expert. Used for the ends of a democratic society, the social mobilization of science is likely in the end to effect such changes in the practice of government—and finally in its theory—as to initiate a new type of democracy. With respect to this alteration, as with respect to the airplane, there is more likelihood of underestimating than of exaggerating the consequences which are to follow.

Another consequence, not directly willed but made necessary as an incident of the war, is the formation of large political groupings. Almost all the nations of the world are now arrayed on one or other of the two sides. Not only is such a world-wide organization including the peoples of every continent a new and unique fact, so much so that the world for the first time is politically as well as astronomically round, but the character of the alliances is quite unprecedented. In order that the military alliance may be made effective, there is in effect if not in name a pooling of agricultural and industrial resources, a conjoint supervision of shipping and hence of international trading, a world-wide censorship and economic blacklist. In addition each nation now has an interest in knowing about other nations, which has put the world as a whole on the map for the citizen of Little Peddlington and Jay Corners. The kind of knowledge and interest that was once confined to travelers and the cultured has become widely distributed. When a million or two young men return from France, the jolt given to our intellectual isolation by the very fact of the war will be accentuated. And Europe, it is safe to say, will have learned as much about us as we about it. The shrinkage of the world already effected as a physical fact by steam and electricity will henceforth be naturalized in the imagination. All of these things mean the discovery of the interdependence of all peoples, and the development of a more highly organized world, a world knit together by more conscious and substantial bonds.

Whatever the immediate decisions of the statesmen who sit in the peace conference at the end of the war, this means that an international state is on its way. Few people realize what a small number of independent states remained in the world even before the war—many times less than there were within the present German Empire a century ago. Consolidation has proceeded with the same certainty and acceleration as in the case of the multitude of small local railway systems which once sprawled over this country—and from the same causes. The war has speeded up the movement, and in the various commissions and arrangements which it necessitated will leave behind mechanisms which are bound to continue in operation—first in order to meet actual post-war needs and then because there is no way of getting rid of them without uprooting too many other things which will have got linked up with them. It is a mistake to think that the movement for the self-determination of nations, the releasing of nationalities now held in dependence, will arrest, much less reverse, the integrating movement. Cultural emancipation of nationalities and local autonomy within a federation are to be hoped for; if they are not attained, the war will have been fought in vain so far as its most important conscious objective is concerned. But even if this goes beyond local autonomy to the point of complete political independence of a new Bohemia, Poland, Ukrainia, Palestine, Egypt, India, it will not militate against the virtual control of the world by a smaller number of political units. The war has demonstrated that effective sovereignty can be maintained only by states large enough to be economically self-supporting. New nations could exist permanently only if guaranteed by some large political union, which would have to be more closely knit together than were the treaty-alliances which "neutralized" (till the war broke out) some of the smaller states of Europe.

To say, however, that the world will be better organized is not—unfortunately—the same thing as to say that it will be organized so as to be a better world. We shall have either a world federation in the sense of a genuine concert of nations, or a few large imperialistic organizations, standing in chronic hostility to one another. Something corresponding to the present anti-German federation, with minor realignments in course of time, might constitute one of these; the Central Empires and southeastern Europe another; Russia, it is conceivable, would go it alone, and the Oriental countries might make a fourth. In this case, we should have a repetition of the Balance of Power situation on a larger scale, with all its evils, including the constant jockeying to secure by threat and bribe the allegiance of Scandinavia, Spain and some of the South American countries to one imperialistic federation or another. The choice between these two alternatives is the great question which the statesmen after the war will have to face. If it is dodged, and the attempt is made to restore an antebellum condition of a large number of independent detached and "sovereign" states allied only for purposes of economic and potential military warfare, the situation will be forced, probably, into the alternative of an imperially organized Balance of Power whose unstable equilibrium will result in the next war for decisive dominion.

The counterpart of the growth of world organization through elimination of isolated territorial sovereign states is domestic integration within each unit. In every warring country there has been the same demand that in the time of great national stress production for profit be subordinated to production for use. Legal possession and individual property rights have had to give way before social requirements. The old conception of the absoluteness of private property has received the world over a blow from which it will never wholly recover. Not that arbitrary confiscation will be resorted to, but that it has been made clear that the control of any individual or group over their "own" property is relative to public wants, and that public requirements may at any time be given precedence by public machinery devised for that purpose. Profiteering has not been stamped out; doubtless in some lines of war necessities it has been augmented. But the sentiment aroused against profiteering will last beyond the war, while even more important is the fact that the public has learned to recognize profiteering in many activities which it formerly accepted on their own claims as a matter of course.

In short, the war, by throwing into relief the public aspect of every social enterprise, has discovered the amount of sabotage which habitually goes on in manipulating property rights to take a private profit out of social needs. Otherwise, the wrench needed in order to bring privately controlled industries into line with public needs would not have had to be so great. The war has thus afforded an immense object lesson as to the absence of democracy in most important phases of our national life, while it has also brought into existence arrangements for facilitating democratic integrated control. This organization of means for public control covers every part of our national life. Banking, finance, the supervision of floating of new corporate enterprises, the mechanism of credit, have been affected by it to various degrees in all countries. The strain with respect to the world's food supply has made obvious to all from the farmer in the field to the cook in the kitchen the social meaning of all occupations connected with the physical basis of life. Consequently the question of the control of land for use instead of for speculation has assumed an acute aspect, while a flood of light has been thrown upon the interruption of the flow of food and fuel to the consumer with a view to exacting private toll. Hence, organization for the regulation of transportation and distribution of food, fuel and the necessities of war production like steel and copper. To dispose of such matters by labeling them state socialism is merely to conceal their deeper import: the creation of instrumentalities for enforcing the public interest in all the agencies of modern production and exchange.

Again, the war has added to the old lesson of public sanitary regulation the new lesson of social regulation for purposes of moral prophylaxis. The acceleration of the movement to control the liquor traffic is another aspect of the same fact. Finally, conscription has brought home to the countries which have in the past been the home of the individualistic tradition the supremacy of public need over private possession.

It may seem a work of supererogation to attempt even the most casual listing of the variety of ways in which the war has enforced this lesson of the interdependence, the interweaving of interests and occupations, and the consequent necessity of agencies for public oversight and direction in order that the interdependence may become a public value instead of being used for private levies. It is true that not every instrumentality brought into the war for the purpose of maintaining the public interest will last. Many of them will melt away when the war comes to an end. But it must be borne in mind that the war did not create that interdependence of interests which has given enterprises once private and limited in scope a social significance. The war only gave a striking revelation of the state of affairs which the application of steam and electricity to industry and transportation had already effected. It afforded a vast and impressive object lesson as to what had occurred, and made it impossible for men to proceed any longer by ignoring the revolution which has taken place. Thus the public supervision and control occasioned by this war differ from that produced by other wars not only in range, depth and complexity, but even more in the fact that they have simply accelerated a movement which was already proceeding apace. The immediate urgency has in a short time brought into existence agencies for executing the supremacy of the public and social interest over the private and possessive interest which might otherwise have taken a long time to construct. In this sense, no matter how many among the special agencies for public control decay with the disappearance of war stress, the movement will never go backward. Peoples who have learned that billions are available for public needs when the occasion presses will not forget the lesson, and having seen that portions of these billions are necessarily diverted into physical training, industrial education, better housing, and the setting up of agencies for securing a public service and function from private industries will ask why in the future the main stream should not be directed in the same channels.

In short, we shall have a better organized world internally as well as externally, a more integrated, less anarchic, system. Partisans are attempting to locate the blame for the breakdown in the distribution of fuel and the partial breakdown in food supplies upon mere inefficiency in governmental officials. But whatever the truth in special cases of such accusations, it is clear that the causal force lies deeper. Fundamental industries have been carried on for years and years on a social basis; for public service indeed, but for public service under such conditions of private restriction as would render the maximum of personal profit. Our large failures are merely exhibitions of the anarchy and confusion entailed by any such principle of conducting affairs. When profit may arise from setting up division and conflict, it is hopeless to expect unity. That this, taken together with the revelation by the war of the crucial position occupied by the wage-earner, points to the socialization of industry as one of the enduring consequences of the war cannot be doubted.

Socialization, as well as the kindred term socialism, covers, however, many and diverse alternatives. Many of the measures thus far undertaken may be termed in the direction of state capitalism, looking to the absorption of the means of production and distribution by the government, and to the replacement of the present corporate employing and directive forces by a bureaucracy of officials. So far as the consequences of war assume this form, it supplies another illustration of the main thesis of Herbert Spencer that a centralized government has been built up by war necessities, and that such a state is necessarily militaristic in its structure. On the other hand, it must be pointed out that in Great Britain and this country, and apparently to a considerable degree even in centralized Germany, the measures taken for enforcing the subordination of private activity to public need and service have been successful only because they have enlisted the voluntary cooperation of associations which have been formed on a non-political, non-governmental basis: large industrial corporations, railway systems, labor unions, universities, scientific societies, banks, etc. Moreover, the wage-earner is more likely to be interested in using his newly discovered power to increase his own share of control in an industry than he is in transferring that control over to government officials. He will have to look to politics for measures which will secure the democratization of industry from within, but he need not go further than this. Reorganization along these lines would give us in the future a federation of self-governing industries with the government acting as adjuster and arbiter rather than as direct owner and manager, unless perhaps in case of industries occupying such a privileged position as fuel production and the railways. Taxation will be a chief governmental power through which to procure and maintain socialization of the services of the land and of industries organized for self-direction rather than for subjection to alien investors. While one can say here as in the case of international relations that a more highly organized world is bound to result, one cannot with assurance say which of two types of organization is going to prevail. But it is reasonably sure that the solution in one sphere will be congruous with that wrought out in the other. Governmental capitalism will stimulate and be stimulated by the formation of a few large imperialistic organizations which must resort to armament for each to maintain its place within a precarious balance of powers. A federated concert of nations, on the other hand, with appropriate agencies of legislation, judicial procedure and administrative commissions would so relax tension between states as to encourage voluntary groupings all over the world, and thus promote social integration by means of the cooperation of democratically self-governed industrial and vocational groups. The period of social reconstruction might require a temporary extension of governmental regulation and supervision, but this would be provisional, giving way to a period of decentralization after the transfer of power from the more or less rapacious groups now in control had been securely effected. The determination of the issue in one sense or the other will not, of course, immediately follow the conclusion of the war. There will be a long period of struggle and transition. But if we are to have a world safe *for* democracy *and* a world *in* which democracy is safely anchored, the solution will be in the direction of a federated world government and a variety of freely experimenting and freely cooperating self-governing local, cultural and industrial groups. It is because, in the end, autocracy means uniformity as surely as democracy means diversification that the great hope lies with the latter. The former strains human nature to the breaking point; the latter releases and relieves it—such, I take it, is the ultimate sanction of democracy, for which we are fighting.

THE CULT OF IRRATIONALITY

Neither the existence nor the positive value of the irrational in man is to be glossed over. All the instincts, impulses and emotions which push man into action outside the treadmill of use and wont are irrational. The depths, the mysteries, of nature are nonrational. The business of reason is not to extinguish the fires which keep the cauldron of vitality seething, nor yet to supply the ingredients which are in vital stir. Its task is to see that they boil to some purpose. To this end, there must be proportion in the ingredients and a certain regulation of the temperature.

It is not surprising nor yet of itself regrettable that the nonrational in human nature is particularly in evidence in wartime. All emotion bears witness to departure from the habitual, to the presence of an emergency or crisis. And in such a vast crisis as war there is something wholesome in the popular feeling which regards marked absence of indignation, and an excessive exhibition of balanced judgment, as signs of apathy as to the ends of the war.

Under circumstances when all the reserves of power have to be maintained in full action, there is something suspicious in a manifestation of pure rationality. To be stirred is evidence that one is a participant; to be wholly and conspicuously reasonable is evidence that one is an onlooker, a spectator. Many will remember how resentful European peoples in the war were when Americans before we entered into it referred to the insanity which had seized Europe. Many Americans now find it impossible to recover their own former attitude in this respect, an attitude even of many who were always pro-Ally in their sympathies. War which once seemed an insanity now seems natural, righteous and reasonable altogether. That which once seemed a disaster now seems a beneficence. The difference is the normal difference between the

[First published in *New Republic* 17 (1918): 34–35. Republished in *Characters and Events*, ed. Joseph Ratner (New York: Henry Holt and Co., 1929), 2:587–91.]

one who looks on from without and the one who shares from within.

It is not the rise of the irrational as such, accordingly, that must give pause to those who would use intelligence as a director of instinct and passion. It is the deliberate cultivation of the irrational. For the cult is not spontaneous and natural; it is intentional and purposeful. It is ulterior, full of design. It raises questions: What design is behind it? Whose interests are concerned in the careful and systematic working up of the irrational? Who is taking advantage of a natural and wholesome stir of feeling to intensify it abnormally till men see only red, and to deflect it till rational criticism of what is politically and economically obnoxious can be represented as lack of patriotic interest in the war? It is the business of deliberate thought to direct the play of emotion to an end. There are many ends, and the value of the deliberate cultivation of emotions depends upon what ends are held. Is irrationality in the mass cultivated by a few in order that the attention of the many may be diverted from something which would otherwise arouse intelligent opposition? Is it being worked up to a boiling point in order that certain securities and guarantees which are hostile to the wishes of an influential class may be overridden, and that when the proper time comes certain schemes, rendered invisible by the prevailing excitement, may be put over? Not the irrational itself, but the systematic cult of it, is, let it be repeated, the sinister thing.

Everybody who has watched the course of events knows that the deepest impulses and emotions of Americans as a body were enlisted in whole-hearted support of the war because of the end which was presented to them. They bore in imperturbed silence the earlier shrill cries of those who would arouse their emotions for the sake of war itself, for revenge and hatred. When they saw before them their own end, a world organized for the possibility of amicable intercourse, because organized on a democratic basis, the whole preciously restrained flood of impulse was let loose. But one has only to observe the present cultivated propaganda of the irrational to discover that an insidious and skilled effort is being made to detach the volume of passionate energy from its original end and to turn the emotion itself from a means into an end.

The spread of the war emotions unfortunately lends itself too readily to such manipulation. As they swell, they tend to blot from view, save in the more thoughtful, the ends for which they came into play and which justify their intense eagerness. The leaders of the cult of the irrational then strive to alter the emotions into those of fear, suspicion and hatred, knowing well—even if they have never thought of it—that when these feelings are excited they will attach themselves to lower ends, ends which better serve the purposes of those who instigate the cult.

A few months ago the average American needed no one to tell him that we had to win the war, and he needed no one to tell him what winning the war meant. President Wilson had voiced his aim and intent, however inarticulate they had been previously. To win the war was to bring about the state of things which should make any similar war impossible in the future, and this state of things meant the destruction or reduction to impotency of arbitrary and secret agencies of governments pursuing aims contrary to the interests of the common man wherever he lived all over the world. Military defeat and military victory were parts of this end just in so far as they should prove to be parts of it—that is, indispensable conditions of its attainment.

Neither sentimentality on our own part nor smooth trickery on the enemies' part were to stand in the way. But the cult of the irrational has striven to persuade us that a military defeat of Germany had only to be complete enough to be of itself a winning of the war irrespective of any further consequences. It has also taught that only a thoroughgoing and absolute military defeat could be a winning of the war irrespective of all other changes in the constitution and disposition of our foes.

Why? What is the hidden purpose? The answer is that powers which never for a moment heartily subscribed to President Wilson's war and peace aims, but which realized the impossibility of a frontal attack, powers which either distrusted democracy or realized what its victory meant for their own class interests, set a flanking movement under way. They have pulled every wire to create a belief that those who regard winning the war as equivalent to winning the objects of the war are defeatists if not actual sympathizers with Germany. They deprecate as presumption and egotism every effort to put forward as a reality the American ideals in the war. They intimate that such conduct shows lack of recognition of the sacrifices made by our Allies and lack of confidence in them. And by our Allies they here mean not the mass of the people who are themselves animated by democratic hopes, but those elements in the governments which have shown themselves as most nearly imperialistic and unreconstructed.

It is easy to foresee the time when the authors of the present cult will come forward with frank disparagement of the League of Nations, and will propose for the prevention of future wars as a substitute a more assiduous devotion to those principles of exclusive and militant nationalism of which Prussia has been the efficient exemplar. The subtle hidden propaganda to this end is already creeping into the open, and it requires no prescience to see that with the imminence of the Peace Conference it will no longer take the trouble to disguise itself. But the cult has another end which will never be avowed. It is the source of the present endeavor to use the war emotions to bring about a suppression of discussion and criticism, which would make objects of suspicion of all who still think and speak honestly even when their thoughts run counter to the immediate passion of the day. We remember the zeal and emphasis of those conservative critics of democracy who before the war loudly proclaimed the need of checks and guarantees against the will of the populace. It is a commentary on their sincerity that not a single voice has been raised from this quarter to protest against the one thing which there is need to be on guard against in the uncertain will of the populace—namely, its intolerance, when aroused, of discriminating discussion. It is just these reactionaries, these constitutional disbelievers in the people, who are now most active in egging on the intolerance of the populace. It is they who take advantage of the increased pomp of authority with which the war has necessarily clothed some men to put a stigma upon all whose liberalizing influence in domestic policies they dread. For it is not so much this suppression of a periodical or that conviction of an accused person which counts. The important thing which the cultivators of irrationality never lose from view is the discrediting which permanently weakens an obnoxious intellectual influence.

Every sensible American is willing to sacrifice something of his ordinary freedom of speech, just as he is willing for the sake of the war to surrender some of his accustomed wheat or sugar. He promptly realized that when many are giving their lives, there is an uncouth egotism involved in an attempt at a literal maintenance of all the privileges of peace. But just as he would resent a discovery that he was going without the food which is usually his own not for the sake of the common good, but in order that some one else might gorge, so will he resent any evidence that the machinery of espionage and restriction, made necessary by the war, is being used for personal and class ends. The war has shown an unexpected voluntary docility in the American people in its willingness to submit to limitations whose purpose is clear. But every incident which indicates that this docility is being turned to private account will breed a sullenness which is as extreme and harmful as the suppression which generates it. Not the least of the many evils bred by the cult of domestic suppression and suspicion is that besides an irrational submissiveness among the cowardly it cultivates an irrational rebelliousness in others. The spontaneous play of non-rational instinct ebbs and flows naturally. Cultivated irrationality is a hateful thing, which easily gets out of all control.

THE POST-WAR MIND

To make plans for the future we need knowledge of operating influences. Especially is a knowledge of the distinctively human response to the situation, of the psychological factor, indispensable. This is the more true in the degree in which our civilization becomes democratic. For every democratic advance means a release of fundamental human qualities and an increase in their power and prestige. In a stratified social order human nature is touched only through fixed and few channels. But the weakening of fixed custom and authoritative imposition takes away the bars and leaves human nature open and accessible. It is played upon more widely and freely by surrounding conditions and displays itself more directly and intensely. Any sound estimate of the social future following the war must attach importance to the question of the immediately uppermost human reactions.

The commonest fallacy in predicting what is genially termed the "new era" springs from projecting the psychology characteristic of wartime into ensuing days of peace. The first condition of any correct forecast is to note that upon the whole the reactions *from* war are contrary to those which occur *to* war. Instead of carrying over into the future the states of mind which the stress of war evokes, we should ask what states are subdued in war, and forced into the background. For when the constraints of war are removed and when the peculiar eagerness it generates dies from want of nutriment, these subconscious and suppressed tendencies will resume their activity. And quite probably the resumed activities will be so enhanced by their enforced inhibition that, until they have evened things up, they will be the dominant factors. A fair way then to estimate the post-war psychology is to take the spontaneous emotional predictions called out by the pressure of war and reverse them.

[First published in *New Republic* 17 (1918): 157–59. Republished in *Characters and Events*, ed. Joseph Ratner (New York: Henry Holt and Co., 1929), 2:596–601.]

Seriousness, determination and constant preoccupation with the future, with what is coming next, mark the human response in war. A great but uncertain issue hangs constantly before the mind, which can dwell neither in yesterday nor, for any length of time, in today. Events are in flux, and the outcome is in suspense. The event which is still to be, the coming defeat or victory, demands attention. The entire attitude is favorable to consideration of coming change. Predictions of readjustments, sweeping changes, flourish spontaneously. For it is some great and final alteration of the face of events to which the mind is attuned. With the let up of war, with the issue determined, the tension relaxes, and the immediate present regains with added force its command. Not the arduous labor of reconstruction but enjoyment of the present, of the gains to be snatched from using the opportunities of pleasure and profit in things as they are, captures the mind. The commercial expansions, the fierce outbursts of "materialistic" money-making that have followed in the immediate wake of most modern wars, are not wholly due to the need of making good the objective losses of war, nor yet wholly to a continuation of the profiteering of war itself. They are in part due to the normal psychology of release from the unnatural strain which war puts upon a human nature, a nature that is capable of infinite heroism upon occasion, but that can no longer sustain the heroic mood when the occasion is past. An Englishman long resident in Japan noted that after the Russo-Japanese war, young men who earlier had had dreams of scholarship, statesmanship and military glory turned eagerly to money-making as the great "sacrifice" which the new condition of the nation exacted of them. This is only an unusually naïve expression of the usual reaction from war.

The concentration upon the future characteristic of war inevitably takes on a rosy hue. To admit the prospect of defeat is the beginning of defeat itself. Till the issue is decided, unconquered hope colors expectation with limitless optimism. This expression of the nerving of a people against present evil and threatened disaster outruns the limited portion of time devoted to war and projects into the future the image of a new day, which is to be happy beyond all the experiences of the past. Every great war is to usher in a time of enduring peace; it is to see the establishment of justice, the dawn of a new era. Millennial expectations are not born in times of prosperity. In such days, the absorbing present is good enough. The millennium is the compensatory refuge of immediate distress and imminent evil. But victory generates buoyancy and buoyancy is likely to find a vent in quick satisfactions. The paradise of surrounding milk and honey displaces the new order that has to be labored for. Most of the glowing prophecies of an inevitable social reconstruction to follow the war merely transfer into the peaceful future the reaction peculiar to war. It will be all too easy to go on cultivating our plots on the verge of Vesuvius till a new catastrophe overtakes us.

The tragedy of war also breeds a certain exaltation of mood hailed by sympathetic observers of a literary turn of mind as a religious conversion. We have doubtless all heard persons of this type lament that America has not been in the war long enough to experience the intensity of suffering that purchases this elevation of feeling, this spiritual exhilaration, which is sometimes referred to as the priceless boon conferred by the war. It is probably no accident that it was the *New York Journal*, most unremitting in urging unforgiving hate of the Germans, that met the end of the war with a sigh of regret that we Americans had not been in the war long enough to suffer the full "chastening of calamity." But a sensible judge of human nature would be thankful that humanity had been preserved not only from unnecessary suffering, but also from the abnormal strain involved in what, by protective psychological coloration, is called chastening. Having been saved this extreme, there is the greater hope that we may be saved the extreme of frivolity and reckless pleasure-seeking which is the usual reaction when human nature is too long on the rack. Even as it is, it is likely that the excessive sexual excitation which heroic literary commentators and civilian journalistic moralists overlook will have far more abiding consequences than the much heralded spiritual uplift which fascinates their gaze.

An intelligent English historian who had written shrewdly of the development of political ideals and practices from Metternich to Bismarck, pointing out the non-fulfilment of the high hopes aroused by the defeat of Napoleonic aggression, greeted the present war, when it was but a month or two old, as the opening of a new era. He traced throughout the realm of international relationships, domestic politics, the relation of the sexes, capital and labor—all the spheres of conflict in fact—the substitution of an era of tolerance and good will for one of intolerance and antagonism.

Already it is easy to see that he wrote under the influence of that over-emphasis of emotion produced in a people in the first glow of becoming "common servants and common sufferers in the same cause," to quote an English philosopher who celebrated the outbreak of brotherly love which is but the reverse side of fighting. The Russians and Germans who experienced the same sense of unity as the outcome of being banded together have now turned their guns on one another. Fortunately we shall not signalize the return to the ordinary activities of life in the same way. But one is building on the sandiest of foundations who expects much help in dealing with post-war problems, domestic or foreign, from the community of emotional consciousness generated by war. Men will resume the opposition of interests where they laid them down. We may indeed count ourselves lucky if these are not intensified by the truce, by the stirrings of hate and suspicion bred by war, and by the extraordinary and abnormal readjustments that have to be undertaken.

These paragraphs are in no sense a prediction of the future. All attempts at such prophecies are vitiated by the same fact. They may foretell, in the degree of the intelligence of their author, the future so far as that is shaped by forces seen to be working contemporaneously. They omit the effects of some force which is so seemingly slight as to be negligible, but which will in the future modify in the most unpredictable ways all the known forces. Mr. Wells, for example, could prophesy the liberalizing of Russia—that was easy because all modern forces were making autocracies out of date. He could not foresee Bolshevism and the subtle ferment it would introduce into all the otherwise calculable factors. In this sense the weak things will always confound the mighty—the future will be determined by the coming event which at the given moment is still so nascent as to escape detection. I am not, then, attempting to tell what is going to happen; nor to play the part of one who predicts that the hopes of a new era are doomed to disappointment.

But it is important to know what we can count on and what will surely elude us. So far as our expectation of a happier future is based upon projecting into the future the conscious states characteristic of war, it *is* doomed. And in large measure it is fortunate that such is the case. For I have said nothing about the uglier reactions of war—fear and its twin, hate. These unhappily are more enduring than most of the emotions mentioned. They are not so much conscious states, superficial and transitory, as attitudes of will, of action, which eat their way into permanent disposition. But even these things pass when persistently confronted by objective conditions. The embittered missionaries of a permanent vengeful punishment and cultivated hatred of Germany should be compelled to retire and undergo a period of historical study. The transfer of international ill will and friendliness as respects England, France and Germany would form an illuminating lesson. But the sequel of our Civil War, the consequences of the "reconstruction" imposed by distrust and hate and the story of the persistence of its bad effects long after the inevitable emotional reconciliation occurred might alone suffice to teach a much needed truth.

To state some of the human reactions from war is not to predict. It is merely to analyze what already exists—human nature. Such an analysis may, however, assist in planning for the future. For it warns us against trusting to the emotions to do a work which only the most laborious and faithful intelligence can accomplish. It will warn us, with respect to our enemies, from planning a future based on suspicion and hostility. It will warn us, in the infinitely complex problems of domestic readjustment, from trusting to the vague aspirations and protective hopefulness produced in wartime. It will teach us that reliance upon such undisciplined desires is one of the chief reasons why the course of events has in the past frustrated the ardent hopes of men in the great crises of human history. It will suggest dependence upon the homelier and less exciting work of an intelligence which resolves problems into their detailed elements and which contrives piecemeal and patiently for their solution.

THE NEW PATERNALISM

The vast scale upon which affairs go on once seemed enough to make men despair of the possibility of their orderly control. They seemed too big to be got in hand. Men felt dwarfed, shrivelled in the face of the vastness of economic and political conditions. The war put the immensity of things in a new light. It became evident that the very size of things had brought with it a centralization already inchoate in private hands, so that about all that was required to consolidate the centralized control was to give it explicit governmental sanction. The economists and business men called to the industrial front accomplished more in a few months to demonstrate the practicable possibilities of governmental regulation of private business than professional Socialists had effected in a generation. They proved that a few fortresses in our day absolutely command the whole industrial field. When they were taken possession of, public direction of industry followed almost automatically. Production could be controlled by taking over the agencies of shipping and transportation, foreign and domestic; by regulating the giving of credit and the issuing of securities; by administering the labor market, through the government becoming itself a wholesale bidder and conscriptor of men. The centralized mechanisms of industrial and economic control built up in modern business are so definite that when these three things were taken over by the government, public control was shown to be almost ridiculously easy. With sufficient experience to make methods of taxation scientific enough to control profiteering, the simplicity of some form of state capitalism (generally called state socialism) would have been demonstrated.

Reaction against the paternalism of this control now that the war is over is prompt, widespread and highly organized. There are too many interests concerned with maintaining a private pa-

[First published in *New Republic* 17 (1918): 216–17. Republished in *Characters and Events*, ed. Joseph Ratner (New York: Henry Holt and Co., 1929), 2: 517–21, with the title "Propaganda."]

ternalistic regulation of other men's affairs, known as personal initiative, to permit this state of things to go unchallenged. But strangely enough there is one form of paternalism stimulated by the war for the continuation of which these same interests are anxiously eager, namely, intellectual paternalism.

The censorship will be relaxed; officially it will be abandoned. Letters will not be so freely opened. Secret service agents of our own and a foreign government will not be so generously encouraged to exercise a kindly supervision of telegraph and telephone lines. The lapse of the Espionage Act will make it less easy for governmental officials, big and petty, to regulate the press by threatening its mailing privileges. The still more efficacious domination of the agencies of discussion by the Pulp and Paper Division of the War Industries Board will presumably be relaxed. But one thing will not be forgotten. There has been a remarkable demonstration of the possibilities of guidance of the news upon which the formation of public opinion depends. There has been an equally convincing demonstration of the effect upon collective action of opinion when directed systematically along certain channels. One almost wonders whether the word "news" is not destined to be replaced by the word "propaganda"—though of course words linger after things have been transformed.

The world has come to a curious juncture of events. The development of political democracy has made necessary the semblance at least of consultation of public opinion. The beliefs of the masses cannot be openly ignored. The immense size of a democracy like our own would make the development of community of sentiment and persuasion impossible unless there were definite and centralized agencies for communication and propagation of facts and ideas. Consequently just at the time when shaping public opinion has become an essential industry, there also exist the instrumentalities for news gathering and distributing on a large scale. Not only so, but business conditions almost automatically force these agencies into highly concentrated forms easily manageable from the centre. The small operator in news and "facts" can hardly exist. Comprehensive undertakings with large capital are required. Capital in one form is naturally friendly to capital in other forms. Aside from conscious and unconscious affiliations and combinations, there is the always influential fact that reflecting the views of the powers that be gives access to important sources of information, while lack of subserviency shuts off such access. And in the background unremittingly works the fact that democracies are controlled through their opinions, that opinions are formed by the material upon which they feed, and that propaganda disguised as the distribution of news is the cheapest and most effective way of developing the required tone of public sentiment.

The governmental control demanded by the exigencies of war has in part merely revealed the scope of influential forces previously operative in private hands. But the war has also increased the prior centralization, and created an atmosphere favorable to feeding the people with just those things and only those things which the authorities believe that it is good for them to know. The tensions of uncertainty and fear produced by the war have developed an extraordinary sensitiveness which works toward strengthening this benevolent paternalism. On the day when the armistice was signed, an article written by a university professor was published in a daily paper solemnly warning the American people that the reports which stated that the Germans were in revolt and were sincerely seeking peace were in all probability more instances of clever German propaganda designed to undermine American morale. The only thing unusual about this warning was the fact that it happened to be printed a few hours after the revolt and the establishment of peace were accomplished facts. When a few scattering and timid voices were raised in this country in behalf of tempering justice with mercy in the case of the economic conditions of the armistice which had to do with feeding Germany, a semi-official warning was sent out from Washington against the new activities of German agents in this country. One's only embarrassment would be in selecting from the multitude of instances of this sort. When the belief of Germans as supermen in other respects began to wane, the persuasion that they were supermen in propaganda only increased.

Most of the persons who shared such beliefs were neither stupid nor sinister. The dread of the enemy provoked by war tends like all emotions to spread like a cloud and envelop everything in any way associated with the foe. There was enough obnoxious German propaganda to create legitimate fear. Gradually it covered everything, and men saw facts like the collapse of Germany through the fog of fear of German propaganda. Students of human nature also tell us that one may judge of a man's own activities by the charges which he most repeatedly brings against others. Accusations blend with unconscious confessions. It is quite conceivable that some of the reiterated charges of propaganda covered another propaganda; and that, for example, Lord Northcliffe or the advocates of Siberian intervention had little to learn from Germany about the technique of creating opinion.

But in any event there has been stirred up a vast anxiety about the kind of facts and opinions which are brought to public attention. There is uneasiness and solicitude about what men hear and learn. This paternalistic care for the sources of men's beliefs, once generated by war, carries over into the troubles of peace. What we do not see in the news cables from Europe is even more significant than what we do see. Who knows just what is happening in Europe? Have the revolutionary Socialists in Italy been calmed into absolute quiet by the revolutionary occurrences all about them? What are the old minority Socialists in France, who became the majority, doing and saying? Nothing? Compare the scanty amount of news received even about the British Labor party with the amount that reaches us concerning Lloyd George, Carson, Milner, et al., and one might almost think that Americans had a vote to help decide the election. The most striking example of course is the surveillance of what issues as to Russian happenings.

No one can well say how much of this new paternalism is a designedly sinister thing and how much is due to a sincere fear that men's minds will be corrupted by hearing of social changes abroad. The fact which stands out is that the war has generated an atmosphere of safety first regarding all facts knowledge of which stimulates social change. No one can tell just how disturbing here an explicit unbiased report of foreign disturbances may be. The times are still troubled. Let us take no chances. Let the masses be benevolently protected against a knowledge which might not be good for them nor for society. The social and economic woods are full of traps; let us walk gingerly and keep out of harm and risk. This is the psychological factor which cooperates with the physical centralization of the agencies of news gathering and distribution to develop the new paternalistic solicitude for the masses who cannot yet be trusted to think for themselves. Let us make democracy safe for the world by a careful editing and expurgation of the facts upon which it bases the opinions which in the end decide social action. The men most active in urging that state paternalism be surrendered in exchange for private initiative in transportation, banking, investments and manufacturing (barring of course benevolence to the poor working man through a protective tariff) will be most vigorous in solicitude to safeguard against private initiative in belief. Heresy is proverbially a contagious disease. To learn anything about the Bolsheviki except their excesses would corrupt an otherwise staid and respectable America. Consequently men who sincerely wonder how, say, the Roman Emperors could have been so cruel and stupid as to try to prevent the spread of Christianity by oppressive means are sincerely anxious to prevent men's minds and morals from being undermined today by the spread of knowledge of heretical social activities. And it must be admitted that the means formerly at command were clumsy and brutal in comparison with those now available.

MORALS AND THE CONDUCT OF STATES

In his recent article on the legal status of war, Mr. Levinson pointed out that according to the older theory of personal relations and the still prevailing theory of national relations, lower interests, material and mundane affairs, may be discussed and adjudicated, while conflicts in higher interests, ideal and spiritual affairs, must be settled by armed force in duel or war. Swift himself never conceived such irony. Comment or amplification can only detract from the completeness of the picture of a world morally upside down. Mr. Levinson's further suggestion of some supernational organization based upon a preliminary outlawing of war suggests, however, a question of morals which may well be discussed. What is the cause of the present separation of private and public morals? What will be the moral consequences of an assimilation of national and private codes to each other?

Lamentations as to the gulf which divides the working ethical principles of nations from those animating decent individuals are copious. But they express the pious rather than the efficacious wish of those who indulge in them. They overlook the central fact that morals are relative to social organization. Individuals have to be moral because they can be. They can be because they are partakers in modes of associated life which confer powers and impose responsibilities upon them. States are non-moral in their activities just because of the absence of an inclusive society which defines and establishes rights. Hence they are left to their own devices, secret and violent if need is deemed imminent, in judging and asserting their rights and obligations. The distance which separates the code of intrigue and conquest permissible to nations from the code exacted of persons measures the significance for

[First published in *New Republic* 14 (1918): 232–34. Republished in *Characters and Events* (New York: Henry Holt and Co., 1929), 2:645–49; and in *Intelligence in the Modern World* (New York: Modern Library, 1939), pp. 508–11, with the title "Preconditions of the Security of Nations," both edited by Joseph Ratner. For article to which this is a reply, see this volume, Appendix 4.]

morals of social organization. The nations exist with respect to one another in what the older writers called a state of nature, not in a social or political state.

The not infrequent saying that international law expresses not true but only moral law is a striking indication of the widespread absence of scientific understanding of morals. The actual fact is that until nations are bound together by the law of a social order there cannot be any truly moral obligations existing among them. The attempt on the part of a particular nation to conceive of its relations with other nations in genuinely moral terms may be a source of weakness. The bald enunciation of any such position as this is, very properly, shocking. The frank acceptance of the double standard of conduct on the part of Germany has seemed to other nations to be an example of that abolition of all morality commonly known as Machiavellianism. But this attitude of abhorrence is effective only in the degree in which it marks an aspiration for the establishment of a social order among nations wherever moral relations may obtain. The moral deadliness of the assertion of a "higher" morality for a nation lies in its cynical contempt for the possibility of a society of nations where moral regulations would exist. Conversely, if the conception of a federated concert of nations obtains more widely and ardently in America than elsewhere it is not because we are so much more moral than others that we can conceive of a higher social state; it is rather that being more highly socialized we can conceive of a new morality.

The plea that nations *ought* to regulate themselves by the moral code which obtains among individuals is likely to degenerate into a sentimentalism which projects action on the base of wishes instead of facts. It escapes this sentimentalism only as it is a symptom of a discontent with the present social order which will momentarily express itself in a demand for a new social organization. To indulge in vituperations at the wickedness of war and in asseverations of the obligations of states to act upon the basis of the most enlightened code is merely to permit one's self a Pharisaic luxury—unless one is willing to fight for the establishment of a social organization which will make moral responsibilities and regulations a fact.

We are still incredibly subjectivistic in our moral ideas. The common assumption of the Protestant world is that men are gifted as individuals with conscience and that this conscience brings into existence acts and social relations which may approximate its high dictates. So far as anything objective, anything external to the individual is recognized, it is usually something supernatural, God or some of those mitigated substitutes for theological supernaturalism which modern thought calls transcendental absolutes and values. A pacifist clergyman in California recently proclaimed his supreme right to follow not only for himself but for propaganda among others the dictates of his own conscience even when they brought him into conflict with the law of the land: his right to do it not only in the sense of willingness to stand the penalties which would follow, but in the sense that the state had no right to inflict any penalties if he chose to obey what his conscience told him was the law of God. He doubtless offended the loyalty of thousands of his fellow citizens. It may be doubted how many of them recognized that he was asserting the essence of moral anarchy, by which I mean a course which would not only lead to practical anarchy but to a destruction of all moral distinctions whatever. For "conscience," that is the aggregate of the moral sentiments and ideas of man, is not the author and judge of social institutions, but the product and reflex of the latter. They are functions of social organization. They reflect criticism of the existing social order as well as approval of it. But in this capacity they are heralds of a changed social order. They are significant only as they become the pivots about which turn active efforts for the reconstruction of the social order. The notion that it is possible to get bodies of men to act in accord with finer moral sentiments while the general scheme of social organization remains the same is not only futile, it is a mark of the subtlest form of conceit, moral egotism.

If only there were a general recognition of the dependence of moral control upon social order, all of the sentiment and well-wishing opinion that is now dissipated would be centred. It would aim at the establishment of a definitely organized federation of nations not merely in order that certain moral obligations might be effectively enforced but in order that a variety of obligations might come into existence. The weakness on the ethical side of previous discussions of international courts and leagues has been that these have so largely assumed that moral considerations are already adequately cared for, and that it remains only to give them, through proper agencies, legal effect. The result was that moral enthusiasm was no sooner aroused than it was chilled by finding only legal technicalities with which to occupy itself, more international laws, treaties, courts, diplomats and lawyers. It wanted machinery to propel a great new idea and it found itself confronting additions to make the old machinery work better, to keep going the old idea of ultimate national sovereignty and irresponsibility. It found itself confronted with negative provisions for making war more difficult to enter upon, but which refrained from dealing in any positively organized way with those defects in social organization from which wars proceed. All proposals short of a league of nations whose object is not the negative one of preventing war but the positive one of looking after economic and social needs which are now at the mercy of chance and the voracity of isolated states, assume that war is the effect of bellicosity—which is exactly on the intellectual level of the famous idea that it is the dormitive power of opium which puts men to sleep.

Warlikeness is not of itself the cause of war; a clash of interests due to absence of organization is its cause. A supernational organization which oversees, obviates and adjusts these clashes, an organization which, as Mr. Levinson points out, is possible only with coincident outlawing of war itself, will focus moral energies now scattered and make operative moral ideas now futile. It will align the moral code of state behavior with the best which obtains as to personal conduct. But it will do more than that. It will give personal conscience a new stay and outlook. It will permit the social principle which is the heart of all morals to find full instead of hampered expression; it will enable it to be courageous because consistent. It will generalize that secularization or humanization of morals which is now so halting and vagrant that it leads many persons to escape supernaturalism only to land in a half-suppressed scepticism as to the possibility of any intelligent and objective morals, anything beyond social convention on one hand and personal taste on the other.

When I said that it is mere sentimentalism to deplore the deviation of the moral standard of states from that of persons unless one is willing to fight for a social organization which will permit moral relations and regulations to exist, I meant fight in every sense of the word. War to put a stop to war is no new thing.

History shows a multitude of wars which have been professedly waged in order that a future war should not arrive. History also shows that as a pacifist, Mars has not been a success. But a war waged to establish an international order and by that means to outlaw war is something hitherto unknown. In just the degree in which the American conception of the war gains force, and *this* war becomes a war for a new type of social organization, it will be a war of compelling moral import.

THE APPROACH TO A LEAGUE OF NATIONS

In official communications regarding the war, the phrase "Associated Governments" frequently occurs. The mere fact that the United States is not technically an Allied Government is doubtless the reason for the use of the phrase. It does not however take a forced interpretation to find something significant in the term. "Allies" is filled with implications of union for offense and defense. It is charged with the militaristic significance of the old order; it conveys precisely that which the foreign policy of the United States has always avoided. For we have never been the "Ally" of any power. The term "Associated" suggests, on the contrary, the new order. It suggests union for the sake of common ends and interests. Although military necessity gave it birth, its overtones are of the modern world of industry and commerce—of voluntary cooperation among equals to attain results which concern all alike.

The contrasting phrases may be used to indicate the two approaches to the future League of Nations, one rooting in political needs, the other in economic necessities. The older conception was not only an expression of purely political traditions, but these traditions were inseparably connected with those military considerations which are the inevitable outgrowth of a world of independent sovereign states whose sole official combinations with one another must perforce be directed, defensively or offensively, against some other combination of states. Not even Mr. Roosevelt has ever said anything harsh enough about the delusions of those who would cultivate unpreparedness for war in a political world so constituted that the sole legally integrating factor among different nations is combination with respect to war. The earlier conception of a League of Nations as an arrangement whose main, if not sole, purpose was to "enforce peace" exhibits the same preoccupation, the same belated ideas.

[First published in *Dial* 65 (1918): 341–42. Republished in *Characters and Events*, ed. Joseph Ratner (New York: Henry Holt and Co., 1929), 2:602–5.]

Those who are skeptical about the possibility of a League of Nations, those who dwell upon all the difficulties which have to be met, generally carry over into their discussions legal-mindedness which reflects the old military-political system. And many of those who argue for it still ignore all the lessons of the war and revert to the notion of a combination whose chief trait would be an extension of the old Hague Tribunal, provision for legal arbitrament plus agencies of conciliation, and, when needed, for enforcement of decisions by combined arms against a recalcitrant state. Yet if the war has made anything clear it is that such a scheme deals with effects not causes, symptoms not forces; that it is negative not constructive, and doomed to fail at some critical moment when most needed. The real problem is one of organization for more effective human association and intercourse. The newer politics signify the social mind carried into questions of human relationships, while the older politics meant the formulations of the legal mind concerned with defense and litigation. Every statesman of the world today, every political thinker, can be categorically placed according as his plans and ideas are formed primarily in the negative terms of protection against opposition and threatening danger, or in the positive terms of association for realization of common interests. Every passing day (and every passing year of the future) will make it clear that what distinguishes President Wilson from the other statesmen of the epoch is his prompt recognition that, given the conditions of modern life, no adequate defense and protection of the interests of peace can be found except in a policy based upon positive cooperation for interests which are so universal as to be mutual.

This means that a system of ideas and activities which expresses contemporary industry and commerce is being substituted for the ancient system which ignored and despised business and magnified the ethics and politics of dignity, honor, aggression, and defense. It is no accident that the formulation of the new order came from this country, which by the fortune of history and geography escaped most completely from the ethics of maintaining a status of established dignity, and which has committed itself most completely to the ethics of industry and exchange. President Wilson's propositions have commended themselves to the average American as a simple and almost matter of course, although unusually eloquent, statement of the very axioms of our own life. Only courtesy, the urgent need for American assistance, and a slowly growing perception of the essential truth of what he says—a perception largely compelled by the increasing influence of industrial workers in the older countries—have veiled their alien and "idealistic" character in the European countries. For the latter are controlled by the older ideas of personal alliance, instead of by the newer ideas of association in common activities.

A League of Nations whose main purpose is to enforce peace by an extension of legal mechanisms of controversy and litigation is idealistic and academic. It would work in periods of recuperation and quiescence; it would break down, in all probability, when confronted with problems of national expansion and a redistribution of the centres of effective power. Taken by itself, it represents simply a consecration of the politics of the particular balance of power which obtains at a given time. But an organization of nations which grew out of common everyday necessities, and which operated to meet the commonplace needs of everyday life with respect to food, labor, securing raw materials for the reparation of a devastated world, and so on—an organization which grew out of wants and met them would, once formed, become so indispensable that speedily no one could imagine the world getting on without it. It would go of itself; it would possess the only final sanction of any human institution—satisfaction of acknowledged needs and furtherance of urgent interests. It would generate in time any legal and political formulations and mechanisms which were needed to take care of the controversies and conflicts of interest that would still arise. But there is all the difference in the world between a system of courts, laws, decisions, and coercive enforcements which rests upon an organized system of wants and satisfactions, and which gives that system added security, and a system which, taking no constructive care for common interests, spasmodically attempts to keep peace by bringing into play legal devices.

It is a commonplace that the present war has revealed the primacy of economic and industrial concerns in even military affairs. It is not so frequently observed that it is this primacy which has already brought into being a League of Nations of a type not contemplated by those who have urged one on legal grounds. Every day the "Associated Governments" are dealing with questions of the distribution of shipping, raw materials, food, money and credit, and so on. Nobody who thinks believes that these problems will be less pressing after peace. On the contrary, they will become more urgent in some respects. For there will be the danger of a disastrous competition among nations now compelled by war exigencies into a coalescence. New problems of the distribution of labor, immigration, production for exportation will emerge. To annihilate or reduce the agencies of international regulation which already exist would be an act of incredible wantonness. Not to stabilize and expand their scope would be one of almost incredible stupidity. But given such an agency of international regulation, defined and authorized by the Peace Conference itself, and there exists in effect a new and international type of government. Can anyone believe that once such an agency were in existence it would not inevitably tend to be employed for all sorts of new purposes not expressly contemplated in its original constitution? Its very utility for recognized needs would render it natural to enlarge its functions to deal with future perplexities of international import. A Hague Tribunal, a legal ordering of international disputes, growing out of and depending upon an international organization of this positive and constructive sort, would not be spasmodic, negative, artificial, and in important matters always too late. It would play the same constant role which domestic courts play in internal conflict of interests.

THE LEAGUE OF NATIONS AND THE NEW DIPLOMACY

The ethics of honor and dignity, the idealization of their assertion and defense, are deeply ingrained in the minds of all the ruling classes—whether their rule is the direct rule of governors or the more efficacious indirect rule of opinion and sentiment. This morale of pride and fear is most deeply embedded in all that concerns the relationships of states to one another. In contrast, the ethics of industry and of reciprocal contractual service are lacking in prestige. They seem too prosaic, utilitarian, and materialistic to possess moral status. They lack glamour and romance; they are not glorified by the halo that reflects historic sacrifice and heroism in their behalf. We cannot easily conceive them as the subject matter of poetry and legend. And so far are men from actuation in their conduct by calculation of self-interest that nothing which does not become the stuff of poetry and passion can command full allegiance.

Those who are skeptical about the possibility of a reversal of moral prestige with respect to these two principles would do well to recall that Germany has sincerely regarded itself as *the* idealist among modern nations, and has contemptuously considered the United States as *the* materialistic and commercial people. This fact may develop hospitality to the recognition that what is morally at stake is a conflict of ideas and idealizations inherited from feudalism with those which express the transition to a democratic ordering of life. This being the case, it requires only a courageous expression of the newer morale of industry and commerce to insure that in time poetry, glamour, and romance will become attached to it also. For these things, important as they are, are not self-generated nor substantial. They are adjectival. They will in the processes of time cluster about any order that commands men's practical allegiance and in consequence their admiration.

The decline of democracy in comparative prestige during the

[First published in *Dial* 65 (1918): 401–3. Republished in *Characters and Events*, ed. Joseph Ratner (New York: Henry Holt and Co., 1929), 2:606–9.]

last generation, the relative eclipse into which it has passed, will be reversed by the outcome of the present war. A war the final outcome of which is demonstrably to be determined by the efforts of a nation that entered the war to make the world safe for democracy will effect a transformation of sentimental valuations. The permanence of this reversal will depend upon whether the democratic movement gives its own case away by continuing an unconscious adoption of the older morale of honor and defense of status, or has the intellectual courage to assert the moral meaning of industry, exchange, and reciprocal service.

These considerations may seem remote from the question of the practicability of a League of Nations in order to end international anarchy. But so to think involves a tremendous underestimation of the practical part played in human life by the imagination and the emotions gathered about it. The past system is not supported by any rational appeal to usefulness; its upholders always decry such an appeal as contrary to its proper elevated and noble nature. Mere external habit would not sustain it in the face of constant exhibition of its deficiencies, were not the idealizations of emotion enlisted in its behalf. Country, fatherland, nation, honor, rights, defense, protection, glory, sacrifice: these are words which express the forces which above all else maintain the established order—or disorder. Against this, the contrary sentimental idealizations which spring from a certain attempt to give Christianity a mild, pacifistic interpretation are pathetically helpless.

But the old order of ideas is implicated in much more definite and positivistic ways in the maintenance of the present system. Let anyone seriously ask himself what he understands by diplomacy and why it is that such disparagement hangs about it, and he will see what is meant. Everywhere outside of the United States, diplomatists have been drawn from the aristocratic class—that is to say, from precisely that class which has preserved most nearly unimpaired the old ethics of honor, dignity, nobility, and purely personal relationships—the class which has preserved in the most intact way the old noble contempt for the impersonal service rendered by exchange of goods industrially and mechanically produced. It is not diplomacy as an abstraction which tragically failed the world at a crucial moment. It was concrete human beings, diplomatists, who showed their ignorance of modern forces and their incapacity to manage them.

This class of persons manifested all the marks of the old moral order. Secret diplomacy is not a mere technical device; it is something more than a mere rule of traditional usage. It carries with it all the signs of a class so personally and professionally set apart that it moves in a high, inaccessible realm whose doings are no concern of the vulgar mass. It breathes contempt for publicity because it springs from contempt for the public. It would maintain the privacy which characterizes the intercourse of gentlemen with one another in matters which are their primary concern.

For the most part the great powers have directly continued with respect to international relations the traditions which developed when the relations of states were matters of the personal relations of sovereigns who owned the states, and when ambassadors were the personal representatives of their personal superiors. It was no iconoclast but an authority like Sir Thomas Barclay who said of the statesmen of Europe who have controlled foreign policies for the last generation: "Present generations who have suffered through the incompetency and failure of their governing classes are not likely to allow themselves to be deluded again as to the realities of war compared with those of peace." But there is no way of surely remedying this evil state of affairs save by transferring the management of international relations from men who are completely, subconsciously even more than consciously, committed to an old belief—whose minds and hearts are wholly possessed by it—over to men whose habitudes of thought have been formed by dealing with the facts of modern industry and the give and take, for common interests, of modern commerce.

A League of Nations which should be conceived primarily in political terms of the old sort would inevitably leave the older type of diplomatists in control. They are on that ground already; moreover the activities it requires have no drawing power for men who think spontaneously in terms of the realities of modern life. For some time to come, as in the past, big financiers and men of business will largely regulate international relationships for the greater part of the time. But there is a constant division of responsibility between them and those who control the political foreign-offices. The latter, in acting as agents for the former in times of peace, produce situations which carry things beyond the wishes and out of the power of the economic rulers. Something would be gained in clarity and responsibility by any arrangement which made explicit, constant, and formal the power actually wielded by business, and which effectively brought the training and technical ability of its representatives directly to bear upon the problems of international intercourse. But such a movement could not end at this point. When international commissions and boards have representatives of big business upon them, because their technical training is required to handle specific questions, they will also have to seat economists and representatives of labor. The scope and significance of the questions which would be turned over to them for adjustment would constantly grow. Just as the war has led many an able and trained business man to put his special abilities at the disposal of the public interest, so a new type of international diplomacy would stimulate the tendency to use the intellectual power generated in modern industry and commerce for something besides personal advantage. No one can afford to ignore or despise this particular sort of ability and training. The decision of the character of the immediate future in both domestic and international matters depends first of all upon whether they are chiefly used in secret and irresponsible ways for personal power and advantage, or whether they are gradually sublimated by being put to public use in behalf of a public interest.

THE FOURTEEN POINTS AND THE LEAGUE OF NATIONS

One has only to study the fourteen conditions of peace set forth by President Wilson in his speech of January 8 to be convinced of two things: in the first place, they primarily concern the conditions of a permanent peace rather than merely the conditions of peace with Germany at the present time; and secondly, they cannot be effectually realized in detail without the continuing support of an international organization which shall be administrative in character, and not merely judicial. The first consideration concerns us here only as it is bound up with the second. The future historian will point out the extraordinary detachment of President Wilson from exclusive preoccupation with immediate war issues. He will note that, while the articles from VI to XIII are concerned with territorial issues which grow immediately out of the alignments of the war, even these are framed within a statement of world issues which might (substituting the name of some other country for that of Russia in article VI) have been laid down at any time of peace in a discussion of fundamental guarantees of world peace. He will then observe that these specific war aims appear as illustrations of the general principles by means of matters which have been made urgent in the course of the war.

Looking in detail at the contents of the fourteen articles in their bearing on the question of the dominant character of a League of Nations, they will be found to run the gamut from those which absolutely require an international agency with legislative and administrative powers to those which can be finally settled by the peace treaty itself. Intermediate are those which can *formally* be determined by the Peace Conference, but which require a permanent international body to insure that the formal settlement becomes an enduring actuality. A study of the fourteen conditions from this point of view will, I think, justify the follow-

[First published in *Dial* 65 (1918): 463–64.]

ing conclusion: there are but two matters which the peace treaty itself can finally adjust. These are the righting of the wrong done France in respect to Alsace-Lorraine, and the readjustment of the frontiers of Italy.

Next come the problems of restoration affecting all the territories invaded by the Central Powers. These would not of course demand a permanent international commission. But the work to be undertaken will certainly cover a period of years, and it will involve many points that cannot be completely covered in advance by any written agreement. If the work of restoration is to be done intelligently and in a way which will not leave behind it disputes and sore points, it will require mixed commissions involving the cooperation of statesmen, economists, physicians, engineers and technicians of all sorts. Since not all questions which will arise can be treated as mere matters of practical detail, the deliberations of these commissions will have to be supervised by some kind of international council.

Trenching more directly upon the issue of a permanent international government is the matter of international covenants and guarantees. These are specifically mentioned in the case of the Balkan States, the Dardanelles, and the new independent Polish State. They are certainly directly implied in the reduction of armaments, and in cooperation to secure for Russia an "unhampered and unembarrassed opportunity," to say nothing of "assistance of every kind that she may need and may herself desire." For convenience and brevity of discussion, these concerns may be summed up in the problems of nationality and of restoration of order compatible with freedom in eastern and southeastern Europe.

Nothing has brought international relations to greater disrepute from the standpoint of law than the tendency to write certain guarantees into treaties of peace and then fail to furnish any methods for making these "guarantees" effectual. In part this is due to the Pickwickian piety which, when "serious" matters are out of the way, may overcome in a moment of sentimental relief even a congress of professional diplomats. But in greater measure it is due to the fact that as affairs now stand—that is, without a permanent international executive body—the attempt to enforce such guarantees might indirectly threaten the peace of the world. An earnest effort from any quarter would be regarded as having back of it some interested nationalistic motive, and would array against it all of the nations on the other side of the Balance of Powers, even if their own national interests were in no way involved. It is much safer to treat the guarantee written into the treaty of peace as a scrap of paper than to run the risk of dropping a spark into a heap of inflammable international material.

Take the case of Roumania and the problem of a guarantee of civil rights to the Jews. On the face of it, it is a simple matter. But then we discover that it is a question of internal political constitution. The great landowners control the politics of Roumania through controlling the franchise. The cities and industrial centres are discriminated against. The Jews are mainly in the latter places. To give them the necessary rights would involve giving political rights to others who are now disenfranchised so as to secure the supremacy of the landed aristocracy. It is hard to see how an adequate guarantee for the Jews is to be secured short of a shift of the centre of internal gravity in the whole country. When one considers the medley of nationalities in eastern Europe and the inheritance of exacerbations along with religious differences and economic rivalries, it is harder yet to avoid the conclusion that it will remain the tinder-box of Europe unless a comprehensive and impartial international government undertakes for a considerable time the supervision of the development of institutions which shall insure an adequate adjustment of rights in this enormously delicate situation.

The strong prejudice against external intervention in domestic affairs is justified as long as the theory of isolated and independent sovereign states prevails in practice. But the United States, at least, has been largely in the war precisely because it is realized that the dividing line between domestic institutions and foreign policies has become wholly artificial. It was precisely the autocratic domestic institutions of Germany which drew us into what, in its origin, was a purely European war. So far as concerns the United States, the war was either an evil job which had to be undertaken from stern necessity, or it was a war for such intervention in the "internal" affairs of Germany as will guarantee us against the recurrence of any such catastrophe. The logic of this situation demands such friendly oversight of the affairs of other states from which world-wide conflagrations might spring as will forestall wars in the future. And since the United States has no intention of becoming a crusading Don Quixote of nations, this demand means precisely a permanent international government whose powers shall be even more executive and administrative than judicial.

It remains to speak of those two articles among the fourteen which imply, in the most open fashion, a League for economic purposes that is concerned with permanent regulation of those economic affairs which cause wars. These are the third and fifth articles, dealing respectively with the removal of trade barriers and the establishment of an equality of trade conditions, and with the impartial adjustment of all colonial problems. It is possible for opponents of the President to interpret the third article as an academic proclamation of the abstract principle of free trade, and to interpret the fifth as applying merely to the German colonies which have been seized during the war. But no such limitations will accord with the principles of the declaration of February 11 regarding the adjustments most likely to bring a peace that will be permanent and that shall not "perpetuate old elements of discord and antagonism that would in time be likely to break the peace of Europe and consequently of the world." In the concluding portion of this discussion these points will be taken up.

A LEAGUE OF NATIONS AND ECONOMIC FREEDOM

Although the previous articles in this series have asserted that the hopeful approach to a concert of nations is along the economic road which should aim to further common interests, rather than by the negative and legal road which should content itself with litigation and the adjudication of disputes, the problem of the economic equality of nations, which constitutes the third of President Wilson's conditions (and with which any real adjustment of colonial problems is bound up) has been reserved for this concluding article. What does "equality of trade conditions" mean, and how is it to be achieved and guaranteed? The President has contributed to clarification of the thesis. It precludes economic boycotts and selfish economic combinations; it precludes, as he unequivocally states, all preferential trade arrangements. Access to raw materials may be assumed to mean guarantees of outlet to the sea, with the free ports and the internationalized railways and watercourses necessary for adequate commercial use of such ports. But obviously equalization of trade conditions among nations demands something more. It has been demonstrated that more is needed to secure freedom and equality of conditions between individuals than to declare them legally all free and equal, while leaving them to unrestricted competition with one another. Immense inequality of power is compatible with formal equality. The same thing will surely develop with respect to any merely legal equality among nations. Certain nations have a tremendous superiority in population, natural resources, technical progress in industry, command of credit, and shipping. Nothing better calculated to develop actual inequality of trade relationship among nations could well be found than a system which set up a nominal mathematical equality and then threw matters practically into the hands of the present big nations. Under the old regime it was at least an object for every

[First published in *Dial* 65 (1918): 537–39. Republished in *Characters and Events*, ed. Joseph Ratner (New York: Henry Holt and Co., 1929), 2:610–14.]

powerful state to attach to itself and its sphere of influence a certain number of the smaller and weaker states. To some extent the former were compelled to bid, by grant of economic concessions, for the support of the latter. A League of Nations which deprived economically weak states of all the advantages as well as disadvantages of the old system of groupings would merely leave them to be devoured by the competition with one another of the three or four big states of the world.

This may account for the fact that as yet nations like Spain and Italy have not been seen to manifest enthusiasm for the project of a League of Nations. How can they be sure that, in effect, it is not a combination of, say, the United States and the British Empire, with incidental concessions to France, to control the commerce of the world, and to achieve, with no violation whatever of political equality, virtual subjugation of all other peoples? The question doubtless puts the matter with harsh exaggeration, but it suggests that a nation like, say, Italy cannot be expected to engage heartily in the new system of international organization unless she has some assurance in details as to how her economic interests are to be protected. Her primary question and that of other nations similarly situated will be: does the new system enable the more powerful peoples to take advantage of our weaknesses, or will it be so constituted as not merely to reenforce whatever strong points we possess with respect to the world's markets, but actually to make good our deficiencies? Shall we be given legally guaranteed access to coal and iron, but exacted at the highest prices that the market will bear (including a virtual monopoly of the world's shipping by other nations), or will administrative commissions of the League equitably survey the whole field and see to it that we get that relative share of the world's resources which an adequate development of our own powers requires? Shall we have to compete under onerous terms for the world's capital and credit, or will there be some assurance that credit will be equitably assigned to us for, say, such a development of our own hydroelectric power as will make us less economically dependent upon the very nations which supply the credit?

Such questions may seem to answer themselves. They may appear to exact a spirit not merely of justice but of altruism toward economically weak peoples, which it is hopelessly Utopian to forecast. Even so, the questions are worth putting even if only to suggest that the basic problems of an effective League of Nations involve more than a surrender of that arbitrary irresponsible political power we call national sovereignty, that they also involve surrender of ruthless economic activities which, to last analysis, rest only upon the possession of superior power due to accidents of position and history. But after all, the questions do not assume a fantastic altruism on the part of the bigger nations. They do assume, however, an *enlightened* self-interest—enlightened enough to see that some price must be paid for an adequate guarantee against the recurrence of wars which, even when valued in the most materialistic of cash terms, are indefinitely more costly than the charges imposed by the economic self-restriction in question. Not only this, but also enlightened enough to look ahead and weigh the advantages of trade, extended over a long period, with a nation growing in internal prosperity, against immediate trade profits based upon taking advantages of a nation's needs and calculated to keep it in industrial subjection.

For in the long run this is the only question. Does trade flourish better and pay better with a weak and impoverished customer or with one having increasing wants because of increasing power to supply them? This, in last resort, is the question of a narrow protectionism versus an intelligent free trade. And thus we arrive, although perhaps by an unexpected route, at the heart of the question of the meaning of equality of trade conditions and the removal, as far as possible, of economic barriers. The classic doctrine of international free trade was hopelessly defective in that it entirely overlooked the need of intelligent supervision and positively controlling action if real equality of conditions is to be secured. The classic doctrine was bound up with the dogma of laissez-faire among nations, and that doctrine was bound to work as fatally applied to nations as when applied to the relation of individuals. The doctrine rested upon the fantastically unreal theological doctrine of the goodness of Nature when left to herself, and of the natural harmony of interests. It ignored the fact that Nature means only the existent distribution of power, and that to fall back on the existent distribution of relative strength and weakness in the present world of states is to leave the destiny of the world at the mercy of rapacious economic prowess. Against such a dogma the protective policy has stood, however stupidly, for the need of some kind of human direction of natural forces.

In other words, any practicable and any desirable general adoption of a policy of international free trade means the development of powerful international administrative commissions dealing with such matters as equality of labor standards, the regulation of shipping, and, for some time to come, of food, raw materials, and immigrants, and above all of the exportation of capital and the distribution of the available credit of the world. Equality of trade conditions means *equalization* of conditions; it cannot be secured without giving to the maintenance of peace the same kind of intense intellectual labor, study, and foresight which has gone to the conduct of the war—the same in kind, but continued and persistent as well as comprehensive and impartial in scope. If a particular nation would gain in trade by keeping up low labor standards, then there must be power to penalize the commerce of that nation as a means of equalization. If it overstimulates science and industry along lines calculated to make other nations dependent upon it at a critical juncture—as Germany developed the dye industry as an adjunct to explosives—then that must be dealt with as an international government would deal with an excess cultivation of an armed force.

The problem is indeed difficult and complex. But its solution is not Utopian. It requires, let it be repeated, exactly the same kind of cooperating ability of experts of all sorts which within a year took America from a peace basis to an effective war basis. The mobilization of the necessary variety and scale of forces was possible because of the faith and devotion behind the cause. That is the issue which faces the world, and especially the United States, with respect to the organization of the world on the basis of international democracy. The resources and abilities are at hand, if we choose to use them. The question is as to the depth and endurance of our desire.

THEODORE ROOSEVELT

In the death of Theodore Roosevelt the America of the generation of 1880 to 1910 lost its typical representative. Indeed, he was its living embodiment rather than its representative. Successful public men are not merely themselves. They are records and gauges of the activities and aspirations of their own day. It is futile to praise them or blame them except as we remember that in so doing we are appraising the time and the people that produced them. Hero worship of the olden type is gone, at least so far as statesmen are concerned. For in a democracy the people admire themselves in the man they make their hero. He is influential with them because he is first influential by them. The ordinary politician is fortunate when by dint of keeping his ear to the ground he can catch and reflect in articulate speech the half-formed sentences of the people. Roosevelt did not have to resort to this undignified posture. He was the phonograph in whose emphatic utterances the people recognized and greeted the collective composition of their individual voices.

To praise or condemn Roosevelt is, then, but to pass judgment on the America which suddenly awakened from the feverish and gigantic expenditures of energy that followed the Civil War to find itself in the face of vast problems and in need of vast reforms. We can better tell the qualities and defects of the period by looking at Roosevelt than in any other way. Through long living in the public eye he had become with extraordinary completeness a public character. It almost seems as if his native individuality, his private traits, disappeared, so wholly did they merge in the public figure. Of every man who goes into political life there gradually grows up a double. This double consists of the acts of the original individual reflected first in the imaginations and then in the desires and acts of other men. Just because Roosevelt's capture of the imagination of his countrymen was so complete,

[First published in *Dial* 66 (1919): 115–17. Republished in *Characters and Events*, ed. Joseph Ratner (New York: Henry Holt and Co., 1929), 1:87–94.]

his public double was immense, towering. One cannot think of him except as part of the public scene, performing on the public stage. His ordinary and native acts gained a representative significance. He shook hands with a locomotive engineer, chopped down a tree at Oyster Bay, hunted big game, or wrote a magazine article on his hunting. Each of the acts somehow swelled with an almost ominous import. Each provoked applause or rebuke, enlisting the partisanships of the crowd. In all of these acts he was delightedly *our* Teddy, ours with admiring acclaim or with disgusted irritation. In these acts, almost equally with those of Roosevelt making a stump speech, writing a state paper, taking a canal, or sending a fleet round the world, he was the man in whom we saw our own ideals fulfilled or betrayed. One of the things that rankled most in the minds of those who did not like him was that they could not get rid of him, even in the innermost recesses of their minds. His representative, incarnating force was such that he stayed by them. Everything in American life reminded them of something which Roosevelt had said or done. The assimilation of the private individual with the publicly assumed figure is so complete that for all except his personal intimates the former is non-existent. All that an outsider can say of it is that it must have been great to permit such thorough identification with the public self built up out of impacts upon others, and out of reflections back into the native self of the successes and failures, the applause and dislike of others. Only an individuality at once mediocre and great could have become so wholly a public figure. In thinking of him one is never conscious of mysteries, of unexplored privacies, reticences, and reserves, hidden melancholies, or any touch of inaccessible wistfulness. His inherited advantages of social position, comfortable wealth, education without personal struggle against obstacles, afforded external conditions from which he could launch himself the more easily, without preliminary apprenticeship and without waste of time, upon his task of representing the America of his day. For this America had grown self-conscious about its pioneer days of log-cabin and rail-splitter learning hardly bought by light of candle-dip. It wanted something less sparse and starved, something more opulent, something more obviously prosperous in culture and social standing. It felt the struggles of the earlier day in the scars it had left behind, and rested easily only in the contemplation of a figure which never reminded it of a past which the nation—for so it seemed—had so happily left forever behind. It was a period of the complacent optimism born of success in overcoming obstacles, and of subconscious irritating memories of the shameful limitations involved in having such obstacles to overcome.

Roosevelt was the Man of Action. In that he incarnated his time. He preached the strenuous life and practiced what he taught. The age was delirious with activity. It wanted not only action but action done with such a resounding thump and boom that all men should sit up and take notice. Bagehot somewhere remarked that a large part of the avoidable evils of mankind had arisen because a number of men at some important juncture had not been able to sit quietly in a retired room until things had been thought out. The generation had no sympathy with such a notion. If evils existed it was because men did not act promptly and intensely enough. Gordian knots exist only to be cut by the sword of sharp and vehement action. As soon as they are cut, we should have statistics of the number of strands, the variety of snarls, of the size of the sword and the number of foot-pounds in the blow that annihilated the difficulty. Refinements and subtleties and shades of distinction are not for such a period.

To criticize Roosevelt for love of the camera and the headline is childish unless we recognize that in such criticism we are condemning the very conditions of any public success during this period. A period that is devoted to action can have but one measure of success—that of quantity and extent. This measure is essentially one of social and political reverberations. It cannot be said that it was reserved for Roosevelt to discover the value of publicity for a public man. But he deeply divined the demand for publicity of an emphatic and commanding kind, and he allowed no private modesty to stand in the way of furnishing it. When one has performed a resounding act it is stultifying not to allow it to resound. While other politicians were still trusting to the gumshoe, it took courage as well as genial sagacity to adopt the megaphone. Irritated critics of Roosevelt's egotism—which they called megalomania—overlooked the fact that a petty deed cannot be made great by heralding, and that his acts commanded publicity because they were in the first place of a quality to command attention.

Probably nothing in Roosevelt's career so won the attachment of the American people as the fact that he had the courage to take them into his confidence. If it now seems a simple thing for a politician to make the people, in form at least, members of his own household, politically speaking, and to share with them at the breakfast table the political gossip of the day, the simplicity of the performance is evidence of the thoroughness with which Roosevelt did his work. He established a tradition which even a man as opposite in temperament as Wilson has felt obliged to follow, and, whatever his practice, to make central in profession. Just as politicians since Lincoln's time have studiously scanned the latter's methods, so future statesmen will copy the style of publicity which Roosevelt's courageous impetuosity created. Thinking out loud, or at least seeming to do so, is one of Roosevelt's permanent contributions to the American political tradition. Lack of occasional spasms of frankness will henceforth be resented as evidence both of lack of courage and lack of trust in the people. And these will become—because of Roosevelt they are already becoming—the cardinal vices to a political democracy. Roosevelt's enemies repeatedly believed that he was politically dead, that he had killed himself. Although the vehemence with which they announced his demise was part of a calculated technique for making their prediction true, they nevertheless sincerely believed that no man could recover from what they took to be stupendous blunders—such as the New Nationalism speech, the recall of judicial decisions, and so on. What they never understood was the admiring affection and unbounded faith with which the American people repaid one who never spoke save to make them sharers in his ideas and to appeal to them as final judges. Because of the power thus given him—combined, of course, with his own power to learn and to grow—probably no public man of any country ever equaled Roosevelt in power to "come back."

Perhaps the best proof of the completeness with which Roosevelt embodied the belief of his generation in action, action unhesitating, untroubled by fine distinctions or over-nice scruples, is the irritation which his personality aroused in academic men. There are a few exceptions, but upon the whole up to the time of the Progressive campaign they followed him with distrust and only, as they felt, from compulsion of circumstances. A mind which apparently never engaged in criticism, certainly never in self-criticism, which in fact identified criticisms with instantaneous assault, was the natural opposite of the mind tangled in the timidities which result from always criticizing, and hence never acting save when external pressure compels.

It would require a history of the life of the United States in the last quarter of the nineteenth century to explain how and why there developed such devoted admiration of action as action, provided only it was on a large scale. But that Roosevelt was a great figure because he was the exponent in word and in personality of this faith there can be no doubt. Nor can it be doubted that power accrued to him because he exemplified his period in thinking and speaking of action exclusively in moral terms. And with Roosevelt as with the type which adores action for its own sake, to think and to speak were synonymous. There are those who think that morality does not enter into action until morality has become a problem—until, that is, the right course to pursue has become uncertain and to be sought for with painful reflection. But by this criterion Roosevelt rarely if ever entered the moral sphere. There is no evidence that he was ever troubled by those brooding questions, those haunting doubts, which never wholly leave a man like Lincoln. Right and wrong were to him as distinctly and completely marked off from one another in every particular case as the blackness of midnight and the noonday glare. Nothing more endeared him to the American people than the engaging candor with which he admitted that in the face of this immense and fixed gulf he was always to be found on the side of righteousness. As he repeatedly confessed, he "stood" for justice, for right, for truth, against injustice, wrong, and falsity. When he did not stand, he fought. Wherever his activities were engaged at all, he saw the combat between the forces of the Lord and of the Devil. The battle at Armageddon was, after all, but the consummating fight in the campaign for Righteousness in which he enlisted when he entered public life. And if upon the whole the moral battle was a cheery thing in which one was stimulated rather than humbled into thoughtful meditation that too reflected the moral simplicity of his generation.

It is true, of course, that the cult of action for its own sake tends to demand for its successful pursuit either a cynical immoralism or the certainty of being on the side of the Lord. No politician in America can be successful beyond the local stage who takes the former course. The good old Anglo-Saxon habit of thinking of politics in moralistic terms was strengthened rather than weakened by its voyage across the Atlantic. Not, however, till the time of Roosevelt were economic problems treated in terms of sin and righteousness. Roosevelt borrowed much from Bryan, but Bryan came from Nazareth in Galilee, and spoke the cruder language of the exhorter and the itinerant revivalist. When Roosevelt uttered like sentiments, his utterances had the color and prestige of a respectable cult and an established Church. It is no part of my intention to appraise what Roosevelt did for our American life in the years around nineteen hundred. But events move rapidly, and if for a time Roosevelt, as the prophet of a new social day, loomed larger than facts justified, it is already easy to underestimate what we owe him. Positively speaking, pitifully little has been done with our industrial inequities and conflicts. But in addition to what Roosevelt did in arresting some of the worst tendencies of the time, he brought men to where they could behold the newer problems. And it is very doubtful if they could have been led to such a place by any other than the moral road, or by any one who did not spontaneously appeal to ethical convictions and enthusiasms. He made the problem of economic readjustment the problem of rebuke of unrighteousness. He endued the cause of the reformer with the glamour of virility and vitality—and all those other terms of romantic energy that come to the lips when Roosevelt is spoken of.

If under the cover of a buoyant and readily vocalized idealism, Mr. Roosevelt took the steps which a "practical man" interested in success would take irrespective of moral considerations, he was in this also the embodiment of his generation of Americans. The generation was not hypocritical—and neither was he. Prosperity is the due reward and recognition of righteousness. Defeat (in that reign of moral law which Americans were brought up to feel all about them) is the sign manual of evil. The cause of righteousness was too precious to be compromised by the danger of defeat; it not only needed to win but it needed the moral sanction that comes from triumph. And Mr. Roosevelt's glory in the fray and his astuteness in discovering the conditions of success blended with his belief in righteousness. He endowed his frequent dickers with machine politicians and compromises with machine politics with a positive moral glow. They were to him proof that he was not as those academic reformers who profess high ideals and accomplish nothing. *His* belief in righteousness was of the sort that "brought things to pass." He trusted—and correctly enough—to a certain ingrained rectitude which would protect him from being compromised beyond a given point; meantime it was the corrupt politicians who took chances, not he. This dualism of theoretical idealism with a too facile pragmatism in action has still to be faced in American life.

When an epoch is closed, the following epoch is not usually generous, or even just, to it. What it achieved is taken for granted; what it failed to do is the outstanding and irritating fact. Roosevelt's period has not wholly passed. The men who fought him are now just beginning to "appreciate" him, and their acclaim mixes with the reverberations from old fights and victories. The fact that the old interests have, in profession at least, moved up to about where Roosevelt stood in his heyday measures the progress made. But it also leaves him by association in a somewhat reactionary light. Above all, men are beginning to realize that our serious economic problems are complicated, not simple; that they have to do with deeply rooted conditions and institutions, not with differences between malefactors of great wealth and benefactors of great virtue; and that for the most part even the most arduous fights of Roosevelt were waged with symptoms rather than with causes. The epoch of "Onward, Christian Soldiers" ended with the Progressive campaign in which it consummated. We are in an epoch of special problems of industrial democracy in farm and shop to which the older idealistic slogans of righteousness and the strenuous life are strangely foreign. Roosevelt's "luck" did not desert him. He has been forever saved from any danger of becoming the figurehead and leader of reactionaries.

JAPAN AND AMERICA

Mr. Creel's critics should have been sent to a foreign country to view his activities in a new perspective. When the armistice was signed the Bureau of Public Information was at its height. Every newspaper in Japan was daily printing about two columns of American news conceived from an American standpoint. And daily newspapers in Japan are many and widely circulated. Small towns that in the United States would depend upon journals of the large cities have sheets of some importance. Practically every Japanese man reads a newspaper. To put it moderately, the international value of publicity is not less in Japan than in other countries. Self-consciousness about foreign affairs and about what other nations think of one's own country is perhaps more intense there than anywhere else. No country is so responsive to the approbation of other peoples, and none more sensitive to slights, real or fancied. It was then hardly a coincidence that pro-Americanism in Japan rose with the rising of news from America, and was at its height when the end of war came.

There was enthusiasm for America's energetic share in bringing peace, and even more for her aims. Sentiment was warmer toward us than any time since the end of the Russo-Japanese war and the days when readers of a Tokyo newspaper voted George Washington and Abraham Lincoln to head the list of the world's great men when that paper took a poll. Such a vote, placing Americans above even the Japanese national heroes, is a surprise to those of our countrymen who regard the Japanese as devoted to a narrow and exclusive "patriotism." But the indication it gives of the almost sentimental responsiveness of the Japanese is more to be depended upon than current opinions that make the Japanese people completely self-centered. On the spot one reaches the conclusion that some at least of the most chauvinistic

[First published in *Dial* 66 (1919): 501–3.]

utterances of her politicians are intended as a makeweight against too ready popular enthusiasms for outside countries.

Today the Bureau of Public Information is out of existence, and Japanese newspapers are largely engaged in an anti-American drive which however already shows some signs of waning, as influential statesmen have issued warnings against it. It is no coincidence that this drive began when news from the United States had been for some weeks at its lowest ebb. The Pacific cable has been broken, and no news has come directly, and none even indirectly from the Associated Press. Hence all knowledge of both America and of the Peace Conference has reached the public through three non-American sources: British, French, and Japanese. The latter two are, so it is currently believed, subsidized. The French Havas service if not anti-American has been steadily anti-Wilson. The Japanese service, both the regular Kokusai and the special cables, has been chiefly concerned with the questions of race discrimination and China. The Reuter service is not anti-American but is decidedly pro-British, and with American prestige at the height it has reached all over the Far East, there is no motive, economic or political, for expressly cultivating its further growth.

As a net result the reader of the press would receive the impression that President Wilson's policies have had a very bad back-set, even if they were not positively discredited; that he has practically failed both at home and abroad in securing an effective following; and that the League of Nations will either fail in the end or be adopted in such a form as to represent a complete defeat for Wilson. Prior regard for the United States was largely due to sympathy with the idealism of Wilson's policies and the wave of liberal sentiment they released. But if they are coming to nothing, the wave naturally subsides. There are also many items which leave the further impression that "humanity" and peace for the whole world were merely disguises behind which materialistic America was hiding her commercial and territorial ambitions in China, Siberia, and other parts of the world. The League of Nations has been held up as a scheme of Anglo-American capitalism to dominate the world without the trouble and expense of maintaining an army. As a reputable publicist recently said, "when the robber is expelled, the swindler is likely to enter"; the menace of

German militarism is destroyed to give way to that of Anglo-American economic domination.

Those whose faith in moral factors as political forces has departed should pay a visit to the Far East. Unless they have become complete cynics their faith will revive. Sentiment will appear as a thing of almost incalculable importance. On the one hand, Oriental diplomacy is an object lesson in the suicidal character of an international politics based on narrow considerations of self-interest. There are no critics of Japan's policies more severe than many of the Japanese, who declare that for lack of sufficient disinterestedness Japan has thrown away in Asia one of the greatest opportunities that ever came to any nation. While the present Hara ministry has tried to repair the evils done by the prior Terauchi ministry, these critics feel that the mischief has been done—and done because of a short-sighted policy of seeking immediate and one-sided advantage. On the other hand, it is evident that American prestige and influence rise and fall in the Far East with belief and disbelief in the generosity and idealism of her purposes. The Americans at home who have advertised opposition to the League of Nations have assumed a heavy responsibility. They have made many intelligent foreigners, previously sympathetic with America, open to the impression, fostered by inadequate news service, that Wilson's professed aims were a cloak. They have done America an ill turn in spreading the conviction that in truth America cares at home only for her supremacy in South America and abroad only for such power as will increase trade.

It is not my intention to repeat the items of the newspaper criticism of the United States that would stimulate a like criticism of Japan. They are referred to for an opposite purpose, to bring out the various factors which at the present time are affecting the formation of public opinion. In part, most Tokyo newspapers are against the ministry whatever it is. Criticism of the United States is thus an easy way of hitting the Government. This is accused on one side of truckling to the United States and on the other of failure to promote Japanese interests properly at the Peace Conference, in Siberia, and in China. There is also a natural reaction in the face of the surprising exhibition of patriotism and power, military as well as economic, manifest by the United States. There is a revulsion of combined suspicion and dread not unlike that which in the United States followed after Japan's victory over

Russia. The result was desired but it seemed unnecessarily demonstrative. Hence events in Korea, in Siberia, in China, where it is possible for imagination to involve America either officially or through private individuals, take on an ominous aspect. The race discrimination issue, which becomes pointed in the virtual prohibition of immigration, suddenly takes on a renewed importance. The reported abolition of conscription seems to be aimed particularly at Japan. Each one of these matters is too complicated to be discussed merely in passing. It is enough to say here that they constitute the headings of the chief charges brought against the United States, adding that the accusations as respects China and Siberia have many sub-headings. Looked at from this point of view, the drive against America ceases to be a mere matter of newspaper recrimination and retort, and becomes a kind of burning glass in which focus all the possible causes of friction between the two countries.

Up to the present the anti-Americanism is, according to the best reports I can get, almost wholly confined to the newspapers. The difference of tone within and without the newspapers is such as to create a feeling that somewhere it is thought that the people are too pro-American, and need to have their sympathies and affections cooled. Especially does it seem suspicious that the only chord which wins a spontaneous popular response should be increasingly harped upon—the race discrimination issue. However this may be, there is one fact that Americans should bear unceasingly in mind when accounts reach them of anti-American propaganda in Japan. The outstanding fact is that the outcome of the war has dealt the militaristic and bureaucratic party in Japan the greatest blow it has ever had. It is not too much to say that only one thing could have shaken its hold to a greater extent, and that is the actual defeat in war of the party itself. If this element of Japanese life, so strong in the past, is not to pass into deeper eclipse and be permanently discredited to such an extent that nothing less than a radical realignment of Japanese politics will occur, it must take steps to recover some of its lost prestige. The easiest way to accomplish this recovery is to foster that dread and suspicion of other nations which is the ultimate source of all militarism, since it is the only thing that will make a nation endure the burdens militarism imposes. There are some symptoms that the discredited party has wavered between Great Britain and the

United States in selecting the danger which only its own reinvestment can avert. But aside from the alliance with Great Britain which still holds, the United States is uppermost in everybody's mind at the present. It was from America that proceeded the cry which made the war one between autocracy and democracy, and the difficulties which Japan is experiencing in Korea, Siberia, and China can most plausibly be attributed to America.

I asked an intelligent and well-informed Japanese friend if he did not think that this situation, together with the absence of authentic American news, explained the present outburst of criticism. He was very sure that it did not. And his reason is so significant that I give it. It is not possible, he said, that the bureaucrats and militarists should be back of the criticisms, for they have so completely lost their authority and influence that they are powerless. I quote the answer because it illustrates that loss of standing and prestige to which reference has been made—a loss so extreme that at first it seemed incredible, but which I am now convinced is the outstanding fact in the present life of Japan. That, however, a party still entrenched in education, the army, and the civil service should be so completely discredited as to surrender without a struggle does not seem probable.

The moral of all this for our own country is almost too obvious to need mentioning. The cause of liberalism in Japan has taken a mighty forward leap—so mighty as to be almost unbelievable. The causes which produced it can sustain it. If they do sustain it, there will be little backward reaction. If they do not continue in force to sustain it, they will betray it. To speak more plainly, the release of liberal forces that had been slowly forming beneath the lid was due to the belief that democracy really stood for the supremacy of fairness, humanity, and good feeling, and that consequently in a democratic world a nation like Japan, ambitious but weak in many respects in which her competitors are strong, could afford to enter upon the paths of liberalism. The real test has not yet come. But if the nominally democratic world should go back on the professions so profusely uttered during war days, the shock will be enormous, and bureaucracy and militarism might come back. One cannot believe that such a thing is to happen. But every manifestation of national greed, every cynical attack upon the basic ideas of the League of Nations, every repudiation of international idealism, every thoughtless word of race prejudice, every exhibition of dislike and unjustified suspicion directed at Japan is a gratuitous offering in support of the now waning cause of autocratic bureaucracy in Japan. Liberalism here has plenty of difficulties still to overcome. Only the liberals in Japan itself, who have now taken heart and courage, can work out the problem. But liberals elsewhere can at least fight against those untoward developments in their own countries which will restore to the Japanese reactionaries the weapons which the outcome of the war has loosed from their hands.

LIBERALISM IN JAPAN

I. The Intellectual Preparation

One heard the word frequently from the mouths of Japanese fellow travelers as one crossed the Pacific—De-mo-kras-ie. The animated, cultivated man, who after wearing the baggiest clothes of the ship blossomed out one day in a general's uniform with rows of medals, and turned out to be one of the heroes of the Russo-Japanese war, confided in you that he was on his way back from France to explain to his countrymen the new world situation and preach the gospel of democracy. An ardent returning student told you of an interview with a distinguished American educator in which the latter had said to him that the future relations of Japan and the United States were secure if both followed the same principles, and who added on his own account, "Yes, the same principles. We have had enough exchange of compliments and fine words. We need to adopt American principles of democracy." And he avowed his intention of becoming an apostle of those principles. The day after landing, another returned student tells you that when he landed just a year before it was not safe to utter the word democracy, as it might send you to prison, but that now everybody was talking it, even coolies and ricksha-men. And the American educator who has lived in Japan fifteen years says that there has been more alteration in the spirit of Japan in the prior six months than he had seen in the whole fifteen years of residence.

But the Japanese tell you that their opinions are unstable; that they are mercurial, easily aroused to follow the last intellectual fashion; that they catch readily but superficially at the latest trend of ideas only to turn to another, even its opposite, when something more "up-to-date" comes along. So Nietzsche had

[First published in *Dial* 67 (1919): 283–85, 333–37, 369–71. Republished in *Characters and Events*, ed. Joseph Ratner (New York: Henry Holt and Co., 1929), 1:149–69.]

given way to Eucken, the latter to James, and James to Bergson in the realm of those who coquetted with philosophy—all in the last few years. Germany had been not merely ingloriously defeated but had collapsed in internal revolution. America had come out with fine words and had surprisingly made its words good in deeds. Autocracy out of fashion, democratic styles were in. Was the change anything more than this?

As one remained and became somewhat better acquainted with the currents of thought—not an easy thing where the language is unknown and where every intellectual is a specialist and assumes similar specialization of interest on your part—one realized that the change was not so sudden as it seemed on the surface. All during the years of the most reactionary conservatism—and they were much more reactionary than the present writer at least had ever dreamed of—there existed genuinely liberal thinkers and teachers. The infiltration of the best Western ideas had been as steady if not as bulky as that of Western shoddy, physical and intellectual. The defeat of Germany had not so much brought about a sudden and superficial change as it had removed the lid. It became possible, almost popular, to say out loud what liberals had been saying quietly and steadily in the class room, or in the public press in language sufficiently veiled to pass the eye of the police. The change of fashion was a fact, was indeed a large part of the situation. But it operated mainly to depress the prestige of the reactionary bureaucrats and to increase that of the liberals so that men were willing, and even glad, to listen to them.

The seemingly abrupt alteration was in largest measure the appearance above the surface of a movement that had been long maturing—assuredly a much healthier state of affairs. All during the war the lines had been drawing. Even before the final defeat of Germany there were a courageous few who dared to take the view that the war was between two systems and that Japan would remain in an anomalous position as long as she was the foe of Germany in war, but her disciple and follower in government and educational methods. On the other hand, even in the midst of war against Germany, influential voices were raised defending German institutions, German thought, and German ideals, and explaining that since Japan had made these her own and built her greatness upon them she was an enemy of Germany only in a military sense, and even that only for certain specific purposes. I was among those who heard Baron Ishii denounce German propaganda as responsible for alienation of feeling between the United States and Japan, and like many more of my countrymen I was much moved thereby. But when I reached Japan I marveled. For I found that intellectually, morally, and politically an active German propaganda had been carried on during the war by Japanese officials. I learned that in the army the conscript recruits had been systematically got together and taught the superiority of German institutions to those of the Allies, and especially the superiority of German militarism and the fact that it could not be defeated. I learned that on the very day when the armistice was declared an important intellectual figure was billed for a public lecture on Why Germany Cannot Be Defeated.

These facts are not mentioned to rake up grounds of offense. They help explain the courage of the liberals who when the war was still undecided had said that Germany must be defeated not merely to oust her from the Far East, but because she was autocratic and militaristic, and begged the Japanese to eliminate from their own government and administrative methods all that Japan had borrowed from Germany lest Japan should in the end find herself also at odds with the whole world. And the fact that the lines had been so openly and stringently drawn made the final defeat and still more the spectacular collapse of the invulnerable state a sensational victory for the liberals against the bureaucrats. It gave liberal and democratic ideas a vogue which they would not have had if there had not been during the war itself a struggle between the partisans and the opponents of German ideals and an application of the controversy to domestic politics.

The highest wave of democratic sentiment in Japan has apparently receded since the winter and early spring months. The Japanese are quick—often too quick—and they have not failed to take home to themselves the lesson of the failure at Paris of the fine words which President Wilson flourished when he took the United States into the war. It may be that the racial discrimination issue was raised at Paris as a smoke-screen to obfuscate the Shantung question—diplomats other than Japanese have been known to raise a moral question when they wished to gain a material point. But there can be no doubt of the immense popularity of the issue in Japan. The interest was clearly in part "accelerated" by politicians of light conscience, like Marquis Okuma, but there is no question of the popularity of the response. When the newspapers gave next to no attention to other problems of the Paris Conference they gave columns to this one. And the defeat of the proposal to insert a recognition of the principle of equality of nations in the Preamble to the League Covenant was a blow to liberal thought. For it made it easy to assert that all the democratic professions of equality and humanity of the Allies during the war were part of a hypocritical propaganda. At the last, the Japanese proposal was whittled down to a Platonic and almost Pickwickian statement. The more those who opposed it believed that it was not offered in good faith but for ulterior purpose, the more willingly they should have favored it—if only as a sop to sentiment and a salve to pride. Its rejection was worse than inhumane; it was stupid. To have accepted it would have been to create good feeling and also a frank and objective basis for a discussion of immigration as an economic and political question, free from entanglements with the question of racial prejudice. As it is, the two questions are still entangled, and the supporter of restricted immigration on economic grounds (and political also till Japan has radically changed its form of government) is hampered by the bad conscience that comes from giving to Japan an opportunity to inject the question of race and color discrimination into the discussion. But for present purposes the consequence chiefly of importance is that the action of the Conference gave a great tactical advantage to the Japanese upholder of things as they were and dampened the ardor for democratic ideas.

The other leading force in giving liberal thought a temporary setback is the raising of the Chinese issue. "Patriotism" is more acute in Japan than in any country of the globe, and the press is more recklessly irresponsible than that of any other country of the globe. And the political consciousness of the people is still immature. Consequently the intelligent and critical discussion of foreign relations, hard enough in any country, is unusually difficult in Japan. In fact one of the ablest of the intellectual liberals in Japan said in spite of his democratic beliefs he dreaded the time when diplomacy should come in Japan more under popular influence, for the professional diplomats were much more enlightened, much more cosmopolitan, more sympathetic with Western ideas and ways than were the people, who are still blindly chauvinistic—as was indicated in the riots that protested against the mildness of the terms of peace with Russia—and who constantly clamor for a stronger foreign policy. Anyhow, it was an easy matter to lead the mass of the Japanese people to think that there is a conspiracy to thwart the true national destiny of Japan in Asia and that nominally democratic countries, especially the United States, are at the bottom of this plot. And the militarist party has not been slow to point the moral or to hold up Japanese liberals as embryonic traitors who would weaken and destroy the national cause. It was not Japan that originated the motto "Our country right or wrong" or that originated the psychology which is sure that our country is always right. Consequently the Japanese liberals who wish to tell the truth about conditions in China—and there are a good number of them—at the same time temporarily handicap the liberal cause because they seem to be identified with an unpatriotic and anti-nationalistic cause.

If the situation can develop in a reasonable, normal way, there is no doubt as to where ultimate triumph will lie. It was European imperialism that taught Japan that the only way in which it could be respected was to be strong in military and naval force. Not its art nor the exquisite courtesy of its people nor its eager curiosity gave Japan the rank of one of the Big Five at Paris. And none of these things brought triumph to its diplomats there. Until the world puts less confidence in military force and deals out justice internationally on some other basis than command of force, the progress of democracy in Japan will be uncertain, because in Japan more than any other country the strength of political reactionism centres in the army, in the ideas which it breeds and in the officials who come, willingly or unwillingly, under its influence. But, barring outside events, two great forces are working on the side of liberal ideas and institutions. One is intellectual, the other economic. Japan is trying, under the leadership of its present rulers, an impossible experiment. It recognizes its dependence on the West for material, technical, and scientific development, and welcomes the introduction of Western ideas and methods so far as they concern these things. But it is trying at the same time to preserve intact its own peculiar moral and political heritage; it is claiming superiority in these respects to anything the West can give it. It is another chosen nation, unique in origin and destiny. With extraordinary toughness and tenacity it has managed somehow to conserve the feudal and even barbarian morale and politics of the warrior, while it has borrowed wholesale the entire scientific and industrial technique of the world. But no nation can enduringly live a double life; Japan shows everywhere the strain of this split in its life. Nor can the Japanese, even with all their power of resistance, indefinitely shut out the entrance of genuinely Western ideas and aims. These have crept in and are expelling the traditional ideas in spite of the most incredibly reactionary system of primary education the world has ever known. The first fruits of this creeping in is that release of liberal ideas which accompanied the defeat of Germany. As one of the intellectual leaders of the new Japan put it, the change that has come over Japan in the last year is not describable in words; it is intellectual, moral, even metaphysical.

II. The Economic Factor

In my previous article I discussed the intellectual change which is furthering the growth of liberalized institutions in Japan. The word "metaphysical" was ventured upon in describing the change. I can imagine the scorn with which some greet the idea that intellectual changes can lead to political changes. People love to stand on their heads intellectually, and so it is that the Marxians, who have given the world its best modern demonstration of the power of ideas and of intellectual leadership, are the ones who most deny that these things have any efficacy. Even the most hardened upholder of the impotency of intellectual and moral forces might however concede that *without* certain changes of mental attitude and disposition, there are certain alterations of society which cannot be accomplished, that intellectual changes are at least a negative condition, a sine qua non. And this concession will be met not with an admission but an assertion that it is fortunate for the prospects of liberalism in Japan that the intellectual modifications already dealt with are accompanied and reinforced by active and aggressive economic changes.

The war tremendously hastened the industrial transition in Japan. In 1918 alone the number of factories in Tokyo doubled in spite of extraordinary increases in prior years. The last five years have practically transformed Japan from an agrarian into an industrial state. For there is today actual shortage of farm labor in that country, although the wages of farm hands have more than doubled. The urban factories have been absorbing labor at such a rate that for the time being at least the old plea for territorial expansion to take up the growth of population does not hold. In consequence of this expedited development Japan has been plunged into the labor problem—and plunged with exceedingly little preparation.

The remote and speculative observer is given to supposing that a new country which is undergoing the industrial revolution at this late date will surely learn from the experience of the other countries that passed through it earlier. Why wait for all the evils of child labor, woman's labor, long hours, unsanitary factories, congested housing, slums, and so forth to show themselves, when experience has demonstrated how surely they follow upon a laissez-faire policy, and also how legislation and administration may at least alleviate their worst evils? Especially would it seem as if a paternalistic government like that of Japan would do something, if only because of the general influence exercised by her model, Germany. But practically no foresight was manifested. Certain factory laws on the Western pattern were indeed passed, but their execution was postponed for a term of years—up to twelve—on the plea of giving capital a chance to adjust itself. As a matter of fact, greed for immediate profits irrespective of ultimate results has taken possession of industrial Japan.

This individualistic force has been reinforced by what seems to me the most harmful force at work in Japan—impatient hurry to become a Great Power at once. The Japanese know very well that a modern Great Power requires developed industry and wealth. Consequently they have "drawn the great red-ink overdraft on the future." Its statesmen have believed that the interests of the nation coincided with the get-rich-quick desires of individuals, and have not only not tried to regulate them but have encouraged them. The most enlightening answer received to the question asked by every foreign visitor as to the difference of political parties in Japan was that the party in power was the Mitsui party, while its rival was the Mitsubishi party. Japan has its "big six"—corporations which combine banking, shipping, mining, manufacturing, and continental exploitation in their various activities. Of the six, the Mitsuis and Mitsubishis are the richest and most powerful, the others being grouped about them. By direct intermarriage as well as in countless indirect ways, these big business interests are woven into the administration of the state. In fact, they on one side and the military and naval clans on the other *are* the State. Perhaps the greatest enlightenment I received as to practical politics in Japan was upon being told that the big business interests did not as such interfere in the Parliamentary elections. They did not care particularly what individuals were elected, for they did business direct with the political overlords. The story of the alliance of big business and politics in Japan would require a book—not a paragraph. Hence there is not much use in citing isolated illustrative facts. But certain items in their system of taxation may be taken as typical. A private individual pays a seven per cent income tax when his income reaches seven hundred and fifty dollars. A corporation pays only seven and a half per cent on an income of half a million. Chapters could not say more as to where control lies in Japan. The theory is that the private individual can do little to make Japan a strong world-power. Big concentrations of capital can really push Japan ahead in building up trade and industry for world competition. And newspapers which devote columns to general denunciation of the government rarely condescend to discuss the significance of such facts as this.

During the discussions by the Japanese newspapers of the League of Nations, they were wont to say that Japan represented the cause of labor, while the Western nations, especially Great Britain and the United States, represented capitalism. But there is no modern state in which capitalism has such unresisted and almost unquestioned power as in Japan today. The fear of the League of Nations as an agency of capitalistic exploitations was in fact a fear of one organization of capital by another—especially with reference to the development of Siberia and China.

It was a cynical Japanese—there aren't many—who told me that Japan's factory legislation was solely for the benefit of the Westerner. Being tired of telling curious visiting foreigners that Japan had no labor laws, they put some on the statute-book and suspended their execution for the most part. The former fact is advertised—and the latter concealed unless the visitor is unusually inquisitive. But the effect of this absence of regulation in conjunction with the rapid development of industry and trade during the past five years has been what every Westerner would have foretold. The labor crisis has arrived and it is unmitigated, acute. The allegedly more liberal Hara government at present in power has not authorized the formation of trade unions, but it has suspended the enforcement of the ban they are under. They now exist in a dim twilight zone, neither forbidden nor legalized. How numerous they are a visitor like myself has no way of knowing. One young radical Japanese told me that Japan was honeycombed with them, even while they were illegal, that even farm hands were unionizing, and that the police no longer reported them because the police had themselves been infected with "dangerous ideas"—a technical term in Japan as well as in certain respectable circles in the United States.

In intellectual circles there is animated discussion of whether Japan must in its economic development pass through the stage of antagonism of capital and labor characteristic of Western development. There is an influential section, representing the old Confucianist oligarchy, which holds that it is not necessary. They conceive that the old feudal principle of master and man, of protection and dependence, can be carried over into the modern relation of employer and employee. They do not content themselves with making appeals to the former to treat their employees better, to assume paternalistic responsibilities. There are countless societies in existence, under the control of employers, for health insurance, sick funds, promoting the welfare of laborers, and so forth. This is known technically as the principle of "kindness." The liberals who have come most under the influence of Western ideas contend that the principle is only a belated feudal relic and is bound to fail. They hold that it is morally as well as economically necessary for the laborers to assert themselves; that they cannot develop unless they organize and win their rights for themselves, instead of accepting concessions from benevolent patrons. This is known as the principle of "rights." But the feudalists of the chosen, unique-nation type counter by saying that it is only the materialism of the West that has made the development of industry take the form of struggle for liberties and rights; that the superior moral standards of the Orient are capable of applying the principle of kindness and sympathy to the growth of industrial relations and thus escaping the class war which has disgraced Western civilization. The Bolsheviks, of course, come in usefully here as well as elsewhere.

But for the moment at least the case is going against the upholders of the doctrine of "kindness." The rice riots were the signal of the beginning of labor and class-consciousness. The high cost of living is even a more acute issue in Japan than elsewhere. Japan has to import a considerable part of its food supply, and rice is not, like wheat, a world staple. It is conceivable that the future destiny of Japan turns upon this fact, for rice costs twelve times what it cost thirty years ago, and over three times what it did at the beginning of the war. Meantime there are all the usual consequences of change from the relative isolation of rural life to close contacts in cities and factories. On every side there are stories of increasing and active friction in shops and factories between foremen and laborers, and as I write there is a perfect epidemic of strikes. The rise in wages has in no sense kept pace with the increase in the cost of living; and the evidences of millionaires new-made from war profiteering abound on every hand. Japan is plunged suddenly and with practically no preparation, administrative or intellectual, into the most acute labor problem. Socialism is under the ban; a socialistic party is legally a criminal conspiracy and is treated as such. But according to all reports the interest in socialism is growing with remarkable rapidity.

In one of the private universities a teacher gave his class in advanced political economy a chance to vote as to whether they would take up for study Commercial Expansion, Labor Movements, or Socialism. The vote was a hundred for the last topic, to three for the first. Considering the avidity of the Japanese for practical topics and the zeal for commercial expansion it is safe to say that before the war the figures would have been reversed. The younger generation of students is becoming infected with radical ideas. The Imperial University is often thought to be the home of intellectual conservatism. A group of its students are publishing a journal called *Democracy*. Some of its professors are the most active members of a society called The Dawn, which is openly carrying on propaganda by public lectures for democratic ideas. Magazines with titles like Reconstruction, The New Society, are born almost every month. During the time of the previous cabinet, when police supervision was more rigid than now, a judge was convicted of lèse majesté, because in attacking the bureaucratic militarists he had said that by coming between the people and the Emperor they tarnished the glory of the Emperor. The suggestion that the Emperor could be tarnished was enough to send him to jail, but his standing and his influence were increased by the episode. A number of like cases could be cited. There have been of late many arrests for possession and circulation of "revolutionary" literature. There are even those who prophesy a political revolution on an economic basis in Japan within the next five years. But they seem to me too sanguine.

Serious as is the situation with labor, it is even more serious with the middle class. So far the industrial revolution in Japan does not run true to form. It is not creating a bourgeoisie, but rather undermining that which Japan used to possess. The Marxian division into the proletariat and the millionaire is rapidly going on. The old hand points out to you as significant that the numerous autos seen on the streets of Tokyo are of the Rolls-Royce and Pierce-Arrow type; Fords are conspicuous by their absence. In the country districts, peasant proprietorship is on the wane; large and absentee landownership is on the increase. The average land holding is about three acres; this hardly supports a family. Since it leaves no rice to sell, the high price of rice does not help the small farmer. Consequently concentration of land as well as of other forms of capital is rapidly proceeding.

Japan has had for some time an educated proletariat, which it has characteristically nicknamed the "European-clothes poor." So far as minor officials, police, clerks, and primary school teachers are concerned, this middle class has been the most staunch supporter of bureaucracy and militarism. But it recently tasted the bitterness of being a salaried class when the cost of living was leaping. Wages have increased; salaries hardly at all. The police began to agitate, and the Government did something for them; their position was too strategic to take chances. The primary school teachers called meetings for discussion in Tokyo and Yokohama; the police, acting under governmental instructions, forbade and then broke up the meetings. A newspaper commenting on the situation asked what would be the effect upon pupils when teachers in school taught conventional ethics, while out of school the teachers went contrary to the ethics they taught? In other words, the burden of what is termed "ethics" in the primary schools is submission to authority, while out of school the teachers were guilty of going contrary to authority in agitating to force the authorities to give them a living wage. The middle class does not of course possess the weight in mass of the laboring class, but it is quite likely that, with its greater education, its weaning from the cause of autocracy to which it has been devoted will have the earlier political results.

The observer can follow the progress of the cause of democracy in Japan by certain outward signs. The first and in many ways the most superficial will be the extension of universal suffrage. The last Parliament passed a bill about doubling the electorate. It was a compromise measure that gave no satisfaction to either the conservatives or the radicals. Unless foreign relations monopolize attention, the struggle will be renewed in the next Parliament. The second sign, and a more significant one, will be a conflict, occasioned either through the extension of suffrage or some similar question, between the lower house and the upper. For the House of Peers was deliberately invented to give the old oligarchy and the new plutocracy power to prevent extravagances in the popular direction on the part of the lower house. An even more serious sign will be the determined effort to make the ministers of war and navy real members of the Cabinet, instead of privileged appointees of the Army and Navy with independent and irresponsible jurisdiction. How far their independence goes came out in a way which would have been most embarrassing in any country except Japan in the closing days of the last Parliament. It was necessary to get the approval of the budget of expenditures of the various governmental departments. That of the War Department called for extra wages to one hundred and fifty thousand soldiers who had been on service in Siberia. Yet the Foreign Office had had a distinct understanding with other governments that only from seven to ten thousand men, a number proportionate to the army of the other Allies, would be sent. There was a temporary excitement, the House went into secret session, the money was voted, and a few days later there appeared in the newspapers a semi-official statement that the number in Siberia had not exceeded seventy thousand. No outsider, and not many insiders, will ever know what the other eighty thousand were paid for. But the meaning of an independent minister of war in a government that is said by propagandists in foreign countries to be constitutional is measured by the fact that he could act in such contravention to the direct pledge of the minister of foreign affairs. Numerous such cases appear, especially in connection with

Chinese affairs; and it is of course impossible to tell how much is collusion with a chance to prove an alibi on the part of supposedly liberal ministers, and how much is due to the undoubted power of the Minister of War (in effect the General Staff) to act without the rest of the "Government's" knowing anything about it. Other convincing signs of the spread of democratic ideas will be a movement for responsibility of the ministry to the Parliament instead of to the Emperor—which means in effect to the Clansmen who constitute Elder Statesmen—and for real legislative initiative on the part of the Parliament. For one has to be near the scene to learn that no important bills ever even receive consideration in the Parliament unless they have received a permit from the Privy Council—a secret and irresponsible body. The canceling of the power of the police, without judicial action or review, to suppress newspapers will be a most hopeful sign.

However, it is not likely that affairs will move in such a logical sequence as has been outlined. It is more likely that something will happen and a general change in the political structure take place all at once. Yet while in its effect, in its consequence, this happening will be a revolution, it is hard to imagine a happening in Japan such as we usually associate with the word "Revolution." There is some quality in the Japanese inscrutable to a foreigner which makes them at once the most rigid and the most pliable people on earth, the most self-satisfied and the most eager to learn. It is wholly conceivable that, with the development of democratic sentiment, a dramatic change may suddenly take place comparable to the transfer in the sixties of power from the old Tokugawa Shogunate to the Satsuma and Choshu clansmen, and the consequent centralized unification of Japan and the surrender of the policy of isolation. To the student of history it now looks very much as if Japan in the seventies and eighties had been very much in flux, and as if with slight changes in the course of events Japan might then have become a genuine and not a simulated constitutional state. But unfortunately in the eighties Europe generally entered upon the imperialistic path, and in the later eighties Japan deliberately adopted from Germany a militarized state, a constitution which gave the form without the substance of a representative government, and a universal primary education calculated to produce what a young Japanese student of English called "obeyfulness," and a secondary and higher system aiming at specialized efficiency in the service of the state. The development of liberation was put in abeyance for thirty years.

III. The Chief Foe

Comparisons of Japan with Germany have become common, perhaps too common. At all events, they usually fail in my judgment to point out wherein the actual and undeniable likeness lies. The similarity is not so much intrinsic and indigenous as it is imitative and acquired. In the seventies and eighties Japan was busy studying the Western world for models, as one thousand years before she had studied Korea and China. From Great Britain she borrowed the idea of navalism, merchant marine, sea commerce and sea power. From France she took the idea of centralized administration as a cure for the remaining ills of her centrifugal feudalism. From Germany she learned a technique for family law (a most important thing in transition from family organization to an individualistic basis); borrowed the aims and methods of an educational system, and the way of setting up an apparently Western or representative government which should not actually infringe in any way upon the autocratic oligarchy of the Choshu and Satsuma clan-leaders. Nor were the latter actuated wholly, nor possibly even chiefly, by personal ambitions. They were sure that only a high degree of centralized power would permit that development of army, navy, and a strong foreign policy which would save Japan from undergoing the same fate at the hands of Western powers that the rest of Asia was undergoing. And in the face of the imperial Europe of the last generation, it would demand a boldness of idealism not possessed by the present writer to declare they were wholly wrong.

Moreover the unification of Japan was only a recently accomplished fact. The foreigner is so used to hearing of the unity and community of the life of the Far East, especially Japan, that he is likely to overlook the socially divisive force exercised by the family principle. In Japan, isolations and animosities had been acute all through the still recent feudal period. Japan had been held together only by the force of the Tokugawas, and by their skill in playing one clan off against another. In connection with the restoration of Imperial unity and the opening of Japan to the outside world, Japan needed some internal and more spiritual bond of union. This she found in going Germany one better. In her past she had had a theocratic tradition which could be revived and put at the service of centralization. Japan has now had over a generation of education in a religion of state and emperor worship. Hence a new moral and intellectual flux can never be as eager, as open to new methods and institutions, as was the Japan of fifty years ago. There is a story told in Japan which does not sound authentic but which has a certain symbolic truth about it. It is said that when Marquis Ito and his commission on a constitution were on their way back to Japan—fresh from Germany and Bismarck—they stopped in London. Ito visited Herbert Spencer, whose advice (and this is authentic enough) to Japan to keep foreign nations at arm's (and armed) length had given him great influence. And Ito, so goes the story, told the philosopher that he was taking home with him plans for a constitution, an educational system, economic development, and so forth—in fact for everything except religion; and that he was depending upon Spencer to supply Japan with plans for that necessity. In reply, Spencer is said to have stated that since Japan had had ancestor worship and since the Emperor had been for ages a religious rather than a secular figure, she did not need to look abroad for plans to construct a national religion.

This particular account of the calculated use of Shintoism as political support of militaristic autocracy may be doubted. But no student can doubt that the Elder Statesmen who in the later eighties set Japan upon its present track deliberately surrounded the Imperial dynasty with all the mystic emotional haloes and sanctions that accompany divinity and divine origin. It is not many centuries since Europe had states based on the divine right of kings; but we have to go back to Imperial Rome to find emperors who are themselves divine and the sons of gods. A Japanese scholar told me that till the publication of the Constitution in 1889 the title Son of Heaven had been reserved for dead emperors, and that the deliberate use of religious myth for preventing the growth of democratic ideas was evident in the fact that in this document the title was for the first time applied to the living ruler. Of course I do not know whether his statement is correct, but there can be no doubt of the completeness of the fusion in the popular mind of political with religious and theocratic ideas, nor of the support the fusion gives to Japanese nationalistic sentiment as against other nations, and to the prestige and power of the ruling dynasty. And since as matter of fact the Emperor is still almost as much of a figure-head as when he was in seclusion in Kyoto, this permeating religious sanction accrues to the benefit of the bureaucracy that actually runs things. And it is interesting to note that one wing at least of the new liberal group is endeavoring to give the religious status of the Imperial dynasty a democratic turn. They do not attack the imperial idea; the attack would not only throw them personally into prison but would render them so odious as to discredit their cause. They claim that traditionally the emperor has been the Father of the People, supremely interested in their welfare; that in the sense of government *for* the people Japan is historically a democracy; and then they attack the oligarchy which has turned Japan aside from its true basis, and which has for its own aggrandizement come between the emperor and his people.

Westerners naturally have not taken Shintoism seriously as a political instrument. They have not taken the theocratic idea seriously. They could not; it is too alien to their ways of thinking. Hence they imagine that it is not taken seriously in Japan itself. They think of it as a kind of poetic embellishment, an additional romantic touch in a romantic land. And of course it is true that educated men in Japan do not believe the political myths in any literal sense. But it is also true that the theocratic point of view governs the consideration of all questions, and that emotions connected with it are so pervasive and intense that Japan *is* a unique country, one whose aims and methods are baffling to any foreigner. Perhaps only the foreigner who makes a study of elementary education, especially of the teaching of history and "ethics," realizes how systematic is the emperor-cult and how completely it becomes a part of the sub-conscious mental apparatus of all the pupils. Those who throw it off may be compared to the few who in Western countries in earlier days threw off, as they grew up, the theological teachings of childhood. The emotional after-effect can hardly be thrown off even then without a simultaneous casting off of patriotism and nationalistic feeling, so intimately religious has the dynastic sentiment become.

Three myths compose the larger myth. First is the notion of

complete racial homogeneity, of common blood, common descent, of common relationship to the gods who established civilization in Japan and whose descendants still rule the country. This is the doctrine which practically has the most truth in it in spite of its ethnological falsity, for in the course of time the various ethnic elements have got wonderfully fused together: Japan has not been an island and an isolated one for nothing. This is also the myth which it is safest to question, for all educated people are well aware of the different types that are found in the population. But it would hardly be safe to draw any political implications or conclusions from the denial of racial unity and common relationship to the emperor. The texts in "ethics" used in the schools teach that citizens of other countries have patriotism and that they also have filial and paternal affection, but that Japan is the only country in the world where the two things absolutely coincide. And a scientific ethnology which was punctilious enough to deny an objective literal basis for this statement would find itself in trouble.

The second myth is that of the unbroken continuity of the imperial dynasty for over twenty-five hundred years—since the first imperial God settled in Japan. As a basis for this statement, children in school are gravely taught a lot of myths about the formation of Japan and its earliest history which intellectually and esthetically are not on a level with the legends of the North American Indians. Then the actual facts of history which prove anything but continuity of blood and unity of dynasty are systematically falsified. The myth of single and pure descent of the imperial house which has existed from time immemorial and which will continue to exist for ages eternal is proclaimed in the very beginning of the German-borrowed constitution of Japan and remains the cornerstone of the Japanese state. The third myth is the consummation of the other two. All that Japan is and can become she owes to the original virtues of the divine founders and to those of their divine descendents. The moral as to what the citizen of Japan owes the imperial dynasty is obvious, and the teaching of ethics and history in the common schools takes no chances that it will not be made plain. It is not surprising that the fanatical apostles of these doctrines have more than once allowed their little charges to perish in flame and smoke while they saved the portrait of the divine emperor.

University teachers in their classrooms tell the historic truth. They fulfill orally the obligations of historic scholarship. But such higher criticism is confined to the confidence of the classroom. Martyrdom is not wooed by setting forth the facts in printed form for general consumption. Sometimes I think that the surest sign of the approach of democracy will be given when we read that a group of intellectuals have braved prison or death by setting forth to the public the truth about such matters.

I am afraid I may seem to have got completely away from my subject. I seem to be speaking not of liberalism in Japan but of the most insidious and influential type of reactionarism. But it is worth while to know the difficulties with which the growth of liberalism has to contend. The knowledge will make us more sympathetic and more patient. The liberalism is there, and it is coming to possess the present generation of university-taught men. Since I began writing, a delegation of Japanese University students has been in Peking to express to the Chinese their entire lack of sympathy with the policy of Japan towards China, and to say that their enemy is a common one—Japanese militaristic autocracy. It is impossible for Japan to engage in trade, to exchange commodities and technical science with all the world, to take a part in world politics, and still to remain isolated from the world situation and world currents. The significance of this fact has been brought home to Japan with increasing acceleration and momentum by the war and its conclusion, and the outcome is the present spread of democracy and liberalism. The imperialistic settlement at Paris has undeniably effected a setback. Every reaction from democracy all over the world will retard the movement in Japan. But unless the world overtly and on a large scale goes back on democracy, Japan will move steadily in that direction. And my own confidence in the resilience, adaptability, and practical intelligence of the Japanese people, as well as in a kind of social democracy which is embodied in the manners and customs of the people, makes me think the change will come without a bloody and catastrophic upheaval.

ON THE TWO SIDES OF THE EASTERN SEA

It is three days' easy journey from Japan to China. It is doubtful whether anywhere in the world another journey of the same length brings with it such a complete change of political temper and belief. Certainly it is greater than the alteration perceived in journeying directly from San Francisco to Shanghai. The difference is not one in customs and modes of life; that goes without saying. It concerns the ideas, beliefs and alleged information current about one and the same fact: the status of Japan in the international world and especially its attitude toward China. One finds everywhere in Japan a feeling of uncertainty, hesitation, even of weakness. There is a subtle nervous tension in the atmosphere as of a country on the verge of change but not knowing where the change will take it. Liberalism is in the air, but genuine liberals are encompassed with all sorts of difficulties especially in combining their liberalism with the devotion to theocratic robes which the imperialistic militarists who rule Japan have so skilfully thrown about the Throne and the Government. But what one senses in China from the first moment is the feeling of the all-pervading power of Japan which is working as surely as fate to its unhesitating conclusion—the domination of Chinese politics and industry by Japan with a view to its final absorption.

It is not my object to analyze the realities of the situation or to inquire whether the universal feeling in China is a collective hallucination or is grounded in fact. The phenomenon is worthy of record on its own account. Even if it be merely psychological, it is a fact which must be reckoned with in both its Chinese and its Japanese aspects. And in the first place, as to the differences in psychological atmosphere. Everybody who knows anything about Japan knows that it is the land of reserves and reticences.

[First published in *New Republic* 19 (1919): 346–48, datelined Nanking, May 28. Republished in *China, Japan and the U.S.A.* (New York: Republic Publishing Co., 1921), pp. 3–9, and in *Characters and Events*, ed. Joseph Ratner (New York: Henry Holt and Co., 1929), 1:170–76.]

The half-informed American will tell you that this is put on for the misleading of foreigners. The informed know that it is an attitude shown to foreigners only because it is deeply engrained in the moral and social tradition of Japan; and that, if anything, the Japanese are more likely to be communicative—about many things at least—to a sympathetic foreigner, than to one another. The habit of reserve is so deeply embedded in all the etiquette, convention and daily ceremony of living, as well as in the ideals of strength of character, that only the Japanese who have subjected themselves to foreign influences escape it—and many of them revert. To put it mildly, the Japanese are not a loquacious people; they have the gift of doing rather than of gab.

When accordingly a Japanese statesman or visiting diplomatist engages in unusually prolonged and frank discourse setting forth the aims and procedures of Japan, the student of politics who has been long in the East at once becomes alert, not to say suspicious. A recent illustration is so extreme that it will doubtless seem fantastic beyond belief. But the student at home will have to take these seeming fantasies seriously if he wishes to appreciate the present atmosphere of China. Cables have brought fragmentary reports of some addresses of Baron Goto in America. Doubtless in the American atmosphere these have the effect of reassuring America as to any improper ambitions on the part of Japan. In China, they were taken as announcements that Japan has about completed its plans for the absorption of China, and that the lucubration preliminary to operations of swallowing are about to begin. The reader is forgiven in advance any scepticism he feels about both the fact itself and the correctness of my report of the belief in the alleged fact. His scepticism will not surpass what I should feel in his place. But the suspicion aroused by such statements as this and the recent interview of Foreign Minister Uchida and Baron Ishii must be noted as evidences of the universal belief in China that Japan has one mode of diplomacy for the East and another for the West, and that what is said in the West must be read in reverse in the East.

China, whatever else it is, is not the land of privacies. It is a proverb that nothing long remains secret in China. The Chinese talk more easily than they act—especially in politics. They are adepts in revealing their own shortcomings. They dissect their own weaknesses and failures with the most extraordinary reasonableness. One of the defects upon which they dwell is the love of finding substitutes for positive action, of avoiding entering upon a course of action which might be irrevocable. One almost wonders whether their power of self-criticism is not itself another of these substitutes. At all events, they are frank to the point of loquacity. Between the opposite camps there are always communications flowing. Among official enemies there are "sworn friends." In a land of perpetual compromise, etiquette as well as necessity demands that the ways for later accommodations be kept open. Consequently things which are spoken of only under the breath in Japan are shouted from the housetops in China. It would hardly be good taste in Japan to allude to the report that influential Chinese ministers are in constant receipt of Japanese funds and these corrupt officials are the agencies by which political and economic concessions were wrung from China while Europe and America were busy with the war. But in China nobody even takes the trouble to deny it, or even to discuss it. What is psychologically most impressive is the fact that it is merely taken for granted. When it is spoken of, it is as one mentions the heat on an unusually hot day.

In speaking of the feeling of weakness current in Japan about Japan itself, one must refer to the economic situation because of its obvious connection with the international situation. In the first place, there is the strong impression that Japan is over-extended. Even in normal times, Japan relies more upon production for foreign markets than is regarded in most countries as safe policy. But there is the belief that Japan *must* do so, because only by large foreign sellings—large in comparison with the purchasing power of a people still having a low standard of life—can it purchase the raw materials—and even food—it has to have. But during the war, the dependence of manufacturing and trade at home upon the foreign market was greatly increased. The domestic increase of wealth, though very great, is still too much in the hands of the few to affect seriously the internal demand for goods. Item one which awakens sympathy for Japan as being in a somewhat precarious situation.

Another item concerns the labor situation. Japan seems to feel itself in a dilemma. If she passes even reasonably decent factory laws (or rather attempts their enforcement) and regulates child and women's labor, she will lose that advantage of cheap labor which she now counts on to offset her many disadvantages. On the other hand, strikes, labor difficulties, agitation for unions, etc., are constantly increasing, and the tension in the atmosphere is unmistakable. The rice riots are not often spoken of, but their memory persists, and the fact that they came very near to assuming a directly political aspect. Is there a race between fulfillment of the aspirations of the military clans who still hold the reins, and the growth of genuinely democratic forces which will forever terminate those aspirations? Certainly the defeat of Germany gave a blow to bureaucratic militarism in Japan which in time will go far. Will it have the time required to take effect on foreign policy? The hope that it will is a large factor in stimulating liberal sympathy for a Japan which is beginning to undergo the throes of transition.

As for the direct international situation of Japan, the feeling in Japan is one of the threatening danger of isolation. Germany is gone; Russia is gone. While those facts simplify matters for Japan somewhat, there is also the belief that in taking away potential allies, they have weakened Japan in the general game of balance and counterbalance of power. Particularly does the removal of imperialistic Russia relieve the threat on India which was such a factor in the willingness of Great Britain to make the offensive-defensive alliance. The revelation of the militaristic possibilities of America is another serious factor. Certainly the new triple entente cordiale of Japan, Italy and France is no adequate substitute for a realignment of international forces in which a common understanding between Great Britain and America is a dominant factor. This factor explains, if it does not excuse, some of the querulousness and studied discourtesies with which the Japanese press for some months has treated President Wilson, the United States in general and its relation to the League of Nations in particular, while it also throws light on the ardor with which the opportune question of racial discrimination was discussed. (The Chinese have an unfailing refuge in a sense of humor. It was interesting to note the delight with which they received the utterance of the Japanese Foreign Minister, after Japanese success at Paris, that "his attention had recently been called" to various press attacks on America which he much deprecated.) In any case there is no mistaking the air of tension and nervous overstrain which now attends all discussion of Japanese foreign relations. In all directions, there are characteristic signs of hesitation, shaking of old beliefs and movement along new lines. Japan seems to be much in the same mood as that which it experienced in the early eighties before, toward the close of that decade, it crystallized its institutions through acceptance of the German constitution, militarism, educational system, and diplomatic methods. So that, once more, the observer gets the impression that substantially all of Japan's energy, abundant as that is, must be devoted to her urgent problems of readjustment.

Come to China, and the difference is incredible. It almost seems as if one were living in a dream; or as if some new Alice had ventured behind an international looking-glass wherein everything is reversed. That we in America should have little idea of the state of things and the frame of mind in China is not astonishing—especially in view of the censorship and the distraction of attention of the last few years. But that Japan and China should be so geographically near, and yet every fact that concerns them appear in precisely opposite perspective, is an experience of a life time. Japanese liberalism? Yes, it is heard of, but only in connection with one form which the longing for the miraculous *deus ex machina* takes. Perhaps a revolution in Japan may intervene to save China from the fate which now hangs over her. But there is no suggestion that anything less than a complete revolution will alter or even retard the course which is attributed to Japanese diplomacy working hand in hand with Japanese business interests and militarism. The collapse of Russia and Germany? These things only mean that Japan has in a few years fallen complete heir to Russian hopes, achievements and possessions in Manchuria, and Outer Mongolia, and has had opportunities in Siberia thrown into her hands which she could hardly have hoped for in her most optimistic moments. And now Japan has, with the blessing of the great Powers at Paris, become also the heir of German concessions, intrigues and ambitions, with added concessions, wrung (or bought) from incompetent and corrupt officials by secret agreements when the world was busy with war. If all the great Powers are so afraid of Japan that they give way to her every wish, what is China that she can escape the doom prepared for her? That is the cry of helplessness going up all over China. And Japanese propagandists take advantage of the situation, pointing to the action of the Peace Conference as proof that the Allies care nothing for China, and that China must throw herself into the arms of Japan if she is to have any protection at all. In short, Japan stands ready as she stood ready in Korea to guarantee the integrity and independence of China. And the fear that the latter must, in spite of her animosity toward Japan, accept this fate in order to escape something worse swims in the sinister air. It is the exact counterpart of the feeling current among the liberals in Japan that Japan has alienated China permanently when a considerate and slower course might have united the two countries. If the economic straits of Japan are alluded to, it is only as a reason why Japan has hurried her diplomatic coercion, her corrupt and secret bargainings with Chinese traitors and her industrial invasion. While the western world supposes that the military and the industrial party in Japan have opposite ideas as to best methods of securing Japanese supremacy in the East, it is the universal opinion in China that the two are working in complete understanding with one another, and the differences that sometimes occur between the Foreign Office in Tokyo and the Ministry of War (which is extra-constitutional in status) are staged for effect.

These are some of the aspects of the most complete transformation scene that it has ever been the lot of the writer to experience. May it turn out to be only an extraordinary psychological experience! But in the interests of truth it must be recorded that every resident of China, Chinese or American, with whom I have talked in the last four weeks has volunteered the belief that all the seeds of a future great war are now deeply implanted in China. To avert such a calamity they look to the League of Nations or some other force outside the immediate scene. Unfortunately the press of Japan treats every attempt to discuss the state of opinion in China or the state of facts as evidence that America, having tasted blood in the war, now has its eyes on Asia with the expectation later on of getting its hands on Asia. Consequently America is interested in trying to foster ill-will between China and Japan. If the pro-American Japanese do not enlighten their fellow-countrymen as to the facts then America ought to return some of the propaganda that visits its shores. But every American who goes to Japan ought also to visit China—if only to complete his education.

THE DISCREDITING OF IDEALISM

It will be recalled that the decision of the Versailles Conference as to Japan's claims in China was announced at the end of April. A few weeks after this time, when I was giving some lectures in one of the chief educational centres of China, the teachers and students were asked to hand in questions in writing. They responded in large numbers. The question asked most frequently, repeated over and over again in different terms, ran about as follows: "During the war we were led to believe that with the defeat of Germany there would be established a new international order based on justice to all; that might would not henceforth make right in deciding questions between nations; that weak nations would get the same treatment as powerful ones—that, indeed, the war was fought to establish the equal rights of all nations, independently of their size or armed power. Since the decision of the peace conference shows that between nations might still makes right, that the strong nation gets its own way against a weak nation, is it not necessary for China to take steps to develop military power, and for this purpose should not military training be made a regular part of its educational system?" At every educational gathering since, this question has been uppermost.

The matter is not referred to here for discussion in connection with China. China can become a strong nation only through industrial and economic development. Any military efforts, apart from this development, would only prolong the present chaos, and at most create an hallucination as to national power. The implications, however, of the question come home to every one who favored the participation of the United States in the war on what are termed idealistic grounds. It comes with especial force to those who, strongly opposed to war in general, broke with the pacifists because they saw in this war a means of realizing pacific

[First published in *New Republic* 20 (1919): 285–87. Republished in *Characters and Events*, ed. Joseph Ratner (New York: Henry Holt and Co., 1929), 2:629–35, with the title "Force and Ideals."]

ideals—the practical reduction of armaments, the abolition of secret and oligarchic diplomacy and of special alliances, the substitution of inquiry and discussion for intrigue and threats, the founding, through the destruction of the most powerful autocracy, of a democratically ordered international government, and the consequent beginning of the end of war. Once having taken sides, vanity is enlisted. As President Wilson is moved to "make the best" of the actual outcome, so all those who favored America's action in the war from idealistic reasons are tempted to make the best of its outcome. And "making the best of it" means blurring over disagreeable features so as to salve vanity. Consequently the pacifists who were converted to war are obliged to undertake an unusually searching inquiry into the actual results in their relation to their earlier professions and beliefs. Were not those right who held that it was self-contradictory to try to further the permanent ideals of peace by recourse to war? Was not he who thought they might thus be promoted one of the gullible throng who swallowed the cant of idealism as a sugar coating for the bitter core of violence and greed? Is the pacifist à outrance, the absolutist of peace, the only one who can make a valid claim to untarnished idealism? Have the ideals of humanity, of self-determination, justice to the weak, been hopelessly discredited through being inscribed?

The defeat of idealistic aims has been, without exaggeration, enormous. The consistent pacifist has much to urge now in his own justification; he is entitled to his flourish of private triumphings. Superficially, his opponent—I mean the one who placed himself also on idealistic ground—has not much to urge except the scant though true plea that things would have been much worse if Germany had won, as she would have done without the participation of the United States. The defeat, however, is the defeat which will always come to idealism that is not backed up by intelligence and by force—or, better, by an intelligent use of force. It may seem like a petty attempt to get back at the pacifist to say that the present defeat of the war ideals of the United States is due to the fact that America's use of "Force to the uttermost, Force without stint," still suffered from the taint of complacent and emotional pacifism. But it may fairly be argued that the real cause of the defeat is the failure to use force adequately and intelligently. The ideals of the United States have been defeated in the settlement because we took into the war our sentimentalism, our attachment to moral sentiments as efficacious powers, our pious optimism as to the inevitable victory of the "right," our childish belief that physical energy can do the work that only intelligence can do, our evangelical hypocrisy that morals and "ideals" have a self-propelling and self-executing capacity.

If the principle of force to the limit had been in operation in behalf of our ideals, complete information would have been had at an early date regarding the secret agreements that were outstanding, and our share in the war would have been made to depend upon a clearing of the decks. This would have shown distrust of our Allies, and an ungenerous wish to take advantage of the hour of their critical need of our help? There speaks our inveterate sentimentalism, our unwillingness to use the force at hand in support of our ideals. Either we and our Allies were fighting for the same ends or we were not. There was no moral generosity in putting them in a position of willingness to use our help for professed democratic ends when in reality they were to use it for imperialistic ends. On our side, if we had had a tenth of the faith in concrete intelligence used at the right juncture that we had in fine phrases, many of the obstacles to securing at the end a peace in accord with our idealism would have been swept away in the earlier months of 1917. It is exceedingly silly to regard as a failure of idealism what ought rather to be charged against our own lack of common sense.

Past history would have shown what any knowledge of the present situation confirms—that the type of man brought forward by war is not the type needed to make peace. The urgencies of war bring to the front the kind of man who can make quick decisions in the face of immediate pressure of circumstance. Such statesmen are bound to be of the aggressive and quasi-gambling type. At best they represent the government of war, not the pursuits of normal peace with its long-time interests and consequences. Mr. Norman Angell and a few others, but Mr. Angell especially, taught all during the war the indispensable necessity of provision for popular representation at the peace conference. Everybody who heard him was impressed with the reasonableness of the proposition. But nothing was done. Was this an intelligent use of the force at our command?

President Wilson as a peace-maker is the exception that proves the rule. Owing to the accidents of our electoral and party system, he was the one figure in the Councils who had not been given his place and influence by the exigencies of war. He represented and upon the whole with more than ordinary representative capacity the normal interests of men and governments in times of peace. Yet in essentials he was overruled. Why? Because it was thought that, by some magic, dumb millions could be given effective voice through him. He seems to have thought that, contrary to all experience of representative government, he could "represent" the unrepresented interests of the common people whose main concern is with peace, not war. It would be difficult to imagine any greater travesty on the use of force to the uttermost than the idea that one man could secure a just decision by appealing à la improvvisatore over the heads of diplomats to the unorganized, scattered and unenlightened peoples of the earth. When he became inclined to act in this way the diplomats had only to point out to him that he would thereby decrease the waning power of governmental authority, increase popular unrest, and run the risk of plunging Europe into the chaos of political revolutions. After that, he could not even speak effectually for himself, to say nothing of "representing" the unrepresented peoples of the earth. He made his popular appeal in the case of Fiume, indeed, but its chief tangible effect was to strengthen Imperial Japan in its encroachments upon the people of China.

There is another force, an immense force, which might have been used in behalf of the war ideals of the United States, a force which might still be employed though less effectually. There is the economic and financial force of the United States. It may be doubted whether the world has ever seen such a spectacle as that of the last few years. The United States has extended money and credit almost "without stint" to governments of Europe irrespective of whether they were supporting the announced policies of the United States, nay, even when those governments were doing what they could to undermine American ends. And doubtless the average American has taken pride in this fact. We are so generous, so disinterested, that we do not bargain or impose conditions. In short we are so childishly immature, so careless of our professed ideals, that we prefer a reputation for doing the grand seigneur act to the realization of our national aims. This is the acme of our sentimentalism. Can we blame the European statesmen if to put it with blank vulgarity they play us for suckers?

Such considerations as these, which might be indefinitely multiplied, show that not idealism but *our* idealism is discredited, an idealism of vague sentiments and good intentions, isolated from judgment as to the effective use of the force in our hands. It may be said that this is not our fault, but President Wilson's. There are a few who are entitled to the benefit of this plea, but only a few. President Wilson is a scape-goat convenient to save our vanity. But he successfully appealed to the American people and led them.

If they—if we—had been different, he would have had to use different methods to get results. History will probably record that his idealistic speeches corresponded to the spirit of the American people; and that the blame which belongs to him is not that of betraying the American spirit but of embodying its weaknesses too faithfully. Take one example. The use of force in behalf of our professed ideals would certainly have involved the use of all the thinking, speaking and writing of the liberals and radicals who in the end could alone give sympathetic and intelligent support to the aims eloquently set forth by President Wilson. Instead, we had a policy of suppression of free speech, of espionage, and of encouragement of the violent unrestraint characteristic of the reactionary. It is easy to blame for this Mr. Wilson's personal desire to play the part of Atlas supporting alone the universe of free ideals. An accomplice his conceit assuredly was, but the American people who revelled in emotionalism and who grovelled in sacrifice of its liberties is the responsible cause. Immaturity and inexperience in international affairs consequent upon our isolation mitigate the blame. But they would not have taken the form they took were it not for our traditional evangelical trust in morals apart from intelligence, and in ideals apart from executive and engineering force. Our Christianity has become identified with vague feeling and with an optimism which we think is a sign of a pious faith in Providence but which in reality is a trust in luck, a deification of the feeling of success regardless of any intelligent discrimination of the nature of success.

It may be that the words idealism and ideals will have to go—that they are hopelessly discredited. It may be that they will become synonyms for romanticism, for blind sentimentalism, for faith in mere good intentions, or that they will come to be regarded as decorative verbal screens behind which to conduct sinister plans. But the issue is real, not verbal. There remains a difference between narrow and partial ends and full and far reaching ends; between the success of the few for the moment and the happiness of the many for an enduring time; a difference between identifying happiness with the elements of a meagre and hard life and those of a varied and free life. This is the only difference between materialism and idealism that counts. And until we act persistently upon the fact that the difference depends upon the use of force and that force can be directed only by intelligence, we shall continue to dwell in a world where the difference between materialism and idealism will be thought to be a matter of opinion, argument and personal taste. To go on opposing ideals and force to each other is to perpetuate this regime. The issue is not that of indulging in ideals versus using force in a realistic way. As long as we make this opposition we render our ideals impotent, and we play into the hands of those who conceive force as primarily military. Our idealism will never prosper until it rests upon the organization and resolute use of the greater forces of modern life: industry, commerce, finance, scientific inquiry and discussion and the actualities of human companionship.

THE STUDENT REVOLT IN CHINA

The depression that bore China down after the Paris decision to hand Shantung over to Japan was fraught with as much pessimism as bitterness. China knew her weakness as against any other large Power of the world. She knew that her political division, with a civil war not yet officially closed, her industrial backwardness, her financial chaos, put her in a position where she could not say a decisive No to any country bent on exploiting her. Accordingly, she hung pathetically and tremblingly upon the deliberations of the peace conference. Morning and night she kept up her hopes by repeating the assurances given by the Allied statesmen of the creation of a new international order and of the future protection of weak nations against the rapacity of the strong. And her hopes needed support, for they were mingled with fears. Better than western nations she knew how far Japan was prepared to go, for twice during the war she had yielded to Japan's barely disguised threat of war. She also knew more about the secret treaties and understandings than did the western nations. Hence it was that the Paris decision created despair rather than the bitter antagonism to America and the other Allies which might have been expected. The outcome just proved that Force still ruled; that Might still made Right in international affairs; that China was hopelessly weak and Japan threateningly strong.

On May 4th a thrill stirred this hopelessness. Somebody had *done* something. Students of the Peking University had demonstrated, and in the course of their demonstration had deliberately attacked and beaten up two of the three Chinese statesmen who are popularly known as traitors because of their part in negotiating various secret treaties and loans with Japan. A stir moved vitally through the national apathy. The weakness, possibly the corruption of Chinese officials, had had a responsible share in the Shantung decision (it is always the Shantung and never the

[First published in *New Republic* 20 (1919): 16–18, datelined Peking, June 24.]

Tsingtau question in China). If China could not count upon other nations, she might at least do something to put in order her own house. The students' act was received not as a chance act of lawless lynching, but as a gesture of righteous indignation. The air was again tense with expectation. Was the Peking event anything more than a passing gesture?

Events followed quickly. The government arrested a number of students. Then their fellows protested; troops were thrown about the University buildings. The city was practically under martial law. The provinces were rife with rumors of the readiness of the Chinese militarist clique to go to any extreme in the way of slaughter to put down opposition; rife even with rumors of an impending coup d'état to fix irretrievably the hold upon the government of the militarist and pro-Japanese party. The Chancellor of the University, whom the militarists hated as the intellectual leader of the liberal elements, resigned and disappeared, because, according to report, not only his life but those of hundreds of students were threatened. Then came the news that all of the students in Peking in institutions above the rank of the elementary school had struck in protest against the action of the government. They had not only struck, but they had made definite demands (of which more below); and they had organized into bands of ten, who were everywhere making open-air speeches, defying the military police to arrest them, and trying to organize the public that listened to them into similar bands of ten to carry on propaganda.

This time the thrill throughout the country was electric. The seventh of May is the day kept as the Day of National Shame. Even the primary schools have banners in them, "Remember the seventh day of the fifth month." This day of national humiliation is the anniversary of the Japanese twenty-one demands. The coincidence of dates had a powerful effect. Students from the Peking University rapidly dispersed through the country, addressing themselves primarily to students in all the large centres. The latter became restless; then they struck; middle (high) school students, normal and technical schools; again everything above the elementary grade. Everywhere the bands of ten were organized, speakers were drilled in what to say and how to say it, and the popular propaganda spread through the provinces. And the multitude heard it gladly.

The unorganized hostility to Japan took form in a boycott. That was one of the themes of the boy and girl orators. They did not content themselves with general exhortations. Lists of Japanese goods were printed and mimeographed by the thousand; classified lists of all Japanese products sold in China. Similar lists of substitute native goods were circulated. In some of the schools the industrial department set to work to discover what Japanese goods could be made in existing shops without additional capital. As soon as models were constructed they were taken to small shops and their mode of manufacture explained. Then, to create a market, other students took these goods and hawked them through the streets, lecturing, exhorting, explaining the political situation at the same time. And as the vacation period comes on these students are dispersing all over China peddling goods and speaking, speaking, speaking . . .

Meantime the government was not idle. Political speeches were forbidden, students' meetings were forcibly broken up, many scores of students in different parts of China were sorely injured, a few were killed. It is not difficult to foresee the future memorial meetings in honor of these martyrs of patriotism, or even the shrines wherein their memory will be reverenced. Then the government at Peking took more drastic measures. Mandates were issued condemning the students, ordering them under penalty of dissolution of schools to return to their studies, to disband their unions, and to cease concerning themselves with what was none of their business, praising by name the men popularly regarded as traitors, warning against the boycott, and in general saying that foreign affairs should be left in the hands of the government. Coincidently several hundred students were arrested in Peking for speaking. With the fatuity which affects militarists in China as well as elsewhere, it was promised that this would put an end to the students' agitation. The next day the number of students speaking on the streets was more than doubled, and the arrests ran to above a thousand. The students planned to go on till every man was in jail. Girl students formed a procession (some of them had to break down gates to get out) to wait upon the President and request the freeing of students; they said they would remain praying for justice all night if he did not hear them. The jails could not hold the arrested students. These were shut up in the University buildings and left with little food and less water, with cordons of troops around them. The faculty met; protested against this military invasion; against the degradation of using halls of learning as jails; against the abuse of patriotic students; and they telegraphed their protest widespread.

Events had been moving outside of Peking. This last arbitrary action was the beginning of the end. Merchants in Shanghai went on strike; shops were closed, including those selling food; the merchants in Tientsin and Nanking joined; those in Peking and other cities prepared to join. There was plenty of evidence that the students had practically succeeded in converting the merchants to their side; that they no longer stood alone, but had effected an alliance, offensive and defensive, with the powerful mercantile guilds. There was talk of a strike against paying taxes. The government capitulated suddenly if not gracefully. Troops were withdrawn from the University grounds and the students invited to come out. They declined, and announced that they would stay in till the students everywhere were guaranteed the right of free speech and until the government officially apologized to them. Two days more saw the end. The government sent delegates to make the required apology; a new mandate was issued saying that the country realized that the students were actuated by patriotic motives, and should not be interfered with if they kept within the law. The "resignations" of the three men called traitors were accepted. Undoubtedly the spread of the strike to the merchants, and the fear of its further extension, were the actuating motives in the inglorious surrender. But the students had managed to get their propaganda into the army. Rumors were afloat that the armies could not be counted upon for further suppressions—especially as pay was far in arrears. After their triumphant march from out their self-made prison, students were heard to lament that the government changed the guards so often they had not been able to convert more than half their jailers.

The original demands made upon the government were few and simple. The students arrested for engaging in the beating-up enterprise must be freed and given immunity from prosecution; the Chancellor who was so obnoxious to the militarist clique must be reinstated. By the time the government was ready to meet these first demands (in outward form, at least), the demands had greatly increased. Instructions must be given to delegates in Paris not to sign the treaty except with reservations as to Shantung, all "traitors" must be dismissed, all secret understandings with Japan abrogated, freedom of speech guaranteed. Within about a month the Student Movement had won all its points except the third and first; and with respect to the first the government had promised to do all that the international situation permitted; and fell back vaguely upon advice received from Great Britain, France and President Wilson to sign, with hopes of later readjustment. Yet there is no evidence that the students are deceived as to the amount of success they have achieved. The military clique is still in full command; the places of the three dismissed men will probably be filled by other men of the same pro-Japanese affiliations. Externally things are much as they were before. No successful revolution in government or in foreign affairs justifies giving this amount of space to the Student Movement.

But the prestige of the militarist faction has received its first great blow—and prestige is the primary feature of Oriental politics. A negative boycott, sure to fail in the end, has been changed into a constructive movement for development of home industry—a movement still in its infancy but capable of effective development. The possibilities of organization independent of government, but capable in the end of controlling government, have been demonstrated. It is hard to estimate the significance of the fact that the new movement was initiated by the student body. Reverence for the scholar is traditional in China. It still holds over from the rank accorded the literati in former days. From the western standpoint it amounts to superstitious regard. Yet this is the first time that students have taken any organized part in politics. Beyond what their speaking and writing have done in organizing public opinion at the present emergency is the abiding effect for the future. Most of the outward signs of the movement—aside from hawking goods and teaching patriotism at the same time—have now subsided. But a National Students' Union has been formed and definite plans have been made for the future. Already attempts are making to unite the people of the divided north and south in a way that will cut under the militarists of both sides. It would be highly surprising if a new constitutionalist movement were not set going. The combination of students and merchants that has proved so effective will hardly be allowed to become a mere memory. Already in some cities it has been extended into a

Four Group Union, and efforts are making to extend this larger organization throughout the country.

Probably a foreign observer would count as the most precious fruit of the movement the awakening of China from a state of passive waiting. A sharp blow has been given the idea that China itself is helpless and must be saved from without. In spite of the charges of which the Japanese newspapers are full that the movement was instigated, and even financed, by foreigners, especially Americans, it was a strictly native movement, showing what educated China can do, and will do, in the future. The spell of pessimism seems broken. An act has been done, a deed performed. Perhaps there is now a healthier, better organized, movement from within China itself for China's own salvation than at any time since the Revolution.

Even if nothing more were to come of the movement, it would be worth observation and record as an exhibition of the way in which China is really governed—when it is governed at all. American children are taught the list of "modern" inventions that originated in China. They are not taught, however, that China invented the boycott, the general strike and guild organization as means of controlling public affairs. In no other civilized country of the present day (leaving Russia out of account now as an exception to all rules) is brute force such a factor in official government as in China. But in no other country could moral and intellectual force accomplish so quickly and peaceably what was effected in China in the last five or six weeks. This formulates the standing paradox of China. But in the past the moral forces which fundamentally control have been organized only for protest and rebellion. When the emergency is past, the forces have again dissolved into their elements. If the present organization persists and is patiently employed for constructive purposes, then the fourth of May, nineteen hundred and nineteen, will be marked as the dawn of a new day. This is a large If. But just now the future of China so far as it depends upon China hangs on that If.

THE INTERNATIONAL DUEL IN CHINA

Everybody knows that before the war the territory and resources of China were the scene of contention among five great Powers. During the war the situation completely altered. Russia and Germany ceased to exist as influential factors. Great Britain and France had their energy, attention and capital mortgaged in a life and death struggle. This left Japan mistress of the field. In accordance with the rules of established international diplomacy, she took full advantage of the unique opportunity to improve her national position. It is hardly sportsmanlike of other nations who have been engaged in the same game to whine about her success. Anyway, they have been her accomplices. Something like an offensive and defensive alliance between Japan and Russia was consummated while the latter seemed to be still a Power. Great Britain and France made secret arrangements with her. In every case, the consideration given Japan was at the expense of China. Until the circumstantial reports of the activities of Ota in Stockholm are confirmed or refuted, the question remains whether Germany, the fifth contender, had not also already entered into negotiations with Japan, also at the expense of China but this time with Russia also as a prospective victim.

Apparently Japan had the field to herself. Yet for over two years a duel has been in progress, a duel which concerns both China's internal policy and her international relationships. The duel concerns the ideas and ideals which are to control China's internal political development. Is it to become a genuine democracy or is it to continue in the traditions of autocratic government?—whether under the name of a republic or an empire being a secondary consideration. Internationally, the question is whether China's integrity can be regained and maintained under some sort of temporary international supervision, or whether China is to follow the course which in the past has made Japan the only

[First published in *New Republic* 20 (1919): 110–12, datelined Peking, July 8.]

Asiatic nation capable of protecting herself against European encroachments and sure of the effective respect of western nations. A duel between ideas and ideals needs, however, to be embodied. The United States and Japan are the bodies through which the duel of ideals is carried on. Force of circumstances, not conscious choice, has determined the figures of the duel.

In details, Japan may perhaps have been a peculiarly adept pupil in the way of secret diplomacy practiced by the western Powers. But she has a right to claim that her ultimate object, controlling every particular step, has never been concealed. Her announced aim has been to free Asia, at least eastern Asia, from foreign, that is, European control. The Monroe Doctrine for Asia, Asia for the Asiatics, is a doctrine as public as it is sweeping. Any Japanese is entitled to claim that if the foreigner has ever taken Japanese guarantees of the territorial integrity of China in other sense than as *against* the European intruder, the foreigner has only his own stupidity to blame. Japan would still hold that she has kept her guarantees of the territorial integrity of Korea—kept them by the only means which under the conditions are effective. In other words, the standing minor premise of the conclusion of the recovery of China by China is the protectorate of weak, unorganized and unprogressive China by organized, militarized Japan—Japan which has adopted western methods in science, industry, education and arms in order to turn them against the West and to preserve the culture and territory of the East, of Asia, intact. Behind every word of the twenty-one demands and of the other negotiations of Japan with China lies the clamorous and luminous unuttered word: Put yourself under the complete protection of Japan, and you shall be guaranteed the same international prestige, the same immunity from projects of partition, concessions, spheres of influence and economic servitudes that Japan enjoys. In no other way can you secure integrity, freedom and respect.

Incidentally of course, great material and industrial advantages would accrue to Japan, to say nothing of the military advantage of command of unnumbered man power. But only the blindness of extreme national prejudice will fail to see that the grandiose scheme has as many ideal aspects as those which have ever clothed the plans of any western Power to fulfill its national destiny and mission. As between Japanese and European domination of Asia, a disinterested and cynical American, barring an eventual menace to his own country, might easily remain a neutral spectator. As it now stands, Japan has won official and governmental China—at least that of the internationally recognized government of the North. This does not mean that assent has been given to the basic idea, or that the very officials who are now playing the game of China do not hope that some time or other something will happen which will loosen the hold of Japan over China. But they do accept the particular acts by which Japan is making her approaches to the realization of her goal, even though they protest vigorously, as in the case of the twenty-one demands, when the pace is too much forced. Patriotism aside, all the interests of their own pockets and of their own local power and prestige require that each specific step forward should be met with obstructions and resistance until Japan is ready to pay the specific price exacted.

The extent to which Japan has won over the officially governing clique of China is evidenced in the circumstances surrounding the refusal of the Chinese peace delegates to sign the peace treaty. With all the concessions which the government made to the students' movement, it never agreed to instruct the delegates to refuse to sign, until a semi-promise was made to an insistent incursion from Shantung to Peking; and instructions in accord with this vague promise did not reach Paris till after the delegates, on their own responsibility and with the moral backing of the country set over against their official instructions, had refused to sign. The government is now putting the best face possible upon the matter and trying to get popular credit on the one hand while it placates Japan upon the other. Quite likely it is still urging the Paris delegates to make a belated signature. But the militarist, imperialist pro-Japanese group has had an almost deadly blow dealt to its moral authority, and it is even conceivable that a signature forced at this time would be a signal for a popular revolution.

In short, the grandiose scheme of Japan failed to reckon with the most essential factor in the situation—the Chinese people. The extent of this failure may be calculated from the fact that Japanese propagandists in the United States sometimes compare their mission in China to that which they benevolently assign to the United States in Mexico. China with her four hundred million population and the author of the civilization of Japan does not see herself as a Mexico waiting for salvation from Japan. Call it pride or ignorance or national conceit or self-respect or a true sense of comparative national values on the part of China, call it what you will, the fact remains that Japan has so misjudged the psychology of China that she has made an implacable enemy of the people while she has been winning over the officials. One thing, and one thing only, can throw China back into the hands of Japan. Let there be a resumption of the old diplomacy of the western nations with respect to China, and it is conceivable that bitter as would be the dose, China would accept the domination of Japan as the lesser of two evils. And it is not enough that the western nations should have good intentions. They must avoid even the appearance of evil, for ingenious propaganda is always at hand to explain to the Chinese how westerners are trying to exploit them. Even avoiding the appearance of evil is not enough. No task more difficult can be found than the discovery and institution of ways and means by which China can be given the assistance which she imperatively needs, which must be given from outside herself without arousing her national jealousies, suspicions, fears, antagonisms and opposition and thus inviting the aid of Japan against the foreigner.

This brings us naturally to the other figure in the duel of ideas and moral influence—the United States. In the main of course it is the logic and especially the psychology of the situation that has put the United States into this position, not anything she has actually done. If the American idea has for the moment won the people as effectually as the Japanese practice has imposed upon the most influential official clique, it is by way of rebound. Idealization is most active when contrasting emotions are deeply stirred. Fear of Japan has bred trust in the United States; dislike of Japan a pathetic affection for America. It is no wonder that Japan with her poor reading of national psychology is bewildered by the present pro-American outburst of China, and can find in it only proof of superhuman ability in intrigue and of the expenditure of countless millions in propaganda. But in fact the situation has made itself. China in her despair has created an image of a powerful democratic, peace-loving America, devoted to securing international right and justice, especially for weak nations. The heroic legend that unified the United States for the war she still accepts, and she has added paragraphs and chapters of her own.

How trustingly naïve is the faith in the United States may be gathered from various addresses of congratulation which were proffered to representatives of the United States on the Fourth of July. Shanghai was the real centre of the patriotic students' movement, and the following are extracts from some of the Shanghai addresses: "Your great nation is now introducing into the international relations of the world those principles of justice and right which have always been the guiding lights of its own national life." This is Platonic enough, but the concrete meaning appears a few sentences further on: "We look forward to the day when China and the United States shall both be in a position to maintain the peace of the Pacific as your country together with that of Great Britain have maintained the peace of the Atlantic." The Canton Guild congratulated the United States upon her leadership of the cause of human rights in the Councils of the Nations, and left no doubt as to its understanding of the character of this leadership by saying "China and America must have the same ideals. China and America must maintain the peace of Asia. We look to America to help in our battle for justice." Another address (this time from women and girls) is even more specific. After remarking that the American navy has never been used to wrest liberty from any people, it goes on to say that "if ever the day comes when China will have to drive the aggressor from its soil, the American navy will throw its influence in the cause of right." The Commercial Federation sounded the same note in a different key: "On this day of independence we call upon the American people to assist us to be independent, to develop our railways, our waterways, our resources, to join with the capital of China to make us free from the commercial bondage under which we have been living."

Of course through all these lines runs the hope of actual assistance against the country believed by the people to be bent upon dominating China under the pretext of helping her. But while the desire for material aid, naval, military, diplomatic, financial, is plainly there, the spirit behind these addresses is something more than national self-interest. The international appeal is bound up with national aspiration for a truly democratic China—

an aspiration up to the present tragically frustrated. For the same situation which has given Japan the role of a despoiler and assigned to America the role of a rescuer, has also made Japan the symbol of autocratic and militaristic government in China itself, while the United States symbolizes the free democracy that progressive China would be and is not. No one can understand the present idealization of the United States by China who does not see in it the projection of China's democratic hopes for herself. I cannot quote again at length but each of the addresses to which reference has been made contains a touching reference to the fact that America's Fourth of July signalizes an accomplished fact, while the nation that offers the congratulations has for eight years fought a battle for a republic and has not yet won her victory. Deceived by the traditional officialism of the ruling clique, Japan has so far failed to see the enormous gulf that exists between her own centralized autocracy and the democratic modes of life of the Chinese masses. This perhaps is no wonder when representatives of western nations have so frequently misconceived China's essential democracy and have longed for some strong ruler to bring her the blessings of peace and order. Although this democracy is articulately held only by a comparative handful who have been educated, yet these few *know* and the dumb masses *feel* that it alone accords with the historic spirit of the Chinese race. And this fact has done for the United States what she could never have done for herself in making her the popular counterfoil to the bureaucratic and autocratic government of Japan.

The situation is one that imposes humility rather than self-glorification upon Americans. Our country will have a hard time living up to the role for which she has been cast. The difficulties are intellectual and moral as well as matters of practical judgment and tact in action. Have we the required fibre and virility? Or shall we once more fall between a clever commercialism on the one hand and a futile phrase-making idealism on the other? Above all it demands stamina and endurance of intelligence to think out a consistent and workable plan and to adhere to it.

So far as the Far East is concerned, the whole question of the attitude of the United States to the peace settlement, including the League of Nations, is how America's action is going to affect her freedom and force of action in behalf of the international democratic ideals she has professed. In China at least there is fear lest America in making the world safe for democracy be herself compromised by too close association with nations who in international matters are not as yet moved by democratic ideals. If the United States in working with the Allies was obliged to surrender at Paris her own convictions on the Shantung question, China prefers to trust a United States which is free from such commitments and entanglements. After all, democracy in international relations is not a matter of agencies but of aims and consequences. Under certain conditions, a United States which was going it alone would, so far as the Far East is concerned, be a much more effective instrument of true internationalism than a United States in a League the other members of which had no belief in American ideals. But League or no League, the task of the United States in the problems of the Far East is not an easy one. The first requisite is a definite and open policy, openly arrived at by discussion at home and made known to all the world. Then we need to be prepared to back it up in action. Idealism without intelligence and without forceful willingness to act will soon make us negligible in the Far East—and surrender its destinies to a militaristic imperialism. We can't, to take one minor illustration, go on loaning money freely to France if France is at the same time supporting the policies of Japan regarding the composition and functions of an International Consortium. This perhaps is but a hypothetical illustration. But it may well be questioned whether the United States has as yet awakened to the enormous power which is now in her hands. That which most impresses a visitor to the Far East is the extent of this power—accompanied by a query whether this same power is not largely being thrown away by reason of stupidity and ignorance.

MILITARISM IN CHINA

"The effect of the decision of the Allies at the Peace Conference to guarantee the claims of Japan strengthens the hold of the militarist party upon the Chinese government and also increases the hold which a neighboring militarist country has upon the determination of Chinese policies." This sentence, with slight verbal changes, can be found over and over again in every liberal paper in China. It comes with a shock to an American who has learned to identify China with inveterate pacifism, and who, under the tutelage of Mr. Roosevelt, believes that Chinafication and supine pacifism are synonymous. China a militarist country? Impossible!

A few statistics may be cited. At the present time, the Chinese government is supporting an army of a million and three hundred thousand at the lowest estimate. And China does not have conscription. This is a paid, standing, professional army. And China sent no troops to Europe and trained no troops to go there. The nearest approach to the war zone was connected with the propaganda for intervention in Siberia after the Russian debacle. Nor is the civil war in China anything more than nominal at present, and in any case the great mass of soldiers never had part in it. From the standpoint of the size of its standing army, then, China is not "Chinafied."

The budget of China tells the same story. The central government spent for ordinary military purposes last year two hundred and ten millions of dollars and for "extraordinary" purposes thirty millions more. Percentages are even more eloquent. This amount is fifty per cent of the entire annual expenditures of the government. And since the total income of the nation, barring loans, is but three hundred and seventy millions, this means that sixty-five per cent of the total state income goes to the army. Figuring still another way, leaving payments for interest on the national debt out of account, China spent almost twice as much for mili-

[First published in *New Republic* 20 (1919): 167–69, datelined Peking, July 28. Also published in *Peking Leader*, 14 October 1919.]

tary purposes as for all other ends put together, fifty times as much as she spent, from the side of the central government, for schools and six times as much as the central government and all the provinces together spent for public education. Moreover China is now spending, in the eighth year of the republic, much more than twice as much on the army as was spent in the last year of the Manchu dynasty. These facts do not point to undue addiction to pacifism.

Still, something more than large military expenses are needed to justify calling a government militaristic. For the term implies a subordination of civil to military control in political affairs generally. This is a matter which cannot be settled by statistics; but it is this matter even more than the size and expense of the army which is referred to in the sentence quoted at the beginning of the article. This militarism goes back to the earlier days of the republic, especially to the ambitions of Yuan Shih-kai. It is hardly a coincidence that the leaders in present Chinese policies are former lieutenants and disciples of the "strong man" who attempted to convert the fruits of the revolution into a family perquisite of a new imperial dynasty. But in its present form it dates actively from two years ago, and particularly from conditions connected with China's declaration of war against Germany. Quite likely the full history of this episode cannot as yet be written by any one. But even a tyro in Chinese history like the present writer may report certain facts which could not be stated and which were not stated in the West—and in the Far East only under the breath—when the war was still on. And the outstanding fact with respect to the growth of militarism is that its present swollen fortunes date from the circumstances under which China entered the war on the side of the Allies. And if this fact is not brought out in books dealing with the recent years of Chinese history it is partly because the writers were so interested in the righteous cause of the Allies that they hardly allowed themselves to perceive the fact, and partly because to have dwelt upon this fact while the war was still going on would have been pro-German in effect, to say nothing of subjecting writers to the charge of promoting German intrigue.

One does not have to go far to find explanations for the opposition in China to entering the war. There existed every reason that operated to bring about the delay on the part of the United

States—except the presence of a large population of German descent—and there was in addition a genuine fear of German victory and subsequent German reprisals of whose nature China had already had sufficient warning. Moreover the German nationals in China were upon the whole more popular personally than those of any other country unless perhaps those of the United States. For however arrogant Germany was as a nation, Germans taken individually were sufficiently bent on successful business to be unassuming, friendly, and attentive to native wishes and customs. Against all the reasons for not declaring war against Germany there were in fact but two intrinsic reasons for so doing. A portion of the genuinely liberal and republican sentiment of China was truly convinced after the United States entered the war that the war was between democracy and autocracy; between a new, just, international order which would guarantee the rights of weak nations, and the old, rapacious, nationalistic imperialism. Thus the historic humanitarian idealism of China actually urged liberal China into the war. Self-interest pointed in the same direction, for participation in the war would give China representation at the peace board, permit her to present her claims for the restoration of Shantung, and in general enable her to start even as a partner in the new international ordering of diplomacy which so many, besides the Chinese, ardently believed in, only two years ago. Immediately after the United States broke off diplomatic relations with Germany, China followed, the Cabinet and Parliament acting in unison. This was done in direct response to the invitation of President Wilson and China was the first nation to make a favorable response.

Then followed weeks and months of intrigue before China on August 14th finally declared war against Germany. What took place during those months was, first, the displacement of the American auspices evident in a severance of relations early in February by Japanese auspices; and, secondly, the struggle between the Premier, Tuan Chi-jui, and Parliament—a struggle ending in the forced dissolution of Parliament and in the outbreak of the still unhealed civil strife between the North and the South. The extent of the diplomatic defeat of the United States by Japan is seen in the fact that on June 7th a warning was communicated to China from the United States that the entrance of China into war was a "secondary consideration" compared with the reestablishment of a tranquil and united China, while on June 12th a mandate was issued at the dictation of military leaders and with the approval of the Japanese legal adviser dissolving Parliament. The immediate outcome was the farcical restoration for ten days of the Manchu boy Emperor. The final outcome was the ousting of President Li, and the defeat, through the coerced dissolution of Parliament, of Constitutionalism, and the beginnings of a civil war which in turn played into the hands of the militaristic cliques.

For the Premier was then, as he is still though now out of political office, the head of the militarist, anti-constitutional and anti-parliamentary faction. The liberal Parliament, which, whatever its defects, was still devoted to republican constitutionalism, grew more and more lukewarm in the cause of breaking irreparably with Germany. Ready to follow promptly in the wake of the United States when American and democratic prestige seemed to be uppermost, it hesitated when diplomatic leadership went over to the Japanese, and when it came to believe that the Cabinet was not thinking so much of the defeat of Germany as of an excuse for building up an army and a military regime which would insure their own continued power.

By one of the ironies of fate, the militarist and anti-democratic factions became the professed spokesmen of the Allies, and a constitutionally inclined Parliament was put in the position of being pro-German. The wheat and the tares were so mixed that even the liberally minded foreign press, tired of the delay and intriguing, welcomed the "strong" action of Tuan Chi-jui in dissolving Parliament simply because it hastened the day when China was officially arrayed with the Allies and when German commercial interests would get a hard if not fatal blow in the Far East. When one sees how wrong was foreign liberal sentiment—with a few notable exceptions—in the case of the Yuan Shih-kai adventure in imperialism and again how wrong it was in the inception of the regime they are now all cursing, in spite in both cases of the warnings of liberal native Chinese thought, one receives a marked lesson in the extent to which Chinese events have been interpreted to the world in the light of supposed foreign interests, and how little consideration has been given to the actual effect of the events in question upon the development and destiny of China itself. One sometimes wonders that the Chinese have retained any faith in the political intelligence of the foreign interpreter of her contemporary history.

At present the militaristic faction whose power was confirmed by the happenings of the summer of 1917 is still in control of the government. There is no doubt that all its members are patriotic enough to have welcomed the restoration of Shantung. But still human nature is human nature, and they have also welcomed the demonstration offered at Paris that might still makes right in the case of weak nations, so that in a strange and subtle way the diplomatic victory of Japan in particular and of imperialism in general has been a vindication of their own anti-democratic and militaristic policy. If the humanitarian international and democratic ideals profusely proclaimed in the war had been realized at Paris, no observer in China doubts that a vast domestic political realignment would already have taken place. The demonstration that national self-interest was on the side of the democracies of the world would have had an irresistible reflex effect upon domestic policies. And few doubt that the realization of this fact was, in addition to the concrete economic advantages at stake in Shantung, one of the reasons why Japan was so insistent at Paris. While her newspapers exaggerated in saying that her national existence was involved in securing a diplomatic victory, the exaggeration covered the fact that her diplomatic defeat, following upon the collapse of autocratic Germany, would have ended for the time being the prestige of militarism in the Far East, and compelled a reconsideration of home policies in China and of foreign policy in Japan. This moral reverberation seems to have been completely ignored at Paris and it may be doubted whether it is receiving the attention it deserves in Washington.

The specific signs of the continuance of the militarist regime in China are many. In the provinces the Tuchuns, military governors, still override civil governors and interests and sacrifice the crying need for education and better transportation to the pelf and power that go with command of a large number of troops. In remote provinces they encourage the growth of opium either for direct revenue or for levying hardly disguised blackmail. They discourage the development of natural resources in mines and manufacturing because their cohorts give them an effective power to demand a large interest in the business. In spite of the universal desire for reconciliation between the North and South, the militarists on both sides (and it would be a great mistake to think they are confined to the North) block all final settlement. The last few weeks have seen the beginnings of a mysterious adventure in Mongolia and an attempt of a Tuchun to obtain a virtual dictatorship of the three Manchurian provinces. But, especially, it is militarist control which keeps China in a condition that invites and rewards foreign intrigue and secret unacknowledged interventions.

No observer thinks that the present condition can last a great while longer. The equilibrium is too uncertain. No sensible person attempts to prophesy what the nature of the change will be when it comes. But if the reader will return to the statistics given early in the article he will note that at present the expenses of China exceed its available income by one hundred and ten millions a year. This means, of course, borrowing money—and when China borrows money she borrows it from some foreign nation by pledging some definite asset. In other words, cut down the army one-half and China's accounts balance. Continue the present army, and the responsibility lies with some foreign nation or group of nations through the loans it—or they—are willing to make for an army which is not and will not be a source of strength to China abroad, and which is eating up China at home. In the case of the continuation of China's militarism, the economic interpretation of history is more than ordinarily obvious. Hence it is hardly prophecy to say that what happens next in China will be determined by financial considerations, and that the decision is in the hands of those who have the power to control the making of loans. As long, however, as some one nation can serve its own interests by making loans, the situation cannot be adequately met on the part of other nations by merely a laissez-faire policy of declining to make loans. Something positive is needed.

TRANSFORMING THE MIND OF CHINA

The beginning of the modern age in China dates from that bloody episode, the Boxer Convulsion. Its outbreak signalized the supreme endeavor of old China to have done once for all with the unwelcome intruder, so that it might return untroubled to its self-sufficiency. Its close marked the recognition that the old China was doomed, and that henceforth China must live its life in the presence of the forces of western life, forces intellectual, moral, economic, financial, political. With its usual patience China set out to adapt itself to the inevitable. But in this case, something more than a patient passivity was necessary. China learned in 1900 that she had to adjust herself to the requirements imposed by the activities of western peoples. Every year since then she has been learning that this adjustment can be effected only by a readjustment of her own age-long customs, that she has to change her historic mind and not merely a few of her practices. Twenty years have passed and the drama does not seem to be advancing. China seems to be marking time. As with the drama of the Chinese stage, the main story is apparently lost in a mass of changing incidents and excitements that lack movement, climax and plot.

But the foreign interpreter comes to the scene with a mind adapted to the quick tempo of the West. He expects to see a drama unfold after the pattern of the movie. He is not used to history enacted on the scale of that of China. When he hastily concludes that nothing is doing, or rather that although something new and unexpected happens every day, everything is moving in an aimless circle, he forgets that twenty years is but a passing moment in a history that has already occupied its four thousand years. How can a civilization that has taken four thousand years to evolve, that has crept about and absorbed every obstacle hitherto encountered, that has countless inner folds of accumulated ex-

[First published in *Asia* 19 (1919): 1103–8. Republished in *Characters and Events*, ed. Joseph Ratner (New York: Henry Holt and Co., 1929), 1:285–95.]

perience within itself, quickly find itself in new courses? We talk glibly about the importance of the problem of the Pacific, and even the school boy can quote Seward, Hay and Taft. But what do we suppose this problem to be? One that concerns a superficial waste of mobile waters? No, the real problem of the Pacific is the problem of the transformation of the mind of China, of the capacity of the oldest and most complicated civilization of the globe to remake itself into the new forms required by the impact of immense alien forces.

Analogies, especially when they are obvious, are as deceptive in the field of political thinking as they long ago proved in natural science. The tempting comparison of the future of China, in its reaction to western ideas and institutions, to the record of Japan is misleading. The difference of scale between a small island and a vast continental territory makes the correspondence impossible. China emerged from feudalism two thousand years ago, but without at the same time becoming a national state in the sense familiar to us. Japan's emergence coincided with its opening to the West, so that its internal condition and the external pressure from other nations enabled it to take the form of an absolute state (with certain constitutional trimmings) externally similar to states produced in the evolution out of feudalism of modern Europe. The development of a strong centralized state, with unified administration and militaristic protection, was as easy for Japan as it is difficult for China. More fundamental is the difference in national psychology. Something over a thousand years ago Japan took on Chinese civilization via Korea and yet remained essentially Japanese. For the past sixty years it has been taking on western civilization. Yet the writers and thinkers most characteristically Japanese tell you that Japan is not westernized in heart or mind. Though it borrows wholesale western technique in science, industry, administration, war and diplomacy, it borrows them with the deliberate intention of thereby strengthening the resisting power of its own traditional policies. It acknowledges without reserve the superiority of western methods, but these superior methods are to be used to maintain eastern ideals intrinsically superior to the foreign. This may seem to the foreigner an evidence of the conceit often associated with Japan, but the retort is easy: Is the European complacent conviction of superiority anything more than the conceit of prejudice? At all events, this doubleness of Japanese life, its combination of traditional aims and moral ways with the externals of foreign skill and specialized knowledge, accounts for the impression of duplicity which so many carry away from contact with contemporary Japan.

It is to be doubted whether such a dualism, such inconsistency of inner and outer life, can be long kept up. Yet its successful achievement marks the record of Japan in its relations to western civilization. And it is precisely this sort of thing which cannot happen in China. She has evolved, not borrowed, her civilization. She has no great knack at successful borrowing. Her problem is one of transformation, of making over from within. Educated Chinese will already tell you that if you wish intact survivals of old China, you must go to Japan—and Japanese tell you much the same thing, though with quite a different accent and import. The visitor is struck by the fact that it is in the public buildings and schools of Japan, not of China, that the eye everywhere sees the old Confucianist mottoes, especially those of the reactionary and authoritative type. China with all its backwardness and its confusion and weakness is more permeated today with western contemporary thought than is Japan. There is some significance in the fact that while the circulation of President Wilson's war speeches was legally forbidden in Japan, they have furnished for the past two years China's best seller. There will be many to say that Japan's retention of the ideas that she took from China in the best days of the latter's history, and then protected against deterioration, is the cause of Japan's strength, and that China's decay is precisely because she has permitted the infiltration of ideals and ideas that are foreign and consequently destructive. This may be true. I am not here concerned to deny it. In any case, it illustrates our proposition: China must run a course radically different from that of Japan.

There will either be decay and disintegration, or thoroughgoing inner transformation. There will not be adoption of western external methods for immediate practical ends, because the Chinese genius does not lie in that direction.

Japan's influence upon China has been enormous. The westerner who has not studied the situation is quite unaware of the extent to which China after the Russo-Japanese war in particular took over Japanese administrative and educational methods. But it is already obvious that they are not working here as they worked in Japan. A large part of the present intellectual and moral crisis in China is due to reaction against this factor in Chinese life. Doubtless it is artificially strengthened just now by immediate political causes. But beneath this surface there is a general intellectual ferment, and a belief that China must resort not to Japanese copies of western forms, but to the original sources of western moral and intellectual inspiration. And the recourse is not for the sake of getting models to pattern herself after, but to get ideas, intellectual capital, with which to renovate her own institutions.

National conceit, national vanity, is a sealed book to the outsider. We are sure that our own is only just pride and self-respect, and that the foreigner's is either ridiculous or a mark of offensive contempt and dangerous hostility to our own cherished ways of life. But dubious as is generalization on such matters, one is struck by certain differences in the group self-consciousness of Japan and China. Its quality is perhaps suggested in certain comments which they pass not infrequently upon each other. A Japanese will tell you that the Chinese do not care what other persons think of them. A Chinese says that Japan has no sense of its "face." The two criticisms are enough alike to be intriguing. But it may be suggested in explanation that Chinese complacency is the deeper seated and hence is not so acute. It is fundamental and taken for granted. It does not need to be asserted in special instances. As long as the Chinese retain unimpaired their own judgment of themselves, their own reputation with themselves, their face is saved, and what others think is negligible. On the other hand, it is humiliating to them to borrow as Japan does. It would be a confession of absence of inner resources. When Japan engages foreign experts, she is interested in results, and so gives them a free hand till she has learned what they have to give. China engages the foreign expert—and then courteously shelves him. The difference is typical of a difference in attitude toward western life. It is a large part of the cause of Japan's rapid progress and of China's backwardness. The Japanese naturally places himself in the stead of the western spectator and is acutely conscious of the criticisms the beholder might pass upon what he sees. He tries to make over the spectacle to satisfy the demands of the western onlooker. He reserves his deeper pride for his national ideals. The Chinese scarcely cares what the foreigner may think of what he sees. He even brings the skeletons in his closet cheerfully forward for the visitor to gaze at. The complacency or conceit involved in this attitude has enormously retarded the advance of China. It has made for a conservative hugging of old traditions, and a belief in the inherent superiority of Chinese civilization in all respects to that of foreign barbarians. But it has also engendered a power of objective criticism and self-analysis which is rarely met in Japan. The educated Chinese who dissects the institutions and customs of his own country does it with a calm objectivity which is unsurpassable. And the basic reason, I think, is the same national pride. His institutions may not stand the criticism very well, but the people who produced these institutions are intrinsically invulnerable. They produced them, and when they get around to it they will create some new ones better adapted to the conditions of present life. The faith of the Chinese in the final outcome of their country, no matter what the despair about the current state of things, reminds an American of a similar faith abounding in his own country.

We are brought around to our main contention. China's slackness with respect to borrowing the technique of the West in civil administration, public sanitation, taxation, education, manufacturing, etc., is quite compatible with an effort on her part to bring about a thoroughgoing transformation of her institutions through contact with western civilization. In this remaking she will appropriate rather than borrow. She will attempt to penetrate to the principles, the ideas, the intelligence, from which western progress has emanated, and to work out her own salvation through the use of her own renewed and quickened national mind. The task is an enormous one. Time is of the essence of the performance. Just because the task is to effect an inner modification rather than an outward adjustment, its execution will take a long time. Will the forces that are playing upon China from without, forces that have contemplated its territorial disintegration, that are desirous of dominating its policies and exploiting in their own behalf its natural resources, permit a normal evolution? Will they stand by to assist, or will they invade and irritate and deflect and thwart till there is a final climax of no one knows what tragic catastrophe? These are some of the elements in the great drama now enacting.

The baffling and "mysterious" character of China to the West is genuine enough. But it does not seem to be due to any peculiarly dark and subtle psychology. Human nature as one meets it in China seems to be unusually human, if one may say so. There is more of it in quantity and it is open to view, not secreted. But the social mind, the political mind, has been subjected for centuries to institutions which are not only foreign to present western customs, but which have no historic precedent. Neither our political science nor our history supplies any system of classification for understanding the most characteristic phenomena of Chinese institutions. This is the fact which makes the workings of the Chinese mind inscrutable to the uninitiated foreigner, and which makes it necessary to describe so many things in contradictory linguistic terms. The civilization itself is not contradictory, but in its own self-consistency it includes things which in western life have been sharply opposed. Then there are intermediate forms, political missing links, which to our grasp must prove elusive; they are vague because we have no comparable forms by which to define and interpret them. Yet the Chinese mind thinks, of course, as naturally in terms of its customs and conventions as we think in ours. We merely forget that we think in terms of customs and traditions which habituation has engrained; we fancy that we think in terms of mind, pure and simple. Taking our mental habits as the norm of mind, we find the ways of thinking that do not conform to it abnormal, mysterious and tricky. We can get the key to mental operations only by studying social antecedents and environment, and this truth holds pre-eminently in an old civilization like the Chinese. We have to understand beliefs and traditions to understand acts, and we have to understand historic institutions to understand beliefs.

It is clear enough that the Korean question is quite pivotal in many of the most urgent external political questions of Asia. Yet Mr. Holcombe has told how the question was complicated in earlier days by the misconceptions which formed the basis of dealing with it by western nations. They knew that there was something of a relation of dependency of Korea upon China. They assumed the kind of relationship with which the West was acquainted, that of suzerain and vassal. When China declined to bear the responsibility of enforcing certain demands upon Korea as being out of her authority, the western nations thought that China was either insincere or else disclaimed all political jurisdiction. That there should be a genuine relationship of dependency, but of an advisory, homiletic, grandfatherly type, was beyond the scope of western precedent and understanding. The early relations of western diplomacy with the Imperial Court at Peking are a record of similar misunderstandings. There were all the insignia of royalty over China, extending even to despotic power. In relation to happenings in the provinces, therefore, it was natural to endow the "Government" at Peking with all the attributes of sovereignty as that is constituted in Europe. That the central government (beyond certain well-established relations of taxation and appointment of civil service) sustained mainly a ceremonial and hortatory connection with a large part of China was beyond conception. These grosser misunderstandings could be multiplied in considering almost every detail of Chinese institutional life. It has to be understood in terms of itself, not translated over into the classifications of an alien political morphology.

The story of the difficulties that had to be overcome in the introduction of railways into China is perhaps the best known of Chinese incidents. But it bears retelling because it affords a typical illustration of the fact that the chief obstacle in the effective contact of West and East is intellectual and moral. Opposition to railways was not a matter of routine conservatism, blind sluggish opposition to the new just because it was new. The Chinese have the normal amount of curiosity, and perhaps even more than the normal amount of practical sense of the advantage to be gained by a novelty which does not conflict with traditional beliefs. A difficulty presented itself in getting a clear right of way for railways, on account of the graves, which, from the western standpoint, are scattered at random. But from the Chinese standpoint, they are located with the utmost science, and to disturb them is to throw out of balance the whole system of environmental influences that affect health and good crops. Moreover, the graves are the centre of the system of ancestral worship, and that is the centre of civic organization. The tale might have been invented to show how completely the forces to be reckoned with are intellectual and moral, and how completely they are bound up with the structure of life. Without a change of national mind it is hopeless to suppose that China can go forward prosperously because of intercourse with the West.

It is a rash enterprise to form a generalization about the factors of the Chinese popular psychology that count most, whether positively or negatively, in the task of regenerating China. But the strong points of a people, as of individual character, lie close to its weak ones. So perhaps it is safe to say that the promise of China's rebirth into full membership in the modern world is found in its democratic habits of life and thought, provided we add to the statement another: the peculiar quality of this democracy also forms the strongest obstacle to the making over of China in its confrontation by a waiting, restless and greedy world. For while China is morally and intellectually a democracy of a paternalistic type, she lacks the specific organs by which alone a democracy can effectively sustain itself either internally or internationally. China is in a dilemma whose seriousness can hardly be exaggerated. Her habitual decentralization, her centrifugal localisms, operate against her becoming a nationalistic entity with the institutions of public revenue, unitary public order, defence, legislation and diplomacy that are imperatively needed. Yet her deepest traditions, her most established ways of feeling and thinking, her essential democracy, cluster about the local units, the village and its neighbors. The superimposition of a national state, without corresponding transformation of local institutions (or better without an evolution of the spirit of local democracies into national scope) gives us just what we now have in China: A nominal republic governed by a military clique, maintained in part by foreign loans made in response to a bartering away of national property and power, and in part by bargainings with provincial leaders whose power rests upon their control of an army and the ability this control gives them to levy on industry and wealth. In fact, we have a state which, if it were taken statically, if it were frozen, would reproduce the evils of the old despotism with new ones added, and which can be saved only because it has released popular forces that make for something better. But it remains to organize these popular forces, to give them play, to build for them regular channels of operation.

Up to the present western thought has confined itself to the more obvious, the more structural, factors of the problem. These are naturally the problems most familiar in occidental political life. They are such things as the adjustment of the power and authority of the central government to that of local and regional governments; the problem of the relations of the executive and legislative forces in the government; the revision of legal procedure and law to eliminate arbitrariness and personal discretion. But after all, such matters are symptoms, effects. To try to reorganize China by beginning with them is like solving an engineering problem by skilful juggling. The real problem is how the democratic spirit historically manifest in the absence of classes, the prevalence of social and civil equality, the control of individuals and groups by moral rather than physical force—that is, by instruction, advice and public opinion rather than definitive legal methods—can find an organized expression of itself. And the problem, I repeat, is unusually difficult because traditionally, in the habits of beliefs as well as of action, these forces out of which the transformation of China must grow are opposed to organization on a nation-wide scale. Take a conspicuous example. To maintain itself as a nation among other nations of the contemporary world, China needs a system of national finance, of national taxation and revenues. But the effort to institute such a system does not merely meet a void. It has to meet deeply entrenched local customs, so firmly established that to interfere with them may mean the overthrow of all central government. To put another system of taxation into force requires the operation of the very national organs which depend upon a national system of public revenues. This is a fair example of the vicious circles that circumscribe all short-cut systems of reform in China. It is another evidence that the development must be a transforming growth from within, rather than either an external superimposition or a borrowing from foreign sources.

There are many, including a rather surprising number of Chinese as well as foreigners, who think that China can get set on her feet and become able to move for herself only by undergoing a period of foreign guardianship or trusteeship. The feeling is sedulously fostered by some persons in a neighboring island, and there is some undoubted response in China, though much less than there would be had the point of view not been unduly identified with the point of a bayonet. There are others who look to some western democracy or to the League of Nations to exercise the needed guardianship. We may waive the question whether at the present time there exists in the world a sufficient amount of disinterested intelligence to perform such a job of trusteeship. We stay on safe ground if we confine ourselves to saying that to be successful such a guardian would have to confine his efforts to stimulating, encouraging and expediting the democratic forces acting from within. And since such a task is almost entirely intellectual and moral, the guardianship is not necessary provided that China can be guaranteed time of growth protected from external attempts at disintegration. All that is necessary is a sufficient international decency and sufficient enlightened selfishness to give China the *ad interim* protection. She may have to sink deeper yet into the slough of confusion before she can get upon firm ground and move about freely. There is only harm in underestimating the seriousness of the task.

The evolution of Japan, as I have already said, offers no fair precedent. The problem is even more perplexing than that of the change of feudal into modern Europe. For medieval Europe was not civilized in the sense in which old China is civilized. There was not the inertia and weight of institutions wrapped up in the deepest feelings and most profound thoughts of the people that is found in China. Moreover, the European transition could take its own time to work itself out. That of China has to be accomplished in the face of the impatient, mobile western world, which, if it brings aid, also brings a voracious appetite. To the outward eye roaming in search of the romantic and picturesque, China is likely to prove a disappointment. To the eye of the mind it presents the most enthralling drama now anywhere enacting.

CHINESE NATIONAL SENTIMENT

Is it possible for a Westerner to understand Chinese political psychology? Certainly not without a prior knowledge of the historic customs and institutions of China, for the institutions have shaped the mental habits, not the mind the social habits. The West approaches all political questions with ideas composed on the pattern of a national state, with its sovereignty and definite organs, political, judicial, executive and administrative, to perform specific functions. We have even made history over to fit into this pattern. We have taken European political development as a necessary standard of normal political evolution. We have made ourselves believe that all development from savagery to civilization must follow a like course and pass through similar stages. When we find societies that do not agree with this standard we blandly dismiss them as abnormalities, as survivals of backward states, or as manifestations of lack of political capacity. Approached with such preconceptions, Chinese institutions and ideas are often given up as a bad job and as a case of arrested development. In actual fact, they mark an extraordinary development in a particular direction, only one so unfamiliar to us that we dispose of them as a mass of hopeless political confusion and corruption, or a striking object of what happens when there happens to be even a high code of ethics without the blessings of a divine revelation.

The attempt to read Chinese institutions in terms of western ideas has resulted in failures of understanding and of action from the very beginnings of our contact. For example, in the early days of intercourse there was ground of complaint of the treatment received by western shipwrecked sailors on Korean coasts. The Foreign Offices knew that there existed some tributary relation between Korea and China. They interpreted this relation of de-

[First published in *Asia* 19 (1919): 1237–42. Republished in *Characters and Events*, ed. Joseph Ratner (New York: Henry Holt and Co., 1929), 1:222–36, with the title "The Growth of Chinese National Sentiment."]

pendence, as Mr. Holcombe has pointed out, in the way familiar to them. They thought of the connection as that of feudal suzerain and vassal. Hence they demanded that China make its dependent behave. When China disclaimed authority, they thought that this was either equivalent to a renunciation of all relationship, or else a wilful piece of deceit in a characteristic endeavor to evade just responsibility. They had no precedent for a relationship which, while one of genuine dependence, was moral and advisory in nature. The whole early history of the dealings of western nations with the Court at Peking is full of similar misconceptions. There was an undoubted monarch. The monarchy was even of the despotic kind; there were none of the checks of constitutional and representative institutions familiar to the western mind. Hence all the attributes of political sovereignty, external and internal, were attributed to the Court. Here again there was no precedent for conceiving of a dynastic rule which was a combination of a primitive tribute-levying empire and an authority of a moralistic, homiletic, hortatory kind. And as we go from such external aspects to deeper conditions we find that China can be understood only in terms of the institutions and ideas which have been worked out in its own historical evolution.

The central factor in the Chinese historic political psychology is its profound indifference to everything that we associate with the state, with government. One inclines to wonder sometimes why the anarchists of the pacifist and philosophic type have not seized upon China as a working exemplification of their theories. Probably the reason is that being preoccupied with the problem of active abolition of government, they have not been able to conceive of an anarchy which should be only a profound apathy towards government. Or else they, too, have been misled by the popular association of anarchy with extreme freedom and mobility, and could not imagine it in connection with the stagnation attributed to China.

According to literary records, the following verse is the oldest poem in the language—a song put into the mouth of a farmer:

> Dig your well and drink its water;
> Plow your fields and eat the harvest;
> What has the Emperor's might to do with me?

China is still agricultural, as it was in the bygone centuries.

Its farmers still go about their own business of tilling and eating, marrying and giving in marriage, begetting and dying. As of old, they attend to their own affairs, and the power of Emperor or President concerns them not. Governors come and go, and fuss about their petty intrigues of glory and greed. But they do not govern the farmers, who are the mass of the population. The only governance known to them is that of nature, the rules of the immemorial change of seasons, the fateful laws of birth and death, of seed-corn and harvest, of flood and pestilence. In the words of perhaps their oftenest quoted proverb, "Heaven is high and the Emperor far away." The implication is that earth is close and intimate, the family and village nearby.

M. Huc tells an incident that dates from 1851; it might, however, have happened at any period in the long history of China. After the recent death of the Emperor, he endeavored without success to engage his fellow guests at a roadside tavern in a discussion of political prospects and possibilities. There was no response, though he exhausted his ingenuity. Finally one of the Chinese replied: "Listen to me, my friend. Why should you trouble your heart and fatigue your head with all these vain surmises? The Mandarins have to attend to affairs of state; they are paid for it. Let them then earn their money. But we should be great fools to torment ourselves about what does not concern us. We should be great fools to want to do political business for nothing." And the anecdote continues: "'That is very conformable to reason,' cried the rest of the company. Whereupon they pointed out to us that our tea was getting cold and our pipes were out." The state, the government, was a special business or trade, less interesting and less important for the mass of the people than ordinary affairs. It was, however, lucrative to those who specialized in it; let them carry its burdens. Meanwhile not merely the wedding and funeral, the sowing and reaping, concerned intimately the life of the people, but even the social consolations of the teacup and the tobacco-pipe were of more importance than affairs of state.

If the people were indifferent to government, the government, which in our western terminology we have to call the state, reciprocated. In theory it was the representative of Heaven, and consequently owned the earth, namely, the soil, and was the symbolic cause of its fertility, exercising a beneficial paternal influence upon the prosperity of the country. In fact, like Heaven itself, the government was high above. In earlier days Heaven may have directly intervened in the affairs of earth, but for outnumbered centuries in later days it had remained discreetly aloof, satisfied with relations long ago established and interrupting the affairs of earth only at great crises. Except for a few purposes well understood by custom, the central government was irrelevant to the life of the people. It was a Court, and its dignity, prestige, ceremony and pleasures had to be maintained. The material side of this life required material supplies and money. The ideal life, the glory and supremacy of the reigning dynasty, could be satisfied symbolically and ceremonially, as the spirits had learned to be satisfied with symbolic money and imitations of servants, animals and food. The primary material function of government was then to receive a tribute from the products of the earth, partly in kind, partly in money. The amount was not onerous, and long custom had converted the tax into part of the regular order of nature, though, like the crops and other phenomena of nature, it was subject to unexpected ups and downs. The moral and ceremonial sovereignty was incarnated in the officialdom of viceroys, governors, heralds and other functionaries, who represented the Imperial Court, and who communicated to the people its mandates and exhortations, composed in the best literary style and manifesting the continuous benevolent solicitude of the representative of Heaven for their morals. These morals were, in turn, the source of the prosperity of the country and of the stability of the Empire. These officials also had to lead a life of a certain symbolic grandeur and glory which cost money, but taxation was kept within limits prescribed by custom, and as a rule the burden was not heavy. Pains were taken that it should fall upon the well-to-do as far as possible, thus serving the double end of keeping down the power of possible rivals and of not arousing the disfavor of the masses. It is possible to trace in the old Chinese theory of politics the survivals of an original theocracy. But in China, even more than in Europe in its most deistic days, God, or Heaven, was remote, contenting itself with a general benevolent oversight. Its lordship was of an absentee nature. And the Court which represented Heaven was contented to imitate the latter's non-interference with the details and customs of life.

The result was that for all practical purposes each province was an independent state, composed, in turn, of a large number of petty republics called villages. In 1900 an English writer, made competent by long residence and intimate experience, wrote: "Each of China's eighteen provinces is a complete state in itself. Each province has its own army, navy, system of taxation and its own social customs. In connection only with the salt trade and the navy certain concessions have to be made to one another under a certain modicum of imperial control." These independent units are traditionally called provinces. But, as the quotation shows, they might have been called principalities, save that they had no orderly lineage of princes. China was not even a confederation, much less a national state or an imperial state, in the sense which history has given those terms in the West.

Again we have no precedents by which to interpret and understand such a situation. We are acquainted with empires that left local customs undisturbed and that contented themselves with levying tribute and exacting booty. But they were military powers, and always existed in unstable equilibrium. They never became so interwoven with local custom as to be a part of the established order of nature and able to dispense with military support. But China has worked out a scheme of remarkable static equilibrium—the most stable known to history. The political life of China went on essentially undisturbed, even though rebellions overthrew dynasties. Such rebellions were themselves as much a part of the established order of Heaven or Nature as was an occasional flood or plague. All such crises had their natural causes and were proper and normal, however uncomfortable or destructive they might be. The texture of life was unchanged; it continued to exhibit the same patterns. The equilibrium was a human and internal one, a moral one, not one maintained by external pressure or military force. The actual government of China was a system of nicely calculated personal and group pressures and pulls, exactions and "squeezes," neatly balanced against one another, of assertions and yieldings, of experiments to see how far a certain demand could be forced, and of yielding when the exorbitance of the demand called out an equal counter-pressure. Long before the time of Sir Isaac Newton, China worked out a demonstration in the field of politics, of the law that action and reaction are equal and in opposite directions. It exemplified the working of the principle in every aspect of human association. Such a social system implies a high state of civilization. It produces civilized persons almost automatically. For the essence of civility, or of civilization, is the ability to live consciously along with others, aware of their expectations, demands and rights, of the pressure they can put upon one, while also conscious of just how far one can go in response in exerting pressure upon others. The Chinese, as long as they were left undisturbed by other peoples, had all the complex elements of the social equation figured out with unparalleled exactness. Their social calculus, integral and differential, exceeded anything elsewhere in existence. This fact, and this fact only, accounts for the endurance of China for almost four thousand years of recorded history.

Then there came the eruption of forces from the outside which were radically new, which were unprecedented, for which the social calculus provided no rules. They were not, strictly speaking, human; they were physical forces of a strange and incalculable kind—battleships, artillery, railways, strange machines and chemicals. At first China was complacent. It remembered the numerous eruptions and invasions which had broken into its system in the past, and recalled how they had been subdued by absorption, how they had been gradually worked into the patterns of adjustments, demands, concessions, compromises and intercourses which constitute China. But gradually it became evident that old formulae would not apply, that a radically new force had been introduced. And it gradually became apparent that the new physical agencies and forces which were so irresistible were themselves the tools and designs of an unaccustomed social and political order. China, a civilization, was confronted by a civilization which was organized as China was not, into national states. The consequences of this contact are written in every problem, internal as well as external, that occupies China today.

There is a story of an intelligent Chinese who asked a foreigner to explain to him the nature and amount of the indemnity exacted from China by Japan after the successful war waged by the latter about the Korean question. After hearing the explanation he reflected a while to take in the full force of the matter, and then remarked in a contented way, "Well, that is the Manchus' affair; it doesn't concern us. They will have to pay, not we." The remark appears to indicate not merely the extraordinary indifference to politics already spoken of, but an equally extraordinary political stupidity. But it is stupidity only to the mind built after the pattern of western political institutions. From the standpoint of Chinese customs the remark was intelligent. Relations with foreign states were the business of the Imperial Court. And any expenses consequent upon such relations had to be met out of the purse of that Court. In the established system of taxation and revenues, the funds accruing from the tariff on imports from foreign countries belonged to the Imperial Treasury. It was nobody's business what the Court did with them. It was a logical conclusion that any debit item was also the exclusive affair of the ruling dynasty. The logic was good. But it was based upon the past, upon premises that no longer hold good. The Japanese Indemnity was followed by the Boxer Indemnity. The whole revenue system was thrown out of balance. The long-established Imperial balance of expenditures and receipts was destroyed. Yet any radical change in the established system of taxation was practically out of the question, entirely out of the question in any immediate or abrupt way such as the situation required. It would have wrenched the whole social system out of order.

Even such changes as had to be introduced had a large part to play in the dissatisfaction with the Manchu dynasty, which led to its overthrow. There was not merely the ordinary opposition felt anywhere to a marked increase in taxation. There was not merely the interference with custom which for immemorial ages had set limits in the game of exactions and resistance. There was an indissoluble association of taxation with the peculiar prerogatives of the Imperial Court, none too popular at best. There was an equally fixed association of increased taxes with "squeezes" on the part of officialdom, with corruption which was not exactly corruption if kept within certain limits of percentages, but which was intolerable when it surpassed them. The internal system of taxation, adequate to all internal emergencies, was not elastic in the face of the externally induced crisis. Foreign loans had to be resorted to. The remedy increased the disease. It gave the opportunity for more and more intervention from without; it invited a multiplication of precisely those dependencies upon foreign power which were the original root of the difficulty. And gradually the entire internal equilibrium has been upset in consequence of the contact with foreign powers. It cannot be regained without a radical transformation of China's historic political system. It has to nationalize itself in some fashion in order to meet the conditions imposed by its intercourse with other peoples who are organized into national states. What is true of the matter of taxation and revenues is true of almost every phase of Chinese life. Public finance but gives a typical example.

There has been discussion of whether the Chinese have national loyalty, whether they have patriotism. Here also our words in their accustomed meanings betray us. In its literal sense the word "nation" is connected in derivation with the word for birth. In the sense of community thus implied, the Chinese are certainly a nation. But in its acquired historical meaning, nation means a people with a certain political organization, a people claiming or possessing sovereignty of a centralized sort over a certain territory. And this is what the Chinese have not, but have to acquire in the face of sharp demands from foreign nations. It is contrary to their own social inertia and momentum, which has been acquired in minute and complicated ways through centuries of adjustments. Patriotism means love of country. In the sense of love of their earth, their native soil, the Chinese are perhaps the most patriotic of all existing peoples. The love may not be acute as with the Japanese, as ardent as with the Poles, but it is interwoven with every detail of life. It is not so much a sentiment, a fact of consciousness, as an unbreakable habit of life. Attachment to soil and birthplace is quite a different thing from an effectively organized allegiance to the state, that political entity which is constituted by political means rather than by matter-of-course habits of daily life and intercourse. It is customary to try to escape from the dilemma of a spontaneous, pervasive and unquestioned love of country that exists without the familiar manifestations of public spirit and political nationalism, by saying that the Chinese have a strong sense and pride of race which does for them what patriotism does for western peoples. Literally, this will hardly work. The Chinese regard themselves as five races, not one, as their flag testifies. In a certain genuine sense the Chinese are profoundly indifferent to race and racial distinctions. They have not been infected as have the Europeans and Japanese with the ethnological virus. While the Revolution was expedited by the fact that the Manchu dynasty was foreign, yet this ground of objection had had no effect for over two hundred years. It became significant only after western contact had aroused nationalistic feeling. What the Chinese abundantly possess is community of life, a sense of unity of civilization, of immemorial continuity of customs and ideals. The consciousness of a unity of pattern woven through the whole fabric of their existence never leaves them. To be a Chinese is not to be of a certain race nor to yield allegiance to a certain national state. It is to share with countless millions of others in certain ways of feeling and thinking, fraught with innumerable memories and expectations because of long-established modes of adjustment and intercourse.

This consciousness becomes loyalty, patriotism, in our sense in just the degree in which it gets transferred to the idea of a national state made after the model familiar to us, a state with an army and navy, a system of regular taxation and public revenue, an organized system of legislation, judiciary and administration, a subordination of all local powers to a central power, and all the other paraphernalia of sovereignty which we take for granted. It is not easy to transform a traditional feeling into nationalism, and then attach it to an object which is largely non-existent, an object of faith rather than of sight.

For this reason nationalistic sentiment has tended to take an anti-foreign color among the Chinese. In spite of the Boxer outbreak and other violent demonstrations against aliens, it may be doubted whether there has been a strong hostility against the foreigner as such. The Chinese, one surmises, are rather unusually tolerant. Their amiable live-and-let-live policy is applied all around. Their normal attitude is that of indifference to strangers rather than of aggressive antagonism. But conditions were such that about the only way in which they could show their devotion to their own civilization was negative. It was the outsider who was disturbing it. The Chinese lacked the positive organs of national life through which to resist foreign encroachments. Their loyalty to their own customs was therefore bound, one might say, to take the irregular and disorderly form of attack upon foreign residents. There are few who think that the Boxer days are likely to recur. The Chinese are intelligent, and they learned the hopelessness of holding their own by such methods. But it is still true that their national feeling can be aroused and concentrated more readily for purposes of resistance and opposition to foreign nations than for constructive purposes.

There are fine illustrations of this fact in recent Chinese international relations. There can be little doubt that the Government had officially instructed its delegates to the Peace Conference in Versailles to sign the treaty, recognizing though it did the Japanese appropriation of German rights in Shantung. National sentiment was, however, tremendously aroused. If Japan had set out to instigate a new national spirit which should overwhelm the old local provincialisms, she could not have proceeded in a more effectual way to accomplish the purpose. The people took the matter out of the hands of the Government. By cablegrams to Paris, by telegraph to Peking, by mass-meetings and agitations, finally by a strike of students and then of the mercantile guilds in the larger cities, they made it clear that national sentiment would regard as traitors all those who should take part in signing the treaty. It was an extraordinarily impressive exhibition of the existence and the power of national feeling in China. It was all the more impressive because it had to work without organized governmental agencies, and, indeed, against the resistance of deeply-intrenched pro-Japanese officialdom. If there still remained anywhere those who doubted the strength and pervasiveness of Chinese patriotism, the demonstration was a final and convincing lesson. But it took a great crisis of foreign menace to focus the feeling; Japan in the last two years has done for China what otherwise might have taken a generation more. But when the immediate task of preventing the signing of the treaty that gave away Chinese rights was performed, the feeling lapsed. Perhaps it remains equally intense, but it has lost in sureness of direction. The outward means and the established habits of thought required for positive determination of constructive national policies are still inchoate.

Everyone knows that the chief instrumentality of foreign encroachment in China has been finance. Russia first conceived the policy of conquest by bank and railway, and other nations joined in. Japan, with her usual alertness, saw the point, and with her usual energy acted upon her perception. The question of finance remains pivotal in any positive national policy for China. Even if China had the capital to take care of her own developments, and she certainly has more than she has used, the denationalized customs work against loaning it to the Government. And lack of trust in the competency and honesty of the officials reinforces the other influences that tell against extending domestic credit for public needs. Clearly, an international financial consortium which should loan money to China in bulk without assigning in return special concessions and spheres of influence to any particular nation is the obvious solution. But it is extremely difficult to arouse any popular interest in this matter. It is, so to speak, too positive and too specialized. On the contrary, it is comparatively easy for interested parties to stir up opposition. They have only to keep saying that this is a move on the part of foreign powers to get complete subjugation of China, and national feeling is excited in the negative direction. The alternative, namely, foreign loans from separate powers, in fact, Japan claiming specific rights and privileges in return, is not faced except by the more enlightened. The masses trust to a *laissez-faire*, happy-go-lucky policy of meeting each stringency as it arises, rather than of committing the country to some comprehensive scheme which, because of the organization involved in it, makes the fact of foreign influence obvious. Habituated to dealing with obstacles and dangers in a piecemeal way, playing off one force against another with great skill, the natural dread that all feel towards the unknown is felt towards organization on a large scale. And the fact that the organization is one on the part of foreign nationalism makes it appear particularly dreadful. And who can blame China in view of its past experiences with foreign influence? There is even now a small section which quite sincerely argues that it would be better to let Japan have Tsing-tao than to make it an international settlement.

The situation is critical. The fear of coming against an organization of foreign nations was sufficient recently to defeat, at least for the time being, the proposition to unify the railways of China. Ultimately it would mean the development of a large national system under exclusive Chinese control. But for the time being it involved a certain amount of international control. Foreign nations interested in maintaining separate spheres were naturally hostile. But their easiest way of working was not to offer public opposition, but to play secretly, through domestic agencies profiting by the existing state of affairs, upon the national fears of China. The same forces are already at work attacking the proposed international consortium and may wreck it. In fact, they will almost certainly succeed in delaying it until it becomes a matter of dire necessity. Yet it seems almost axiomatic that as long as

China is dependent upon foreign loans it is much better for her to be dependent upon a combination of powers that have agreed to forgo special privileges, and who will have to use their funds to build up China as a whole, than upon single separate powers that loan money only in response for special concessions and command of strategic points. These points are strategic not only economically, but in a political and military way. It seems at first sight very unreasonable that China should prefer to continue a system, or lack of system, which has brought her to the present pass. And it is unreasonable. But we need to understand that China has now reached a point of intense national feeling and a position where she can act with assurance as a nation. Feeling is feeling. It is comparatively easy to arouse national aspiration and national fears. It is not so easy to secure a national understanding of and agreement of any comprehensive or constructive plan of operations. And the reason is obvious, for there are no national institutions, no national organs, to supply the material of understanding and afford the basis of enduring faith and confidence. This union of intense national sentiment, with absence or lack of channels and organs of national action, describes the dilemma in which China finds itself today, both internally and externally.

It is especially important that the United States should sympathetically comprehend the situation. Just now there is a warm wave of pro-American feelings, especially outside of the governmental circles, which have become involved in Japanese intrigues. It is genuine. Yet it is largely a rebound from the prevalent anti-Japanese feelings. It is in any case a national feeling, not a national idea. It will be subjected in the future to the forces which always operate to make feeling, as distinct from thought, a fluctuating affair. Because of past history and because of economic interests, the United States stands against the policy of partitioning China, whether overtly or by means of spheres of influence and special interests. That is all to the good with respect to China's feeling towards us. She also stands, as in the case of unifying railways and combined financial aid, for organized international assistance. With an ordinary amount of decency and good will, this policy should build up China rapidly and get her to the point where she can dispense with foreign control. But for reasons just explained, China will hesitate and object and postpone. She may conceivably completely balk, and prefer to continue the policy of playing one nation off against another, in spite of the fact that that will mean for the time being an increase of Japanese control. It is most important that America should understand the causes of this attitude and should be patient and persistent in its policy, instead of being swayed by an emotional gust of revulsion at "ingratitude." Revulsion and withdrawal of active interest on our part, because our advances and plans do not meet with an immediate and hearty approval, will only play into the hands of those countries who desire special and selfish rights in China, and who for this reason, and because of lack of faith in the political capacity of the Chinese, always carry in the back of their heads a scheme of ultimate partition and subjection. We need to realize that it is just because the Chinese have great political capacity that the problem of national redirection is difficult and slow. For this capacity has been committed to definite lines which are contrary to those that fit into the present situation. It will help an intelligent sympathy to remember that China has not advanced on the path of modern political nationalism to the point where national feeling is warm and intense, but where definite organs of national thought and action are only in the early stage of formation.

THE AMERICAN OPPORTUNITY IN CHINA

The average American probably regards the past course of the United States in China with complacency, and imagines that we have won a like admiration from the Chinese. Even the casual newspaper reader knows of the return of the Boxer indemnity, and supposes in a hazy way that our declaration in behalf of the Open Door in China succeeded in arresting the partitioning of China. The better informed reader takes pride in the consistently enlightened diplomacy of the United States exemplified in Cushing, Burlingame and Hay, and the insistence upon comparatively mild measures after the Boxer revolt had been put down. Our entire course, we readily fancy, is one that has secured for us the grateful confidence and respect of the Chinese. Our treatment of Chinese immigrants on the Pacific coast and our exclusion act may occur to us, but we quickly put such disagreeable thoughts out of mind as so much past history.

It is worth while to ask how far our notion of the Chinese attitude towards us corresponds with the facts. Or if this way of putting the matter implies a false assumption regarding the universality of public opinion in China, then what is the attitude of an influential section of public men, and what are the grounds upon which it is based? The result of the inquiry even if unflattering will be a necessary preliminary to the conception of a proper policy for the future. To give the uncomplimentary answer in a few words, our prior behavior has left with many Chinese, especially those who have not been in the United States, the impression that we are not, in our foreign dealings, a very practical people; that we lack alertness, quickness of decision in emergencies, promptness of action, and especially persistence. And all this even where our own interests are at stake. We are thought of as,

[First published in *New Republic* 21 (1919): 14–17, datelined Peking, September 12. Republished in *Characters and Events*, ed. Joseph Ratner (New York: Henry Holt and Co., 1929), 1:296–303, as the first part of "America and China."]

upon the whole, a well disposed people, but somewhat ineffectual in action. Even gratitude for our refusal to enter into the game of grabbing China is colored by a suspicion that perhaps we lacked the energy and skill to engage successfully in the game.

The immediate background of this feeling is connected with the contest of Japan and the United States in the past two and a half years for prestige and moral authority, a rather passive contest, to be sure, as far as the United States is concerned. Some parts of the record have a definite bearing on the obstacles that are in the way of a successful American policy in the Far East. The expressed objectives and ideals of the United States in entering the war and the vigor with which we went in aroused the greatest enthusiasm in a certain section of Chinese public men. For a time it looked as if there were to be a powerful liberal party with pro-Americanism for one of the most important planks in its platform. Enthusiasm for the Allied cause ran high. Even the militarists who are now in control were anti-Japanese in the early months of 1917. Eloquent testimony is given by the fact that diplomatic relations were broken off with Germany without consultation with any of the Japanese representatives. In fact the Japanese minister being out of China at that time, Japan did not know of the event until it was an accomplished fact. There was then much zeal for an active participation of Chinese troops on the western front. The militarists wanted it because of the training that the army would get; the liberals because they were pro-Ally and pro-democracy; all because they saw the advantage for China of a share in the international negotiations at the end of the war. Plans were made to use the seized interned German ships for transporting troops. But the Allies were short of shipping and parcelled out the ships themselves. If American diplomacy made any effort to help the Chinese carry out their own plans, it was either defeated or no knowledge of the effort came to the ears of the Chinese.

Then China needed money, and needed it badly. She needed money not only for internal reorganization but for active participation in the war. The United States was making regular advances to the other Allies. China wanted a loan and got nothing. The Japanese overwhelmed her with financial proffers. Current gossip insists that more or less of the funds stuck in the pockets of corrupt Chinese officials. But in the larger sense the accuracy of this allegation is negligible. The outstanding fact is that Japan came forward when the United States did not. From this time dates the hold of Japan upon Chinese official circles. Another fact cooled the ardor of even the military people for an active share in the war.

After August of 1917, the military fortunes of the Allies sank to their lowest. Many Japanese leaders became convinced that German victory was either inevitable or that the war would end in a deadlock which would be almost equivalent to German victory. Responsible statesmen, men who had been prime ministers and heads of the foreign office, publicly stated that while Japan would be faithful to her allies throughout the war, an international re-alignment was almost certain after the war. Japan had already undertaken the necessary rapprochement with Russia, obviously undertaken in part with a view to resisting the growth of American influence in the Far East. Where would China be after the war in the case of an alliance offensive and defensive between Japan and Russia and Germany? It was obvious prudence for her to tread softly and give no offence to the powers which in the near future were likely to dominate the Far East. It is, I am convinced, impossible to exaggerate the influence of this factor in determining the present position of forces. For while the forecast did not come out according to specifications, in the meantime a situation was created which was pro-Japanese and indifferent to America. Even recently the man who is credited with being the head of the pro-Japanese military party in the government circles (and who is known as an incorruptible man) said that China had to be pro-Japanese, because Japan was so powerful in army and navy and also so nearby. "If the Pacific shrinks to a pond we shall be pro-American."

This is the concrete background upon which to project more general considerations regarding Chinese opinion of American policy. While Americans commence their account with, say, the benevolent return of the Boxer indemnity, the Chinese are likely to recall that as a positive force the United States opened its Far Eastern career with proposals for the neutralization of the Manchurian railways, and then met a defeat at the hands of Russia and Japan. This in itself was nothing very important. All countries receive diplomatic checks. But as it looks to the Chinese, after proposing a large scheme and meeting initial rebuffs, the American government neither made use of its check to secure a compensating advance elsewhere, nor did it try other means to maintain the principle it had laid down.

The affair of the Hankow-Peking railway strikes them also as an example of the tendency of the American government to conceive rather grandiose schemes and then fall down or withdraw when resistance is encountered. Through the American Red Cross valuable flood relief work was done. But there was also a large engineering plan for the regulation of the water-ways. After an original flourish, that too dissolved. The Siems-Carey railway projects may not be a case in point, for they may be in a state of suspended animation rather than of death. But the fact remains that the United States is the only great power that has nothing to show in China in achievement on a large scale. Or rather our one decided achievement is in the educational line where confessedly we are far ahead. But this success is not of a kind to be impressive when it comes to determination of international affairs. The cases given must stand as samples of the facts that have led educated and influential Chinese to feel that America could not be seriously counted upon. The Chinese have not, like some other nations, set us down as bluffers. But the cases mentioned, together with our failure to do much except utter words in behalf of the "Open Door," have led to the feeling that we readily emit large and good schemes, but are ineffectual when it comes to the test of action. The Chinese do not carry sentiment into practical matters. They judge by results not by intentions. In contrast with ourselves, they have found the Japanese constantly on the job, never allowing anything to get by, taking advantage of every opening, stimulated by obstacles only to renewed or redirected effort, quick, patient, persistent, unremitting. If Japan had not blundered hugely in estimating Chinese national sentiment, China might already have put its foreign policies mainly into the hands of Japan. For if China has to depend upon some outside power, there was much to say for relying, even at great cost to itself, upon a nation that was acute, vigorous, vigilant, and that never abandoned a plan after it started to realize it. To the Americans, Baron Shibusawa's proposal for Japanese-American cooperation in China, the United States to furnish the money and Japan the brains, did not seem altogether tactful in form of expression. But it is not likely that the great Japanese financier-philanthropist meant to imply that universally speaking Japanese intelligence is superior. He spoke rather on the basis of the fact that the Japanese have used their brains actively and persistently in pushing their policies in China, and Americans have not.

Now, of course, the reply to all this from an American standpoint is easy. We have never had large enough interests in the Far East to make it worth while to keep our attention and energy concentrated. We have never, beyond the Monroe Doctrine, gone in for a continuous foreign policy, as have other great powers. We have had so many other profitable ways of investing capital that it paid better to switch off to any other scheme than to bother too long in putting through a railway or other plan in the face of constant irritating and delaying obstacles. And in addition it is to our credit that we have never had the close alliance of business enterprise and governmental action which has characterized the policy of every other great power in dealing with economically backward countries and with China. From the American standpoint, excuses, and good ones, are as plenty as blackberries. But after all, as has been indicated, justifications and reasons do not concern the Chinese when it comes to their formulation of policy in foreign relations. They are interested in past results, in the actual outcome, as a means of forecasting the probable course of the future.

The war has now conclusively demonstrated that the United States can act promptly, efficiently and on a large scale in its foreign affairs. Unfortunately the contrast between President Wilson's words and the concrete results of the Peace Conference—a contrast that circumstances make glaringly conspicuous in China—tends to restore the older idea about the United States. Yet not wholly; there is a new interest and a new expectation on the part of important leaders while the masses of people look pathetically toward us for their redemption. The historic friendliness of sentiment toward the United States is so reinforced that it is an asset of great potentiality. The problem is the practical one of turning it to account by a constructive policy in action. It cannot be said that there is any single specific political act which is absolutely indispensable. But there is a line of action which would be fatal, at least for a considerable time. After so much talk about Shantung, to allow matters to go by default, or to permit them to drift, would be to confirm the worst opinions about the instability and futility of our policies. Some kind of definite course, persistently followed up, is a necessity unless China is to fall into practical vassalage to another nation. For help from without China must have. While the peace settlement has made the political international issue most acute for the moment, the financial and industrial question is the important one in the long run. Here lies the great chance of the United States. The introduction of a unified comprehensive currency system, a unified comprehensive railway system, improved modern harbors and terminal facilities, the reconstruction of the inland water-way system to improve transportation and avoid destructive floods—these are samples of the important tasks that must be undertaken. At the present time the United States is the only country that combines the requisite capital, engineering ability and executive talent.

The important thing is that by undertaking big things on a large scale the United States will get around much of the competition that breeds irritation and suspicion. If the scale is big enough, there will be no competition. Japan is not prepared to take hold of these matters on a large scale. A negative policy that can be interpreted as putting obstacles in the way of the legitimate development of Japan is fraught with dangers. To concentrate upon big enterprises in a constructive way will leave Japan plenty of opportunities, while it will once and for all avert the possibility of rendering China a virtual subject of Japan—a danger which the best friends of Japan must admit to be real as long as the militaristic-bureaucratic element continues to dominate her policies. The serious source of evil in the present situation is the likelihood that the United States will have sufficient interest in the Far East to talk a great deal, to act in minor ways but upon the whole in ways which can be construed with more or less justice as having for their main object to thwart the ambitions of other countries, especially Japan.

It is not necessary to say that the next few years are crucial. In China as elsewhere reconstruction is imminent, but for the time being things are in solution. Distance has its disadvantages in all the lesser relations. But it can be made an advantage if the attention of America is fixed on large scale undertakings. A considerable part of past friction in accomplishing things under foreign direction in China is due to failure to secure the administrative cooperation of the Chinese. American enterprise should be reasonably free from the temptation to fill such positions with economic carpet-baggers. The Chinese students who have studied and who are studying in America supply a definite nucleus for administrative cooperation. If there are not enough such trained persons among the Chinese then business plans should include an extension of educational facilities to train the required number. The great stumbling-block of the past, the lack of active alliance between business interests and political governmental authority, can also be converted into a positive asset. The Chinese, like the Americans, have the tradition of industrial self-help; they are constitutionally averse to governmental activities. To get around the government, with its almost unbreakable traditions of procrastination, obstruction and corruption is an advance step. And this can largely be effected by enlisting the cooperation of Chinese voluntaryism. It cannot be done however by sending subordinates to carry out plans made without Chinese consultation. Leaders must come whom Chinese leaders recognize as their equals and who are intellectually prepared to deal with Chinese leaders as equals. And the plans must be on such a scale that it is evident while ample security and reasonable profit are given foreign investors the outcome will be to make China the mistress of her own economic destinies. When this is accomplished, she will have no difficulty in looking out for herself politically. Just because the controlling factor in the policies of other nations has been to cultivate the economic subjection of China, the United States has an unparalleled opportunity to pursue the opposite course. Has it the imagination and the energy?

OUR SHARE IN DRUGGING CHINA

Of the millions who associate opium and China probably only few know, beyond a vague impression of England's part in an "Opium War," that from the very beginning, the responsibility for the introduction and spread of the use of narcotics lies with foreign nations. Few know how repeated and consistent have been the struggles of responsible Chinese authorities to prevent the importation of the drug, nor the obstacles that officials of other nations have thrown in their way. Even when poppy growing became general throughout the Empire (and there is no denying that it did), fairness compels the acknowledgment that the Chinese had reached the conclusion that since it was impossible to prevent the introduction of opium from India, they might as well have a share in the profits themselves. In 1906 began the last great campaign against the growing of poppies and for the total eradication of the drug habit, cooperation of Great Britain regarding the importation of opium from India being secured. Even the foreigners who are most pessimistic regarding the capacity of the Chinese to carry through any general reform make an exception of the anti-opium fight. The vigor with which it was conducted was equalled by the ingenuity and skill with which offenders were detected and dealt with. What was accomplished in five years speaks wonders for the capacity of Chinese administration when it is in earnest, and for the adaptability of the Chinese people. There are few instances in history where such a sweeping reform was carried through so rapidly and thoroughly.

Belatedly and under the pressure of criticism and in opposition to the protest of business against "sentimentalism," other countries agreed to cooperate with China. They forbade the exportation of opium save under strict regulations to secure legitimacy of use. China enforced as well as made these restrictions. Since 1905 only about forty ounces a year have passed through

[First published in *New Republic* 21 (1919): 114–17, datelined Peking, October 6.]

the Chinese customs. This amount is taken accordingly as the standard of proper medical use by physicians, hospitals and chemists. It is hard, however, for law and morals to keep up with the advance of science and business. The above figure cannot be taken to measure the state of the drug-using habit in China.

As the importation and use of opium decreased, science provided substitutes in the way of derivatives, especially morphia, heroin and codein, while cocaine was added from a new source. And the use of these forms of "dope" is spreading so fast that they are likely to outdo the ravages of opium at its worst. Opium-smoking is expensive. It is an indulgence now confined to the wealthy. The use of the syringe is as cheap as that of the pipe is dear. Injections can be had for three coppers a "shot" and the profit to the dealer at that rate is over a thousand per cent. Opium-smoking was an aristocratic vice; the needle reaches the coolies. It was not difficult to discover the opium-users. The dweller in any large city of the United States does not need to be told how difficult it is to detect the seller of forms of modern dope. Ingenuity when profits are at stake is not less in China than in America. On every hand one hears of the tricks employed in smuggling and distributing morphia and heroin. The sale is made easier because the Chinese are great takers of medicines, and the licensed practitioner in our sense hardly exists. Opium derivates are sold in all kinds of pills, and itinerant pedlars introduce pills and injections without the ignorant victim knowing what he is getting until after the habit is well fixed. And the weight of evidence is that the effects of morphia, cocaine and heroin are more completely demoralizing to the body, mind and character of the average dope user than were those of opium-smoking. Add the comparative minuteness of the dose for injections,—a single case of detected smuggling in Shanghai lately yielded enough for over twelve million "shots"—and it is easy to see that the new menace is worse than the old.

Since, however, the drugs now reach China only by the medium of smugglers, it might be thought that there is no longer national responsibility for forcing this evil on China—that it is now simply a matter of the individual wickedness of the smuggler and dealer. Unfortunately for the good repute of the western nations, such is not the case. Putting it mildly, carelessness and neglect in drawing and enforcing regulations regarding manufacture, transportation and exportation of opium products are such as to make the nations accomplices in guilt. In 1912 an international convention forbade the further exportation of morphia into China. Before this time the exportation from Great Britain into Japan was 30,000 ounces a year. This was a large enough amount in all conscience, and the most of it undoubtedly found its way to China. By 1917 it had jumped twenty-fold—to 600,000 ounces. Over fifty tons got from Scotland to Japan in four years, these figures being official custom statistics. It does not have to be pointed out that both the British and the Japanese governments knew that this amount was infinitely above legitimate needs—or that its destination was China, to which country exportation was nominally prohibited. But division of moral responsibility was at work. The British were far from the retail trade and the ultimate consumer. Their profits were in Indian revenue where the opium was raised, in Edinburgh the manufacturing centre, and in the shipping trade. The Japanese did not have (at that time) the responsibility for producing and exporting; they merely served as intermediaries. It is easy in such circumstances to pass on blame, and difficult to make an effective appeal to conscience. Only international cooperation would work. The Hague passed excellent resolutions—and Great Britain, the offender at the source, declared that she would put them into force when every other nation did.

In 1917, however, the appeal to the conscience of the British government was sufficiently strong, so that regulations were put into effect by which opium derivatives could be shipped into Japan and its leased territory in Manchuria (the latter being one of the chief centres whence morphia reached the Chinese) only when licenses were given to the exporter. And these licenses were to be given only after receipt of a certificate from Japanese officials that the morphia was for medical use only, and was destined for consumption in Japan itself or its leased territory. The latter proviso made Japan an underwriter that the goods should not reach China. The next year there was a great falling off. Still in view of the fact that Japan was by this time manufacturing more than enough to supply its own medical needs, it is disconcerting to find that one hundred and fifty thousand ounces were imported into Japan. The fact argues an easy conscience somewhere. But this statement does not cover the ground.

In the first place, Great Britain exacts no such license for exportation by means of parcel post—and a single postal package can easily carry stuff for a hundred thousand injections. British subjects in China accuse their home government of wilful omission and evasion. In the next place, the British authorities in both Hong Kong and Singapore farm out the opium product business, receiving in each place two millions of revenue annually for the concession. Now there are well established facts proving that the concessionaire can make his business pay only by getting contraband into China proper. It is obvious that no one would pay two millions a year for the privilege of making opium to be sold only in the city of Hong Kong. So many facilities are given to the concessionaire for smuggling into China that there are those who say that the British licensing regulations for the Japanese trade were adopted not for moral reasons but to protect the "opium farmers" who were having difficulty in meeting Japanese competition in contraband and who appealed to the British government for protection in their rights.

So much for Great Britain's share. As to Japan. Leaving out of the question the neglect of the government in Japan in issuing licenses, and the charges that advantage was taken of the lessened British trade to encourage poppy growing in Japan and Korea, there is the fact that for Japanese territory on Chinese soil, namely in the leased territory of "Dairen and vicinity" and in Tsingtao, licenses are issued by minor officials and irresponsible officials. In a single year there were imported "for medical use only" in "Dairen and vicinity" sixty-six thousand ounces of morphia. The figures are conclusive that the Japanese administration was an accomplice to making its Manchurian territory a point of departure for sending contraband into China. In general Japanese control of the retail and distributing trade has of late years become so complete that they have gradually come to be regarded as the chief if not the only sinners. One cause of present anti-Japanese feeling is found in the fact that Shantung has now become a centre for distributing dope.

Now enters the American participation in the crime of poisoning China. The British require no license for exportation to the United States. Our laws are such that when the stuff arrives at one of our ports it is only necessary to put the goods into bond for transhipment to avoid payment of duty. And while the morphia could not be directly exported under our own laws into China, our laws regarding transhipment make no inquiry into the nature of the goods. They need only be described in a general way. All the morphia now manufactured in Scotland could readily pass through the United States into Japan thence to reach China illicitly if labelled "pharmaceutical products." Remember they could not go direct to Japan from Great Britain. If this is allowed to continue after the attention of our custom officials and of Congress has been called to it, we share with Great Britain and Japan the burden of sinning against China.

But not all our guilt is indirect. The morphia seized in the recent smuggling case in Shanghai was all manufactured in Philadelphia—a fact verified in open court by a lawyer of the International Anti-Opium Association. It would be a criminal offense to ship this direct to China. But there is no law against shipment to Japan. American traffic through the two channels of British goods in bond and our own products has reached vast proportions already. The official statistics show that for the first five months of the current year, twenty-five thousand ounces of morphia reached the port of Kobe from American ports. But the *Japan Chronicle*, published in Kobe, is responsible for the statement that the manifestos of ships arriving in Kobe during the same period show about ninety thousand more ounces not appearing in the custom house returns. The conclusion is certain. This amount was transhipped in Kobe harbor to be smuggled into China. That this shows gross connivance on the part of Kobe port officials may be argued. But the primary responsibility is with the laws and administration of the United States. We have become a large partner in the contemptible business of drugging China at the time when China is making heroic efforts to emancipate herself from the narcotic evil.

Our holier than thou attitude towards Great Britain and Japan must be abandoned. We have as yet no vested industrial and commercial interest possessing great political influence. It requires only a slight amount of interest in the evils of the traffic and a slight amount of energy to frame laws and administrative regulations that will compel adequate registration of all opium products reaching American ports, and make it a criminal offense to transport such goods for re-export. We can easily take steps that will make it impossible for morphia and heroin of American production to be exported to Japan thence to reach China. We can see to it that our post-office at Shanghai cannot be employed for sending narcotics into China by parcel-post (as we do not do at the present, thus making ourselves criminal accomplices in the breaking of Chinese laws and the poisoning of the Chinese people).

The International Anti-Opium Society has worked out plans which if adopted would effectually control the whole nefarious traffic not only for China but for the world. These plans start from the fact that control from the side of retail distribution and the ultimate consumer are so difficult as to be almost hopeless. But control at the source is simple. The growth of poppies can be put under supervision, and every grain of raw opium that leaves them be accounted for and traced. It is possible to determine the amount of narcotics that is required for legitimate medical use. The manufacture of this necessary amount should be put under government licensing and constant inspection. Then by serial numbering of uniform packages and records of sale all distribution could be traced. No opium products are to be shipped anywhere to the Far East except upon receipt of a requisition from the importing country certifying to the intended use, and upon *prior* notification to that country of the nature and date of the shipment meeting the order.

Our own interest is not a purely altruistic one, nor is it confined to doing our obvious duty by China. We have the drug evil with us, and its growth in our country is one of the most disconcerting of present events. We cannot insure ourselves against this evil till we take the measures that will guarantee China against it. The laws and regulations for the control of importation, transhipment, exportation, manufacture and wholesale merchandizing that are needed to protect China from our partnership in the crime of undermining her life are the exact means of safeguarding our own health and morals. Until we have cleaned our own house we cannot take the part that we should take in urging upon other nations, especially Great Britain and Japan, effective international action. The Paris Conference promised China that the League of Nations would take up the opium and morphia traffic. Shall the United States continue its partnership in crime until forced by outside action to abandon it? Shall it enter the deliberations of the League of Nations Assembly with unclean hands?

AUTOCRACY UNDER COVER

In days now so remote, before the war, the mayor of a large city appointed seven members of a school board. There was one Swede, one Bohemian, one Pole, one Norwegian, one Russian Jew, one Irishman and one "American." The mayor explained that it was necessary to recognize the various nationalities, and there was none to question. The distribution covered religious as well as national differences. There is a certain squeamishness, a certain provincial snobbishness which often poses as Americanism. As against this my sympathies are with the mayor of those former days. But, alas, one has to doubt whether the appointments were made because of any recognition of representative contributions to the rich diversity of a developing American life. The reasons had rather to do with recognition of men who could deliver votes en masse, or who would speak for groups in a block. The appointments were a reward for past services in keeping a group so isolated and fixated that it could easily be handled. They put a premium on further segregation and the maintenance of an obnoxious hyphenatedism. Such "recognition" is but a mask for the failure of American life to achieve a true recognition of the value brought by immigrant groups.

Let the incident stand as a symbol. I fear that at the back of the minds of many Americans there is a half-formed picture of aliens wilfully herding together for fear of becoming transformed into genuine Americans. The picture conceives of an open, inviting, hospitable America on one hand and of an obstinate devotion to alien habits and ideals on the other. Even when obstructions due to difficulties of language, economic limitations and exclusiveness on the part of native Americans are sympathetically sketched in, the final background is left out: the conspiracy of economic, denominational and political forces with personal ambition and love of prestige to keep the newcomers isolated and out

[First published in *New Republic* 16 (1918): 103–6.]

of a real share in American life. The measure of their segregation into distinct blocks is likely to be the measure of the ease with which they can be converted to the uses of special interests and self-seekers.

This idea has been made poignantly concrete through a study with which I have been associated in the last few months of a large Polish settlement in the city of Philadelphia, consisting for the most part of hardworking, thrifty people, unusually prosperous at the present time because of steady employment and high wages. They are very patriotic; enthusiastic about the war, which they feel to be intimately their war. Because of President Wilson's pronouncement in behalf of a free and united Poland, to fight for the United States and to fight for Poland have fused in a single flame. In details, they have the ignorance of a peasant population to whom education was made difficult in their native land plus the burden placed upon them by a plunge en masse into a congested industrial centre. In vague generality, they have an eager and emotional knowledge of the glories of historic Poland and a vivid consciousness of the possibilities of its redemption. This is a story of how their ignorance and their knowledge have combined to make them the readier material for subjection to alien uses. At least, it is a typical chapter of that story.

A convention of Poles is to be held in Detroit in the last week of August. The convention is heralded as the visible sign of the united will of the four million Poles of America. Its conclusions will profess to voice authoritatively the desires of all patriotic Poles concerning the next steps to be taken in behalf of free, independent and united Poland.

This ostensibly representative organization of all the Poles and of Poland is called by a self-constituted circle of men centering in Chicago who for the time being are playing Providence to the destinies of nations. They come from the Polish National Alliance, the Roman Catholic Polish Alliance and some Polish-American (the hyphen is inevitable) politicians who keep the Polish vote almost solid for the Republican party in local and national politics. This self-formed and self-styled Executive Committee of the National Polish Department then appointed a Committee on the Convention, consisting in part of its own personnel and of others identified with the same interests. This committee assumed of course authority to determine the constitution of the convention and the selection of delegates. Roughly speaking, the method is as if the bosses of a political machine like Tammany should graciously decide that all of its own minor and local clubs should be allowed to select delegates to a thoroughly representative convention, the leading officers being thrown in as delegates ex officio. Moreover the committee has arrogated to itself the right to decide whether any given organization falls within the vaguely worded rules and whether therefore it is entitled to send delegates. Such local societies as may send delegates have their meetings called by parish priests; the meetings are generally held within the churches and are presided over by the parish priest if he so desires. These facts exclude automatically all inconvenient elements. There are also so-called territorial delegates, but their selection is controlled by rudimentary machine devices.

The committee was not content to determine the make-up of the convention. It also took upon itself the burden of managing the affairs of the delegates after they come together. The regulations for the conduct of the convention might arouse envy in the hearts of the most astute managers of a political steam roller. The phrase that recurs most often is "no discussion." With one exception, the general meetings are for hearing routine reports and for high oratory—Mr. Paderewski being, naturally, the fountain head. The actual business is conducted by seven sectional meetings. The topics for their consideration are thoughtfully prepared by clerks appointed several weeks in advance by the managing committee. The Chairman of the convention will appoint the chairmen, secretaries and nine members of every section. The last general meeting, which is the one that actually does business, cannot take up any measures not reported back to it from the sections, and there can be no discussion of even their decisions, except upon *written request of one-third of the delegates.* No chances are to be taken even with a packed convention.

Such is the technique of calling and operating a convention which, in the words of its inspired creators, will be the "greatest political and national event for all Poles in America, a visible external expression of the will of the entire immigration." As such its decisions will be represented to the American public through the American press.

The sources of the power so to impose itself are a lesson in the relation of the immigrant to this country. The glamour of a great name and personality, the ordinary ambitions for place and prominence plus the extraordinary opportunity due to working in a corner and under the cover of a press not read by Americans, the deliberate exploitation of a segregated group, work together. But after all the chief reinforcement comes from the too willing ignorance of those who claim the first right to the title of American.

To know more, to take the pains to be better informed, would involve overcoming the instinct which leads men to withdraw from the "foreigner." But it would also involve the inconvenience of assuming the responsibilities which knowledge and intercourse would bring. Ignorance compensated for by well intentioned effort at "Americanization" is the easier course. And this course is so uncomprehending of causes and so concerned with superficial symptoms that it evokes the sort of response of which the following is fairly typical: "After leaving us alone when we needed close contact with you, personal and human contact, a lot of you Americans are now trying to get us to speak a jargon which is neither good English nor good native tongue, and to adopt the use of chewing gum and other American customs." This whimsical expression of the feeling that an attempt is made to impose external habits upon the immigrant instead of bringing about an association of equals and between equals is widespread. The situation of compartmental life that evokes it is the situation which too readily throws the more energetic and able of the immigrants into contact mainly with politicians and others who have something to gain. Thus are generated alliances which produce such phenomena as the operations of the "representative" Convention of American Poles.

Even in times of peace, and when matters concerning exclusively the domestic affairs of the Poles—if there are any such—were to be considered, the methods described put the problem of Americanization of immigrants in a light different from that in which it is ordinarily viewed, and a light I venture to think immensely more significant. For it concentrates attention upon the forces which work unceasingly to maintain segregated masses in a block amenable to ready exploitation by autocratic managers. Thus the oppressed nationalities of Europe have their literal counterparts here, and there is the same need for self-determination and unhindered access to materials—in this case, human materials.

In the typical case selected, namely, the convention, it is easy to see that genuine American interests are concerned. One of the occasions, if not aims, of calling the convention was a conflict of opinions concerning funds raised for Polish war relief, political propaganda, etc. The determination of the destination of funds is mainly in the hands of one set of men; raising the funds is in the hands of another set who have direct contact with the mass of the immigration. Leaving out of account as unedifying reciprocal insinuations and recriminations as between these two forces, there is here a conflict of interests which needs adjustment. The mere fact that this important financial matter concerns the war establishes the vested interest of America, for it makes a great difference whether these matters are so handled as to bring Americans and immigrants together or to continue and even increase separatism.

It is a moderate statement to say that in the case of the Poles so far as concerns raising and employing funds the opportunity for closer unification has not been taken adequate advantage of. It is not necessary to accept the view of one side in the controversy just referred to, namely that the cause is that an alleged interest in relief of war victims has been subordinated to interest in using funds for political ends, much less the numerous insinuations of graft. The facts speak for themselves. In spite of the devotion of American Poles to the war—over ten per cent of the killed in the American Army in France up to the present time are Poles—in spite of the awful suffering of Poles in Polish territory during the war, and in spite of the great generosity with which calls coming from Belgium, Serbia and other suffering countries have been heard, funds raised in this country for all Polish uses growing out of the war have been lamentably small—hardly one-tenth of what has been raised for Armenian relief, for example. It certainly is a matter of concern to all Americans interested in the most effective prosecution of the war, whether the convention merely makes a personal adjustment or compromise of financial interests, or whether it takes such action as will enlist the complete confidence of both Poles and Americans in the financial conduct of Polish affairs in this country and thereby reverse the poor record made in the past. While American money has gone for relief to Europe not with ulterior ends but because of misery and destitution, everybody knows what the effect of American generosity has been among the populations reached. This effect has not been produced in Poland up to the present time. It will not be produced, unless all the conditions which up to this time have kept down the response to appeals for money are resolutely and courageously swept aside, and Polish unity under American auspices achieved. Will the convention rise to this height? Unfortunately, the methods expressed in its formation give scant ground for optimism.

The same opportunity and the same query present themselves in reference to the political policies to be endorsed by the convention. These concern not fundamental objects but the methods of their attainment, which in this case as so many others, have such a direct bearing upon the attainment of objects. All Poles are agreed upon a free, independent and united Poland, with access to the sea. All, even radical socialists, are agreed in opposition to the Bolshevik regime in Russia. All, in this country anyway, are agreed that the United States is the natural and most effective guardian of the interests of Poland at the Peace Conference. With this unity of ends, it would seem an easy matter to attain practical unity. But historical causes have created among Poles partisan divisions which are unusually acute and numerous, these being complicated by the struggle of individuals to be the pivot upon which shall turn the achieving of Poland's new destiny. If you suppose the many-party system from right to left of any European country cut across by parties due to a partition among these powers, and influenced by the intrigues of those powers, you have a rough picture of Polish politics. With the hoped-for approaching advent of a new State, great are the stakes involved in advantage of position in controlling the formation of its government. It would hardly be truthful to say that Polish partisan and personal politics have been "adjourned."

Will the convention have the intelligence and the loyalty to act upon the fundamental points of unity? If so, it will come out strongly for an international commission, consisting of all the various party elements; for the closest possible contact with all parties who are truly loyal to Poland in Poland itself; and for the centering of the Polish question in Washington, where as all admit in private conversation is Poland's most powerful and disinterested friend. But if influences too strong in the past continue to operate, the mask of seeming authority to speak for all Poles will be taken advantage of to strengthen the power of faction, to glorify personalities, and to subordinate America's influence and authority to that of other countries—and thereby perhaps to jeopardize the future of Poland itself. So subtle and strong are the connections between the forces which separate and subject a particular group in America and the forces which determine the ultimate execution of American national policy.

PRELIMINARY CONFIDENTIAL MEMORANDUM

Polish Conditions in this Country

RE DETROIT CONVENTION

Pending the preparation of a more extensive report, as asked for by the Military Intelligence Branch, I beg leave to submit a preliminary report concerning activities in connection with the Detroit Convention. This Convention is convened for August 26th, and accordingly presents the only immediate and urgent phase of the matter.

I. Character of Convention

The Convention is called by a committee having headquarters in Chicago, calling itself A National Department. This central committee appointed a pre-convention committee, consisting in part of its own members and in part of other individuals affiliated with them, which issued rules concerning both the appointment of delegates and the actual conduct of the convention when called. It will be noted then that the conduct of the convention is not under its own control. The convention, ostensibly called to express authoritatively the "external will" of the entire Polish immigration regarding the Polish press, including a large number which have supported the National Department in the past and societies affiliated with it, shows a great deal of friction and discontent. The vagueness and complexity of the rules regarding the appointment of delegates, the assumption of authority on the part of the National Department to decide whether a given organization comes within the list of those who are entitled to send dele-

[From typescript in Edward M. House Papers, Yale University Library, New Haven, Conn., dated 19 August 1918; first published in Louis L. Gerson, *Woodrow Wilson and the Rebirth of Poland, 1914–1920* (New Haven: Yale University Press, 1953), pp. 149–53.]

gates, appear to justify the suspicions and criticism that the convention is not in fact what it purports to be. The rules for conducting the convention place the actual business of the convention in the hands of six sections, the President, Secretary, and nine members of which are to be appointed by the Chairman of the Convention; moreover, the pre-Convention committee appoints in advance clerks who draw up a list of topics to be considered by these sections. Only at the last day of the convention does the convention as a whole take action beyond listening to speeches and reports, any discussion of which is officially discouraged. On the last day the entire convention can take action only upon resolutions reported to it from the section. There can be no discussion of these section reports excepting upon the written request of one-third of the members of the convention.

These facts explain the very general criticism and unfavorable comment of a very considerable portion of the Polish press. Unless very great care is taken in the actual conduct of the convention to allay suspicion and mistrust by a frank and open policy they render it practically impossible for the convention to speak with that authority and unity which are most desirable. It should be clear that the criticisms to which reference is made are in no sense confined to the K.O.N., or radical faction.

II. The Convention and Polish Finances

There is an immense dissatisfaction among practically all groups of Poles with the management of their financial affairs. There are constant recrimination and counter-charges, leaving entirely out of account the accusation of misuse of funds; these charges concern extravagant salaries, unnecessary duplication of societies and offices, and failure to discriminate between funds raised for distinctly relief purposes, for propaganda and presswork, for political and for army purposes. There is jealousy at least between the Chicago headquarters, which handles funds, and the large number of the local organizations that raise the funds. Since the parish priests who are in closest contact with the mass of Polish population are largely instrumental in the raising of local funds the charges and counter-charges are having a decidedly bad effect upon the mass of Polish immigrants. It is reported,—and so far as we can determine, correctly,—that funds collected last May are still withheld from transmission to headquarters. All Poles are much dissatisfied with the relatively small amount of money that has been raised for Polish purposes in this country. Attempts to explain this small fund have led Poles now very influential in the conduct of their affairs in this country to attack Americans for lack of interest, to attack the conduct of the Red Cross, and to the recriminations among themselves to which attention has already been called.

The situation has lately been further complicated by the introduction of the so-called "White Cross." Although in France the corresponding society for the relief of Polish soldiers works under the French Red Cross, the so-called "White Cross" in this country is working independently. The masses of the Polish people do not understand why they should not work with the American Red Cross, and the attempt of the authorities of the White Cross to answer questions and criticisms leads to attacks on the American Red Cross. In addition, the duplication of offices and salaries is criticised. It is a part of the task of the Convention to straighten out these various matters, secure unity and efficiency, of raising and distributing funds. According to all information at our hand this can really be accomplished only in one way,—namely, unification under representative Americans who have the confidence both of Polish immigrants and of generous Americans. Anything short of this will be regarded by very numerous sections of the Polish immigrants as merely an attempt to perpetuate with minor changes the confusion and rivalry which has so unfortunately existed in the past. The interest of the American Government and policy in this matter is obvious. The present situation reacts unfavorably upon the recruiting and support of the Polish Army, of the American Red Cross—of which the President of the United States is President—, and tends to create totally unnecessary divisions and quarrels of the Polish civilian population, which is enthusiastically united otherwise in support of the war. Moreover, the comparatively small amount of funds raised for Polish affairs as compared with that for other oppressed nationalities of Europe reacts unfavorably upon American prestige abroad.

All factions of the Poles are so committed to the expressed policies of President Wilson about the war in general, and the future of Poland in particular, that it would be an easy matter for a few words from the right sources to bring about the required unity and efficiency under definitely American auspices. Obviously any hesitation in acceding to such a request would indicate that personal or factional ambition is more influential than loyalty to the United States or even to Poland.

III. Political Aspects of the Convention

Some weeks ago a bill was prepared to be introduced in the Senate of the United States, one of the provisions of which was a clause which virtually constituted a committee located in Paris as the State and War Department of the new united and independent Poland. It is reported that this bill was prepared or transmitted through the agency of the Polish press bureau of Washington. Our information is to the effect that the actual introduction of this bill was delayed at the suggestion of high governmental authorities. Our information is also to the effect that an important representative of one of the foreign military commissions in this country stated that the General Staffs of both France and Great Britain were desirous of securing such recognition of the Paris Committee, but that the American Government up to this time had blocked such action. We have Mr. Paderewski's personal statement that attempts to make the Paris Committee more representative by including members of the parties of the Left, and a very influential representative of the Austrian socialists, (who while on Austrian soil had come out strongly for a free and united Poland with access to the sea), had been overruled by representatives of the military staff of Great Britain and France,—a fact which would presumptively indicate an interest of the American War Department in this whole situation.

In view of the fact that the persons in control of the convention had prepared the resolution which purported to voice the will of the entire Polish immigration in this country in favor of making the Paris Committee the Foreign and War Department of the New State of Poland, it is a fair inference that one of the main objects of the convention was to bring pressure to bear upon the American Government. If this had been done at the request of the President through the State and War Department there is, of course, nothing further to be said; but if the resolution was prepared without a frank and complete understanding with the State and War Department the resolution appears to indicate a willingness to subordinate American to foreign interests.

In this connection it is appropriate to call attention to two facts: One is that President Wilson and the American Government are the only authorities which have the complete confidence of all Poles in this country and abroad. President Wilson, in his speech of January 22, 1917, was the first statesman to go out for a free and united Poland. Moreover, owing to past historic complication the United States is the only country which is trusted by the Poles here and abroad as completely disinterested in its policy in the peace settlement as that affects Poland. Under such circumstances American leadership is as natural as pressure from a convention misrepresenting itself as the voice of all Poles in behalf of foreign leadership would be distressing and unfortunate. The other fact is that Mr. Paderewski is the official delegate of the Paris Committee to this country; that he speaks of himself as a "plenipotentiary," and is freely spoken of by his immediate associates as Ambassador of Poland to the United States.

IV. Summary

It is in the interest of complete Polish unity in this country and of American influence and prestige abroad, both in general and with reference to Poland in particular, that the Detroit Convention be postponed until there is adequate assurance that it is genuinely representative in its make-up and truly parliamentary in its procedure, and is committed to the policy which has the antecedent sanction of the State and War Department of the United States.

If such postponement is now impossible, then it is important that the convention, through the comparatively small group in control of it, be guided in the direction indicated above. Namely, first, financial reorganization and unification, with sufficient active, not merely nominal, American representation to secure confidence and supervise methods and details of collection, distribution and accounting, together with added Polish members drawn from persons not identified with any of the present contending interests; there are a number of these who have withdrawn because of disgust at squabbles and personal intrigue. Second, with reference to foreign affairs a resolution calling for an American commission which shall have as its object the unification of all Polish groups and parties in behalf of the declared policies of President Wilson, and which shall—through authorized representatives—get in touch with similar groups abroad, including those in Poland itself. We are assured by representatives in high standing of both the more conservative and the more radical party groups in this country, that in spite of German occupation such communication is entirely feasible, and in fact is now maintained.

The willingness to accede to such a proposition would be an acid test of whether the interests of the United States primarily, and of Poland secondarily, are uppermost, or whether these interests are subordinate to something personal and factional. This test should be applied to the representatives of all groups whatsoever, and they should be judged by results.

If there are weighty and important objections to the course outlined it certainly would be a simple matter to pass a resolution stating that the Poles of this country unitedly and enthusiastically entrust the future interests of their country to the leadership of President Wilson. If instead of such a resolution any individual prefers a resolution in behalf of any committee on foreign shores, no matter how influential in the past it would seem to fix his status beyond further discussion.

August 20, 1918. Later information shows that one faction plans to eliminate Madame Paderewski from financial and internal activity. If she declines, it will be put up to Mr. Paderewski. If he refuses, he will be told that he also must withdraw from connection with financial and American Polish affairs; that he is to be "promoted" to Washington to take care of the international end, in view of the fact that he is a delegate from the Paris Committee.

The significant bearing of this is in connection with the proposed resolution recommending making the Paris Committee the State and War Departments of the new State of Poland. The larger number of the Poles are not particularly interested in the international complications, or are ignorant of them; this element would have favored the passing of the resolution simply as a method of eliminating the Paderewski influence in domestic and financial affairs of this country. This comes in part from the section which is honestly disgusted with the Paderewski regime, and in part from those who wish to have the management of funds in their own hands, in this country.

All of this strife is, of course, within parties nominally supporting the present Paderewski and Chicago Groups.

SECOND PRELIMINARY CONFIDENTIAL MEMORANDUM

Polish Conditions in this Country

PUBLICITY

The question of publicity for Poland and Polish affairs is urgent.

1. There is immense dissatisfaction among the Poles with the *amount* of publicity given to the Polish cause. Poland is both the largest and the most important from all points of view of the oppressed nationalities of Europe for whose freedom we are fighting. Poles point out that it will rank, even immediately after the war, next to Spain, or form the seventh country in population in Europe; that its geographical position makes it the key to the future war and peace relations of eastern and even southeastern Europe; that its political problems are more complicated than those of any other oppressed nationality, owing to its past division between three great powers, and of the peculiar importance of the relations of Poland to the Jews, Lithuanians, and Ruthenians. In addition they point to the antecedent sentimental interest of Americans in Poland, which would have been intensified by an adequate knowledge of the sufferings of Poland as great as those of Belgium or Serbia. The domestic American interest is pointed to in connection with the fact that the Poles are about one-twentieth of our population, one sixth or seventh of our total immigration population, and that the Labor and Immigration problems after the war, as well as those of establishing the best commercial relations with the new State of Poland, make wide publicity most important.

After reciting such facts as these, they point to the great ignorance of Polish questions among even educated Americans,

[From typescript in Edward M. House Papers, Yale University Library, New Haven, Conn., dated 23 August 1918; first published in Louis L. Gerson, *Woodrow Wilson and the Rebirth of Poland, 1914–1920* (New Haven: Yale University Press, 1953), pp. 154–56.]

and to the fact that there is next to no publicity. They compare the amount of space given to Polish affairs to that, say, of the Czecho-Slovaks, and show that what does find its way into the American press almost always comes through regular foreign press channels, and that no attempt is made to show the meaning or bearing of this material from week to week and day to day.

2. The blame for this state of affairs is put upon the Polish Press Bureau or so-called Polish Associated Press located in Washington. Charges of both ignorance, inefficiency, and lack of vigor are freely made. It is said that Mr. White's past record does not justify his being head of the Bureau, that he owes his position there to Mr. Paderewski's influence and financial support rather than general ability or special knowledge of Polish affairs; that Mr. Wedda, an American Pole, is not expert in the Polish language and that he owes his position to his former connection with Mr. Smulski. As there is reported friction between the Paderewski group and the Chicago group headed by Smulski (in spite of external show of harmony), it is said that they are there to see that both factions receive attention. There is said to be a Pole connected with the Bureau who is much better informed about Polish affairs and abler, but who is very lazy—unfortunately I have mislaid the memorandum of his name. In connection with the charge of lack of energy brought against the whole Bureau, it is pointed out that of the issues of *Free Poland*, a monthly in the English language for publicity among Americans, the June number did not come out till well in August; the charge of ignorance is specifically supported by the instance of the appeal for funds in that issue for support of the Polish army in which the simple facts about the army were misstated and had the effect of discouraging recruiting as well as casting reflections upon the French management of its affairs, on account of gross understatement of pay, privileges, etc.

3. In addition to claims of ignorance and inefficiency as accounting for the lack of adequate publicity, it is said that the Bureau is much more concerned with furthering the fortunes of a faction of Poles in this country than of presenting the interests of the Polish cause; that it has permitted itself to become the headquarters of intrigue, malicious gossip, and other activities calculated to divide the Poles. I have in my possession a memorandum coming from quarters directly connected with the Polish Press

Bureau supporting this charge. The factional tendencies among Poles are already so strong that it is impossible to overstate the dangerous and un-American character of all activities that tend to further dissension and discord.

4. As also accounting for the absence of genuine publicity through this Bureau, the close personal relations mentioned above, between its members and Messrs. Paderewski and Smulski are pointed to. It is generally believed—this among Poles of almost every faction—that the Bureau has concerned itself more with personal press agency work for Mme. and Mr. Paderewski than with systematic and whole-hearted general Polish propaganda. This general belief is doing so much harm that it should be looked into, so that the situation may be radically changed if the charge is true, and authoritatively put to rest if it is at fault. The inquiry should not rest with personal assertions pro or con but include examination of financial support and expenditures.

5. The Government has a double interest in this situation, in addition to the general interest in adequate publicity, and in addition to the bearing of this publicity upon the matters already pointed out, namely, (a) better relations between Poles in America and other Americans, (b) discouragement of factions and securing of unity, (c) recruiting for the Polish army from Class Five. These are—

I. The War Department now refers all press inquirers and others to the Bureau for all information regarding the Polish army. This tends practically, if not officially, to give it a semi-official status for Washington reporters as sources for all Polish affairs.

II. Mr. Wedda is the Chairman of the section of the C.P.I. for Polish affairs, and his office in such capacity is adjacent to his office in his capacity as member of the Polish Press Bureau.

Recommendations

1. An official inquiry into the efficiency, intelligence and affiliations of the Bureau. This should, as stated above, go into matters of finance as well as effect some showdown as to what the Bureau has been accomplishing.

2. An immediate termination of Mr. Wedda's connection with the C.P.I.

3. The development of a well-considered and effective organization for Polish publicity whose main objects should be:

1. Securing and publishing full information about all phases of the Polish problem general knowledge of which among Americans and the Polish Immigration would unify and intensify support of the war.

2. Bringing about greater unity among the Poles, reducing and eliminating so far as possible their cut throat and factional methods.

CONFIDENTIAL REPORT OF CONDITIONS AMONG THE POLES IN THE UNITED STATES

Introduction

OCCASION OF REPORT

I received a telegram signed General Churchill on August 15, 1918, requesting me to come to Washington to place at the disposal of the Military Intelligence Bureau any information in my possession on conditions among the Poles in this country. At various conferences held on August 17 and some days of the ensuing week I met Captains Uterhart and Dalrymple and Lieutenant Horgan. During these conferences it appeared that the information which I had to report covered a variety of the branches of service and also a number of matters that fell primarily within the province of the State Department. Accordingly, Major Hunt asked me to make out a written report of the whole situation.

Two preliminary reports covering more urgent phases of the matter have been handed in, one on August 19, regarding the Detroit Convention, and another on August 23, on publicity for Polish affairs. It will be found necessary to traverse some of that material in the following report.

In preparing this report it has been necessary to choose between such condensation as might fail to bring out the significance of the material and restatement of historical and other facts which are already familiar as matter of record. In view of the diversity and complexity of interests concerned, it has seemed better to err, if at all, in the direction of undue explanation.

SOURCES OF INFORMATION

Mr. Albert C. Barnes, of Philadelphia, spoke to me in New York City last April regarding the possibility of securing some well-trained post-graduate students from Columbia University to undertake a study during the summer months of conditions

[First published in Philadelphia (?): privately printed, 1918, 80 pp.]

among an immigrant group in Philadelphia. The Poles were selected. The main object of the inquiry was to ascertain forces and conditions which operate against the development of a free and democratic life among the members of this group, to discover the influences which kept them under external oppression and control. To quote from a letter written by Mr. Barnes: "The idea would be to work out a practical plan, based upon first-hand knowledge, to eliminate forces alien to democratic internationalism and to promote American ideals in accordance with the principles announced by President Wilson in his various public communications." As to method, he emphasized simply the importance of competent scientific impartial inquiry. Neither then nor at any other time did Mr. Barnes give any instructions as to specific points to be investigated, much less as to any particular kind of results to be attained.

In accordance with his request the following persons were selected and after about a month's preliminary study on their part of conditions in Philadelphia the following assignment of topics made:

Mr. Brand Blanshard, religious conditions and the activity of the church; Miss Frances Bradshaw, educational conditions, including both public and parochial schools; Mrs. A. Levitas, conditions affecting family life and women; Mr. Irwin Edman began with a study of general intellectual, esthetic and neighborhood activities, but in connection with developments related below gradually diverted his energies to a study of conditions as affected by international politics. In May, Mr. Barnes asked me to act as adviser and general supervisor of the undertaking. The inquiry itself was set on foot on the fifteenth of May, 1918. In addition to the persons mentioned above, one of whom, Mrs. Levitas, is herself a Polish immigrant, persons were engaged both permanently and for stated periods to act as interpreters and translators. Other persons have been engaged in library research from time to time. All of the active investigators lived in a house in the Polish district during the study of the immigrants.

Quite early in the inquiry a number of facts were discovered which were blind and confusing. In spite of the unity among the Poles in support of the war, there were marked symptoms of strife and unrest which nothing on the surface accounted for. Briefly stated, we discovered much fear and intimidation in a certain part of the Polish population, much manipulation and exploitation in another part, together with much criticism of leaders whom they were nominally following with much enthusiasm. An attempt to get at and understand these conditions obliged us to extend our investigations to New York City and to Washington. What was there discovered necessitated an extension of the study to European and international conditions which were reflected upon this side. It will be understood that this extension was not originally contemplated and was entirely an outgrowth of local facts and events unexpectedly encountered.

During the course of the inquiry various members of the organization have talked with scores of Poles, including leaders and important persons of all factions so far as they were within geographical reach. Owing to the attempts spoken of below, which were largely successful, to represent the Progressive and Democratic party among the Poles as pro-German, the data used in the following report have been derived from the conservative or Paderewski-Smulski faction or confirmed from that source unless otherwise indicated. In studying the European situation we have relied as far as possible upon books and documents of an independent source and upon English, French and Swiss periodicals and newspapers. In dealing with the European side we have had to rely more upon the statements of the radical than of the conservative faction because of the admittedly greater learning of the former. Material from the radical source has, however, been used only where it was possible to check it up by independent documentary material.

The order of statement in the following Report reverses the course taken in our inquiries and discoveries. The Report begins with European conditions and then takes up American conditions as influenced thereby, and finally takes up local, specific and immediate conditions among the Poles in America which have a bearing upon the disposition and morale of the Poles with respect to the war, in that they breed dissension and disturb the unity which is desirable for efficient prosecution of the war.

In brief, the European aspect of the matter is the record of a struggle which originated long before the war between a party of the Poles whose chief policies were monarchical, reactionary and clerical and a party which was radical, often revolutionary and socialistic, anticlerical and republican. As will appear below, neither of the parties is especially favorable to the cause of the Jews but the record of the conservative party is much the more aggressively anti-Semitic. Both parties share the tendency among all Poles to exaggerate territorial claims based upon events of past history, some of them as old as the twelfth century, but the conservative party is the more imperialistic and extreme, being "Pan-Polish." Since the Russian Revolution particularly, the radical party has moderated its claims.

Upon the American side what we discovered was an alliance, avowed and active, between that portion of the Polish clergy which is opposed to and admittedly afraid of Americanization along with a political group centered in Chicago, in the past chiefly interested in the finances of Polish organizations, with the conservative European group. The prominent heads of this alliance were Mr. and Mrs. Paderewski and the people immediately associated with them.

On the other hand, there was a much smaller group of radicals affiliated with the revolutionary socialistic group in Europe which had been discredited by accusations of pro-Germanism to such an extent that the Intelligence Bureau of the Government was practically shut off from receiving information from it and precluded from using its influence in industrial centres to allay industrial unrest.

The local conditions observed in Philadelphia were found to have their origin in the conflict between these two factions and in discontent under external show of harmony with the Chicago-Paderewski leadership. The bad conditions were accentuated by the campaign of misrepresentation, public and private, carried on against the members and adherents of the radical party.

A. General European Conditions as Affecting the Poles in the United States

1. It is unnecessary to recite the effects of the partition of Poland between Russia, Germany and Austria except insofar as a statement of the much more favorable condition of affairs in Galicia under Austrian control throws light upon events related below. Bearing in mind then that four million of Poles are German

subjects, four million Austrian and twelve million Russian, we have the following marked contrasts between Austria and Russia:

In Austria every group of Poles has its own public schools, supported by public taxes, where the teachers are Poles, the Polish language is used and Polish history, geography and literature are regular school subjects. This holds of both elementary and high schools, while Cracow has its own Polish university. In Russian Poland there is not a single public Polish school and no Polish language or literature is allowed in any school. Polish universities once existing have been closed, and when the Russians conquered Galicia the Polish university at Lemberg was changed over into a Russian one. In Galicia wherever the Polish population predominated, the judges in the civil courts are Poles and witnesses are allowed to use the Polish language. The civil service throughout Galicia consists of Poles or Ukrainians. Polish political clubs flourish freely. There is complete manhood suffrage and many delegates were elected to the Austrian Parliament. Moreover, Galicia had its own provincial legislative Assembly which in turn elected its own executive officers for the province, generally four Poles to one Ukrainian. All of these features contrasted sharply and almost absolutely with the conditions under which the Poles lived in Russian Poland. The first Duma had a parliamentary representation of Poles consisting of 36 members, but in the third this was arbitrarily cut down to 12. Moreover, the whole policy of Austria was to cater to the Poles. In so doing it was following its traditional policy of setting the various nationalities in the Dual Kingdom over against each other. Thus the Poles were doubtless favored at the expense of Bohemians, Ukrainians, and Jugo-Slavs. Almost every Austrian ministry had at least two Poles in it. In fact, excepting for a certain amount of economic exploitation and oppression, Poles under Austrian rule enjoyed practically complete autonomy while in Russia they were subjected to the most exacting repressive measures. In addition there was religious harmony between Poles and Austrians, while in Russian Poland there was sharp religious and ecclesiastical discord. In this connection it should be noted that the so-called Constitutional Government in Russia was little more favorable to the Poles than strict autocracy had been and that the Constitutional Democrats under Miliukov had no intention of granting Poland political independence or freedom, contenting itself with assurances of Home Rule under Russian control.

2. There was considerable economic and political friction between the Poles and other subject nationalities. Germans and Russians alike played the Lithuanians off against the Poles while, as already indicated, the Austrian Government stimulated antagonism between the Ukrainians and the Poles. Even before the war Germany had favored the Ukrainians wherever possible against the Poles and had built up a strong pro-German party in Ukrainia which fact was later taken advantage of in the separate treaty with Ukrainia.

The Jewish question is particularly acute in the Kingdom of Poland—that is, Russian Poland. Poles claim that the Russians had systematically used the Jews to foment internal discord and that after the Jews were expelled from Russia great masses of the Jews took advantage of their migration into Poland to bring about an economic exploitation of the Poles, especially in the country districts. Even the liberal Poles claim that some Jews are not contented to agitate for personal and civil rights but wish distinctive political rights as a national group on Polish territory. They also claim that Russia has instigated them to this policy and that the older generations of Jews born on Polish soil are entirely loyal to the political cause of Poland. The Jews complain not merely of economic boycotts and civil disabilities but also of actual persecution modeled after the Russian pogroms.

Up till recently there has been friction between Poles and Bohemians. The Bohemian radicals have directed their revolutionary activities against Austria and have pursued upon the whole a pro-Russian and pro-Slav policy. In so doing they have frequently argued against the independence of Poland, saying that Poland should become united under the domination of Russia. It is a matter of much grief and considerable resentment among the Poles that Professor Masaryk, now the leader of the Czecho-Slovaks, formerly expressed himself in this sense. Since the Russian Revolution and since the pronouncements of the Italian Conference at Rome and of Secretary Lansing, the relations between the Poles and the Bohemians, in this country at least, have undergone great improvement, and Czecho-Slovaks and Jugo-Slavs and Poles seem now to be united in demanding political independence and freedom for all three nationalities.

3. Aside from the ordinary division of political parties into conservatives and progressives or liberals, the party situation in Poland, especially the Austrian part, was complicated by parties whose main interest was in looking after the economic interests of certain groups. In Galicia the peasants were especially well-organized. Aside from these divisions, the important one and the one which has affected American conditions was that into Activists and Passivists. Up to the time of the war, or at least two or three years previously, practically all the population in German Poland, much the greater mass in Russian Poland and a considerable majority in Galicia were Passivists—that is to say they had practically given up all hope of political independence and were concerned simply with obtaining from their respective governments concessions regarding the use of language, educational facilities, economic improvements and nationalistic cultural development in general.

For a long time practically the only Activist Party was that headed by a group which started in Paris a revolutionary movement in 1892. This party combined moderate socialism with aspirations for a free and independent Poland. Their main activities were directed from the start against Russia as the country which was most reactionary and which held the largest part of Poland in subjection. Their socialism was of a nationalistic, not an internationalistic, character because the party aimed first at securing a new national state for Poland. It was of a moderate progressive rather than an extreme radical character as may be seen from the platform adopted in 1892 to which this radical party has since adhered.

> An independent Polish Democratic Republic based on the following principles: Direct, general and secret suffrage; legislation by the people, including the initiative and referendum; equality of all citizens, regardless of sex, race, nationality and religion; progressive income tax; an eight hour working day, minimum wages, equal pay for men and women, prohibition of child labor; gradual socialization of land, of the means of transportation and production and of communication.

The first factor in their strictly political program was attack upon Russia. This group was very active in the abortive revolution of 1905–6. They allied themselves with the revolutionists in Russia proper and finally succeeded in stirring up an agitation in the Kingdom of Poland which extended far beyond their own group.

When the revolution was crushed this manifestation of dislike of Russia by Poland was used to increase the oppression of Poles and was also taken advantage of by the conservative and Passivist Party to discredit the radical faction. The revolutionary activities of the latter were pointed to as evidence of political immaturity and bad judgment which, in turn, were declared to be the causes of the failure of Russia to yield a greater amount of political freedom and local self-government to the Poles.

The second item in their policy was the utilization of the great amount of intellectual, civil and political freedom granted the Poles by Austria to secure a jumping off place for the future struggle for the freedom of Poland. They thus made Galicia, especially after 1906, the headquarters of their revolutionary propaganda, extending even to the training of young Poles in the manual of arms and military tactics. They also used Galician autonomy to foster the idea of a new Poland consisting of Russian and Austrian Poland which, while independent, should be friendly to Austria and a buffer state against Russia. There were and are various things in the internal policy of Austria-Hungary which made such a policy not impossible of realization. It constitutes even now the basis of one of the so-called Austrian solutions of the Polish problem as over against the German solution.

The third item of the program was the addition of Prussian Poland to the new state. This was especially desired for economic and industrial reasons on account of the mines in Prussian Silesia. The fourth and final aim was the formation of a federation which should extend from the Baltic to the Black Sea. The Lithuanians and Ukrainians were to be encouraged to be self-determining, as were also the Esthonians and Letts, and then all were to be encouraged to join a federation which should extend clear from the north to the south of Europe, making a complete barrier between Russia and all the country to the west. Poland would be the largest and naturally the dominating state of this federation. This entire program was planned, of course, to cover a very long period of years in its realization. Its comprehensive scope caused this party to be attacked as theorists and dreamers, while its gradual step-by-step nature lent it to the opposite charge that the party was exclusively devoted to the interests of Austria, or even of Germany. This latter charge was based upon ignoring all phases of the movement excepting one, namely, the use of Austria as a basis of attack upon Russia so as to secure the independence of Russian Poland.

B. European Developments during the War

I. RELATIVE TO RUSSIA BEFORE THE REVOLUTION

Immediately upon the outbreak of the war the conservative or Right Wing Polish parties in Russia adhered enthusiastically to the cause of Russia. The National Democrats, Realists and Polish Progressives issued on August 7, 1914, a manifesto calling upon all Poles to rally to Russia against Germany. After the proclamation of the Russian Grand Duke in favor of the autonomy of Poland under Russian sovereignty, members of this group issued a manifesto on November 25, 1914 in which the following language is used:

> One object confronted the Nation: the unification of Poland under the sceptre of the Russian Monarchy. Upon this object our Nation concentrates itself; toward this end turn all its endeavours. . . . Therefore the undersigned this day unite to form a Polish National Council, thus laying the foundation of Poland's political organization.

Partly because of the prevalence of the Passivist attitude in Russia, but even more because of the thoroughness of Russian conscription, a very large army, said to amount to 700,000 soldiers, was recruited in Russian Poland.

The renunciation of a completely free and independent Poland in favor of home rule under Russian sovereignty naturally placed the conservative parties which joined in signing it in good favor not only with the Russian Government but with the Entente Allies, especially Great Britain and France. It aroused, however, the distrust of the Polish parties of the left. The latter constantly pointed out that the proclamation was a purely military one, being issued by the Commander-in-Chief of the Russian Army, and had no political sanction or authority. They pointed also to instructions sent from Petrograd to local Russian authorities in Poland indicating that the Grand Ducal proclamation was to make no difference in the methods of dealing with Polish subjects. At the beginning of 1906, Mr. Maklakoff, who was later the Russian Ambassador in France, declared in the Duma that the promise of autonomy for Poland was a hypocritical farce. The treatment of the Poles in Galicia after the Russian conquest of that country strengthened the conviction of a large number of Poles that the Russian pretensions were insincere and that at most it was intended to give even autonomy only to German Poland.

This belief affected the attitude of the Poles, who wished for a completely free Poland, through the Allies. There was general discontent with the failure of the statesmen of the Allies in their speeches claiming that the Allies were fighting for the freedom of oppressed nationalities to make any specific reference to Poland. This discontent was strengthened by the official reply of the Allies of January 10, 1917 to President Wilson's request for a statement of war aims, since the reply merely referred to the attitude of Russia in the matter. In the French press a complete censorship was exercised as to any discussion of the Polish question. This and other facts made the Independent Poles believe that there was a definite understanding on the part of the Allies to leave the settlement of the Polish question wholly to Russia. This belief was of course confirmed upon the publication by the Bolsheviki of the so-called Secret Treaties in which the Entente Allies committed themselves to an agreement with Russia that the problem of Poland should not be raised at the Peace Conference. The critical attitude thus developed toward the Entente Allies is largely responsible for the misrepresentation of the Poles who wish a completely free Poland as pro-German. It is generally claimed that it was the failure of the Entente Allies to make an unambiguous proclamation in favor of a free Poland which gave Germany its opportunity to institute the Council of State and later the Regency in Russian Poland and to carry on its propaganda to persuade the Poles that the Central powers were the truest friends of an independent Poland.

II. RELATIVE TO AUSTRIA

The Radical Poles in Austria were persuaded in the first years of the present decade that a war between Austria and Russia was inevitable. Because of the favorable status of Poles in Austria, the extreme Russian oppression of the Kingdom of Poland and the larger population and size of the Kingdom, they decided to favor Austria against Russia. An anti-Russian propaganda was carried on, young Poles were instructed in military tactics and the nucleus of a Polish Army formed. In 1912 a delegation was sent from Galicia to London stating that in the case of a European war the Polish Independents would favor Austria against Russia, and a delegation was sent to the United States to enlist the support of the Polish migration in this country. (See the paragraphs below regarding the formation of the K.O.N.) When war was declared, Polish military companies were among the very first to cross the boundary line and attack Russia. Of the Legions, the more radical were grouped under General Pilsudski, the more conservative under General Haller. The further fortunes of the Legions are related below, but at this point it may be remarked that it was until very recently the policy of the National Democratic group in Europe and of the clerical Paderewski-Smulski party in this country to denounce Pilsudski as a German agent in spite of the fact that he is the idol of very large numbers of Poles and that his name is acclaimed with that of Kosciusko. Since, however, General Haller has found his way to Paris and has become a member of the Paris Committee, these earlier tactics have become embarrassing, so that they have been dropped and there is a tendency to speak more enthusiastically of General Pilsudski. At the same time his supporters both in this country and abroad are still denounced as essentially pro-German.

III. EFFECT OF THE RUSSIAN REVOLUTION

There were three stages in the development of the international politics of Poland as affected by the Russian Revolution. In the first stage there was a much more generous and sincere recognition of an autonomous Poland than the Tsar's government had ever given expression to. This was coupled, however, with two conditions:

First, that the boundary lines of the new state of Poland were to be fixed by the Constituent Assembly of Russia without any representation of the independent state of Poland; second, that there should be a military union for the future between Russia and Poland. The Council of State of Poland (see below) issued a proclamation welcoming the new Russian Government and its recognition of the principle of independence for Poland, but protesting strongly against the two conditions attached. The Committees of the parties of the Centre and the Left also protested.

The second stage of development was constituted by the Social Revolutionary Government under Kerensky. This government made an out and out pronouncement in favor of a free, united and independent Poland, made arrangements for a joint commission between Russia and Poland to liquidate outstanding affairs, and began a movement to influence the Entente Allies to change their former attitude and come out for a free and independent Poland.

The third stage was constituted by the Bolsheviki Government. The parties of the Left in Poland were highly sympathetic with the Kerensky Government. Exactly the opposite is true of their relations with the Bolsheviki Government. This is accounted for on the following grounds: (1) As just stated, the radical parties in Poland were sympathetic with the Kerensky party. They were national socialists, not international socialists of the type represented by Lenine. There had been much previous friction between the leaders of the socialist party in Poland and the international socialists. (2) There was and is still a general belief that the Bolsheviki leaders were directly under the control of Germany, and a universal belief that the disintegrating social condition into which Russia was thrown was playing directly into the hands of Germany. (3) The Bolsheviki conspicuously ignored the cause of Poland and its leaders in their peace negotiations with Germany. With reference to the other oppressed nationalities in whose self-determination the Bolsheviki professed great interest, it agreed in article three of the peace treaty with Germany, that as respects territory occupied by German troops: "Russia undertakes to refrain from all interferences in the internal affairs of those territories and leaves it to the Central Empires to determine their future fate in agreement with their populations." Poland was of course one of these occupied states and the Poles regard this article of the treaty as a cynical betrayal of their own interests. (4) The Poles regard the Bolsheviki as largely responsible for the cession of the province of Chelm to Ukrainia.

The following quotations from the official protest indicate its general tone and show how far the Regency is from acting as a mere subservient instrument of German interests.

> The independent existence of Poland, her political life, her political and economic vitality are made empty phrases. Her interests and rights are ignored and her territorial integrity is not respected. We swore to God to stand guard over Poland's happiness, liberty and power. Conscious of our

> oath we today raise our voice in protest before God and the world, before mankind and the tribunal of history, and before the peoples of Austria and Germany, against the new partition of Poland, refusing to sanction it and branding it as an act of brutal violence.

In the resignation of all the ministers headed by Mr. Kucharzewski, constituting the Cabinet as a protest against the same measure the following language is used:

> We judged it our duty to do everything in our power to gain some influence on the course of the peace parleys, but we must state that it was beyond the power of the Polish Government to overcome the forces which were hostile to Poland, forces which combined to deal a blow against Poland by means of the treaty of Brest-Litovsk. In view of the peace treaty concluded by the two Central Powers with Ukrainia, a treaty which effected a new partition of Poland, it is impossible for us to remain any longer in our respective offices. . . . Today is the moment of greatest urgency for the people of Poland to consolidate itself and to rally around the supreme national authority because of the blow which has been dealt the Polish people. That supreme authority basing itself upon the broadest masses of the people will mark out the road for the nation to follow.

These statements are not meant in any way as a defense of the Regency as a genuinely representative government of Poland. Under German occupation it is clearly impossible for it to be completely a government of a free and independent Poland. But the facts, which could be multiplied almost indefinitely, raise a question as to the motives which prevent the Polish Agencies under the control of Messrs. Dmowski and Paderewski from making known to the world the gallant struggle which the Regency has put up under extremely hard conditions and still more the motives for insinuating that any attachment whatever to it is proof of pro-Germanism. In the end, these facts get back to Poland and this gratuitous misrepresentation perplexes the loyal Poles and reacts to the advantage of Germany. Those who engage in these insinuations are playing a part Germany would have them play.

In spite of the antagonism of the Poles to the Bolsheviki which is so extreme among all factions, conservative and radical alike, that all have been in favor of strong, Allied, and even Japanese intervention, the Russian Revolution marks a turning point in the evolution of Polish international politics. It put an end to the distinctly anti-Russian policy of the radical group and made them ready to turn against Germany. It freed Austrian liberals, including the Poles, from fear of Russia and made them willing to change from their advocacy of Trialism (Poland as a third state of the Empire on the same level as Austria and Hungary) to an independent Polish state consisting of the Kingdom of Poland and Galicia. Its influence upon the Polish socialists and radicals in the Austrian Parliament can best be brought out in connection with the next topic, for its effect was closely combined with that of the address to the Senate of President Wilson of January 22, 1917.

IV. EFFECT OF PRESIDENT WILSON'S DECLARATION OF JANUARY 22, 1917

The effect of the statement of President Wilson, that he assumed that the statesmen of all nations were agreed upon the necessity of a free, autonomous and united Poland, may perhaps be judged from a paragraph from the telegram to President Wilson of the Temporary Council of State of Poland under German occupation:

> For the first time in the present war the head of a mighty neutral power who is the supreme representative of a great nation declared officially that an Independent Polish State is the only just solution of the Polish question and an indispensable condition of a lasting and just peace. For this wise and noble suggestion the Temporary Council of State, as the nucleus of a State which is again coming to life, brings you, Mr. President, in the name of the Polish Nation and its own name expression of its most profound gratitude and respect.

The Municipal Council, the Polish National Council and the associated democratic parties all telegraphed from Warsaw to the same effect. Demonstrations took place in Warsaw before the United States Consulate. The demands of the Council of State upon the German Governor-General were more urgent and positive from this time.

A still more marked effect (in conjunction with that of the Russian Revolution) was that upon the Polish Parliamentary Club in Galicia, an organization consisting of all of the Polish representatives in the Austrian Parliament. Up to this time the Poles had voted for the budget and in general, in return for concessions, had supported the Austrian policy. Early in May Mr. Daszynski, the head of the Polish Socialist Party, stated that the Polish Parliamentary Club was losing the confidence of the public and that it must now either openly declare for the government or for the opposition and declared that no timidity must prevent the Poles from safeguarding the honor and dignity of the Polish nationality. On May 16 and 17 the Polish Parliamentary Club held a meeting in Vienna at which three motions were presented, the first from the conservative party in favor of a free, independent and united Poland under the Hapsburg dynasty; the second, that, since the government had declined to unite Galicia with the Kingdom of Poland, the Polish Parliamentary Club would no longer support the government. Neither of these motions passed. The third was a general resolution in favor of a free and united Poland with access to the sea and declaring that the Polish Parliamentary Club would no longer support the government unless there was a larger participation of Poles in the administration of Galicia. Shortly afterward, demonstrations were held in Cracow and resolutions passed in favor of the re-establishment of an independent Poland with access to the sea and declaring that the re-establishment of the Polish state with the help of Austria would secure for the latter a natural and enduring ally. In spite of the fact that access to the sea could be obtained only at the expense of Germany the Austrian Government took no steps to interfere with the demonstration. Since this time the radical party under the head of Mr. Daszynski has become even more active in opposition to the Austrian Government demanding that the latter should cooperate in the formation of a free and independent Poland. The cession by Austria-Hungary of the Polish province of Chelm to Ukrainia accentuated the antagonism of the Polish parties against the Austrian Government.

V. THE GERMAN OCCUPATION, THE COUNCIL OF STATE AND THE REGENCY

On November 5, 1916, the Central Powers issued a proclamation in favor of the independence of Poland, meaning of course Russian Poland. At the same time they began an active effort to get Poles enrolled in the German army. This was immediately opposed by a proclamation of the parties of the Left demanding that the new independent state have its own government and its own army under its own control and headed by General Pilsudski. In January the secret military organization of Pilsudski placed the Polish National Legions, which previously had been fighting with Austria against Russia, under the control of the Council of State.

In February the Council of State sent a telegram to the Emperor of Austria demanding the transfer of the Polish Army. When, in March, there was a rumor that Austria intended to recall the Polish Legions into Austria, the Council of State threatened to resign in a block on the 30th of March. The Russian Revolutionary Government recognized the independence of Poland and the Council of State replied as mentioned above. In April an Imperial Austrian decree was issued placing the Legions under the command of the German general von Beseler. Soon after the Council of State demanded the nomination of a regent and suspended its activities until a reply from the Central Powers should be received. At the same time the Congress of the National Council demanded a government and a national army together with a convocation of a parliament. In July the agitation for the Regency increased and also the demands for a less ambiguous attitude on the part of Germany. The representatives of the parties of the Left (that is to say—the parties more directly connected with General Pilsudski—see the section on the K.O.N. below) resigned. On the 9th and 10th of July the Polish Legions under Pilsudski refused the oath of brotherhood with the German army and were interned, while on July 20 Pilsudski was arrested and has been in a German prison ever since, in spite of the frequent demands of the radical parties that he be released as proof of the good faith of Germany. In view of the constant accusations of pro-Germanism brought against this radical party, the following quotation from the proclamation of the parties of the Left of August may be quoted:

> This new violation of our rights by the Central Powers is only one link more in the chain which has been forged by their Polish policies. Our belief will none the less persist in spite of everything and will not permit this terrible war to strengthen its chains. The will of the nation will triumph over the tactics of the invaders. During the war the nation has learned to appreciate better than ever before the value of an independent existence. It will oppose with all of its energy a policy of annexation which violates its rights. We salute therefore the Legions, stolen from the country by the brutal force of the Austrian-German alliance and cry aloud: "Long Live Independence, long live Pilsudski and down with the invader!"

The Legions which did not threaten to revolt were withdrawn into the Austrian Empire and for a time fought on the Italian border. Subsequently they also first declined to obey orders and later on actively revolted because of the treaty by which Chelm was ceded to Ukrainia. Some who revolted were shot, others put into prison, while a small remnant under General Haller fought its way through, and General Haller is now a member of the Paris Committee, associated with the factions which accused General Pilsudski of pro-Germanism and are still making the same accusation against the political party which is following Pilsudski. There is no reason to doubt the honesty and patriotism of General Haller and his followers. But the fact that they took the oath when the more radical element refused it, shows lack of sincerity on the part of the conservative faction which is now pointing with great pride to the hero, General Haller, as one of its own members.

After much hesitation and temporizing, the German authorities under the pressure of the threat of the Council of State to resign in a body, consented on the 12th of September, 1917, to the formation of a Regency. The three members were the Archbishop of Warsaw, whose position placed him outside all party strife, Prince Lubomirski, a representative of one of the aristocratic families of Poland who up to the time of the war had belonged to the Passivist Party but who had become an Activist under the stress of the war, and Mr. Ostrowski, a distinguished jurist, one of the former six Polish members of the Russian Council of State and the first president of the Conservative Realist Party, connections with which, however, he severed upon becoming a member of the Regency. The Prime Minister was Mr. Kucharzewski. He belonged to the liberal Activist section, having left the National Democrat Party in 1908 when the leader of the latter, Mr. Dmowski, adopted a policy of conciliation toward the Russian Tsarism.

In order to quiet the constant use of insinuations concerning the pro-German character of the Regency and of all who give support to it, it would be well to ask from Mr. Paderewski and his leading supporters a written statement as to whether they regard the Regency as other than loyal to Poland, doing the best it can under difficult circumstances, and what evidence they have of its being pro-German or consciously or unconsciously a German tool. Such a written statement would make the issue one of ascertainable facts and take it out of the realm of vague insinuations and personal attacks. It should be noted that the National Democrats in Petrograd who have been in close contact with the Regency sent their congratulations to the Regency saying that "it hails with joy the taking into your hands of national affairs."

In spite of irresponsible rumors and insinuations to the contrary, no responsible authority has ever charged the Regency with ever being pro-German or as interested in anything else than an independent and free Poland. Mr. Seyda, a recent delegate from the Paris Committee to this country, expressly relieved the Regency from any accusation of pro-Germanism. The Regency, however, is attempting to maintain a government in a territory which is under the military occupation of German forces and is subject to constant pressure from the German authorities. Under its conditions, it has pursued a balanced and somewhat compromising policy. It has devoted itself mainly to matters of internal improvement and education, reconstruction and civil administration, and while claiming for itself the right to maintain its own foreign department, sending ambassadors to other countries, and the right to maintain a national army, it has not pressed these claims with any great vigor. While regarding itself as a nucleus of the future government of the Polish State, it has not been accused by any party of attempting to usurp the rights of the future government.

All Polish parties in Poland welcomed the formation of the Regency as furnishing at least the basis for the development of a future free state. The radical parties soon withdrew from active support in all domestic matters and in the main have abstained from any participation in politics under the Regency. At the same time they recognized the Regency as a nucleus of Polish sovereignty in distinction from any party group which is formed in non-Polish soil. They justify their refusal to cooperate with the Regency upon the ground that this policy enables the Regency to bring greater pressure to bear upon the German authorities and wring more concessions from them. If the report is correct that the Regency has recently protested against the action of the Versailles Council, it looks as if the Regency had yielded more to German pressure than it had done earlier. On the other hand, it is claimed that vacillating policy of the Regency has largely grown out of the failure of the statesmen of the Allies to make a joint proclamation repudiating in effect their previous policy of entrusting the future of Poland to Russia and putting this squarely beyond the policy of President Wilson for a free, united and independent Poland. Meantime the press reports from Europe show increasing friction between Germany and Austria over the future of Poland and an increasing willingness on the part of Austria to consent to a union of Galicia with the Kingdom of Poland as an independent state whose king, presumably, would be the Austrian archduke, Charles Stephen, who is regarded as having distinctively Polish sympathies. It is not likely that Germany will consent to this move as it will render the Dual Empire much less amenable to German control in the future, and will also stir up a continually increasing desire of the inhabitants of German Poland for secession and union with the new state. Should, however, Germany be forced to yield, the new kingdom would reinforce the demand for a definite official statement on the part of all the allied governments regarding the future of Poland in order to maintain the loyalty of Poles in Poland to the Allies.

C. The Paris Committee and its Policies

I. THE NATIONAL DEMOCRATIC PARTY

This party which constitutes the backbone of the Paris Committee described below, had branches in all three parts of divided Poland. After an early period in which its aspirations conformed more closely to its name it became in each of the three divisions a party of accommodation whose purpose was, through a good understanding with the governments of the respective countries, to secure concessions regarding language, education and religion, a betterment of economic conditions, etc. In short, it was a leading Passivist party. Mr. Dmowski was the intellectual and practical leader of this party in Russian Poland. Their general politics were also monarchical and distinctively conservative in all internal and economic matters. The following from Leroy-Beaulieu, author of *Empire of the Tsars*, is an impartial statement from an authoritative French writer having much sympathy with the views of this party. Speaking of the National Democrats elected to the Russian Duma, he says that they were—

> the most conservative of all the parties assembled at the Taurida Palace. In a notorious article, Björnson, in the *Courier European*, even accused them of being secretly in the service of the Russian Government. There are of course Socialists, Radicals, Progressives, and Revolutionaries in

Poland as in all other countries, but in this case they had boycotted the elections and the electors were loyal and Catholic Poles. Almost alone in the first Duma they opposed the new agrarian laws, passed in the interests of the moujiks, while in the second they acted with the parties of the center. Thanks to their agreement, the Budget was seriously considered and its passage rendered certain. They explained that they voted for a large army, because they believed in a strong Empire.

Between the second and third Dumas the National Democrats under Dmowski's lead became so conservative that they ceased even to work with the Russian "Cadets" for constitutional reform, and became allied with the Octobrists. This affiliation with Tsardom was so extreme that it led to the secession spoken of above. At the beginning of the war Mr. Dmowski and others of his party came out for a Poland under the control of the Tsar in the manifesto referred to above. After an earlier period in which the centre of Mr. Dmowski's political activities was in Austria, he stood consistently for a pro-Russian and anti-German policy, endeavoring to persuade the Russian authorities that the German menace was such that it could best be met by concessions to the Poles that would make them strong adherents, political and military, of Russia. This policy met with practically no success. It is universally believed that Germany and Russia had a common understanding with reference to the treatment of Poland, namely, that neither country should make any concessions to its Polish subjects and would use all its influence to discourage agitation, even among the Polish subjects of its neighbor. Many believe that this understanding continued even during the war, up to the time of the Russian Revolution.

Mr. Dmowski was also well known in connection with anti-Semitic activities in Poland. His enemies claim that he promoted the introduction of Russian methods of persecuting the Jews, including the organization of Black Hundreds and pogroms. His supporters indignantly deny the latter charge and claim that aside from literary attacks upon the Jews, he has confined himself to the organization of an economic boycott. In connection with the German occupation of Russian Poland there was a general exodus of politicians to Switzerland and Paris.

II. FORMATION OF THE PARIS COMMITTEE

In May, 1917, the Lausanne Agency of the National Democrats and allied parties sent a memorandum of instructions to the affiliated group in Warsaw, in which there is sketched the plan for the organization which later developed into the present Paris Committee. The occasion for the formation of this group is stated in the memorandum as follows:

> In Paris, unfortunately, there are certain Poles who are working political mischief there, since they have the greatest influence. They are called "franc-tireurs" by some representatives of the French Government but they have openings everywhere and enjoy a good repute. To counteract their obnoxious activity it is planned to organize in Paris a Polish representative body which will, as a group, take upon itself the work carried on by individuals. This collective body will be known as the Polish House. Its director in Paris will be Count Zamoyski.

It is understood that the influential body of Poles whose mischief-making activities had to be counteracted were the Union of Polish Democrats, who constituted the least extreme branch of the Republican Left among the Polish parties. Dr. Motz and the distinguished scientific woman, Mme. Curie, were among the leaders of this group. The politician with whom they are said to have too great influence is understood to be Clemenceau, who at that time was outside the Government. The memorandum of May, 1917, contains a general survey of the politics of the Polish situation, including the relations of the various governments of the Allied Nations to the Polish question. The report boasts particularly of the great influence of the National Democrats with the British Government and says: "The center of gravity of the Polish cause lies in London."

It deplores the fact that Lloyd George is not yet won over to the Polish cause and claims that he is under the influence of Liberal Jewish circles. Regarding the United States, it says that the United States is pursuing a bold and far-seeing policy in Russia and is thinking of commercial expansion there. With reference to domestic politics it says:

> The Poles here voted for Wilson at the last election and he is grateful to them for it and values them highly. Paderewski has considerable influence on him and when conversing with him the President called the Act of November 5th a "dirty German trick." From this incident arose the famous and sincere declaration of the President; the influence of the United States in view of its entrance into the war will be predominant. . . . The Polish Central Council has elected a National Department which works hand in hand with the Lausanne Agency (see below). This department has declared that the Polish Nation is its first leader and after that

the Lausanne Agency. It demands the creation of a powerful national government outside the boundaries of Poland to whose authority it wishes to submit itself. Mr. Smulski, who possesses great influence, is the President of the National Department. Here, as everywhere, the Jews harm all work done for the benefit of Poland. Fortunately, a strong anti-Semitic movement is under way here.

In view of the attacks of the conservative party affiliated with Dmowski's group both in Europe and in this country upon the radical party for criticizing the Allies' subordination of the Polish question to Russian interests, it is interesting to note the following:

> The attitude of the Quadruple Alliance to Poland is not based upon the ideals of the freedom of Peoples, the rights of nations, etc., but upon national egotisms, the interests of the states of the Alliance, individually and collectively.

III. COMPOSITION OF THE PARIS COMMITTEE

The efforts of Mr. Dmowski and his associates were successful to the extent of gaining a certain official recognition of the Paris Committee on the part of the French and British Governments and through them of the United States Government. Although, as will appear below, the recognition so far extended is much less than that desired by the Paris Committee itself. Beside Mr. Dmowski and General Haller, who was also a National Democrat, the following are among the more important members of the Committee: Mr. Seyda, who was for a long time the editor of the National Democratic organ in Posen, in German Poland, and who, in conformity with the policy of the National Democrats, used the paper to bring about better relations between German Poland and the German Government. His brother, at last reports, was at the head of the Polish Parliamentary Club in Berlin, which has stood for the same policy. Mr. Piltz was, in the 80's and 90's, not merely a political supporter of the Russian Government, but is said to have been directly in the pay of Russia. At all events, in 1901, a pamphlet was issued in Russia under the auspices of a group with which Mr. Dmowski was at that time associated which reprints freely from the pages of a memorial submitted by Mr. Piltz to the Russian Government in which he recites the services which he and his journal had rendered to the Russian cause, including attacks upon Poles who had dreams of the reestablishment of Poland. Mr. Piltz is the member of the Paris Committee upon whom most bitter personal attacks are made because of his prior record. Mr. Skirmunt who, in earlier days, was a member of a party of Compromisists with Russia of such an extreme type that in 1908 they were criticized even by Mr. Dmowski. Count Zamoyski, a National Democrat, not previously active in politics, but one of the richest men in Poland and indeed in Europe. Mr. Kozicki, a former editor of the organ of the National Democrats in Lemberg, Galicia. Mr. Rozwadowski, a cousin of a former Austrian Consul in New York, also a National Democrat from Galicia and a landed proprietor. Major Fronczak is a representative from the United States, formerly a health commissioner in Buffalo, but not otherwise especially prominent in American or Polish-American affairs. Mr. Paderewski, the great musical artist, is also a member of the Committee and its official delegate in the United States. He had earlier relations with Mr. Dmowski and his associates in Switzerland, and is charged by his enemies with having shared Mr. Dmowski's anti-Semitic proclivities, especially through ownership of an anti-Semitic journal in Warsaw. This he denies.

In view of the ten or a dozen different political parties in Poland, and the fact that the National Democrats are only one of the several parties of the Right Wing, the very large number of National Democrats on the Committee is striking. When followers of the Paris Committee, including Messrs. Paderewski and Dmowski, were asked about the apparently one-sided nature of the Committee and their attention was called to accusations that it was unrepresentative, the replies took the following form: First, a denial that it was unrepresentative and a statement that but four or five of the eleven members of the Committee were National Democrats. This calculation seems to be based upon including only National Democrats from the Kingdom of Poland and treating National Democrats from Galicia and Prussian Poland not as National Democrats but as representatives of these two parts of Poland. After a general denial it was admitted that members of the parties of the Left and even of the Moderate Democrats of the Centre were not found upon the Committee.

This lack of representation was said to be due to the fact that these parties had no statesmen of sufficient prominence or else had a pro-German record. When attention was called to politicians of considerable prominence outside the National Democratic Party, the third and final position taken was that the present Committee had made an attempt to become more representative by including persons from groups not now represented but (*a*) that groups invited had refused to send delegates unless they had a sufficient number to control the Committee and (*b*) that the suggestion of representatives like Dr. Motz of the Union of Polish Democrats and Mr. Daszynski, the leader of the Austrian Socialists, had been turned down either by the British Government or by the General Staffs of the British and French Armies. The radical groups on the other hand claim that every effort has been made to keep them from having any membership on the Committee and, more than that, to carry on a malicious campaign of misrepresentation which would shut them out from any hearing and influence with the Allied Governments. It is obviously impossible for anyone excepting a person having some official authority to get at the truth of these varied statements and counter-statements.

In view, however, of a war waged in behalf of democracy and the freedom of oppressed nationalities, the query naturally persists as to why a group which is monarchical, representative of conservative economic interests and largely anti-Semitic should occupy such an important semi-official political status? The inferences which occur on the face of the matter and apart from official knowledge are that the pro-Russian interest of this group before the war and in the early years of the war gave them a somewhat privileged position as long as Russia was one of the Allies and in a position to dominate the attitude of the Allies on the Polish question. This group had access to the Russian ambassadors in Paris and London denied to the representatives of the Democratic, to say nothing of the radical and socialistic groups. This privileged position, having once been obtained, naturally persisted in spite of the changes brought about by the Russian Revolution and the entrance of America into the war.

In this connection it may be noted that Mr. Paderewski is quite indignant because the radical press harps upon the fact that he invited Mr. Iswolsky, the Russian Ambassador at Paris and a well known enemy of the Polish cause, to act as Chairman of the French Committee of Relief for Polish Sufferers. He says that Mr. Iswolsky is a personal enemy of his and that he did not invite him until numerous and high French political authorities had told him that it would be practically impossible for a committee to be formed under the sanction of the French Government until it had first received the sanction of Mr. Iswolsky. Moreover, any committee once formed, which has received any official acknowledgement whatsoever tends, from the very conveniences of the situation, to have its powers enlarged. Especially is this true on the military side. The Polish Army made it necessary to have someone who would speak with some official weight on Polish matters, and the military authorities would not be particularly interested in the political constitution of the committee as long as the committee existed with which it could do business. I do not know of any reason for attaching especial weight to the claims of the instructions of the Lausanne Agency, that Messrs. Seyda and Horodyski, at present an official in the English Foreign Office and formerly connected in some way with the National Democrats, have had a predominant influence in London. The same memorandum states, however, that the *Posen Journal*, edited by Mr. Seyda, is carefully read at the Foreign Office and is one of the chief British sources of information about Polish affairs.

In case any Continental power is persuaded that a monarchy of some sort is to be restored in Russia, and that a conservative regime is to emerge from the present chaos, the interest of such a power in the independence of Poland might be subordinate to its interest in a Poland which should be in quasi-military vassalage to Russia in order to secure a stronger opposition to the pretensions of Germany in the east. Considering, however, the understanding that there has always been in the past between Germany and reactionary Russia over the Polish question, and considering the great probability that a reactionary Russia would sometime in the future become an ally of an imperialistic Germany, this would be a short-sighted policy in comparison with the policy of encouraging a number of federated free states which should come between Germany and Russia and which would be the natural allies of western democracies.

In any case, the ambition of this Paris Committee to become the Foreign Office and the War Department of the new government of Poland is established through the utterances of representative members of the Committee, especially through an authoritative interview with Mr. Seyda when in this country. The furtherance of this ambition through securing the support of the American Poles was one of the chief reasons for the calling of the Detroit Convention. Although Mr. Seyda disclaimed the desire of the Committee to be itself the government of the new state of Poland, the Polish press agencies spoke of it during the Detroit Convention as the Polish Provisional Government. The effect of this ambition and claim has been to accentuate factional animosities. The representative character of the Paris Committee has been denied by a great majority of the Polish groups in Poland, by the Poles in Russia proper, by the majority of Polish societies in France and by the largest Polish Club in London. The democratic and radical groups accuse the Paris Committee of taking advantage of the somewhat accidentally won privileged position to favor their own political ambitions and the fortunes of a faction which is ultra-conservative. It is argued that if the group realizes its ambition to be recognized by the Allied Governments as the Foreign and War Departments of the new State of Poland it would logically entitle this group to take its place at the Peace Conference as the official representatives of the new State of Poland, and that this fact explains their great present activity, particularly their violent denunciations of all those who will not render them full allegiance. As is stated below, an alliance consummated in 1915 at Lausanne between this group and the representatives of the clerical party among the American Poles has given this Paris Committee great prestige and influence on American soil and is largely responsible for the bitter dissensions which now exist. While opinion which is not *ex parte* is difficult to get, there is good ground for believing that any further recognition of this Paris Committee would weaken the cause of the Allies in Poland proper and produce an alienation which would be particularly disastrous in case Germany should accede to the Austrian proposition of an independent Poland under Charles Stephen.

D. Polish Conditions in the United States

I. CHARACTER OF POPULATION

The census does not of course list Poles as Poles. Consequently there is a great variation in the estimates of the population, of Polish birth and descent in the United States, the figures running from three and a half to four and a half and even five millions. A fair estimate puts the number at 3,800,000. Polish immigrants are largely of peasant origin and although now largely located in industrial centres, continue their prior devotion to owning land. One of their chief ambitions is to own their own houses, and while they come to this country in large measure intending to return, as a rule they change their minds and settle down after becoming household owners. There is general agreement among the Polish leaders that the change from peasant conditions to congested city life has a deteriorating effect, intellectual and moral, upon the immigrants, especially the children of the first generation. Any governmental or semi-governmental agency which would secure a distribution of Polish peasants through the rural districts of the United States with the opportunity of owning their own farms would be generally welcomed. The Poles are especially represented in the mining and steel industries, and at the present time they are prominent in ship-building and munition making. So far as the great mass of the Polish population is concerned, the question of origin in Russian, German or Austrian Poland respectively is of no special importance. The unity of language, of religious worship and of devotion to past national history outweigh the differences of origin. At the present time, however, this latter difference is a source of considerable friction because Austrian and German Poles are, technically, alien enemies. The number of German Poles is comparatively small, but the Austrian Poles who feel themselves as patriotic as the Russian Poles feel that they are being discriminated against, especially in important war industries, without justification.

II. ORGANIZATION AMONG AMERICAN POLES

Preliminary to a brief sketch of the main organizations which will be given below, in the next section, it may be said that Poles in this country are not well organized. They compare very unfavorably in this respect with the Jews, Bohemians, Russians and even Italians. Considerably less than 10 per cent. of the Poles belong to any organization having a national membership of any kind, beneficiary, ecclesiastical or political. This fact makes it easier for the leaders of the small number of organized Poles to manipulate the Poles as a whole and to profess to speak in their name. The history of Polish organizations in this country is very complicated. It presents a series of secessions, alliances, splits and fights within organization. Three factors seem to have chiefly operated in bringing about the succession of changes.

1. *Financial.* The largest and most important organizations have had to do with beneficiary funds. The primary aim was to assist newly arrived Polish immigrants in facing their strange and difficult economic conditions. These beneficiary activities include building and loan associations, protection against sickness, death, etc. In the years immediately preceding the outbreak of the war, an organization was formed for raising and sending funds to Europe to be used there for propaganda and in behalf of a free and independent Poland and for military training in connection therewith. The war itself has of course added the raising of funds for Polish relief.

2. *Clerical.* This head cannot be strictly separated from the previous, for the first great split, that between the Polish National Alliance and the Polish Roman Catholic Alliance came about through dissensions concerning the control of finances which led to the formation of the Roman Catholic Alliance as a new organization. In general, these organizations are clerical in the sense of interesting parish priests rather than involving general church policies or the activities of the hierarchy. In fact in domestic matters there is a good deal of friction between the Polish priests, the Irish priests and the hierarchy. Poles point to the fact that they have but one Catholic bishop and claim that Irish and Germans are constantly favored at their expense. There is also a good deal of friction between the Polish clergy and the Irish on the subject of Americanization which the latter favor, and the former, especially the parish priests of the older generation, who were themselves born in Poland, oppose. So far as any general statement can be made on such a complicated matter, the fear of Americanization is not directed at American political and social life as such but is due to the belief that Americanization would lessen the personal and direct control of the parish priests over their own flock. While there is a numerous and powerful Protestant group in Prussian Silesia, the Protestants are not represented in any number among the Poles in this country. This has the unfortunate effect of encouraging factional strife along religious lines for, there being nothing which might be called a religious middle

class, there is a sharp division into clericals and anti-clericals, running through the whole intellectual and moral life of the Poles, including the Polish press.

3. *Political.* This, upon the whole, has been a decidedly subordinate factor, especially so far as domestic politics are concerned. Upon the whole the Polish population has given its votes to the Republican Party. The headquarters of Polish affairs in general are in Chicago, and Mr. Smulski, who has been very influential in Polish affairs, has been closely affiliated with the local Republican machine. In the Philadelphia district, with the exception of a socialistic group, the Poles were practically entirely under the control of the Penrose machine until some of the Polish clubs recently went over to the Vare faction. In the campaign of 1912 the advertising agent of the daily which was the organ of the Polish National Alliance took the sum of $5000 for backing the Republican candidate for president of the United States. Although a motion was passed at the convention of the Alliance that the money should be returned, it is stated that the Polish National Alliance never complied with the resolution, due, it is charged, to the influence of Smulski.

III. CHIEF ORGANIZATIONS

The Polish National Alliance was the first formed and is still the largest. It was formed in the 30's to promote the general interest of the immigrants which, for a long time, it did very successfully. During the Civil War it made a fine patriotic record. The next largest organization is the Polish Roman Catholic Alliance or Union, which, as already stated, split off, due primarily to a dispute as to whether laymen or priests should have primary financial control. For a number of years a fierce struggle was carried on between the National Alliance and the Roman Catholic Alliance, until, under considerations related shortly below, the Roman Catholic Alliance virtually got control of the National Alliance. Up to 1912, the only organization of Poles in the United States which took an active interest in European Polish politics was the Alliance of Polish Falcons or Sokols. The original purpose was the military training of youth with an ultimate view for the struggle for Polish independence. As the prospects for Polish independence became more and more remote the societies became more of the nature of the German turnverein. The athletic interest was not very strong and the societies did not prosper. Moreover, about 1905, there was a split between the so-called free Falcons whose headquarters were Pittsburg and the old line Falcons, whose headquarters were Chicago and who were pretty closely affiliated with the Polish National Alliance. In 1912 the development of a revolutionary movement in Galicia began to have its reflex effect upon this side and a convention was called to meet at Pittsburg to reunite the two branches for the purpose of again engaging in active support of the revolutionary movement abroad. At the same dates a meeting was called, also to convene at Pittsburg, under clerical auspices, to represent all the Poles of America. Meantime representatives of the Pilsudski radical party in the United States came to an understanding with the more nationalistic part of the Polish National Alliance and with a minor group, the Polish Young Men's Alliance, to attempt to bring about a union not merely between the two groups of Falcons but between them and the larger convention of Poles. The aim was to unify all immigrant groups in America whatsoever in support of the European movement for a free and independent Poland. Mr. Debski, a naturalized American citizen, represented General Pilsudski at the convention and so great an enthusiasm for an independent Poland was created that a new and unified organization was formed. This was the Committee of National Defense generally known from the initials of the corresponding Polish words, K.O.N. This organization was created then in Pittsburg, December, 1912, and was the first general organization in this country having the independence of Poland as its object. The following resolution was passed:

> Since we are thousands of miles away from our native country and cannot actively participate in the national policy, we submit to the direction of the united independent parties in Poland who were represented at Zakopane in the fall of 1912 by their delegates and who are now creating a military fund for the Polish Army. In accordance with the political program of the above mentioned parties, we pledge ourselves to assist by all means the revolutionary movement against Russia, the greatest enemy of Poland, the representative of oppression, barbarism, darkness and absolutism in Europe and of de-nationalization. For the purposes of giving our help to this movement we herewith create the Committee of National Defense. Long live the armed struggle, long live liberty. Long live the independent Republic of Poland.

The above resolution was accepted with a sworn oath by representatives of all Polish parties in America. The president of the Polish National Alliance was elected president, the president of the Polish Catholic Alliance treasurer, and Bishop Rhode was made its honorary president.

In view of these facts, which can easily be substantiated by reference to historical documents, it appears either that those who now represent the K.O.N. as having been formed under Austrian auspices and through the activities of Austrian delegates in this country, and even financially supported by the Austrian Embassy, are guilty of wilful falsification, or else that the representatives of the Polish Alliance and of the clerical organizations who are now making these statements about the K.O.N. were themselves in 1912 wilfully guilty of representing a movement undertaken in behalf of Austria as one undertaken in behalf of a free and independent Poland. As between these two alternatives, choice is easy.

In June, 1913 the clerical members of the K.O.N. seceded. Their opponents claim that the secession was due to inability to control the new organization for their own purposes. At the same time the National Council was formed. The character of this National Council is seen in the following words taken from their own official report: "The National Council has been created by organizations at whose head stands the Polish Roman Catholic Alliance under the protection of the holy heart of Jesus." Meantime, the Polish Alliance found itself between two fires, that of the more radical element among the immigrants together with those most interested in the revolutionary struggle for free Poland, and the Catholic Alliance on the other hand. In the years of 1913 and 1914 it practically surrendered to the Roman Catholic Alliance and in the latter year also seceded from the K.O.N. The subsequent official report of the Roman Catholic Alliance congratulates itself upon the virtual surrender of the National Alliance.

Meantime, in the spring of 1914, representatives of the more reactionary groups went to Europe and there formed the connection between the Polish National Alliance and the National Democratic group which is referred to in the Lausanne memorandum of May, 1917, as stated above. The foreign politics of the Alliance then ceased to be anti-Russian and became pro-Tsar. The existence of this affiliation is confirmed from American as well as European sources. The report of the National Council uses the following language:

> We address ourselves to those who represent in all three partitions the decisive majority of the nation and who are united in their aims, the National Councils in Galicia and in German Poland and the National Democracy in the Kingdom. Our press bureau is in close contact with the corresponding institutions of the National Council in London, Paris, Rome and Zurich.

Omitting the flourish about the "decisive majority," this passage shows clearly the conservative affiliations of the National Council. Although it became under these auspices pro-Russian, it did not take a stand in favor of the Allies. It warned the Polish immigrants from sending their hard-earned money for relief purposes to any of the countries visited by the war excepting Poland.

The National Council came out at the same time openly and avowedly against Americanization.

> The Poles from the fourth part of Poland, the Poles in America, must above all struggle against the abuse of American liberty. From this grows an indifference toward Poland and, at last, total Americanization.
>
> We have here English-American educational institutions which blind us with their official status and perhaps appeal to our pocketbooks by means of their free education. Thus they kill the voice in the depth of our conscience which causes us to sacrifice ourselves for our native country.
>
> We give our children to be guided by strangers; we transplant them into a strange soil where they unfortunately assimilate strange fluids, lose their Polish elements and gradually are lost. American-Poland thus loses her children and if the movement goes on that terrible moment will finally come when the Poles in this country will cease to be called the fourth part of Poland, for they will be finally lost.

After the Polish Victims' Relief Committee was formed (see below), under the direction of Mr. Paderewski, it was combined with the National Council and constituted the so-called National Department, which has since then arrogated to itself the control of Polish affairs in this country. For a short time this National Department was a sub-branch of the National Council and the Polish Victims' Relief Committee, but later on the relationship was suddenly reversed and these two societies became branches of the National Department. So far as we have been able to discover the new organization was formed at the desire and wholly by the action of a few leaders. In any case, it brought about that hopeless mixture of different lines of Polish activity which is largely responsible for the present difficulties and harmful factors in the Polish situation. For it combined without any definite division of labor or proper coordination relief activities due to the war, general philanthropic and insurance activities of domestic concern among the Poles, political activity, both domestic and, through the relation of Mr. Paderewski to the Paris Committee, foreign, and the ecclesiastical organization of the Roman Catholic Alliance. It would be difficult to have invented an organization more calculated to introduce confusion and one more fitted to lend itself to purposes of manipulation from the top. This "Holding Company" constituted the basis for calling and managing the Detroit Convention and for the organization for the permanent control of the Poles which developed therefrom. (See below.)

We thus have the definite cleavage of Polish parties in America lined up in association with the cleavage in European politics. On the one hand the remnant of the K.O.N. which remained true to the principles of a struggle for Polish independence directed primarily against Russia and laid down in 1912, is associated with the political policies of the radical group headed by General Pilsudski, now in a German prison. On the other hand is the priestly and conservative faction which, since 1914, has been directly connected with the National Democratic party in Europe and engaged in endeavoring to mould the mass of the Poles in this country in support of that faction, an arrangement which was consummated at the Detroit Convention of August, 1918, described below.

To clinch its control upon the American situation, the conservative faction has consistently denounced the K.O.N. as either actually pro-German in desire and principles or, in their more guarded statements, as pursuing a policy which is pro-German in effect. These denunciations are based in part upon ignoring the historical European facts related above, in part upon falsification of facts regarding the formation of the K.O.N. in 1912 and in part upon mistakes in policies of the leaders of the K.O.N., although it must in fairness be stated that those now opposing the K.O.N. shared earlier in many of these mistakes. These mistakes as to policy have to do with the Polish Army (spoken of below); the attitude toward the Regency, and the criticisms of the Allies, especially Great Britain.

The K.O.N. has taken a too favorable view of the Regency as a legitimate provisional government of an independent state of Poland, glossing over too much the effects of the military occupation of Germany. This mistake has lent itself to misrepresentations on the part of the enemies of the K.O.N., based partly upon insinuations of the definitely pro-German character of the Regency and partly upon misstatements of the motives of the K.O.N. The extent and nature of the attachment of the K.O.N. to the Regency have been much exaggerated. In domestic policies, the K.O.N. in common with the parties of the Left in Poland itself are strongly opposed to the Regency, because of its clerical, monarchical and aristocratic constitution, as well as a matter of strategy in enabling the Regency to bring greater pressure to bear upon the German authorities. In foreign relations, they have claimed that being on Polish soil the Regency had a claim for recognition possessed by no body of immigrants on foreign soil. This claim is due partly to matters of historical consistency. Because of the number of past Polish insurrections and rebellions, the issue as to whether the provisional governing body should be on Polish soil or not is an old one. On this position, the K.O.N. has maintained the former position of the radical wing, while Mr. Dmowski has shifted. The other and probably the chief reason of the claim is that the radical parties preferred the Regency in spite of its conservative character to the domination of the group controlling the Paris Committee. While individuals have at various times unwisely urged the official recognition of the Regency by the Allies, the May, 1918, convention of the K.O.N. in Philadelphia went no further than the declaration:

> We express our highest respect for the Regency of the Kingdom of Poland, the only present authority in Poland, for its dignified protest and struggle in counteracting German aggression against Polish independence and its struggle against attempts to form so-called Polish governments abroad without the authorization of the Polish Nation.

The last clause is clearly aimed at the Paris Committee.

At the present time the issue of the Regency so far as Poles in America are concerned is a dead one. The K.O.N. leaders have recognized the unwisdom of their former policy and ask now only for a commission of representatives of the different parties among the Poles under the control and supervision of the United States and the Allies to get into contact with all groups in Poland, including the Regency. Members of both the conservative and the radical parties have stated to us that through various underground channels via Switzerland and Stockholm such contact is entirely feasible.

The criticisms of Great Britain and France are due to two causes. In the first place, there is strong emotional sympathy between Poles as representing an oppressed nationality and the Irish. The radical Poles have thus associated themselves to an undue extent with the extremists among the Irish in this country. The other cause is the committal by the Allies of the cause of Poland to Russia, the great historical enemy and oppressor of Poland. This source of friction was largely removed by the entrance of America into the war and the belief that American influence would dominate in the Peace Conference the influence of any European country, and by the pronouncements of the Versailles Council. There is a tendency not confined to the radical element to criticise the Allied Governments for not reinforcing the declaration of the Military Council. The leaders of the K.O.N. at the present time have agreed to forgo all further criticism of the Allied Governments and to use all their influence with their adherents throughout the country to discourage such criticism.

Much has been made by the enemies of the K.O.N. of their socialism. The purpose was to link up the K.O.N. with the unpatriotic attitude of the official socialist party of this country as stated in the St. Louis Platform, and thus strengthen the accusation of pro-Germanism, or at least of indifference to the war. In fact the K.O.N. in this country, like the radical party with which it is affiliated in Europe, is not in orthodox socialistic standing because it puts nationalism before internationalism. The adherents of the K.O.N. in this country have been officially expelled from the socialist party. Before the United States entered the war, Polish socialists in Pennsylvania were disciplined because they collected money and sent it to General Pilsudski, the orthodox socialists objecting that this showed a militaristic and nationalistic spirit. While in Chicago in the last municipal election the radical Poles mainly supported the socialist candidate for mayor, in

New York City, where the loyalty issue was more definitely raised, they supported Mr. Mitchel and denounced Hillquit bitterly.

While there may be individuals among the K.O.N. who were distinctively pro-German in their sympathies and while there may even be German agents among them as among other elements of our population, I cannot speak too strongly of the malicious campaign of insinuation, misrepresentation and personal attack carried on against the leaders of the K.O.N. These leaders in New York are three, Mr. Kulakowski, who is evidently the scholar and intellectual leader of the group, Mr. Debski, an editor and man of action, and Mr. Sosnowski, whose European associations were more distinctly military. I have had no personal contact with the last named, but it is striking that the stories about him concern matters of personal character not matters of loyalty, and that disparaging personal reports are then used to insinuate a probable pro-Germanism. The stories reflecting upon Mr. Sosnowski's personal and financial integrity are denounced as maliciously false by his friends including reputable Americans, and I am credibly informed that a Pole from Warsaw who (when in this country) was the source of these reports declined to meet Mr. Sosnowski to make his charges face to face. In my judgment if these reports are deemed relevant to the situation, as they are by Mr. Paderewski's associates, the charges should be put in writing and Mr. Sosnowski and his accusers brought together under impartial auspices.

I have seen personally enough of the first two named to be convinced of the falsity, the malicious falsity of reports disseminated—such as that Mr. Debski owes a farm which he owns in New Jersey to the assistance of Mr. Dumba, the former Austrian minister to the United States, a story so demonstrably lacking in any basis of fact that only malice can account for its circulation; also that a photograph exists of him "in an Austrian uniform," in spite of the fact that the uniform is one of the Polish Army and was taken when Mr. Debski at the risk of his life visited Warsaw when it was under German occupation to strengthen the hands of the Polish Nationalists against German intrigue. Both of these men were engaged in struggles for the independence of the Poles in Europe, both of them have risked imprisonment, their fortunes and even their lives in behalf of the cause of free Poland, in a period when those who are now bitterly attacking them were making no sacrifice at all and were living in ease and prosperity and on good terms with the oppressors of Poland. In spite of this and of the fact that Mr. Debski is the official representative of General Pilsudski in this country, no insinuations are too base to be made against these men.

I add merely one illustration of the methods employed because a number of the officers of the Military Intelligence Bureau were witnesses of the episode. At an interview in Washington on August 17 with Messrs. White and Wedda of the Polish Press Bureau, Mr. Stalinski, a civilian agent of the M.I.B. and former chief dragoman of the American Embassy in Petrograd, was present at the invitation of the M.I.B. Mr. White made insinuations against the nature of Mr. Stalinski's interest in the Polish question and in this connection, as if it were a final proof of the unworthiness of Mr. Stalinski, asked if it were known that he had been associated with Mr. Lednicki in Petrograd. When I told him that I knew nothing whatsoever about Mr. Stalinski's relation to Mr. Lednicki, but would Mr. White please explain in what way that reflected upon Mr. Stalinski, in case he had been associated in any way with him, Mr. White replied, "We will not go into that now." Now it happens that Mr. Lednicki is the leader of the Polish Democrats among the Poles in Russia; that, like others of this group, he was in very good relations with the Kerensky Government; that he was appointed by the Regency as the chairman of a commission to come to some settlement of matters between Poland and Russia under the Kerensky regime; that the Bolsheviki declined to recognize him, presumably because of pressure from the German Government—that Mr. Lednicki is, in short, a man of integrity, force and character, the only thing to be said against him being that he is a radical, though not an extreme one, instead of a conservative. I mention this incident not because it compares with the accusations of graft, high living, personal crookedness, etc., brought against Mr. Kulakowski and Mr. Debski, but because it offers an excellent illustration of the method of innuendo and insinuation which has been used, and in dealing with Americans ignorant of foreign politics, used very successfully, to discredit all individuals and activities which would not supinely surrender themselves to the Syski-Paderewski-Smulski combination in this country.

The methods are such as to invite scrutiny and cross-examination of the motives of those who employ them in such a way as to close, so far as they are efficacious, to the United States Government important channels of information and influence; and to breed strife and dissension among Poles in this country at a time when the maximum of unity is indispensable. There is considerable reason for thinking that in addition to personal and partisan motives, some of the leaders of opposition to the K.O.N. have been unconsciously used by German influences, for nothing would help the German propaganda among the Poles here and abroad more than to discredit the radical group of the Poles by attaching to it the stigma of pro-Germanism. While the K.O.N. group is numerically smaller among the organized Poles than the National Alliance or the Roman Catholic Alliance, it contains, by the common consent of its adversaries, the "ablest and brainiest" among the Poles in this country and has the greatest influence among all of the more intelligent and skilled workingmen. The only reason greater harm has not been wrought by these malicious persecutions is the thorough-going loyalty of the leaders of the K.O.N. to the American Government. They are so persuaded that the hope of a future free and independent Poland lies with the United States that they have submitted with unusual calm and patience to a campaign of misrepresentation. The critical attitude taken toward the Allies already spoken of has its other side in an intense belief in the unity of the cause of Poland and the United States in the present war. This belief in the United States and the policies of President Wilson has been represented by their enemies as an attempt at a belated camouflage of their pro-Germanism. The somewhat extended study of the material put forth by the K.O.N. throughout the war has completely convinced me that this charge is a falsehood, whether due to ignorance or deliberate malice.

It can be established by sufficient documentary evidence that the K.O.N. is less responsible for the present strife and dissension than its opponents. The latter have been in the position of greater advantage and began the attack. In addition, the K.O.N. has repeatedly in the interest of the unified waging of the war made advances for a truce and combination of forces, and these advances have been ignored or turned down by the Smulski-Paderewski faction. In October, 1917, such a proposition was made by representatives of the K.O.N. to officers of the National Department provided the latter would agree to the condition that the United States should "take over the matter of Poland and direct it on behalf of the Allies." In an "Open Letter to Mr. Roman Dmowski" under date of September 9, 1918, it is proposed that the "Committee of Paris should join in with the representatives of the party of the Left, organize a consulting body which should assist with its wealth of information and its various connections an Inter-allied Commission for Polish affairs, with headquarters at Washington." It also proposes meetings for the joint discussion of methods of bringing about the realization of common national aims, a representative of the United States Government to be present at all the parleys, "since it is the United States Government which has the exclusive right of control over any and every political activity undertaken and conducted on American soil." It sometimes seems as if in addition to personal quarrels and cut-throat factional methods, the devotion of the K.O.N. to American leadership in dealing with the Polish question were one of the motives for the attempts to discredit its leaders by means of false statements.

IV. METHOD OF UNDERSTANDING AND INTERPRETING POLISH CONDITIONS IN THE UNITED STATES

In dealing with activities among the Poles, whether in the press, conventions, public discussions or private rumors or reports, the following considerations need to be borne constantly in mind.

1. The mass of the Poles are unorganized and have no articulate means of expression. The war has brought about a sharp cleavage among the organized Poles into the clerical and conservative party on the one hand and the anti-clerical and radical on the other. Since the mass of the Poles are good Catholics, it is comparatively easy for the priestly party to profess to speak for them and to manage matters so that this profession will seem to be substantiated by the facts (see section on the Detroit Convention below).

2. Conditions and activities among the Poles in this country cannot be understood excepting as they are projected upon the European background. As previous statements show, three factors are of chief importance in this background: First, the division among Poles into the relatively liberal policy of Austria and the

almost absolutely illiberal policy of Russia; second, the division into Activists, who are in favor of keeping up the revolutionary struggle for the independence of Poland, and the Passivists, who are in favor of giving up the struggle and reaching a *modus vivendi*; third, the conflict between the monarchical and economically conservative party and the democratic, radical and anti-clerical party—a division largely coinciding with the last, namely, that between the Activists and the Passivists.

3. The historic sequence of events must always be borne in mind. No statements about any person, condition or activity can be correctly interpreted unless it is placed in its proper historic sequence. The important dates are: the abortive revolution of 1905–06 and the developments in connection with the constantly increasing withdrawal of constitutional government in Russia; 1912, as the time when revolutionary activities came definitely to a focus in Galicia; the beginning of the war in 1914 and the Russian attitude toward Poland together with its acceptance by the Entente Allies; and 1917, with the speech of President Wilson, the Russian Revolution, and the entrance of the United States into the war. To ignore the changes and re-alignments brought about by this succession of events is to lose the clue to understanding the events in question.

Conclusions

1. Owing to the long duration and the intensity of the factional struggle between the conservative and radical parties, all statements, charges, accusations, etc., proceeding from one side against the other should be made in writing, and the statements made so specific and definite, together with the evidence therefor, that the authors of them can be held definitely responsible in case further inquiry shows that there is ignorance or misrepresentation. In every case the past record of any person or movement mentioned should be fully investigated, and all statements made cross-examined and motives for making them carefully scrutinized. If this course is followed, the various details thus presented will be found gradually to fit together and to give a fairly complete and accurate picture of the course of events among the American Poles. I have attempted in this report to give an outline which is

fairly comprehensive and as correct as possible in its main features. The course which I have just recommended would serve to fill this outline and, in fact, to test its correctness. If additional details brought to light by the method suggested fit into the outline, that fitting in will establish its accuracy; if they do not, it will prove that we have been misled. I gladly submit the report to such a test.

2. There is not the slightest doubt that the great mass of Poles in this country, including those who are nominally following the Paderewski-Smulski leadership, are firmly convinced of the importance of American leadership in the war and peace policies regarding Poland. This point of view has been repeatedly stated to us, even by those who at the Detroit Convention voted in favor of committing the Poles in this country to direction by the Paris Committee. This conviction is due both to President Wilson's attitude on the Polish question when the statesmen of the other Allied Nations were silent and to the fact that historical conditions and geographical position make the United States disinterested in a sense in which no European country can be. There is good reason for believing that both the Poles and other oppressed nationalities regard the question of American leadership in exactly the same light and are perplexed and discouraged by the apparent subordination of American leadership to that of a group of exiles in Paris. When this general issue was raised with Mr. Paderewski, he took in the course of the conversation the following positions: First, that there is no need of accentuating American leadership, because there is complete harmony and agreement at the present time; secondly, that he himself made this proposition in connection with the formation of a Polish Army almost a year and a half ago and was turned down; that the leadership of the Paris Committee is now an accomplished fact and that the recognition of this committee by France is so definite that it would create friction even to have an American Commission on Polish Affairs; third, that the United States is the natural guardian of the interests of not only Poland but of all of the oppressed nationalities of Europe, but that he as an official plenipotentiary to this country of the Paris Committee could not suggest any change in the present arrangement; that any change would have to come from the initiative of the United States, and that if it came, he would "in principle" accept it. In his public speeches and private conversa-

tions, Mr. Dmowski also emphasized the great importance of the United States in connection with the future of the Polish question. The willingness of Poles to accept a distinctively American commission which should bring about a unity among the different factions of the Poles, make a special study of the Polish question and get into relation with Polish conditions abroad, would seem to be a fair test of whether any Pole or group of Poles put foremost their personal and factional interest or their desire for a free and independent Poland. The notion that such a commission need in any way interfere with the Paris Committee and the status which it now officially possesses is, of course, absurd. An American commission would naturally cooperate with the Paris Committee and with all other Polish organized groups. The only things that an American commission would interfere with is the ambition of the Paris Committee to become a provisional government for Poland and to be its representative at the Peace Conference; and the desires and activities of those Poles in America who are so afraid of Americanization that they actually prefer allegiance to a group on foreign soil to an active interest in the Polish question on the part of the United States embodied in a distinctly American commission.

E. The Detroit Convention

A brief account of this convention will exemplify in a specific, concrete instance the operation of the forces which have been described.

I. THE OBJECTS OF THE CONVENTION

There were three closely intertwined causes for calling this convention to meet in the city of Detroit in the week beginning August 26. The first, the financial one, is described at greater length below. It involves at least four factors: the funds of the Polish Victims' Relief Fund, of the Military Commission, of the Chicago headquarters and of the local Citizens' Committees and parish groups immediately concerned in raising funds; second, a triangular quarrel carried on under an external show of complete harmony so far as the American public and press are concerned, between Mr. Paderewski and his immediate associates, the Chicago group of which Mr. Smulski is representative, and thirdly the group of priests of which Bishop Rhode and Father Syski are said to be the more prominent leaders. The execution of the plan formed in 1914 to have the Poles in this country work under the direction of the conservative National Democratic party of Europe is the feature to which attention will here be directed.

In July, Mr. Seyda, a highly conservative member of the Paris Committee and the one reputed (as stated above) to have very great influence with the British Foreign Office, was sent to this country with a definite mission. Whether or not he reported to any of the governmental authorities in Washington I have no way of knowing. On July 16, 1918, the Executive Committee of the National Department held an official interview with Mr. Seyda. After this, it passed the following resolution:

> The Executive Committee sees in the National Polish Committee the political organization which controls Polish affairs. Under its direction it will work, as it has done heretofore, for the Fatherland. The Executive Committee recognizes this Polish National Committee as the only competent authority in all matters of national Polish politics and the National Polish Army.

The context shows that this resolution was passed in connection with the preparation of the National Department for the Detroit Convention. At the same meeting a telegram was sent to Mr. Dmowski, inviting him to come to the convention.

Fully to understand this resolution and the cable to Mr. Dmowski in its bearing upon the convention reference should be made to contemporaneous events in Washington. Some of the American daily papers of the date of July 18 carried an account of a bill to be introduced in the Senate by Senator Hitchcock. This proposed bill, in addition to recognizing a free, independent and united Poland, carried a clause which expressly recognized the "Polish National Committee whose headquarters are in Paris, France, as the official representative of the Polish people." The bill expressly gave this Committee the power to send diplomatic representatives to this country. Its representatives here were among other things to have the power to determine whether Poles having technically the status of enemy aliens should be continued in that status or should be regarded as citizens of a friendly state. (It later appeared that the draft of the bill was not intended for publicity and was given to the press only through the carelessness of a clerk in Senator Hitchcock's office.) At the same time it came to our knowledge that representatives of both the British and the French Government in this country expressed the desires of the British and French Government to have the Paris Committee officially recognized by all the Allies as the Foreign and War Departments of the new State of Poland and that some of these representatives in private were criticizing the American Government quite freely for obstructing the execution of this desire. These facts appear to establish beyond question the purport of a resolution which was prepared, as was acknowledged by Mr. White at the joint interview at Washington, for introduction at the Detroit Convention: a resolution strongly recommending the recognition of the Paris Committee *as the Foreign and War Departments of the new free and independent state of Poland.* It is in the light of these facts that the affiliation of 1914, the visit of Mr. Seyda, the resolution of July 16, the cabling of Mr. Dmowski and his appearing in this country to attend the convention, have to be understood. (It should be added in this connection that according to information coming from Senator Hitchcock's office, the draft of the bill was sent to him through the medium of the Polish Press Bureau in Washington which represents the interests of Messrs. Paderewski and Smulski respectively.) During the visit to Washington previously referred to, it was urged upon Mr. White of the Polish Press Bureau that this resolution was open to construction as an attempt to bring pressure to bear upon the American Government to do what up to the present time it had declined to do voluntarily. I was informed by Captain Uterhart that in view of this consideration, Mr. White informed him that the proposed resolution would not be offered.

II. THE CONTROL OF THE CONVENTION

In order to give the resolutions due weight, the convention was represented in the call issued for its convening as "the greatest possible political and national occurrence for all Poles in America without exception, a visible, external embodiment of the external will of the whole immigration." As a matter of fact, the convention was kept wholly within the control of the small committee constituting the National Department. The means of securing this control were twofold.

1. The rules for electing delegates. These rules were so vague and complicated that they were freely criticized during the month of August by a majority of the Polish daily newspapers in the United States, including those which have been in the main hearty supporters of the Paderewski-Smulski faction, as well as the independent or so-called business Polish press. The clerical papers were the only ones which unanimously and heartily defended the rules. In the first place, very generous provision was made for honorary or *ex officio* delegates. In addition to two organizations mentioned by name, "the presidents of all clerical groups and all secular national organizations having groups in different Polish communities" are included. Also local Citizens' Committees and the local centres of the National Department which pay dues are entitled to *ex officio* delegates. Again, the organizations which are entitled to elect delegates were not stated by name. What was the object of leaving the provision vague and ambiguous cannot well be determined, but there is no doubt that the effect was to increase the control of the Executive Committee in Chicago. In Philadelphia, for example, an organization having a state-wide membership had its elected delegates refused credentials on the ground that this organization was not one of those entitled to send delegates. This ruling was later reversed because of pressure brought to bear, but it showed the powers which the Central Committee took upon itself even before the Convention had met and appointed its own committee on credentials. It is noteworthy that there had been friction between the Pennsylvania organization and the Chicago committee over the handling of funds and that in Philadelphia this refusal of credentials was regarded as a disciplinary measure.

The control of the Roman Catholic Alliance is seen in the following regulations. The boundaries of election districts for local delegates are to follow closely the parish boundaries. The electoral meetings of societies and local communities were to be called by the parish priest and were to be presided over by him unless he delegated the office to somebody else. In the rules for the conduct of the convention it was expressly provided that priests' societies should not be called upon to render an account of funds collected for public purposes. While, nominally, provision was made for mass meetings, these were conspicuous for their absence in Philadelphia, as well as in other places from which we had direct reports, the delegates chosen being practically self-elected by a very small group of persons who were directly affiliated with the organizations calling and controlling the convention.

2. The care taken to control the convention is even more obvious in the rules laid down in advance by the National Department for the conduct of the convention. With the exception of one day, the general meetings of the convention were devoted to listening to speeches and to hearing general reports, financial and otherwise, from different Polish organizations. In each case the rules specified that the speeches should be heard and reports listened to without discussion. The actual business of the convention was put in the hands of seven sectional meetings. For six of these, the important ones, clerks were appointed at least four weeks in advance by the Executive Committee of the National Department and these clerks drew up the topics and projects to be considered by these sections. Rules made it difficult for any delegate to present new material. The members of these sections were not elected but appointed by the chairman of the convention. While the general convention took final action on resolutions, etc., at the last day of the meeting, rules provided that nothing could come before this full meeting excepting what had been previously passed upon at one of the sections. Moreover, no discussion could be had by the general convention of any of the measures thus presented excepting at the written request of at least one-third of the voting delegates of the section.

The rules were obviously designed in the first place to exclude the possibility of any adequate representation of the K.O.N. and of the dissenting non-clerical factions in general. They were also designed to keep under cover the various elements of friction and dissatisfaction which existed within the more conservative party on account of the triangular quarrel already referred to. In conversations with the leaders of the factions, they justified the rules for electing delegates and conducting the convention on the ground first, that they were at all events no worse than those frequently employed in American political conventions and secondly that the situation was so delicate and "explosive" that it was in the interests of Polish unity and harmony to keep control in strong hands and to keep public discussion and criticism down to a minimum.

III. DECISIONS OF THE CONVENTION

It is not possible to report the activities of the convention in any great detail. An air of secrecy, or at least privacy, rather than of publicity hung about the convention. The reports in the Detroit newspapers were meagre and for the most part general, being to a considerable extent of the nature of press agency notes. The *New York Evening Post* and the *Christian Science Monitor* were the only American newspapers having correspondents present. Requests to a news clipping bureau for all items regarding the convention have brought forth only notices from Pittsburgh, Pa., and Utica, New York, papers, both mainly occupied with speeches of Mr. Paderewski. Up to the present not even the Polish press has, so far as our inquiries extend, made any adequate report of the actual conclusions of the convention. So far as information is accessible, the following are the chief results of the convention:

1. The control of the present organization of the National Department was confirmed, Mr. Smulski of Chicago being elected permanent chairman of the National Department. All Polish affairs were confided to this organization having five branches: military affairs, relief, financial, press and educational. To some extent, the demand for greater supervision of funds was met by providing for the election of a supervisory body composed of one delegate from each state to meet annually. The control of the present organization was clinched by a provision that the credentials of the delegates to the Detroit Convention should be good for all other assemblies and conventions held during the next four years. According to the report in the *Christian Science Monitor* there was friction between the representatives of the Roman Catholic Church and the Independent Polish Catholic Church. "The main point of contention between the clericals and the loyalists is the domination or attempted domination of the Poles in the United States by the priests. The main objection and indeed the only objection to the Polish Legions is the domination of its organization by the clericals." According to the same paper, about one-third of the thousand delegates were Roman Catholic priests and the rest of the delegates were so largely Roman Catholics that the priests dominated the convention.

2. With reference to the war, it was planned to raise an army of half a million, forty thousand or fifty thousand to come from

this country and the great bulk of the remainder from Siberia and Russia. It was voted to raise a million dollars a month for relief funds, funds for insurance, etc., in connection with the army. How this was to be done, in view of the small amount raised in the past, public reports have not made clear.

3. Mr. Dmowski was present as representative of the Paris Committee and according to press reports dominated the convention. Some reports state that, according to Mr. Dmowski, consulates are to be formed in the various cities of the United States which shall issue certificates of Polish Nationality to Poles in this country who are not American citizens. The press reports that he stated that this plan has already the authorization of the State Department of the United States. The resolutions, besides calling for a free, united and independent Poland including Dantzig, were less imperialistic than previous utterances of the National Democrats in that they welcomed the "freedom of Poland's sister, Lithuania." Pains were also taken both by Mr. Dmowski and the final resolutions to assure the Jews that they would not be oppressed in the new State of Poland.

F. Specific Points of Friction and Discord

I come now to the particular sore points and causes of dissatisfaction and dissension, the local evidences of which in Philadelphia first led to the inquiries whose results have been stated above. I have included only such points as tend to produce conditions which slow down activities connected with the war or introduce such strife as is generally unfavorable to the morale of the Polish population and which lends itself thereby to carrying on of anti-American and even pro-German propaganda. While different heads are treated separately, most of the matters touched upon cut across each other. This is particularly true of the relation between the first head, that of personal differences, and financial matters, relief funds, White Cross and publicity for Polish affairs.

1. PERSONAL

Personal differences centre very largely about Mr. and Mrs. Paderewski on the one hand, Mr. Smulski and the politicians allied with him in Chicago on the other, and a few of the priests whose ambition for personal control and prestige are said to be disturbing factors. We personally have come into contact only with the first and accordingly that is the only one discussed and with regret that the situation makes it necessary to repeat what under ordinary circumstances would be gossip of an objectionable sort. But at present, these personal matters have crystallized into public opinion which is a material and influential fact.

No one questions the eloquence, personal charm and influence of Mr. Paderewski nor his ability in handling in a diplomatic way matters which are brought to his personal attention. The value of his name and high standing as a musician are also recognized as constituting him the best known of all Poles in American circles. In fact it is generally said that he owes his prominence primarily to the fact that his is the only Polish name which is widely known among the American people. This position of his personality is said even by those who criticize his methods and regret his influence to make him an inevitable figure-head for Polish politics and relief activities in the United States. The gist of the criticisms might be said to be that he would make an admirable constitutional monarch who should reign but not govern and reign on condition only that he be surrounded by a strong cabinet of competent advisors and efficient executives. This condition, however, is very generally stated not to be fulfilled—and it should be understood that the criticisms here related come from persons who are outwardly devoted followers of Mr. Paderewski, many of them delegates to the Detroit Convention. It is said that his vanity is such that he can be easily played upon and used for personal ends by those who surround him. There is evidently considerable competition among members of the different circles who have access to him, for in private conversations they freely deprecate the influence of others over Mr. Paderewski and not infrequently refer to those in some other circle as crooks. It is also generally recognized that, while a great artist, he is not a business man and that he has not insisted upon the development of strictly business-like methods on the part of those about him.

The strongest criticisms and the most general ones are directed against Mrs. Paderewski. It is pointed out in the first place that she is not a Pole, but the daughter of a Russian father and Roumanian Jewess mother. It is stated that her influence over Mr. Paderewski is inordinate, and that he is given to yielding in important matters of general policy to her personal desires; that she is a very strong and energetic person who insists upon having her finger, directly or indirectly, in every form of Polish activities, and that where she cannot rule she attempts to ruin. The mildest criticism of all those made against her that we have heard is that she is hysterical and lacks business sense; the strongest that she has an insane egotism which stops at nothing to secure personal prominence for herself. The alleged anti-Semitic activities of Mr. Paderewski so far as they do not follow from his connection with the National Democratic party are said to be due to her influence.

The criticisms directed against her are shared by her son and Mr. Paderewski's step-son, Mr. Gorski. He is President of the Polish Victims' Relief Fund. It is said that there is nothing in his past record or present activity to justify his holding this position, which he is said to hold simply through the personal influence of his mother. His lack of energy, influential acquaintances and executive ability is freely criticised as one of the causes of the comparative failure of the Polish Victims' Relief Fund. Reports are freely circulated to the effect that he draws a very large salary, variously stated at from \$150 to \$300 a week, \$200 being the usual statement, for acting as President of the Relief Fund, although giving but an hour or two to its affairs. In reply it is stated that his salary does not come from the Relief Funds but from his mother's own funds. Then there is the countercharge that Mme. Paderewski pays him herself from a fund of \$20,000 transferred to her from the finances of the Polish Military Commission. I cannot too strongly state that we have no evidence whatsoever regarding any of these charges or countercharges, but that the effect of their constant circulation is extremely undesirable and that some authoritative investigation and statements which would put them all to rest once for all is much needed.

Leaving out of account the pettier personal matters, the criticisms of Mr. Paderewski are that he is so easily influenced by persons who have at a given time his ear that he does not pursue a consistent and comprehensive policy but shifts unaccountably from time to time; that he has been too closely affiliated with pro-Russian and pro-Tsar persons and influences—in this connection the Iswolsky incident related above being referred to and also an interview which he gave to the British press before coming to this country in which he spoke in fulsome terms of the "divine clemency of the Tsar's soul" toward Poland; and that up to comparatively recently he had too many sympathizers with Germany in his immediate surroundings and that he was, in ways in which he was not himself aware of, made use of by German influences. His former close relations with Mr. Knaap, the owner of the *Wolna Polska*, which is popularly regarded as his personal organ, are cited in this connection.

II. FINANCIAL MATTERS, RELIEF FUNDS, ETC.

There is very general dissatisfaction with the financial side of Polish affairs in this country. This dissatisfaction concerns the amounts raised, the methods used in raising funds, the way in which funds are managed, expended and accounted for, and the attempts which have been made to retain a monopoly of the prestige, publicity, etc., connected with war and relief funds in the hands of the Paderewski family.

1. The published statement in the *New York Times* for September 8th of the amount of money received by the Polish Victims' Relief Fund is somewhat less than $1,100,000. Considering the number of Polish immigrants in this country, the prosperity of their wage earners during all of the recent years of the war and the fact that they have not been able to send money home as they were accustomed to doing before the war; considering, also, the enormous suffering in Poland and the sentimental interest of Americans in Polish affairs, together with their sympathy with all European sufferers, this sum is regarded as pitiably small. Its meagreness is compared with the amount raised for the relief of other nationalities who have suffered from the war, especially the Belgians, Jews and Armenians. The smallness of the net amount has led to criticisms and recriminations which are directed not merely against the Paderewskis but against Americans. The tendency is for those who are criticised to defend themselves by laying blame on American citizens for indifference to Poland. There are even claims made of covert antagonism on the part of Americans, an antagonism which is said to have worked constantly against Polish interests. The friction between the Paderewski group, the Smulski group and the Polish priests previously referred to seems to be connected in large measure with diversity of opinion about financial matters and methods, but it would be difficult for anyone not having official authority to determine the

exact nature of this friction. Aside from lack of energy and executive ability and aside from a tendency to subordinate an interest in Poland to the public prominence of various groups of individuals, the real causes for the comparatively small amount of money raised seem to be found in the considerations which are stated in the other paragraphs of this section.

2. There is considerable disgust and resentment at the methods used in raising funds, since these are said to cheapen the whole Polish cause. It is particularly objected to Mme. Paderewski's activities that instead of presenting the importance and significance and the real sufferings of Poland, she diverts attention to secondary, trivial and often personal matters. Her devotion to bazaar methods and to the sale of dolls is cited in this connection. More serious are the criticisms passed in connection with the so-called May Drive conducted under the auspices of the Paderewskis for the sake of raising funds to be used in connection with the support of the National Polish Army. Great preparations were made and much attention given to the matter in the Polish press and pulpits. Up till at least the Detroit Convention, no public statement of funds received in this drive had been made. The charges and countercharges in connection with these funds played a large part in the financial reasons previously alluded to for calling the Detroit Convention. It was repeatedly stated to us that the local Citizens' Committees and the priests who were influential in raising the funds declined to send their money to the Chicago headquarters because funds previously sent were still unaccounted for, the reason being that these funds had been spent for secret diplomatic and political purposes which it would not do to make public. The local organizations holding funds said that such expenditures might be perfectly legitimate, but they ought to have the right to send and keep delegates in Chicago who could oversee this use of secret funds so as to avoid abuse. Rather, so it is reported to us, than to consent to this supervision, the Chicago headquarters proposed a convention which should arrange for a new and more satisfactory method of handling funds. The specific criticism of Mme. Paderewski in connection with the May Drive relates to concerts which were organized under the Paderewskis' auspices and given under the direction of a Pole named Wronski. It is said that he was paid the very high salary of $350 or $400 per week which, of course, had to come

out of the funds raised and which used up a large part of the funds, and that these concerts were conducted after the amounts raised did not even cover expenses including his salary. The subject matter of the talk or lecture accompanying the concert in which the appeal for funds was made was, to put it mildly, of a trivial and undignified character. Of the twenty slides shown, not one had to do with conditions in Poland or even directly with the Polish Army. In addition to slides of the Paderewskis, the caption for Mr. Paderewski being "Our Pride, Our Glory, Our Leader," most of the slides had to do with a so-called Golden Book to be taken by Mr. Paderewski and deposited in the Royal Castle in Cracow after the war. The slides told of the various diplomas that would be granted by the parish priests for gifts to the fund and the ways in which the name would be written in the book.

3. Method of managing and expending funds. It is claimed that there is unnecessary duplication of offices and salaries through a multiplication of organizations; that there is neither a sharp line of division between the activities of these different organizations nor yet a coordination among them; that this duplication and overlapping not merely increases expenses but also lends itself to looseness in financial methods and to a crossing or switching of accounts between the various societies. This last charge is the most serious one which we have heard made on the financial side. In support of the charge of unnecessary duplication it is pointed out that in New York City alone there are expensive offices at the Hotel Gotham, the Aeolian Hall and at 70 Fifth Avenue, and it is said that the work could be done not only more cheaply but much more efficiently if the different offices were adjacent to each other. It is asked why, since, by an order of the War Trade Board, funds can be sent to Europe only through Mr. Paderewski, local organizations should have to transmit their funds first to Chicago. This lack of unity and organization and accompanying publicity is, discounting the charge that there is actual graft and misuses of funds, the chief reason for the various rumors and charges which are afloat.

It is unfortunate that no sharp line of division exists between the distinctively relief activities and funds, those connected with the Military Commission for the support of the Polish Army, the political and propaganda funds and those used for publicity regarding Polish affairs in general and Mr. Paderewski and Mme.

Paderewski in particular. This lack of definite organization gives rise to charges that funds raised ostensibly for relief purposes are devoted to other uses, military or political or press publicity. In a particular instance, a gentleman who gave one thousand dollars to the Emergency Aid fund to help Polish sufferers was asked afterward if he were willing to have the money given for Polish army purposes. He consented, but the impression left was not a favorable one since the whole matter was handled through the Polish Victims' Relief Fund which was supposed to concern itself only with the relief of victims. The organ of the National Polish Alliance, regarding the funds of the May Drive already referred to, publicly announced that instead of the funds being used in connection with the army—the ground on which the appeal was made—they will be reserved for use in connection with the Peace Conference. Local societies in Philadelphia had been accustomed to send their funds direct to the relief committee in Vevey, Switzerland, because, as they explained, they got prompt and satisfactory accountings and also were given due local credit. Finally they were directed to cease sending their funds direct to Switzerland, although the committee there was formed with Mr. Paderewski himself as one of its sponsors, and to send their money to Chicago. The refusal to conform to this order was said by Philadelphia Poles to be the cause of the refusal, referred to in connection with the Detroit Convention, to accept certain delegates. These and other similar incidents which we ran across quite incidentally illustrate both the current dissatisfaction and discontent and the cause of this friction in the absence of proper unification and coordination of the societies raising, handling and expending funds.

4. Perhaps the most serious stories that have come to our notice in connection with relief funds concern the alleged jealous desire of Mr. and Mrs. Paderewski to monopolize all of the glory connected with the raising of funds and to keep things quite strictly under their own control. A brief history of the organization connected with Polish relief since the outbreak of the war may throw light upon this matter. At first the Central Polish Relief Committee was established in Switzerland to send money to the starving population in Poland. This Committee consisted of Messrs. Sienkiewicz, Osuchowski and Paderewski. In America the National Polish Alliance collected money through its section called the Independent Section, the Roman Catholic Alliance

through its section the National Council, and the Polish Falcons through the Kosciusko Fund. In 1915 these societies consolidated and established the Central Polish Relief Committee in America. Mr. Paderewski was at that time in Paris and was cabled to to permit his name to be put among the honorary members of the Committee. He replied by cable that it would be inadvisable for him to do so. He was then in Paris and this was the period in which he formed the Committee under Ambassador Iswolsky previously referred to. When he arrived in New York the American Committee sent him a telegraphic greeting to which he did not reply, claiming afterward, when the matter was brought to his attention, that he had never heard of the Committee.

Mme. Sembrich had been elected president of an organization for Polish relief formed in New York City including in its membership a number of Americans with important banking and social connections. This society was succeeding in raising money and at one entertainment at the Biltmore raised something like $10,000. Mr. Paderewski was repeatedly urged by Mme. Sembrich and others to join this committee and help. He declined on the ground that he had been sent by Poland and that representing the whole of Poland he could not take the place of merely a member of an American Committee and that a committee on which he served must be national in its composition. He also announced that on a reorganized committee no Poles excepting himself and those whom he might name could serve and that instead of sending funds to three organizations in Poland, as well as to a relief committee in Switzerland, all funds must be forwarded through "his" Swiss Committee. He particularly objected to sending funds through the Supreme National Committee of Cracow on the ground that the military branch of that committee was responsible for the Legions fighting under Pilsudski against Russia. It was in this connection particularly that charges were made against General Pilsudski as a German agent, Mme. Paderewski claiming, so it is stated, that he got a mark from the German Government for each Polish soldier who joined the Legions. Mr. Paderewski then set out to organize a committee of his own, diverting, so far as possible, the influential members of the committee of which Mme. Sembrich was the head to his own rival organization. About the same time insinuations were made against Mme. Sembrich of pro-German sympathies and even that she was a paid German agent. Soon after this Mme. Sembrich suffered a nervous collapse and in consequence thereof withdrew from connection with Polish relief. A number of influential Americans, disgusted with the general turn of events, withdrew also and have not since given any attention to Polish sufferings. A few members in protest attempted to form a Polish-American relief commission, but it did not live long.

A somewhat similar story concerns the activities of Miss Naimska. Miss Naimska is a modest and unassuming woman and has suffered so much in connection with her endeavors to aid sufferers in Poland that she personally declined to talk, as did her brother-in-law, Dr. Lewinski-Corwin. Dr. Lewinski-Corwin is Secretary of the New York Academy of Medicine and the author of *The Political History of Poland* which is spoken of in the July, 1918, number of the *American Historical Review* as the best history of this phase of Poland yet published. In spite of the high character of both of these people, when they declined to subordinate themselves to the Paderewski interests they were reported as pro-German sympathizers and engaged in pro-German activities. The story which follows was obtained from friends and, I have every reason to believe, is reliable. Miss Naimska went to Poland to help in work for Polish women and children in the early summer of 1916. She was invited by the Women's League in Poland, which was the largest women's organization there, to represent them in America and to collect money for the orphans and the starving children of Poland. She returned to America with the proper credentials and in a very short time cabled $2000 for Poland and formed branches of the Polish Women's League in fifty-three different cities. In spite of Miss Naimska's credentials and of the fact that she had proper vouchers for every cent collected and sent to Poland and that in addition her accounts are audited and sent to the Charity Organization Society in New York, her work suffered constant opposition and she herself underwent constant persecution. The organs of the Paderewski interests stated that she had never been in Poland, that her authorization papers were forged and that the money collected was sent not to Polish children but to German children. At the present time the organization to which she belongs is holding the sum of $17,000 because the money was largely given by people who distrust Mr. and Mrs. Paderewski and who made it a condition of their gifts that the money should not pass through the Paderewski channels. There seems to be no reason to doubt the statement that a very much larger sum of money could easily have been raised among the Polish women in this country together with American sympathizers if so much time and energy had not had to be spent in overcoming accusations and rumors started by opposing factions.

The Countess Turczynowicz is an American woman married to a Polish gentleman and has also published a book, *When the Prussians Came to Poland.* When she began independent activities under the auspices of the American Y.W.C.A. for Polish reconstruction work, she encountered opposition from Mrs. Paderewski. Countess Turczynowicz's first activity was to raise money for Polish sanitariums. This was to have been done under the Polish Military Commission, and Mrs. Turczynowicz was made a member of the Polish Sanitary Commission, but suddenly Mrs. Paderewski ordered the Polish Military Commission not to permit the Countess to have any more meetings. She was, however, offered a position with a salary of $500 a month and travelling expenses to work under Mme. Paderewski and raise money. Upon asking what would be done with the funds she would raise she was told that that was none of her affairs. She was also told to turn over all the money she had already raised, or otherwise the Military Commission would warn the Polish people against her and she would not be allowed to do any further work, and soon after this personal attacks appeared upon her in the papers allied with the Paderewski faction. This story may be found in some detail in the *Kuryer Polski* of Milwaukee, Wis., of June 9, 1918. So far as we can learn the essentials of the story have never been denied, and the main features Countess Turczynowicz has confirmed to us. Mrs. Turczynowicz, being an American woman and of a different temperament from some other persons who have engaged in Polish relief work, has not been intimidated and is continuing her activities. She is, however, so far as we can learn, the only exception to the statement that the Paderewskis and the people immediately associated with them have attacked and in the end driven out of activity every organization which they could not personally dominate.

Other instances of the attempt to maintain a monopoly are said to be shown in such instances as the following: President

Wilson proclaimed January 1, 1916 as a Polish Day. The money raised was, however, to be sent through the Red Cross and not through the Paderewski committee. The result was such antagonism that only a few thousand dollars were collected throughout the whole country. In the early part of 1916 reports were current that it was impossible for money and clothing to reach Poland, and the Paderewski committee in this country took no steps to contradict the reports which were having an injurious effect on the raising of funds. In reply to a cablegram to the Vevey Committee (of which, it will be recalled, Mr. Paderewski was one of the original members), a message was received on March 7, 1916, stating: "We are able to forward money and supplies to Poland without impediment."

Independent organizations that attempted to have Tag Days in Polish communities for raising funds were antagonized in ways which often were obscure or even secret. In some cases the police were asked to interfere. In one case, that of Newark, a direct connection was established between one Miukowicz and Mr. Gorski in New York. This Miukowicz, having been rebuffed by the Poles in Newark when he tried to get the collection of funds stopped, reported to Mr. Gorski and then returned with a number of Poles to Newark and drove about the city doing what they could to discourage the collection of funds. The following letter signed W. A. Pawlowski, Los Angeles, Calif., dated Aug. 3, 1918, is characteristic of the methods everywhere employed. The letter is addressed to the treasurer of the Polish Women's League of Los Angeles and reads:

> In reference to our recent conversation regarding raising funds on the streets some time in September, I wish to advise you that your society will have the heartiest endorsement from the Allies' committee in this work as soon as it has procured the proper credentials from the official Polish representative, His Excellency, I. J. Paderewski.

Not only do the followers of Paderewski speak freely of him as ambassador, plenipotentiary and excellency, but, as will be seen from the quoted letter, his official status as representative of the Paris Committee is used to maintain the monopoly of his own relief society when other means fail.

III. THE WHITE CROSS AND THE RED CROSS

The creation and activities of the so-called White Cross appear to afford another case of the ill-advised activities of Mrs. Paderewski undertaken with the support of her husband. In the month of April of the present year the Polish press in this country which support the Paderewski leadership announced that a Polish Red Cross was to be organized in the United States as a branch of the Polish Red Cross in France which was working in connection with the Polish National Army, and that Mrs. Paderewski had been named as the President of the Polish Red Cross in France and would accordingly act in a similar capacity in the United States. Mr. Helinski of the Polish Military Commission was even named as the authority for this statement. Since, of course, no such action had been taken, the inference is that the statements were made in order to prepare the way for some such action. The scheme, however, came up against certain obvious insuperable obstacles, such as that there could be a French Red Cross and an American Red Cross, but until Poland was an independent state there could be no Polish Red Cross, and even if there were, its sphere of activities would have to be confined to Poland. The scheme was, however, soon revived in another form. About the middle of the month of July the friendly Polish press announced that a Polish White Cross had been formed in France and received the official sanction of the French Government and that Mme. Paderewski had been appointed its American head. In France, however, it was announced that a White Cross had been formed in America and would work in connection with the Committee for Aid of the Polish Wounded which operated under the auspices of the French Red Cross. The fact that the French Government has not permitted on its own soil any organization which did not work under the French Red Cross appears clearly in the cablegram from Paris of the date of July 12, which gives the authorization under which the White Cross in this country is operating.

> The French-Polish Military Commission, coöperating with the Polish National Committee, have formed a Committee known as the "Aid for Polish Wounded." This Committee will work in close connection with the affiliated societies of the French Red Cross and also directly with the Polish organization in the United States of which Mme. Paderewski is president.

The statement of July 29 of the French Ambassador in Washington, M. Jusserand, is to the following effect:

> The French Ambassador takes pleasure in stating that he has been

informed that the Polish White Cross (having the same aims of the Red Cross in other countries) organized in the United States by Mme. Helene Paderewski, president, has been accorded full recognition in France and is acting in conjunction with the Committee for the Aid of Polish Wounded in Paris of which Count Potocki is head.

These official documents make it clear that Mme. Paderewski first formed a society in this country of which she made herself president and then secured for it recognition from France, a recognition, however, which is absolutely confined to America and does not give a Polish White Cross any official status whatsoever on French soil. Under such circumstances, the misleading statements published in the Polish press and practically universally believed among Poles and especially the Polish women in this country who are immediately affected, are, to say the least, very unfortunate. In this connection it should be noted that efforts are being made wherever sewing circles or other organizations of Polish women exist which have been working for the Polish wounded to turn them into Helene Paderewski Circles of the White Cross. In some communities, at least, these organizations are being informed that they cannot continue unless they become Helene Paderewski branches of the White Cross.

There is no reason to think that the facts as we found them in Philadelphia are at all exceptional. Judging from these facts, the formation of the White Cross, which is operating practically as a rival of the Red Cross, was most undesirable. The Polish women were working mostly under the auspices of the Pennsylvania Emergency Commission which was officially constituted in order to take care of suffering which might arise in connection with any families speaking foreign languages which were represented by the allied armies in France. The women of the weaver district in Philadelphia where the men largely belong to the K.O.N., were working directly under Red Cross auspices. We found absolutely no trace of any desire anywhere for any new organization; in fact a great preference for existing organization and positive resentment at having a new one forced upon them.

In addition, certain specific evils have shown themselves: (1) There is an increasing belief that interest in Poland is being subordinated to personal glorification and ambitions. (2) Polish women are being more and more segregated to work independently of American interests and of American women, when the war would naturally have otherwise thrown these women into closer contact with Americans and with the cause of America. Thus the war is being used to arrest instead of to facilitate the process of Americanization. (3) Much ill-advised and harmful criticism and misrepresentation of the Red Cross has been aroused. The cause was the necessity of justifying the White Cross against criticism and answering questions as to the necessity of a new and duplicate organization having new offices, officers, and, presumably, salaries. In order to answer these questions and show that the White Cross was necessary, a campaign of misrepresentation of the Red Cross has been carried on, in a veiled way in the Polish press, in a more open way in personal and private conversations. It has been variously stated that the American Red Cross would only look after American soldiers in France and that the White Cross was necessary to see that the wounded in the Polish National Army were cared for. It has been stated that the Red Cross would not support the hospitals for the soldiers of the Polish National Army. Since the American Red Cross especially offered to support such hospitals but naturally made the condition that the hospitals be under its own management and not under that of an independent organization, the animus of this accusation is clear. Reports have also been circulated that the American Red Cross is not as much interested in general Polish relief as it is in the relief of other oppressed nationalities; it is insinuated that an official now connected with the Red Cross but formerly connected with Paderewski's relief organization has used his influence against the interests of Polish victims and of Polish wounded. Finally, it is charged that since the White Cross has received official recognition the Red Cross is so jealous and antagonistic that it refused to permit surgical and other relief material to be sent to France if shipped by the White Cross for the Polish National Army. Judging from analogous episodes, it is safe to say that if the White Cross does not become a marked financial and social success, such accusations as these will increase in number and intensity.

IV. THE POLISH ARMY

On the face of it, the importance of the issue of the Polish National Army in this country is due to the attitude of opposition formerly taken on the part of the K.O.N. and the order of the

United States Government through the Military Intelligence Bureau after the Philadelphia Convention of May, 1918, that the K.O.N. should disband unless it ceased its opposition. Beneath this question, however, there are a number of matters of greater importance as indications of fundamental conditions and as influencing the attitude of Poles toward the war and toward the United States.

1. The chief military argument for the existence of a distinctively Polish Army is the effect of the existence of such an army upon the efforts of the German authorities who are occupying Poland to recruit Poles for the German Army, as well as to arouse enthusiasm in Poland and among Poles everywhere for the cause of the Allies. These reasons are accepted by all parties as making desirable the existence of a Polish Army. Differences and disputes concern the location of authority over the army. The National Democratic Party, having secured its recognition by means of the Paris Committee, has pushed an army under the French Military Commission and under the Paris Committee as a means of furthering the recognition of the Paris Committee as the War Department of the New Kingdom of Poland and thereby improving its own position in the future struggle for the control of Polish politics. In the public press members of this party talked in large terms of a Polish Army of half a million to be recruited largely from the United States. In more sober official communications they appear to have committed themselves to a claim that a Polish Army could be raised consisting of 100,000 to 150,000—a claim which, as will appear below, has affected in an unfortunate way the nature of the recruiting campaign in the United States.

On the other hand, the opposition to the Polish Army by the radical party in Europe and by the K.O.N. in this country is due to the fact that this army is now virtually under the control of what the radical party regards as a one-sided and unrepresentative faction and that this control so increases the prestige of the National Democratic Party as to give it an unjustifiable advantage in the determination of the question whether the future Poland shall be a monarchy or a republic and whether it shall be economically imperialistic and reactionary or democratic and progressive. It is freely asserted that the virtual control of the Polish Army by the Paris Committee has been the chief factor in retarding the formation of an effective army to fight on the side of the Allies out of the Poles who previously fought on the side of Russia. It is estimated that there were 700,000 Poles on the side of Russia. But it is generally claimed that the great majority of these Poles, owing to previous sentiment and still more to the recent rapid growth of radical sentiment in Russia, so distrust the National Democrats that they are unwilling to fight under its auspices. The claim is freely put forth that with a more official recognition of a free, independent and united Poland by the Allies and the formation of a comprehensive and representative commission of all parties, it would be comparatively easy to enroll a large army from Russian Poles. We have not of course been in any position to investigate the merit of these claims, but they are made so positively that they would appear to be worth looking into by those who are in a position to ascertain the real facts.

In any case, the claim to control of the former Polish soldiers in the Russian army is becoming a matter of increasing interest. On account of the relative failure of recruiting of Polish legions in this country, the party of Paderewski and Dmowski is now making great claims concerning them—see the section on the decisions of the Detroit Convention—in spite of the fact that evidence available (which is not adequate for a full judgment) tends to show that the soldiers are upon the whole radically inclined. General Dowbor-Musnicki, the Commander of a Brigade in the First Polish Army Corps who is himself a National Democrat, has issued the following statement which seems to put at rest the claims of any persons—like those of some young officers who have recently come to America—to speak officially for the Polish Army of Russia: "Since the dissolution of the First Polish Army Corps, no organization in Poland or outside of Poland, or any individual or group of individuals has the right to represent or to express any opinion in the name of the Army Corps or to speak or to act in its name."

2. Friction in the United States. The opposition of the K.O.N. to the recruiting of a large National Polish Army under the auspices of the Paris Committee and the cessation of this opposition at the request of the United States Government are well known facts. It should be understood in connection with these facts that the leaders and press of the K.O.N. and the radical parties in the United States were at the same time carrying on a very active campaign for enlistment in the United States Army. According to

our investigations there is not the slightest justification for the assertion freely made that these efforts to recruit for the United States Army were an insincere camouflage. They appear to have been undertaken in good faith and carried on very energetically. The facts show that quite independently of any opposition of the K.O.N., the cause of the Polish National Army has not been popular with the Poles in the United States. Instead of the large numbers talked about (Polish recruiting officers and one branch of the Polish press talks loosely about an army of fifty or sixty thousand), only about fifteen thousand have been recruited. Too much has been made of the alleged fact that enemy aliens in Class Five who were not eligible to enlist in the United States Army constitute a natural reservoir for the Polish Army. As a matter of fact, statistics regarding Poles recruited in New York for this army show that over 80 per cent. come from the Kingdom of Poland and would therefore in any case have been eligible as volunteers in the United States Army. It is noteworthy that the same statistics show that less than 6 per cent. of the same recruits belong to the National Polish Alliance; three times that number to the Polish Falcons who, while they have recently broken loose, were earlier affiliated with the K.O.N. The comparative unpopularity of the cause of the Polish Army seems to be due in the main to the natural preference of the great majority of Poles to ally themselves with the American Army. There is, however, a great deal of dissatisfaction among the Poles, including the officers of the Polish National Army, with the character of the local recruiting stations in the United States. Charges of incompetency, lack of energy, etc., are freely made. Dissatisfaction with the management of the Military Commission located at 70 Fifth Avenue has also been much in evidence. Some of the army men have claimed that they seem more interested in politics and in maintaining their affiliations with the Paderewski-Smulski group than in disinterested work for the Polish Army. Such evidence as we have been able to gather indicates that this so-called Military Commission has spent much more of its time and energy in trying to collect funds to be used in connection with the army, insurance, relief of dependents, etc., than in stimulating recruiting and a direct interest in the army. The dissatisfaction with its failure to make a public statement of funds collected has already been referred to. The methods of the Military Commission in dealing with the local recruiting officers are also criticized. It is claimed that the Military Commission compels the local officers to advance funds out of their own pockets. This charge is not made in connection with accusations of graft but as indicating a desire on the part of the Military Commission to keep the local officers under their own political management.

In order to make good the extravagant promises made in France regarding a Polish Army to be raised in the United States, Messrs. Paderewski, Seyda and many of the officers of the Polish Army in the United States have agitated in favor of the following:

(*a*) That all declarants, all who have not completed their full naturalization, should be compelled to go into the Polish Army instead of the United States Army; (*b*) that all Poles who are citizens but who did not speak and understand English freely, should be taken out of the American Army and turned over to the Polish Army; (*c*) that the large number of persons who, under pressure or enthusiasm, enroll in the Polish Army and then do not report for duty should be treated as military deserters.

While, naturally, the American Government has not acceded to any of these claims, their constant urging has created more or less friction among the Poles. While this does not usually culminate in physical violence, cases have been reported to us from Chicago where the ill-feeling became so great that Poles in the American Army and in the Polish Army beat each other up and strife was produced among the civilian members of their respective families. Additional friction has been caused because the American adherents of the Paris Committee, in order to justify themselves for their meagre success in getting recruits, have freely criticized the United States Government for failing to accede to the three requests spoken of above.

The somewhat curious greater devotion of the civilian Military Commission of 70 Fifth Avenue to raising funds rather than to raising an army has been associated with some misrepresentation of the actual status of the soldiers in the Polish National Army. In order to stimulate the raising of funds, the pay of soldiers by the French Government, the amount of protection afforded their dependents, etc., have been much understated. In this connection, a full page advertisement in the periodical

Free Poland, for the month of June, which misstates the facts in such a way as to throw discredit on the French Government, is pointed to.

3. The United States shares of course the interest of all the Allies in the maintenance in Europe of Polish troops sufficient to neutralize German efforts in Poland and actively to attach the interests of the Poles everywhere to the cause of the Allies. There are good reasons for doubting whether the present methods are the best for this end. A somewhat aggressive Polanizing and de-Americanizing campaign has been carried on in connection with efforts to secure recruits for the Polish Army in this country—in order, that is, to get those in Class Five who are eligible to enter the American Army to enter the Polish instead. Polish officers in speaking to us have made no attempt to conceal the fact that they are first and always Poles and that they regard it selfish of the United States not to encourage the transfer of Poles from the American Army to the Polish Army. No such Americanizing campaign is possible in Camp Niagara as is effectively carried on in American camps such as Camp Gordon. The small number recruited for the Polish Army makes this de-Americanizing movement of comparatively slight importance, although it tends to spread to the families and friends of those concerned.

If for this de-Americanizing tendency there could be substituted conditions which would appeal to the American sympathies of the mass of the Poles, recruiting for the Polish Army would, in my judgment, be greatly stimulated. The great industrial importance of Polish labor in this country must be borne in mind and the fact that there will be a shortage of labor after the war and that there is already a movement under foot (which should be carefully looked into) to stimulate the return of Poles and others of foreign birth in Southeastern Europe to their native lands after the war. With the sharp commercial competition that will necessarily take place after the war, any tendencies which on the one hand de-Americanize and on the other hand strengthen the allegiance of those of foreign birth to the United States deserve careful attention. The question may be raised whether, in view of the change of the draft age and the great number of new recruits for the American Army thus made available, and in connection with the comparative ease with which an American commission could handle the question of Poles who are enemy aliens, technically, a readjustment of the Polish Army question might not be advantageous. Without interfering in any way with the existing Polish Army under French Military control, Poles from this time on might be encouraged to join a Polish Army under directly American control. These new Polish Legions could easily be affiliated with the proposed Slavic Legions under American control. There is every reason for thinking that the better pay, provision for insurance and allotments for dependents, together with the much better educational conditions at American camps, would soon bring about the recruiting of a large Polish Army and thereby make up for the comparative failure of the present Polish Army.

V. POLISH PUBLICITY IN THE UNITED STATES

There is much dissatisfaction with both the amount and the quality of the publicity given to the cause of Poland in the United States. Intelligent Poles feel, and apparently with great justice, that the cause of Poland is, after that of Belgium, the most important of the issues of oppressed nationalities for which the war is waged—that, in ulterior importance, it ranks even higher than the cause of Belgium because of the greater extent and larger population of Poland and its extraordinary strategic position as the key to future war and peace issues of Europe. In spite of this importance, the cause of Poland receives comparatively little publicity. The responsibility for this is placed pretty directly upon the Polish Associated Press, of which Mr. James C. White is the director, located in Washington. It is said that this press bureau is more interested in acting as a press agency for Mr. and Mrs. Paderewski and other prominent individuals than it is in securing public discussion of forces and facts about Poland and that instead of acting as a just medium of communication and expression for all Polish interests, it is rather a centre of gossip, tittle-tattle, and intrigue of one faction against another. (For additional matter on this subject see the second preliminary memorandum handed in August 23, 1918.) The veil of privacy and secrecy which was thrown about the doings of the Detroit Convention and the absence of any reporting of this convention which purported to represent the interests of four million Poles in America shows, so it is argued, either their complete inefficiency, or else that the Polish Associated Press is not really interested in publicity for Poland at all but simply in serving personal private ambitions and the interest of a faction.

General Conclusions

There is unity among the different groups of Poles regarding the war and regarding the purpose of establishing a free, united and independent Poland with access to the sea. Differences among them concern primarily the means and methods to be employed in attaining this end. But these differences as to method go back to different conceptions of the nature of the new state of Poland. One party is Pan-Polish and talks freely about a population of thirty and even thirty-five million—a number which could not possibly be reached without annexing non-Polish elements in large numbers. It desires a strong monarchy and conceives of Poland largely as a buffer state between Russia and Germany; looks forward to the reestablishment of a monarchy though not a Tsardom in Russia and expects to be, if not directly under the influence of Russia, at least closely allied to it. In the main it is Pan-Slavic as well as Pan-Polish. By access to the sea it understands a breakup of eastern Prussia by the insertion of an actual continuous wedge of Polish territory. This party has, chiefly through its prior good standing with the Russian Government due to its Russophile policy, established very friendly relations in Paris and London and has through its Paris Committee, the so-called Polish National Council, acquired up to a certain point an official status.

The other party, while inclined to extend the boundaries of Poland on the basis of the ancient historic territories of the State of Poland, yet contemplates the probability of independent states of Esthonia, Livonia, Lithuania, Ukrainia, etc., looking forward to voluntary federation later. While it would doubtless like to see Dantzig completely Polish territory, it would be contented with some kind of neutralization or internationalization which would make it a genuinely free port for Poland. It looks forward to a Republican State with a democratic form of government and a moderate socialistic policy in industrial matters. Owing to its strength with the peasants as well as with the skilled laborers in Poland, it is much stronger in Poland than any other single party, though not as strong as all of its opponents combined. In foreign politics it has in the past been strongly anti-Russian and inclined toward Austria; in the future its relations in case the Dual Empire were broken up would probably be closer with Hungary than with the German portion of Austria. Outside of Poland and Russia this party has no official status nor any great influence in Europe although in France the majority of Poles who belong to the Moderate Democrats are more friendly to it than they are to the National Democrats and the Paris Committee. This faction has the great prestige that comes from the name of General Pilsudski, the present National hero of Poland.

The causes of discord carried over on American soil from these European conditions have been much intensified by the struggle between clericals and anti-clericals for supremacy in American Polish organizations and affairs and by the campaign of misrepresentation carried on by the majority faction against the radical party. The causes of this campaign are, for the most part, past quarrels, many of them going back many years before the war, which are both personal and partisan. The effect of this campaign of misrepresentation has been threefold: (*a*) To create discord and intensify strife; (*b*) by discrediting a number of men of great vigor, intelligence and learning, to close important channels of communication and information to the American public and even the government of the United States; (*c*) to deprive the government of the most active aid which the leaders of this group are capable of giving the Government in the Liberty Loans, Red Cross Drives, and particularly in allaying industrial unrest and speeding up factory, mining, shipwork, etc., connected with the war. For it must be remembered that while this group is a minority of the organized Poles, it possesses by common admission of its opponents the ablest Poles in this country, is stronger with the organized and more skilled Polish workers than the conservative faction, and that large numbers of Poles who are not nominally affiliated with it are sympathetic toward it—namely, those Poles who, without having broken from the church, are opposed to the activity of priests in politics. Intelligent Poles outside of both factions inform us that while the K.O.N. is under a cloud at present, due mainly to the campaign of misrepresentation spoken of, the extremely exclusive and autocratic methods pursued by the conservative party are in reality giving added strength to the

K.O.N. and that it is only a question of time when a very marked reaction in its favor will take place. Should the republican parties in Europe get the better of the conservative and monarchical in the new State of Poland, these independent observers believe that the K.O.N. will, as in 1912, again become the nucleus of the political organization of Poles in this country.

The mass of Poles who, as it has been repeatedly stated, are unorganized, are also indifferent to European party strifes, and would not have been drawn into the corresponding American dissensions were it not for two causes: First, the control of Polish organizations by the affiliation worked out in 1913–14 and consummated at the Detroit Convention between the Smulski political group and the non-Americanizing group of the priests. The mass of the Poles, being Catholics, the influence of the priests upon them is naturally, and, when exercised outside of politics, properly, strong. One of the most unfortunate features of the whole situation as we have found it by personal contact is that, because of conditions described above, the war has had the effect of increasing instead of decreasing anti-American influence among the Poles. Second, the influence of the prestige and standing of Mr. Paderewski among Americans. This influence has been constantly reinforced by the money at the command of people immediately associated with Mr. Paderewski and by vigorous press agent work has imposed itself as a Polish press and publicity bureau. It is clinched, however, by the quasi-official position occupied by Mr. Paderewski as "ambassador" of the Paris Committee, constantly represented to the Poles as the Provisional Government of the new State of Poland. Many influential Poles, including men who as delegates to the Detroit Convention voted to sustain the present state of affairs, have personally deplored Mr. and Mrs. Paderewski's influence on the ground that it tended to subordinate the interests of Poland to personal glorification, but have stated that they were powerless to do anything as long as Mr. Paderewski presented himself to them as having the official support of Great Britain, France and the United States. Just as Mr. Dmowski's control of the Detroit Convention came, on one hand, from his alleged influence in Europe and will, on the other hand, be used to strengthen his power in Europe by enabling him to claim that the four million Poles in this country are unanimously behind him, so Mr. and Mrs. Paderewski constantly use their hold on Americans to discourage and suppress criticism among the Poles and then, on the other hand, employ their supposedly universal popularity among the Poles to function more prominently among Americans.

American repute, prestige and influence are definitely involved in this Polish situation, in addition to the concern due to the bad influence of the Polish dissensions upon the morale of the Polish civilian population. At home this bad reflex effect is seen in everything that has to do with relief work, with the White and Red Cross and with the army. The pains taken by the conservative faction to exclude the radical from representation on committees having the Liberty Loan in charge would have had a harmful influence were it not that the loyalty of the leaders of the K.O.N. is so great that their exclusion from official committees has only stimulated them to greater voluntary activity. The bad reflex effect in Europe is due to the representations of the conservative faction that the United States is completely tied to its cause. This not merely increases dissension among Poles abroad but it enables German propagandists to cast discredit upon the purposes and aims of the United States in the war. It tends directly to strengthen the influence of that party of the Poles in Poland who, short of some guarantee of a free, united and independent Poland, would welcome one of the two "Austrian solutions," particularly if it took the form of the union of Galicia to the Kingdom of Poland under the rule of Charles Stephen.

It is the general impression among the intelligent and independent Poles as well as of Americans who have observed the situation that the Polish factions are now so bitterly opposed to each other that they can be really united only under outside American pressure. It is also the conviction that they would not remain united excepting through American mediation and under American auspices. An American Commission for Polish Affairs which had representative Americans upon it would be able to secure and maintain also in its membership a union of the Poles. Refusal of any faction or important Pole to join would indicate that he put personal ambitions or partisan interests before the cause of Poland, or else that he put allegiance to some foreign group before his allegiance to the United States. In our judgment, this test should be applied impartially to the representatives of all factions whatsoever and their final status should be determined by the way in which they respond to this test. In addition to putting an end to dissension and accelerating the civilian preparation for war, such a Commission could undertake also to great advantage activity in some or all of the following directions:

1. Bring about a financial organization or unification which would command the confidence of Poles and Americans alike.

2. Institute machinery under proper legislation by which Poles who are really loyal to the cause of America and the Allies could be relieved of the technical status of enemy aliens.

3. Stimulate recruiting from Class Five for Polish regiments under distinctly American control.

4. Form a basis for considering the problems of labor, immigration and emigration, which will be immediately urgent after the war.

5. Provide methods by which information from all Polish sources can be secured and organized and by which the causes of industrial unrest can be immediately detected and the unrest allayed.

6. Get in contact with all organized Polish groups abroad, including Poland, and thereby also make clear the active and directive influence of the United States in the Polish problem, quieting German and Austrian propaganda and keeping the Poles in Poland faithful to the cause of the Allies.

For reasons sufficiently indicated in the body of the report, the United States is the one country which is universally regarded as disinterested and the one country therefore which would unqualifiedly win and retain the confidence of Poles in Europe.

Reviews

CREATIVE INDUSTRY

Creative Impulse in Industry, a Proposition for Educators
By Helen Marot. New York: E. P. Dutton and Co., 1918.

This book has ideas in abundance. Since it is composed of less than one hundred and fifty pages, this means that it is intellectually compact. Writers whose own intellectual store compels them to great thrift in order to make a showing would make a number of bulky volumes out of the material Miss Marot exposes. The reviewer could easily fill his allotted space by amplifying such texts as these: "Every established institution contributes fixed ideas as well as fixed customs and rules of action. Schools and colleges circulate and interpret them." "The absence of fear rather than the absence of work determines the capacity of men to play." "Undigested relationships are to-day the outstanding menace to civilization." "A society too enfeebled to use its own experience will not have the power to use the experience of another people or time"—a saying that embodies the best way I recall of disposing of the gentry who would cure the ills of the present by recourse to the habitudes of the past. But while, I hope, such isolated extracts may send the reader to the book from which they are drawn, they do not do justice to the main idea of the book and the forceful skill with which it is developed. So it may be enough to remark that without any flourish of psychology this book contains more sound social psychology, more insight into the workings of human nature, than the professed treatises on the psychology of industry and trade. For it is written from the standpoint of common, that is, universal, human nature, and not from the standpoint of the employer who wants to get all he can out of his labor force, or of the salesman who has goods to sell at a profit.

In her own language, the proposition which Miss Marot presents to educators is that "it is for educators, together with engineers and architects, to demonstrate to the world that while the idea of service to a political state may have the power to accom-

[First published in *New Republic* 17 (1918): 20, 23.]

plish large results, all productive force is artificially sustained which is not dependent on men's desire to do creative work." At present we do not seem to be even aware that industry is the great field for adventure and growth, because we use that field for purposes of exploitation, the capitalist and the laborer alike at the present time being interested in work and materials not for what can really be *made* out of them, but for what can be *got* out of them either for purposes of personal enjoyment or, as in Germany, for the ulterior purposes of political empire. As a consequence the industrial arrangement is carried on not only without the force of productive or creative intention, but against a disinclination to produce. This is the final indictment of our present industrial order.

Educators have largely opposed the attempts to vocationalize education because those who have, with the greatest prestige, urged the movement have merely attempted to harness schools to the existing régime of "business." Hardly more than business men themselves have they been able to conceive of industry which is not subjected to business or money-making, industry carried on for the sake of developing productive initiative and ability. Even the movement for "scientific management" got no further in its psychology than the importance of standardizing methods of production; it never perceived the importance of enlisting the cooperation of the workers in discovering and fixing these standards for themselves. It has relied upon external incentives; it has not had the courage or the wisdom to make use of the incentive, the stimulus, which resides in productive work itself. As education is undergoing transformation by transferring itself from reliance upon external incentives of reward and punishment to reliance upon intrinsic interest in initiative and accomplishment, so must industry be transformed. But the first step is for educators to cease taking industry at the valuation to which its pecuniary exploiters have reduced it, to perceive its possibilities for promoting growth, and then to organize schools—especially those for adolescents—upon the basis of productive industry, just as the most vital schools for little children are organized upon the basis of creative play.

In developing this proposition, Miss Marot makes an effective exposition and criticism of German education in relation to the type of life for which it prepares and points out that many good

Americans are virtually committing themselves to educational ideas which, if widely adopted, would mean the Prussianization of American life; she sketches, in concrete detail, a plan for a school organized with reference to promotion of creative impulse and effort. She is not the first to recognize the possibilities of an educational utilization of modern industry for instruction in scientific method, for supplying avenues to knowledge, and for gaining a social point of view. But in one highly important respect she has carried the discussion further than any previous writer, so far as I know. She lays chief stress upon the importance of such conditions and methods as will give each student-worker personal experience in the *administrative control* of the processes of production and marketing. Here, as she rightly points out, is the greatest field for adventure and the creative impulse. Only as modern society has at command individuals who are trained by experience in the control of industrial activities and relationships, can we achieve industrial democracy, the autonomous management of each line of productive work by those directly engaged in it. Without such democratization of industry, socialization of industry will be doomed to arrest at the stage of state capitalism, which may give the average laborer a greater share in the material rewards of industry than he now enjoys, but which will leave him in the same condition of intellectual and moral passivity and perversion as that in which he now lives. And with such lack of development on the part of its citizens social democracy would be but a name. I hope I have said enough to indicate to the reader that in this little book he will find the most sincere and courageous attempt yet made to face the problem of an education adapted to a modern society which must be industrial and which would like to be democratic.

The Life and Work of George Sylvester Morris: A Chapter in the History of American Thought in the Nineteenth Century

By R. M. Wenley. New York: Macmillan Co., 1917.

Professor Wenley has accomplished a difficult task with rare skill and success. The meaning of his sub-title is amplified in the following statement from his preface, where, speaking of Professor Morris, he says:—"His intellectual history, despite its sudden end, epitomises that of many minds in his day, because it embodies a representative human experience peculiar to the second half of the nineteenth century, particularly in the English-speaking world." Mr. Wenley's achievement is measured by the fact that his biography actually sets forth in a living form this epitome of a great intellectual experience of the later nineteenth century. The reader is not simply told about it. The development of the generation, its intellectual transition and struggle, is depicted as it was embodied in a personality of wonderful sincerity. Sympathetic insight, delicacy of touch, fidelity of portraiture, have combined with hard work and an understanding of the spiritual questionings characteristic of the transition out of Puritan Evangelicism, to produce a work which is both a faithful biography of an unusual human soul and a contribution of signal value to the history of American thought. The task was not made easy by materials ready at hand. In Professor Morris, the traditional constraint and self-consciousness of New England Puritanism had been sublimated into a spiritual detachment from all that narrowly concerned his own ego. He had learned to consume his own smoke, to transmute his personal experiences into something of impersonal meaning, and he would have found it indelicate and impossible to dwell on the incidents of his personal history. As a consequence, it was hard to gather together even the main external facts of his life, to say nothing of the intellectual crises through which he passed. Professor Wenley's scholarly *pietas* surmounted

[First published in *Philosophical Review* 28 (1919): 212–13. For Dewey's contribution to *The Life and Work of George Sylvester Morris*, see *Middle Works* 10:109–15.]

the difficulties. The result is a book which it is to be hoped will serve as a precedent for later records of other American scholars and teachers. There are traditions which are harmful, and there is equally in American life a lack of tradition which is harmful. Studies which should unite as does Professor Wenley's book the biographical element with the significant movements of the time would supply a much needed sense of the continuous ties that bind our present to the past. Few things would so well lend richness and distinction to the intellectual life, which in spite of vigor will be meagre till it is fused with a sense of the labors and achievements of the bygone generations who have worn the roads along which we may press forward to new goals.

If I have said more about the book than about its subject, Professor Morris, it is because to write of the latter in this place would be but to summarize the book itself. George Sylvester Morris was leaving Dartmouth College just as the Civil War was breaking out. Twenty years later he assumed the Chair of Ethics and History of Philosophy in the University of Michigan. In 1889 came his untimely death. During this period, a much greater transformation came over America than it is even yet possible to realize. Mr. Morris suffered the spiritual conflicts of the transition. For himself he achieved, by means of a combination of Greek and German thought, a triumphant reconciliation of traditional religion with rational intelligence, of the older New England individualism with devoted loyalty to the purpose and meaning of objective institutions, of moral faith with the pronouncements of science. This generation finds the solution too easy; the formula of reconciliation too much a product of desire; the combination too much a mixture of incompatible factors. But Mr. Morris's personality, his spirit, was a prophecy of the possibility of a true union of substantial tradition and the free life of thought. No person ever came under his influence without attaining a greater faith in both of these things. In education he was a power among the scholars of those days who led the American College away from its provincialism into broader fields of learning, and keener methods of criticism. His old pupils and friends will rejoice that his life has found such a worthy record, that others may also come within the range of his learning and charm.

Miscellany

SYLLABUS OF EIGHT LECTURES ON "PROBLEMS OF PHILOSOPHIC RECONSTRUCTION"

In the months of February and March Professor John Dewey delivered a course of eight lectures at the Imperial University at Tokyo on "Problems of Philosophic Reconstruction." The following is the syllabus prepared for the audience to which the lectures were addressed. We understand the lectures are to be printed in Japanese. It is to be hoped that Professor Dewey will publish them in English at his earliest convenience.

Lecture I

Conflicting Ideas as to the Meaning of Philosophy

I. THE ORIGINS OF PHILOSOPHY

1. Since man is primarily a being of desire and imagination, his primary beliefs spring from his hopes and fears, successes and failures, rather than from observation; they are poetic and religious, rather than scientific. 2. These ideas when fixed and organized under community tradition and authority became the material out of which philosophy developed.

II. POSITIVE OR MATTER-OF-FACT KNOWLEDGE

1. Information regarding nature, and the natural conditions and consequences of human acts, is necessary to life. This knowledge grows up around the practical arts which give to man the use of the natural environment. 2. After a time the incongruity between this knowledge and the body of emotional beliefs is so great, that some reconciliation is sought for. Then philosophy proper arises. This fact is illustrated in the development of both

[First published in *Journal of Philosophy, Psychology and Scientific Methods* 16 (1919): 357–64. The lectures were published as *Reconstruction in Philosophy* (New York: Henry Holt and Co., 1920); see *Middle Works* 12.]

Greek, medieval, and modern German philosophies. Matter-of-fact knowledge is (i) specific, limited, hard and cold; (ii) accurate and quantitative, and useful; and (iii) consists of tested facts; while poetic and traditional beliefs are (i) universal and comprehensive; (ii) qualitative, vague, but socially fundamental; and (iii) concerned with meanings and values rather than with facts. Hence arise

III. THE CHIEF TRAITS OF CLASSIC PHILOSOPHY

It is (i) apologetic and "compensatory"; (ii) formal and rigorously systematic, or dialectical; (iii) concerned with the difference between absolute, universal Reality and Knowledge and that which is relative, partial and empirical.

IV. THE NEWER IDEA OF PHILOSOPHY

This (i) recognizes the impossibility of reconciling the traditional beliefs with modern scientific developments, and (ii) recognizes the origin of philosophic questions and interests in social conflict and needs, and hence conceives of philosophy as an organ or instrument of social direction.

Lecture II

Knowledge as Contemplative and Active

I. CONTEMPLATIVE PHILOSOPHY

1. Man forms pictures of an ideal world by conceiving a state of things in which only the satisfactory or complete exists. Reflection analyzes the features of such a world, and finds them to be permanence, unity and harmony, and thus creates a noumenal real-ideal realm of being.—Plato. 2. In contrast, the existent and evil empirical world is one of multiplicity, partiality and change. The primary function of philosophy is to lead the mind from belief in this world to contemplation of the ideal-real world. This contemplation leaves the phenomenal world unchanged, but assimilates the mind to true Reality. Aristotle's theory of true knowledge and its influence.

II. ACTIVE PHILOSOPHY

1. Its "realistic" phase consists in willingness to study and to take into account existing facts, regarded as obstacles and means in achieving desired changes. They are not treated as things to be escaped from nor yet to be acquiesced in. Direction of change is the great problem. 2. Its "idealistic" phase consists in cultivating suggestions, ideas, or ideal possibilities and meanings as methods and plans for transforming and improving existing conditions. Forecast of a better future is the pragmatic substitute for the noumenal world in contemplative philosophy. Ideal meanings are thus not separate or ultimate, but are instrumental and need to be tested by consequences.

III. THE SPECIAL FUNCTION OF ACTIVE PHILOSOPHY

While the function of all knowledge is to rectify troubles, that of the sciences is technical, while that of philosophy is social and human or moral. Why knowledge is objective, impersonal and universal. Philosophy is comprehensive and ultimate in the moral sense of going below prejudices, traditions and purposes which divide classes, races and peoples and trying to discover moral adjustments.

Lecture III

Social Causes of Philosophic Reconstruction

The two previous lectures have dealt with the contrast of the classic and the modern conceptions of the nature and function of philosophy. The next two consider the reasons for the growth of the newer point of view, the present one dealing with the more general historical and social factors, the next with the more special scientific factors.

I. THE PHILOSOPHY OF FRANCIS BACON

This may be taken as exemplifying the transition from the classic to the modern point of view. It had for its chief features the ideas that: 1. Knowledge is power, not contemplation. Yet this knowledge is obtained only by "obeying nature," not by "anticipating" her. 2. This knowledge can be obtained only through cooperative and organized research, not by mere individual ability which results only in disputations or ornamental knowledge. 3. The end of knowledge is the relief and improvement of the human estate.

II. SOCIAL FACTORS IN THIS POINT OF VIEW

1. Industrial, matter-of-fact activity and invention had reached a point where the idea of constant and systematic progress through control of natural forces was possible. Travel, exploration, discovery of a new world. 2. The beginning of the breakdown of feudal class divisions, and the rise of national states with a corresponding release of the individual from the bonds of custom. The contract theory of the origin of the state. 3. The beginnings of freedom of criticism and conscience in matters of religious belief and worship. Belief in the power of Reason and Thought was transferred from the conception of the formation of the Universe at large to concrete things and human institutions. Idealism ceased to be cosmic and objective and became in Bacon's successors individual and subjective.

Lecture IV

Modern Science and Philosophic Reconstruction

The growth of science since the seventeenth century has revolutionized our ideas of (I.) Nature and (II.) the Method of Knowing.

I. THE CONTRAST AS TO NATURE

1. The classic view, formulated by Aristotle and adopted by medieval thought, held (1) that nature is a closed whole, finite, and composed of parts qualitatively different, and arranged in a hierarchy of higher and lower; and (2) that there are a definite number of fixed classes or species, each having its own immutable form which controls its movements and growth, so that (3) individuals which change and perish are real only as members of fixed and universal classes. 2. The modern view asserts (1) the infinity, uniformity and homogeneity of Nature, thus substituting a democracy of elements for an aristocracy of classes, (2) that

motion and change are more important than fixity and (3) the universal subordinate to individuals.

II. THE CONTRAST AS TO METHOD OF KNOWING

1. Classic method emphasized the importance of definition, demonstration, and syllogistic reasoning—the inclusion of particulars within the conception of the class. Sense perception was knowledge of perishing particulars and had to be subsumed under the rational knowledge of conceptions. 2. Modern science is interested in inquiry and discovery rather than proof, and hence insists upon experimental analysis of all sense observations, and the experimental verification of all general ideas which are regarded as only hypotheses till verified by experimental production of individuals. Control of change is both the object and the test of knowing. Pragmatically, infinity is equivalent to possibility of indefinite progress.

III. EFFECT UPON PHILOSOPHY

For a considerable period, the effect of the change was limited to physical matters and hence was technical and industrial rather than humane and moral; or, in the latter region, the influence was skeptical rather than constructive. Now the influence is extended to the moral and social.

Lecture V

The Changed Conception of Experience and Reason

I. EARLIER HISTORY OF THE NOTION OF EXPERIENCE

1. To Plato and Aristotle, experience meant an accumulation and gradual organization of a multitude of particular acts and perceptions into a kind of practical insight and ability, like that of the builder or physician. The "empirical" versus the scientific. 2. The early modern, British, notion of experience was under the influence of sensational psychology, and eliminated all traits of organization save those supplied by casual association and blind habit. It was a powerful tool of skeptical criticism, but was impotent for construction.

II. THE EARLIER HISTORY OF THE NOTION OF REASON

It was framed to meet the weaknesses in the current idea of experience. 1. To the Greek philosophers, Reason was the faculty of insight into the universal, the law, cause or principle, which was the only source of scientific explanation and demonstration and of sure direction of conduct. Historically, this "rationalism" became formal, the source of neglect of empirical observation, and the originator of a pseudo-science of simplification and abstraction: "rationalization" as explaining away and covering up. 2. Kant responded to the sensationalistic idea of experience with the theory that Reason is a faculty of organizing the chaotic details of experience through *a priori* fixed concepts as categories. Effects in developing absolutism of thought and action in Germany.

III. RECENT IDEAS OF EXPERIENCE AND REASON

Modern psychology has destroyed the sensational notion by bringing out, under biological influence, the active and motor factors in experience. Experience is doing, trying, and sensations are clews to adjustive behavior which modifies the environment. Experimental method has destroyed ancient empiricism by emphasizing projection and invention instead of accumulations from the past. Reason thus becomes Intelligence—the power of using past experience to shape and transform future experience. It is constructive and creative.

Lecture VI

The Reconstruction as Affecting Logic

The problem of logical theory is important because it involves the question of the possibility of *intelligent method* in determining man's attitude toward his environment, both natural and social. Logic has to be rescued from abstract formalism on one side and from sterile epistemology on the other. Reconstruction emphasizes:

I. THE CONNECTION OF THINKING WITH BEHAVIOR

1. Thinking originates from problems and perplexities, and these arise in conflicts. The intellectual as distinct from the emo-

tional solution of conflicts involves a technique of observation, hypothesis forming and testing, ratiocination, *etc.* 2. The function of thinking is to develop methods of dealing with specific situations; the "idea" is a hypothetical plan of action to be tested by consequences. 3. Science or disinterested inquiry is an indispensable form of practice; meaning of thinking for thinking's sake.

II. INDUCTIVE AND DEDUCTIVE ASPECTS OF METHOD

Their traditional separation resulted from the traditional separation of experience and reason; hence they are now to be treated as mutually complementary. 1. Induction comes at the beginning of a complete inquiry, for experimental observation is needed to analyze the conditions which constitute a problem, and also to test the theory or hypothesis. 2. Deduction is indispensable as the intermediate step of developing an intelligent method. Abstraction liberates; generalization extends and applies; system, classification, prepares an orderly set of instrumentalities, ready in advance for dealing with emergencies as they arise.

III. THE CONCEPTION OF TRUTH

This is a consequence rather than a foundation of other logical features. From the instrumental character of reflection it follows that only theories, ideas, can be true or false, and can be true or false not in themselves but in their application or use. The mark of consistency has to do with the deductive development which works out an applicable conception; correspondence is practical, not epistemological.

Lecture VII

The Reconstruction as Affecting Ethics and Education

I. GOODS AND ENDS ARE SPECIFIC AND ACTIVE, NOT GENERAL AND STATIC

1. Each situation requiring action has its own good depending upon its peculiar needs and conditions. Comprehensive and general ends are of value as instruments of better insight into these specific situations; similarly, principles and standards are tools of analysis and understanding, rather than direct rules of

conduct. The effect of the doctrine of the plurality of unique goods is to increase responsibility of intelligence; to decrease formalism, moral dogmatism and Phariseeism. 2. Ends and goods are *within* each situation, not external. An aim or purpose is a working hypothesis for directing the development of a situation, and is tested by consequences. Hence ends themselves are developing, not fixed. An ideal is a sense of the possibilities of a situation, and is of value only as inspiring action and directing for ameliorating its evils; meliorism as compared with optimism and pessimism. Happiness is found not in possession or fixed attainment, but in the active process of striving, overcoming and succeeding; failures are to be turned to account, and are not incompatible with moral happiness.

II. VALUE AND DEFECTS OF UTILITARIANISM

It has the merits and defects of a transition from one point of view to another. It made the end and good, natural and social, and subordinated law to ends. But in resolving happiness into a mass of pleasures it was made something fixed and uniform in quality, and something to be acquired and possessed. Thus utilitarianism emphasized security of acquisition and possession rather than power and security in creative achievement.

III. EFFECT ON EDUCATION

Education comes to be regarded, accordingly, as not only the method by which moral and social ends are realizable, but as identical with the end, namely, growth and development. The purpose and test of social institutions is their educative effect, while education, in its narrower sense, becomes the primary method of social progress.

Lecture VIII

Reconstruction as Affecting Social Philosophy

From the conclusion that the moral test of institutions is their educative effect there follow other conclusions of importance for social philosophy.

I. RELATION OF INDIVIDUAL AND SOCIAL

The three historic theories of subordination of individual, subordination of social, and "organic" relationship suffer from the same error. They regard individual or social as fixed, given ready-made, instead of as developing and therefore as objects to be continuously worked out. When the individual self is treated as isolated and fixed, social arrangements can only be external means to its pleasures or possessions. But in fact institutions, legislation, administration, *etc.*, are necessary to the release and operation of the capacities that form the individual. Society also means not a fixed organization, but reciprocal and growing sharing or communication of experience. Organization is subordinate to association. The political state is only one of a number of forms of association, each having its distinctive value. The state is instrumental rather than final.

II. RELATION OF RIGHTS AND DUTIES, OR FREEDOM AND LAW

Neither is ultimate, because both are conditions of effective furtherance of a community of experiences, of common ends and values. Unless all the capacities of the individual are liberated and used, society is static and impoverished. Personality develops only through assuming of responsibility, and responsibility is limited except as persons have a share in deciding the matters that are of ultimate importance at the given time. Law is a statement of the order upon which fruitful association depends. British "Individualism" made liberty an end in itself, and German Political Philosophy made Law and the State absolute.

III. RELIGIOUS ASPECT OF RECONSTRUCTION

As the changes described take deeper hold on emotional disposition and imagination, they get a religious coloring; till this happens, the classic philosophy will seem to have the advantage in ideality. Religious value of personality and of the community; place of Nature.

INTRODUCTORY WORD

Many persons have pointed out the strain which has come upon human nature in the change from a state of animal savagery to present civilization. No one, it seems to me, has grasped the meaning, dangers and possibilites of this change more lucidly and completely than Mr. Alexander. His account of the crises which have ensued upon this evolution is a contribution to a better understanding of every phase of contemporary life. His interpretation centres primarily about the crisis in the physical and moral health of the individual produced by the conflict between the functions of the brain and the nervous system on one side and the functions of digestion, circulation, respiration and the muscular system on the other; but there is no aspect of the maladjustments of modern life which does not receive illumination.

Frank acknowledgment of this internecine warfare in the very heart of our civilization is not agreeable. For this reason it is rarely faced in its entirety. We prefer to deal with its incidents and episodes as if they were isolated accidents and could be overcome one by one in isolation. Those who have seen the conflict have almost always proposed as a remedy either a return to nature, a relapse to the simple life, or else flight to some mystic obscurity. Mr. Alexander exposes the fundamental error in the empirical and palliative methods. When the organs through which any structure, be it physiological, mental or social, are out of balance, when they are uncoordinated, specific and limited attempts at a cure only exercise the already disordered mechanism. In "improving" one organic structure, they produce a compensatory maladjustment, usually more subtle and more difficult to deal with, somewhere else. The ingeniously inclined will have little difficulty in paralleling Mr. Alexander's criticism of "physical culture methods" within any field of our economic and political life.

[First published in F. Matthias Alexander, *Man's Supreme Inheritance* (New York: E. P. Dutton and Co., 1918), xiii–xvii. For Randolph Bourne's review, see this volume, Appendix 1; and for Dewey's reply, see pp. 353–55.]

In his criticism of return or relapse to the simpler conditions from which civilized man has departed Mr. Alexander's philosophy appears in its essential features. All such attempts represent an attempt at solution through abdication of intelligence. They all argue, in effect, that since the varied evils have come through development of conscious intelligence, the remedy is to let intelligence sleep, while the pre-intelligent forces, out of which it developed, do their work. The pitfalls into which references to the unconscious and subconscious usually fall have no existence in Mr. Alexander's treatment. He gives these terms a definite and real meaning. They express reliance upon the primitive mind of sense, of unreflection, as against reliance upon *reflective* mind. Mr. Alexander sees the remedy not in a futile abdication of intelligence in order that lower forces may work, but in carrying the power of intelligence further, in making its function one of positive and constructive control. As a layman, I am incompetent to pass judgment upon the particular technique through which he would bring about a control of intelligence over the bodily organism so as not merely to cure but to prevent the present multitudinous maladies of adjustment. But he does not stop with a pious recommendation of such conscious control; he possesses and offers a definite method for its realization, and even a layman can testify, as I am glad to do, to the efficacy of its working in concrete cases.

It did not remain for the author of these pages to eulogize self-mastery or self-control. But these eulogies have too frequently remained in the hortatory and moralistic state. Mr. Alexander has developed a definite procedure, based upon a scientific knowledge of the organism. Popular fear of anything sounding like materialism has put a heavy burden upon humanity. Men are afraid, without even being aware of their fear, to recognize the most wonderful of all the structures of the vast universe—the human body. They have been led to think that a serious notice and regard would somehow involve disloyalty to man's higher life. The discussions of Mr. Alexander breathe reverence for this wonderful instrument of our life, life mental and moral as well as that life which somewhat meaninglessly we call bodily. When such a religious attitude toward the body becomes more general, we shall have an atmosphere favorable to securing the conscious control which is urged.

In the larger sense of education, this whole book is concerned with education. But the writer of these lines was naturally especially attracted to the passages in which Mr. Alexander touches on the problems of education in the narrower sense. The meaning of his principles comes out nowhere better than in his criticisms of repressive schools on one hand and schools of "free expression" on the other. He is aware of the perversions and distortions that spring from that unnatural suppression of childhood which too frequently passes for school training. But he is equally aware that the remedy is not to be sought through a blind reaction in abolition of all control except such as the moment's whim or the accident of environment may provide. One gathers that in this country, Mr. Alexander has made the acquaintance of an extremely rare type of "self-expressive" school, but all interested in educational reform may well remember that freedom of physical action and free expression of emotion are means, not ends, and that as means they are justified only in so far as they are used as conditions for developing power of intelligence. The substitution of control by intelligence for control by external authority, not the negative principle of no control or the spasmodic principle of control by emotional gusts, is the only basis upon which reformed education can build. To come into possession of intelligence is the sole human title to freedom. The spontaneity of childhood is a delightful and precious thing, but in its original naïve form it is bound to disappear. Emotions become sophisticated unless they become enlightened, and the manifestation of sophisticated emotion is in no sense genuine self-expression. True spontaneity is henceforth not a birth-right but the last term, the consummated conquest, of an art—the art of conscious control to the mastery of which Mr. Alexander's book so convincingly invites us.

REPLY TO A REVIEWER

Sir: "R. B.'s" review of Mr. Alexander's *Man's Supreme Inheritance* exhibits such ingenuity in evading perception of its significant points that it seems worth while to make a statement for the protection of readers who might otherwise be misled. Mr. Alexander's book is not concerned with setting forth instrumental, pragmatic or evolutionary philosophy, within which is wrapped a personal intuition or quasi-magical personal knack. His critical contention is that the remediable ills from which humanity suffers on the physical side (with the intellectual and moral ills that result) are due to disassociation of the "higher" nervous structures and functions—those which are at the basis of our conscious life—from the "lower"—those which are involved in the execution of bodily postures and movements. Roughly speaking, the latter represent our animal inheritance, "instincts," which have been changed into our habitual attitudes and acts (the "subconscious") without conscious perception and control. The former represent the distinctly human additions up-to-date, our acquired civilization. Mr. Alexander contends that our education, which covers, of course, infinitely more than our schooling, has proceeded as if the centres of conscious activity had been merely superimposed upon the neuro-muscular structures which represent our heredity from the lower animals. As a result we get evils which are unknown to the animals and to the savages whose intellectual achievements have not become sufficiently complex to override the animal functions. But civilized persons, especially the intellectuals and specialized persons who are leaders, cultivate their "brains" as if they were separate from the rest of the body. Meantime, muscular coordinations, or habits, are formed under the novel conditions of civilization. Hence, they work neither in their natural estate nor with the advantage of control by

[First published in *New Republic* 15 (1918): 55. For review to which this is a reply, see this volume, Appendix 1.]

intelligence, the functioning of the higher centres. The net outcome, in Mr. Alexander's contention, is the larger number of physical disorders which inflict themselves exclusively upon civilized man, and the large number of neuroses which express themselves in intellectual and moral maladies. The claim is sweeping and as simple as it is sweeping. If the book is worth reviewing, the thesis is worth stating.

Mr. Alexander's positive principle is, in effect, an education which will integrate the functions now so disastrously divided. The principle is experimental; it can be asserted and rendered intelligible in a book; proof lies in *doing* it. From the book the idea which the *reader* can get will be but a more or less clear "intuition." To say, as "R. B." does, that it is an intuition with Mr. Alexander is to intimate that he is either the most self-deluded of mortals or that he is deliberate faker of the first magnitude. The cleverness which presents a principle which claims to be one of conscious control, as if it were a matter of personal intuition, is not a cleverness which I envy "R. B."

With adults the integration which is accomplished by the technique at Mr. Alexander's command, is obviously a re-education that is at best remedial and more or less palliative. With subsequent generations it can, to the degree in which it is utilized with children, become positive and constructive. If Mr. Alexander is wrong, the name given to the estate of humanity which would ultimately be produced is of no consequence. If he is right, the change would be so great, the stage introduced into the history of humanity would be of such crucial significance that the use of the word evolution in connection with it is at most a mere matter of literary taste.

"R. B." says that the task suggested is "a little appalling," that "if the school must wait till every one of its children has learned conscious guidance and control, the next step in evolution will be very long delayed." It would be hard to find a greater tribute to the integrity of Mr. Alexander's method than is conveyed in this unconscious confession. It marks the difference between reliance upon some scheme of magic and the more than a "little" appalling task which confronts man if his civilization is not to end in a tragedy. Certainly one of the prime effects of acquaintance with the method of "conscious control" is to make one realize the superficial and over-hasty character of the methods upon which we are relying, and the corresponding importance of a fundamental-method of education, one which in the course of slow generations will integrate into harmonious coordination our animal inheritance and our distinctively human capacities of intelligence.

JOHN DEWEY

Appendixes

Appendix 1

MAKING OVER THE BODY
by Randolph Bourne

Review of Man's Supreme Inheritance *by F. Matthias Alexander. New York: E. P. Dutton and Co., 1918.*

Mr. Alexander rather needs the delighted "introductory word" of Professor Dewey's to justify his own philosophical exuberance. For without such a ratification, the reader is bound to question whether the author of *Man's Supreme Inheritance* has been able to put his mind into that state of delicate balance and harmony into which he can put other people's bodies by his system of conscious muscular guidance and control. The practice seems more significant than the philosophy. Mr. Alexander seems to have demonstrated, in Australia, in England, and latterly in his work with experimental schools in this country, that he possesses a rare physiological intuition and a technique of re-educating the body out of the bad muscular habits into which it has unconsciously fallen, and which impede self-expression and are often the cause of serious functional disturbances. Professor Dewey himself testifies to the successful working of the technique in concrete cases. The old muscular movements, the wrongness of which ordinary "physical exercises" only reinforced, are inhibited, and then the right movements are produced by conscious direction of the will. The body becomes a genuine instrument, and spontaneity, self-expression, become for the first time intelligible terms.

But is it not a mistake, when you have so valuable a pragmatic intuition and power, to let your enthusiasm wrap the idea up in a cosmic and evolutionary philosophy which could not, in the nature of the case, be half so persuasive as the technique itself? Mr. Alexander insists upon presenting this technique as the symptom of a conscious guidance and control which is to be humanity's next step in evolution. The old unconscious days are to be over, and intelligent manipulation is to reign in their stead. But is not the task he suggests a little appalling? For if this next

[First published in *New Republic* 15 (1918): 28–29. For Dewey's introductory word, see this volume, pp. 350–52; and for Dewey's reply, see pp. 353–55.]

step in evolution is to mean anything it means that every separate human being must make over his bodily coordinations. And the secret of that making-over lies—we must conclude—almost exclusively in the rare intuition and skill of Mr. Alexander. If the school must wait until every one of its children has learned conscious guidance and control, the next step in evolution will be very long delayed. Mr. Alexander's application of his idea to the large problems of social evolution, and the shortcomings of civilization, shows an attentive modern ear. But do we any longer think of evolution as a road along which mankind moves abreast in solid phalanx onward and upward forever? Isn't mankind, if it is anything, a pitiful and straggling army, strung along by degrees all the way between heaven and hell, between rationality and instinct, between attainment and futility? Will it ever be anything else? Is an era of world-war, in which statesmen are proving as blind and helpless as the manipulated masses, quite the most convincing time for so far-flung a philosophy of conscious control? Of desire, will, revolt—yes; but not the anticipation that we begin a new era of human intelligence. Mr. Alexander thinks the war is the product of too much reliance on instinctive guidance in human affairs. Is this any more plausible than Dr. Jung's theory that it is a revolt of the "collective unconscious" against an era of too much rational and deliberate control?

Philosophy is a dangerous quicksand. Professor Dewey's instrumentalism has held out to Mr. Alexander a helping hand, but has scarcely saved him from getting at times beyond his depth. He has a physiological technique which is apparently a kind of reversed psycho-analysis, unwinding the psychic knots by getting control of the physical end-organs. A unity and balance of the body is worked for to produce an integration and harmony of the mind. Man's supreme inheritance is the ability to control the circumstances of his own life. But Mr. Alexander's empiric idea and practice are too valuable to be wrapped up in a philosophy that is not just as vigorously integrated and intelligently guided as the muscular system which he skillfully directs towards perfect functioning.

Appendix 2

DEWEY AND URBAN ON VALUE JUDGMENTS

by Ralph Barton Perry

There is an important class of theories according to which value is an object of judgment. This does not mean simply that values, like other things, may be and are judged; but that in this case, at least, the object is created by the act of being judged. Valuation is judgment, and to be valuated is to be valuable. It is possible to hold that all judgment is, in keeping with this view, either valuation, or to hold that valuation is a special kind of judgment. The latter or dualistic view of judgment is familiarly expressed in the antithesis between the "practical" and the "theoretical" reasons, or between "appreciation" and "description," or between "normative judgments" and "judgments of fact," or between "*Beurteilung*" and "*Urteilung*."[1] The former view is exemplified by Schiller's view that all judgments are "practical,"[2] and by Rickert's view that judgment is essentially an act of acceptance or rejection.[3] Most dualistic views are only provisional, a stage in the reduction of all judgments to the type of valuation. This is broadly true of all those theories of judgment that appear in voluntaristic philosophies, such as pragmatism and Fichtean idealism. The practical version of judgment is first distinguished from a popular or traditional version of judgments of fact, after which the latter is corrected and reduced to the former.

Among the views which regard the practical or valuating judgments as constitutive of values, it is important to distinguish two classes, the humanistic and the absolutistic. The former construe judgment in an anthropological or psychological sense, the latter in a transcendent, metaphysical or "logical" sense. According to the views of the former class, values are created by the

1. Windelband, *Präludien*, third edition, pp. 52–53.
2. F. C. S. Schiller, "Are All Judgments 'Practical'?" this Journal, Vol. XII, p. 682.
3. ". . .der eigentliche logische Kern des Urteils, das Bejahen und Verneinen, ein Billigen oder Missbilligen, ein Stellungnehmen zu einem Werte ist." H. Rickert, *Der Gegenstand der Erkenntniss* (1904), second edition, p. 108.

[First published in *Journal of Philosophy, Psychology and Scientific Methods* 14 (1917): 169–81. For Dewey's reply, see this volume, pp. 3–9.]

actual judgments of men, with all their relativity and variability; whereas according to views of the latter class, values are created only by some qualified, standard, or universal judgment which is somehow immanent or presupposed in the fallible judgments of finite minds.

To the former, or humanistic class, belongs the relatively crude view of Westermarck, and the more sophisticated and circumspect views that have recently been set forth by instrumentalists and pragmatists. Professor Dewey may be assumed to speak representatively if not authoritatively for this school. He presents the crux of the matter when he states that "practical judgments" imply "the seeming paradox of a judgment whose proper subject-matter is its own determinate formation." "To judge value," he says, "is to engage in instituting a determinate value where none is given." In other words, "the object of a practical judgment is some change, some alteration to be brought about in the given, the nature of which change depends upon the judgment itself and yet constitutes the subject-matter of (the?) judgment."[4] This means, I take it, that in this peculiar and "paradoxical" case value is both that which is judged, in other words the objective component of the judgment, and also a larger whole which embraces or involves the judgment. This is, to say the least, paradoxical, and could scarcely be regarded as a satisfactory disposition of the matter even though no other account of the facts should appear to be possible.

It is fair to state that Professor Dewey disclaims any intention of dealing with the nature of values. "I am going to deal with valuation," he says, "not with value."[5] It soon appears, however, that he regards "valuated objects" as the only values worth studying; and he continually speaks of values when he means valuated objects, as though the two expressions were interchangeable. Thus, for example, he speaks of value as "practical," "existent," "objective," and as a factor in "completing a situation," when the whole force of the argument depends on identifying value and valuated object. It is true also that he takes pains to distinguish two senses of "valuing." There is, on the one hand, the attitude of "prizing," or "esteeming," merely, which is a "practical, non-intel-

4. J. Dewey, "The Logic of Judgments of Practise," this Journal, Vol. XIII, pp. 516, 517, 521–522. [*Middle Works* 8:35, 36, 47.]
5. *Ibid.*, p. 512. [See *Middle Works* 8:499.]

lectual attitude"; and there is the attitude of "appraising or estimating," which implies a judgment. The two are commonly merged and confused in the conception of "appreciation."[6] But though he calls attention to the confusion and deprecates it, he does not, as we shall see, avoid it. And though he does not deny that the simpler emotional attitude defines values of a sort, he does at any rate clearly affirm that the judicial or intellectual attitude also determines values, and it is to these values that he confines attention in the present paper.

In examining the examples upon which Professor Dewey bases his contention, and which he thinks have been strangely neglected in the orthodox accounts of judgments, it is very important to bear the following general consideration in mind. *It is impossible to interpret any judgment merely from its verbal record.* What is judged in any given case depends upon what is intended at the time by the judging mind. A dozen different judgments may be expressed in the same linguistic form. This is peculiarly true of the very complicated judgments which the author cites. He would himself, I take it, be the last person to deny this; nevertheless his failure to specify in each case just what the judge may be supposed to mean by what he says, gives to his whole discussion an ambiguity which assists his argument, but does not clarify the issue. Take, for example, his favorite instance, the judgment "I should consult a physician." This might mean: 'In view of the general practise of mankind, this is a case for medical advice.' One would be mistaken in this judgment provided one were misinformed as to the general rule of procedure, or provided one had exaggerated one's symptoms. There would be no reference, express or implied, to the probable outcome; and should the act prove fruitless, one's judgment would in no wise be proved at fault. Or this same linguistic form might mean: 'My state of health being such as it is, if I consult a physician I shall probably be cured.' In the case of such a judgment of probable outcome, while there is a future reference, the contingent event would still not affect the truth of the judgment. Though one should in the sequel not be cured, one's cure would still have been probable in view of the statistical evidence. Or one might mean: 'If I consult a physician I shall be cured.' Here again, al-

6. *Ibid.*, pp. 512–513, 520. [*Middle Works* 8:25–27, 45.]

though there is a hypothetical reference to a future event, the non-occurrence of that event would not disprove the judgment, in case I did not fulfil the condition and consult the physician. Or, finally, one might mean: 'Because I am going to consult a physician I shall recover my health.' This is evidently a complex judgment, one component of which does depend for its truth or error on a future contingency. It should be analyzed into two judgments, because either one of two independent facts would disprove it. If there should be no causal relation between consulting physicians and the recovery of health, I should be mistaken; or if I should not as a matter of historical fact recover my health, I should be mistaken, but on different grounds.

In other words, the identity of a judgment depends not on its verbal form, but on what it virtually appeals to for its disproof or verification. Every judgment has objective reference of two sorts, both of which are necessary as an act of judgment, independently of its being true or false. In the first place, it is "about" something, whose reality is not in question, and which serves as the locus of verification. In the second place, there is something judged. A judgment, in short, is like a promissory note, which has its date and place of maturity, and its amount. The first of these factors has usually been termed the "subject" of the judgment, because it is commonly named by the grammatical subject. If, however, we regard the judgment as an act of mind directed to some feature of its environment, it is more convenient to term this the "object" of the judgment. It must somehow be equally compatible with the fact which would prove the judgment, and with the fact which would disprove it. It may, perhaps, best be regarded as a constituent of both alternative facts. Thus, in judging that "the Emperor of Austria is dead," there is "the Emperor of Austria," in any case, as the common constituent of his being dead or alive. The object of the judgment is "the Emperor of Austria" in the sense that both the verifying fact and the discrediting fact would concern him. I am judging something *about* "the Emperor of Austria"; who constitutes, therefore, the quarter to which one must resort for evidence relevant to this particular judgment. Were there no such person, then the judgment would be no judgment; or it would be analyzable, as Mr. Russell has shown, into two judgments: "there is an Emperor of Austria," and "he is dead." I leave open the possibility that all judgments may ultimately be reducible to the form "there is so and so," or "this is so and so." In this case all judgments would be like a promissory note redeemable at any time or place. But if one were forced to this conclusion it would be owing to the very principle for which I am here contending, the principle, namely, that every judgment is about something whose existence is given or unquestionable.

But in every judgment there is not only what the judgment is about, but *what is judged about it*. Thus the judgments "the Emperor of Austria is dead," and "the Emperor of Austria is alive," are both about the same object, but in the one case one thing is judged about him, and in the other case something else. This we may term the "objective" of the judgment. It is that hypothetical state of the object which would verify the judgment, or fulfil the expectation which the judgment expresses. It is not a fact, simply, but a hypothetical fact. In other words, it is a component of the more complex fact of my judgment. It is that toward which my motor set or determining tendency is directed; but *only in the sense of being the direction of that set or tendency*. It is adverbial in character, a qualification or description of the judgment; in short, the way I judge.[7]

It is because, then, of such a virtual appeal to the same object, and such an identical expectation with reference to that object, that it is possible for two or more minds, or the same mind at different times, to judge the same. Thus the outcome of the present war is the object of many contemporary judgments. Some of these judgments are, furthermore, such that the victory of the Allies would fulfil the expectation that underlies them. In that case, though they be expressed by different minds, at different times, and in different languages and grammatical forms, they would be said to constitute the same judgment. Unless this sort of epistemological identity were possible, knowledge could have no history and no social status. It would not even be possible for a hypothesis to be verified, for it could not be the same hypothesis which was first entertained, and then held persistently in mind

7. I can not here enter into a detailed analysis of this type of process. I am confident that it can be dealt with in behaviorist terms, provided we recognize that all behavior has to be described in terms of direction and goal, as is implied in the use of such terms as "set," "tendency," "*Aufgabe*," *etc*. The function of words requires the same sort of analysis. For a further discussion of these matters, *cf.* my articles on "The Truth-Problem," this Journal, Vol. XIII, especially pp. 561 ff.

until the appropriate evidence should be forthcoming. It would not be possible for old judgments to be overthrown, or for one scientist's judgment to be confirmed by another's, because the same judgment could not be reconsidered or tested by different investigators.

Professor Dewey's failure to state precisely what constitutes the identity of a judgment and makes it just that judgment, gives to his whole discussion an elusiveness and fluidity that makes it almost impossible to criticize it. The critic must first formulate the view for himself, and since he can not certainly be sure of exhausting the possible meanings of an ambiguous text, he must always run the risk of missing the point. I shall endeavor to put that construction on the text which reflects its characteristic motive, and which at the same time sheds most light on our general problem of value.

Suppose a situation in which I suffer from ill-health and hope to recover through the agency of a physician. There are several items in this situation which must be distinguished. I suffer from ill-health and am aware that I dislike it. I desire recovery and am aware that I desire it. I believe that consulting a physician conduces to recovery. I adopt the course of consulting a physician, as a course conducive to my recovery. I believe that I am going to recover, and since in this case the object of belief and of desire coincide, I hope that I am going to recover. Subsequently, because of what I dislike, desire, and believe, I do consult the physician, and thereupon, in consequence of having consulted the physician, I recover. There are evidently many more or less independent components in this very complex process, some of them judgments, and some of them "non-intellectual" affective or motor attitudes which condition values. But there is no case so far as I can see of a value's being constituted by a judgment of it, or of value's being both cognized and created by the same mental act.

In so far as I dislike my present symptoms, they are evil. My judging that I dislike them does not make them evil, but simply refers to their being evil as a fact. It is like any perceptual judgment, except in respect of its peculiar degree of certainty.

In so far as I desire recovery, my future recovery is good. It is good relatively to my present desire, and its goodness would not be undone even though I should perish in the very moment of desire. This is the kind of value that attaches to all ideals, however quixotic, though they be "unrealized" or even unrealizable. That I should have dreamed a dream is sufficient to impart to the content of that dream a value that is quite independent of my rude awakening. Owing to this fact, which no theory of value can afford to disregard, it is evident that the realm of values exceeds that of existence. It is necessary to attach the predicate of value to "prospectives," possibilities, hypotheticals, or subsistents. That I should be aware that such is my desire introduces no new value, but merely makes me cognizant of the fact of my desire.

The belief that the consulting of physicians conduces to recovery is like any belief in a law or general rule. It is not peculiar to a practical or valuing situation, and it conforms to the ordinary and unparadoxical notion of judgment as referring to a given and independent state of things to which the judging mind appeals and defers.

The act of adopting the proposed plan as conducive to the desired result may seem to introduce something new, but that is only because it requires further analysis. We must distinguish the act of adoption from the judgment which justifies it. In so far as my adoption of the projected course of action implies that I give it preference or take a favorable attitude to it, it possesses value. Though doubtless weak in intensity, this is a case of what Professor Dewey calls "prizing" or "esteeming." It invests its object with value, but it does not judge or cognize value; though it might, of course, be accompanied by a reflective awareness of the attitude. The judgment as to the sequel does cause me to take the attitude. I do adopt the plan as one believed to conduce to a certain result; but that which in this case gives value to the plan is not its relation to the sequel, but the affective attitude to it which my judgment as to the sequel has led me to take. Or, it is because my judgment as to the sequel has caused me to take the attitude, that the plan possesses value. Though a judgment led me to the attitude which invests the plan with value, *that* value was not what I judged.

But does the mediating judgment in this case possess another value as its object? In a certain sense, yes. The judgment that the plan will bring the desired result, does attribute to the plan a transferred or indirect value. There is no objection, so far as I can see, to extending the realm of value to include things which, though not valued themselves, are instrumentally or causally related to things which are. But in this case it is evident that the transferred value in question is owing not to the *judgment* of its causal relation, but to the *fact* of that relation. The plan would not have this kind of instrumental value, unless the causal judgment were *true*. The existence of the judgment is not sufficient if the judgment is erroneous; and the plan would have the value in question even if there were no judgment. It follows that while the judgment is in this case in a certain sense a judgment of or about value, it does not create the value which it judges.

The attitude of hope is, as we have seen, a mixed attitude. It is desire qualified by belief. But its object possesses value by virtue of the component of desire. Beliefs as to the future, predictions or expectations, have nothing to do with value, except in so far as they are affectively tinged. Desiring recovery, that future contingency possesses value independently of the element of belief with which it is here associated. It would not be less valuable in the case of despair than it is in the case of hope. The expectation or prediction does undoubtedly refer for its verification to events that have not transpired at the moment of the judgment; but this is equally the case with scientific predictions in which one is not in the least emotionally concerned. Such verifying events must be awaited, but their futurity does not contradict their given or independent character. They are not the products of the judgment, but are facts to which the judgment is prepared to submit.

When the whole performance is consummated, as we suppose it to be, by my recovery of health, we have value in two new senses. In the first place, the state of health is good as having been antecedently desired. Its value is not determined by an act of judgment, but by what we call the "fulfilment of desire." The same state may also possess value, although this is not necessarily the case, as something now presently liked or enjoyed. Its value in this respect also would be independent of any act of judgment. In these two senses, as fulfilling and terminating desire, and as being the immediate object of feeling, an existence may be said to possess value. To judge value of this type would involve the additional act of reflective awareness of the desire as satisfied by the existence, or of the feeling as directed to it. While it might plausibly be maintained that such a reflective awareness invariably accompanies the affective attitudes in question, it is in any case a different and distinguishable thing, having a different object. The difference of object is the same difference that must be supposed to obtain in any case of introspection between a mental state and the observation of it.

Finally, we have to consider the fact that the outcome of the performance, the condition of health itself, was due to the antecedent judgments concerning it. In this case, we appear to have a judgment or a series of judgments which bring to pass their own object. I judged that I was going to recover my health, and then for my very judging of it, I do recover my health. How can my judgment have had its object, when that object still lay in the future, and when through its being causally dependent upon the judgment, it could not come into existence until after the judgment had had time to operate? We seem to have a judgment which is somehow antecedent to a part of itself. Here, as I understand it, is Professor Dewey's paradox.

But instead of allowing ourselves to be driven to a paradox, we should, I submit, insist upon such an account of the matter as shall avoid the paradox. We must deny that that future contingency which is the objective component of the judgment, and which is indispensable to the judgment's occurring at all, is *not* the same as that later event which may or may not occur, or which if it does occur is conditioned by the previous occurrence of the judgment. We must, in other words, supply enough entities to go round. This is entirely possible if we provide an *objective*, or *hypothetical*, or *possibility*, as the content of the antecedent judgment, and distinguish it from the later existence; precisely as we would distinguish the hypothetical payment or failure to pay which is defined by the face of the note as what would honor or dishonor it, from the actual conduct of the payer. These two objects must sustain a peculiar and intimate relation to one another, in that the latter must be the case that "satisfies" the former. It is even true, as we have seen, that the two must intersect, or possess some common constituent, which constitutes the judgment's "maturity," or locus of verification. In the example before us this common constituent comprises the time of the recovery vaguely marked as later than the consultation with the physician, and the particular individual whose health is in question. Health is *now due from this individual*, according to the terms of the judgment. These, and doubtless other factors as well, enter into both the objective and the historical occurrence, and without them neither the judgment nor the occurrence could exist. But even though the constituents of the objective and of the fact should coincide altogether, it would be necessary to attribute to them some difference of ontological status. I have proposed above that the objective should be regarded as a description of the behavior of the judging organism, a goal defined by its set or determining tendency. In some sense this sort of thing must be provided for, and however we provide for it, it must be entitatively distinguished from that actual occurrence or event which would realize it. An objective sustains two relations, one to the act of mind which intends it, the other to the existence which exemplifies or is, in the mathematical sense, a value of it. It may sustain the former relation before it sustains the latter, or even in cases when it does not sustain the latter at all.

In some such way as this the paradox may and must be avoided. We should then have a judgment not bringing about its own objective component, but bringing about the existence which exemplifies its objective component. And the value which is prospectively created by antecedent desire, and prospectively apprehended by the judgment which illuminates and guides that desire, would be different from that value which eventually comes to pass.

I submit, then, that the character of practical judgments requires no amendment of our ordinary notions of judgment. Judgments of value do not create that value-object which they judge; nor are they causes of their own component parts.

In a recent article,[8] Professor Urban professes, albeit darkly and dubiously, to be of one mind with Professor Dewey. I shall not attempt to determine whether two views, both of which unfortunately impress me as dark and dubious, are or are not identical. But since Professor Urban "thinks" they are "in agreement," I shall take his word for it and assume that the following remarks are not irrelevant.

Professor Urban comes out expressly for the doctrine that the "value-judgment" is to be distinguished from all "judgments of truth and fact."[9] Unlike most of the authorities he cites (includ-

8. This Journal, Vol. XIII, p. 673.
9. *Ibid.*, p. 683.

ing, I should suppose, Professor Dewey) Professor Urban is a dualist in respect of judgment. But what he means by the antithesis is far from clear. What is a "judgment of truth"? Is it a judgment which predicates truth of a proposition? That would surely be too occasional a form of judgment to constitute a type coordinate with valuation. It is more probable, since he links judgments of truth with judgments of fact, that he means to refer to judgments which *are* true or false. The antithesis would then be between judgments that are, and judgments that are not, either true or false. But since it is customary to mean by judgment that act of cognition that is distinguished by the alternative of truth or falsity, valuation would appear to be a judgment that lacks the generic judgment character. Certainly the antithesis must remain hopelessly obscure until one has defined what one means by judgment in general, and has distinguished this cognitive form independently of the accident of truth or error. It would seem much more in accordance with usage to say that if valuation is neither true nor false, it is something other than judgment.

But let us consider some of the motives that have induced Professor Urban to set up his antithesis. In the first place, he points out that value attaches not to objects, but to objectives, that is, to complexes of the type "that x is ϕ."[10] But this is peculiar neither to value nor to judgment. Factuality certainly attaches to complexes of the same sort, as when we say, "It is a fact *that, etc.*" This would be regarded as a case of judgment, but not of value. On the other hand, that which is desired, hoped, feared, commanded, forbidden, or otherwise regarded in dozens of ways that constitute the commonest affective-motor attitudes, is also "that so and so shall be." In these cases we have values, but not judgments. It is undoubtedly true, as Meinong, Russell, and many others have recognized, that these attitudes require the admission of *Gegenstände* that are not objects or things in the ordinary sense. But they furnish no criterion by which to distinguish judgments of truth and fact from other judgments, nor valuing from non-valuing attitudes.[11]

In the second place, Professor Urban argues that there are

10. "That" is here used as a conjunction.

11. I find nothing seriously objectionable in Professor Urban's contention that "value is an objective" ("Value and Existence," this Journal, Vol. XIII, p. 464); although I think its universality to be doubtful, and I think it undesirable to leave objectives as entitative finalities. But I do object to the supposition that this in the least argues for the uniqueness of "value judgments."

certain *a priori* "propositions about value" (are these propositions truths or facts?) which are independent of the particular psychological facts about interests, and which are coordinate with the *a priori* propositions about being. Thus, he contends that all objects have either positive or negative value, and that of any two values one must be higher than the other. But it seems perfectly clear upon an examination of the argument, that these alleged *a priori* propositions are either applications of *a priori* propositions concerning being, or are obtained from the empirical character of interest. That every object must possess positive or negative value, can be regarded as *a priori* only in so far as it is derived from the law of excluded middle, negative value being regarded as the non-possession of value. To argue that all objects possess value requires an appeal to the empirical character of interest. "All objects, as objects, are of interest either actually or potentially, and wherever there is interest there is value."[12] But how does Professor Urban know that all objects are as such capable of being objects of interest? If he knows it at all, which is doubtful, it is because of the actual ubiquity of interest as a modality of consciousness, or the psychological possibility of associating an attitude of interest with any other attitude by which a thing becomes an object.

The necessity of a value's being "higher or lower" than any other value is derived, if at all, either from the empirical fact that values have all-commensurable intensive magnitude, a contention that has often been disputed; or from the empirical fact that interest is always psychologically associated with preference, that is, from the fact that interests are always (?) so interconnected with other interests in one subject that the expression of one interest implies at least the momentary subordination of other interests. In other words, Professor Urban's generalizations about value are facts about value, which are either of the general logical sort common to all facts, or of a particular sort derived from the special peculiarities of that sort of psychophysical fact known as interest.

In the third place, Professor Urban insists that the conception of "ought," which he believes to be peculiar to value-judgments, is irreducible to the categories of being and non-being.

12. *Ibid.*, p. 675.

"The value-judgment," he says, "is not '*A* is as it ought to be,' but rather 'that *A* ought to be.'"[13] But Professor Urban must be aware that the difficulties, if any, attaching to this form of judgment, are not peculiar to value. What is required is a judgment that shall assert something only hypothetically or contingently existential. But that is the case with all judgments involving variables. Suppose that one says that "*x* is a man implies *x* is mortal." One does not assert that "there is a man," or that "this is a man." Nevertheless, one is judging either truly or falsely concerning a logical or implicational fact. One may express it, if one wishes, by saying, "if a case of man should occur, it would be mortal." And similarly with obligation. Some purpose requires or implies *x*. This can equally well be expressed as "*x* ought to occur," or as "if *a* occurs and is a value of *x*, then it is such as ought to occur." Similarly, "the comet ought to be visible in such and such a place at such and such a time," or "the key ought to be of such and such a shape"; meaning that the law of the comet's motion and the shape of the lock determine the conditions of visibility or fitness, whether or not these conditions are fulfilled by existence. Judgments of this sort are not peculiar to value, nor are they distinguishable from judgments of truth and fact.

The *prospective* character of judgments of "ought" is even less calculated to prove what Professor Urban wants to prove. "It is the very nature of the value-judgment," he says, "that it apprehends, not something completely given, but rather something to be. Value is not a determination of being, but a direction of becoming."[14] It is incredible that Professor Urban should propose to restrict judgments of truth and fact to judgments concerning the completely given. The commonest of all scientific judgments are those concerning the future, the so-called judgments of prediction. And only less common than these are judgments asserting a direction of becoming, such, for example, as the generalization based on the second law of thermodynamics, or such laws as Spencer believed to determine cosmic evolution. The most familiar biological phenomena, such as growth and instinct, can not be judged at all except in such terms. Are such judgments, then, value-judgments? And are they not judgments of fact and truth?

Professor Urban accuses me of confusing "the qualities of an

13. *Ibid.*, p. 687.
14. *Ibid.*, p. 687.

object on account of which it is valued with the value itself, the fact that it ought to be."[15] Now whether we prefer to use the substantive "value" to denote the object which is valuable, or the fact that it is valuable, is a matter of no importance. In any case, Professor Urban's essentially sane habits of mind prompt him here to identify value with the *fact* that a thing ought to be. A judgment of value would then be a judgment regarding such a fact. Like any other judgment, this would be true if the fact were as judged, and otherwise false. This leaves one quite in the dark as to the constituents of this particular kind of fact, whether, for example 'ought' is an intuited ultimate, not further definable, or whether, as I think, it consists in an implicative relation of interests. But at least it makes it perfectly clear that there is no differentia of value to be found in the analysis of judgment.

I still believe that the underlying cause of this whole muddle is a confusion of the essential act of judgment with the motor-affective attitudes with which it is psychologically associated. This is almost invariably betrayed by an author's fondness for such hybrids as "appreciation," "approval," "acknowledgment," *etc.* If one wishes to emphasize the fact that in our experiences of value, judgment, affection and will are intimately associated, well and good. But then let the essential character of judgment be first distinguished from its accidental associations. Fact, existence, truth, object, objective, are terms belonging to the analysis of judgment as such. The structure and function of judgment can not be described without reference to them. Then, and then only, after one has discriminated judgment abstractly, can one safely venture into the perplexing field of the subjective and objective varieties of judgment. Then one may, if one wishes, collect and label a whole menagerie of judgments, not only value judgments, but verbal judgments, visual judgments, private judgments, public judgments, German judgments, American judgments, and German-American judgments,—with some guarantee that at least they are all judgments.

15. *Ibid.*, p. 685.

Appendix 3

VALUE AND CAUSALITY
by Wendell T. Bush

The exchange of views[1] between Professor Urban and Mr. Schneider has impelled me to take from a pigeon-hole a paper written originally as a contribution to the discussion between Professor Sheldon and Professor Perry at the New Haven meeting of the Philosophical Association in 1913.[2] Some changes and additions have been made to connect it with the issue that has been raised by Professor Dewey's theory of value as it appears in his *Essays in Experimental Logic* and which appears to be the point on which Urban and Schneider amiably but vigorously disagree.

It is not surprising that the discussion of values tends to become more and more complicated. Four years ago at New Haven the issue was very clear-cut; it might have been named the place of realism *versus* the place of individualism in a theory of value. At that time realism was still a thing of experiment and adventure, while idealism, or whatever you like to call the type of thinking that still took subjectivism into account, was beginning to look decidedly conservative, and one of the interesting features of the meeting was that the realistic paper was read by one supposed to be, whether rightly or wrongly, an idealist (*pace suo*), while the position in which subjectivism is supposed to survive was defended by a militant realist.

Of these two papers, the former, by Professor Sheldon, gave a definition of value in which the ego, to use a term now sufficiently discredited to be safe, is entirely superfluous. Professor Perry took the opposite ground and assured us that "it is held at the present day with something approaching unanimity that value in the generic sense has to do with a certain constant called bias or interest."[3] It is because this old issue crops up, as I think, in the Urban-Schneider discussion and it is because further dis-

1. This Journal, Vol. XIV, pp. 701 and 706.
2. This Journal, Vol. XI, pp. 113 and 141.
3. *Loc. cit.*, p. 149.

[First published in *Journal of Philosophy, Psychology and Scientific Methods* 15 (1918): 85–96. For Dewey's reply, see this volume, pp. 3–9.]

criminations are usually possible, and because that meeting at New Haven was a very pleasant occasion, that I revive its problem.

I fancy we need no longer feel alarm at what may seem affinities with either realism or idealism. The traditional flavor of "subjective" and "objective" should not impel us to dialectical preferences. The out-door habit of mind has become so natural that the old bogey of labels is rather attractively amusing than otherwise. The above reference to a shop-worn antithesis is, accordingly, only to notice that it has found its place on the shelf of metaphysical curiosities.

As the more recent of the discussions I have alluded to began with a paper by Mr. Schneider, I will venture a word or two about that. Mr. Schneider's point of view is that of what might be called a pragmatic theory of value. This point of view is stated at some length by Professor Dewey in his article[4] "The Logic of Judgments of Practise." Now this context limits the range of the discussion very precisely. Professor Urban could, I think, easily have pointed out that while many things about value do illustrate the logic of judgments of practise, other things do not, but just because they do not, they can not be recognized in a theory of value that is part of a theory of judgments of practise. In so far as value facts come within the region of intelligent behavior, Mr. Schneider's account is, I think, entirely acceptable. But may there not be much of value that falls outside that region? Mr. Schneider appears to assume that whatever is valuable is valuable for something. Of course whatever is valuable in the context of judgments of practise must be valuable for something, but surely many things are prized and enjoyed without reference to any utility or end or completed situation. I do not wish for a moment to dispute Dewey's and Schneider's analysis; I do, however, point out that their analysis applies only to the subject-matter that instrumentalism applies to, and this leaves out of account, I take it, one whole half of experience. I mean that instrumentalism, and its corollaries, applies to what has reference to the future; I do not see how it can apply to what we call the present when we disregard its causalities and potentialities. What I have in mind is the old contrast between beauty and use. Instrumentalism certainly

4. This Journal, Vol. XII, pp. 505 and 533; and *Experimental Logic*, pp. 349–389. [*Middle Works* 8:23–49.]

suggests causality made use of, and the instrumentalist account of value, in the desire to escape the harmless bogey of subjectivism, tends, I think, to equate value with causality. The old problem as to the necessity of an appreciating ego in a value-generating situation seems to be making for the shelf too, but my paper was written when that problem might still be occasionally mentioned, and so my own remarks are conceived in a confessedly reminiscent vein. I shall use the word value in a sense quite the opposite to that preferred by instrumentalism, but a detail of usage is not, I take it, the point at issue, and whether the *word* "value" is given one meaning or another no relevant fact will be modified, and the circumstances alluded to ought not to be obscured.

Instrumentalism is, it seems to me, realistic in an empirical or phenomenal sense (these terms imply nothing metaphysically), and idealistic in the sense that it is interested in human situations, activities, and methods. In the former respect, the instrumentalist theory of value is somewhat in line with Professor Sheldon's paper mentioned above, and in the second it moves in the atmosphere of Professor Perry's paper. While an instrumentalist may claim, I think, that the problem of the presence or absence of an ego does not concern him, he may claim this because he has already decided the question and decided it in favor of Professor Perry's position. The instrumentalist, as such, is primarily interested in the data of what I call below an ego-centric situation, but as an instrumentalist he is somewhat too indifferent to the non-instrumental data of that situation.

The idealistic thesis that the landscape is a function of the ego is familiar and historically intelligible. The thesis of the realist that the ego is superfluous for the landscape is equally familiar. It may be worth while to remember that, in any case, the ego and the landscape often do go together, and that when they do, the situation is not quite identical with what it is when they do not. Using Professor Perry's very neat adjective, the more complex of these two might be called an ego-centric situation. I need not insist that the ego-centric situation is an entirely empirical one with which no one of us is unfamiliar. The originality of Professor Sheldon's paper lay in his effort to emancipate value from ego-centric situations. Let us start, therefore, without assuming any ego, bias, or interest.

Let us conceive, imagine, or define a section of nature where there is nothing that can be aware of a preference or an aversion, no sentient organism that can feel pleasure or pain, comfort or discomfort, or any impulse whatever. The seasons come and go, vegetation thrives and starves in response to rain, sun, and drought. Everything happens that conceivably can happen except that nothing happens to an ego. Does not the term causality cover all the influences here of one thing on another? We can, to be sure, say that the rain is good for the ferns and desirable for the moss, and that the drought was very bad for the wild flowers. We can apply the terminology of value as much as we like and we shall not be misunderstood, for it will be clear that what we are talking about is causality. And it will probably be always more natural to say the rain is good for the crops than to say it is good for the weeds. In a strictly realistic world, however—realistic in the sense that it contains no ego-centric references whatever—does not the word causality describe all the cases in which one thing can affect another? However we may specify or complicate cases of causality, are they, under these conditions, any less or any more than causality?

Now when we introduce a creature subject to bias or interest, impulse or preference, is anything new introduced, and what is it? Does something now happen that did not happen before? If there is now something new, the ego-centric situation calls for a new word, a word which, just because it denotes something that world number one did not possess, should not be applied to cases of world number one type. Things are not now merely causally effective; they are disagreeable and agreeable, sought or shunned for themselves and their effects.

If now something new is introduced when *bias* or *interest* is introduced, if the relation of things to this bias or interest is a new relation, that is, a relation to a new term, it is, of course, merely a question of terminology whether we indicate this new relation by one word or by another. Suppose we extend the term "value" to mean causality under certain definite circumstances not including necessarily any subject of interests or preferences; the word value can then not be used to designate the new relation, and another word will have to be found to do so. Nothing will have been done except to identify value with certain cases of causality and to adopt some other word to do the work that naturally belongs to this one. I can not help concluding, then, that the presence of *bias* or *interest* defines a type of situation where something happens that is not a case of causality merely. What happens is that things acquire value, and if the relation of things to interest and preference can not exist apart from ego-centric situations, what virtue can there possibly be in seeking to ignore this fundamental circumstance?

Another commonplace of the subject (as I had supposed) is the distinction between "intrinsic" and relative values. We experience, enjoy, or endure the present, we anticipate and seek to control the future. These may, to be sure, be viewed as different aspects of a complex present. The present is intrinsically as good and as bad as we find it, and it contains the resources, the causative or relative values that enable us to treat the future as an object of enterprise. This terminology should, perhaps, not be taken too literally; it should not be taken to mean that we value values and not things. Things are complex and acquire value from one property or another; when they do so they may be regarded often enough as individual instances of this property. But within the ego-centric situation intrinsic or immediate values may depend upon all sorts of circumstances, and a classification of them may be indefinitely complex. It is intrinsic values that are "matters of taste," the kind of thing about which disputing is likely to be futile and argument banal. I suppose no one will deny that there are individual peculiarities of taste, and it is quite certain that such peculiarities are most respected by those who have gradually achieved a capacity for varied appreciations.

The causalities of world number one persist, but they no longer influence merely indifferent facts; they are or may be causes of value and so acquire value from the intrinsic character of their consequences. The shortest and simplest word to indicate this new relation is, perhaps, the word "use." Is there anything singular in saying that "use" comes in with the "ego-centric" situation? With use, however, we are in a region of values where discussion is not irrelevant, because causality does not depend upon the ego-centric situation; only the value of causality depends upon that. The ego-centric situation added something to world number one; it did not take anything away from it. Man can not, of course, live in any portion of nature without being seriously interested in the mechanics of his environment, and we can and do study and debate the mechanics by means of which intrinsic values can be obtained. But what is thus studied and debated is mechanics and causality, not value in the strict sense.

Is one more interested in the quality of the present or in the potentialities of the present? The wise man is, no doubt, interested in both. Nevertheless, most of those that are really interested in either are not, as a rule, altogether "wise." Some there are who view things as a vision; others see in things the instruments and the raw material of change. The distinction above insisted upon, that of enjoyment *versus* use, may seem to be overcome in the fact that in actual experience the things that are useful or dangerous have in addition some esthetic quality, or may have; also that the esthetic value of anything is complicated by the future consequences it may reasonably be expected to produce, and that it is a corrupt taste,[5] or at least a crude and inexperienced one, that is indifferent to a thing's "relative" value. This is, however, only to point out what is as obvious as anything else, namely, that things are complex and bear upon the future as well as exist in the present, and that taste is capable of education that does not contradict intelligence, but fortifies it. And it is equally clear that a community should make its instrumentalities esthetically tolerable, for if the present is never possessed, instrumentalities are a futile pretense. It is to the intrinsic values that sacrifices are ultimately due. In a greater or less measure we are continually mutilating the present for the sake of the future, and compromising the future for the sake of the present. That is, we are constantly sacrificing value to use and use to value, and what makes the difference between these so real and so well worth marking is the fact that both the present and the future are such empirical actualities. All this may not be worth dwelling upon, but the distinction ought to be maintained in subsequent generalizations.

The distinction between value and causality will not remove or complicate the discussion of any genuine problem. Only such problems as might result from equating value with causality will be extinguished, and it is the apprehension that artificial problems might be created by a definition that must account for all this display of shop-worn goods.

What I have called relative values (instrumental values might

5. Santayana in *Reason in Art*, p. 207.

be a better term) may seem to be a special case of those values that depend upon presuppositions. I may value and use a disagreeable medicine because it will cure a cold. I may like the Mona Lisa because Da Vinci painted it. These are, to be sure, both presuppositional values, but to class them together is to make a logical rather than an empirical identification. It seems to me their difference is greater than their resemblance. If I may venture to propose a pair of terms, I would suggest independent and dependent values; instrumental values would then appear as a particularly important class of dependent values. Dependent values are good for what can be gotten out of them, and there is nothing startling in saying that independent values are good for nothing. That does not mean that they have no value; it means only that they are the type and source of all value. And if I may repeat, the distinction between independent and dependent values does not in the least imply that things do not have both together. So many things are agreeable but harmful, disagreeable but beneficial; the attitude of esteem is so often spontaneous *and* complicated by various considerations.

Any one who studies the problems of value is likely to approach the topic with a dominant interest in either esthetics or ethics, an interest rather in what I have ventured to call the quality of the present or the potentiality of the present. The difference marks two temperaments that are likely to misunderstand each other unless the distinction between independent and dependent values is kept clearly in mind. Is truth a value? Perhaps. If we say that it is, I suppose we must mean that particular propositions have the one sort of value or the other, or both. It is when propositions acquire independent value that discussion becomes difficult. Certain it is that one who comes to the subject chiefly from esthetics will give ample recognition to what I call independent values. This happens to be the case with the present writer. I do not know that it was the case with Professor Perry, but in his paper,[6] the strong emphasis on independent or intrinsic value is accompanied by an illustration from the field of art. And when Mr. G. E. Moore is cited as denying the necessity of interest, the reference is to a work on ethics.[7]

This fact of special preoccupation leads to another considera-

6. *Loc. cit.*
7. *Loc. cit.*, p. 154.

tion, which is that when a definition of value is attempted, the chances are that it is a case of some one seeking light in one direction or another, and it would usually be helpful to know in which direction the definition is intended to lead. For where the interest is genuine and the subject complex, where one is really thinking one's way ahead, it is not likely that one seeks to make a definition and let it go at that. There will be farther work to do, a great deal; the definition is only getting started. I should expect that those who are more interested in the potentiality of the present, in the control of situations by intelligent behavior, would take very kindly to definitions of value of the type proposed by Professor Sheldon. "Given any tendency, in dead nature, in living organisms, in conscious minds, which presses toward a certain end; any other tendency that furthers this is for it a good, and any that resists it is for it bad."[8]

A definition like this lends itself very well indeed to the interests of those engaged upon that aspect of experience called the future, but it is entirely useless to those engaged upon that other aspect, no less real, called the present. And in the interest of candor, I may add that the view I have stressed received such meager formulation as I have given it, not in the context of ethics where the ideas of intelligence, control, and direction are dominant, but in that of esthetics where one topic of empirical importance is the education of discriminating appreciation, the attainment of progressive connoisseurship, that possession of the present without which it is hard to see how there can be a real possession of anything.

It is only in the field of independent values that the great battles of taste can take place. One generation often hardly understands another. What would the public of Haydn have said to the music of Strauss? But the question of the comparative efficiency of different methods to bring about an objective change produces not a storm, but an experiment.

The emphasis upon independent values may seem, at first, embarrassing for philosophy, for philosophy is committed to discussion. Against that emphasis there is, says Professor Perry, "perhaps one fundamental motive after all; the desire, namely, to discover a criterion by which superiority or inferiority shall be as-

8. Professor Sheldon's article, p. 121.

signed to values themselves—the desire to justify a criticism of the natural or empirical values. It seems to be necessary to provide for a scale or hierarchy in which inclination shall be subordinated to duty, impulse to a 'norm,' or enjoyment to an ideal."[9] And elsewhere (p. 155): "The objectivity or commutability of judgments of value in some sense must be saved, not for the benefit of those debating societies, for which he (Santayana) has so poor an opinion, but in order that we may read and enjoy essays like his own, and understand him even when he says 'that good is not an intrinsic or primary quality, but relative and adventitious.'" But what are the values that can be justified or criticized? Evidently values of instrumentality. And what are the judgments of value that have any objectivity that can be conserved? Clearly, it would seem, judgments of dependent value, judgments which result from a consideration of consequences. But independent values are, so to speak, the premises of specific value syllogisms. They can not be criticized while they remain premises; the experiences that contain them must be construed from the point of view of their consequences, that is, they must be taken instrumentally, with reference to a future. Independent values can not be discussed; this is what gives a certain effectiveness to the sort of popular "pragmatism" that seeks to insure anybody's religious preferences. "For as Moore points out, if each party to the discussion is referring to his own interest, no two can ever be referring to the same thing. This is the genuinely vicious sort of relativism which puts an end to discourse, and is contradicted in the very act of generalizing it."[10] The relativism is certainly there, but it is troublesome only for those who want to treat an independent value as though it were a dependent value. What we can do is to call attention to the things or to the aspects of things which have for us independent or intrinsic value in order to see if it will not then happen that the value is recognized. If the bias, or interest, or sensitive organization is the same or sufficiently similar, then the valued object is in practically the same relation in each case. It seems to be the slightly intolerant assumption that there is a definably normal type such that its values and preferences are normal and authoritative. This essentially

9. Professor Perry's article, p. 156.
10. *Loc. cit.*, p. 154.

academic ideal is a hard one to get rid of, especially, I suspect, for those of us whose business is teaching.

Santayana puts the case for the cautious souls when, writing of Shelley, he says: "The question for Shelley is not at all what will look nicest in his song; that is the preoccupation of mincing rhymsters, whose well is soon dry. Shelley's abundance has a more generous source; it springs from his passion for picturing what would be best, not in the picture, but in the world."[11] What more important subject of discussion than what would be best in the world, and who having the mission to discuss, criticize, and examine all things would not be likely to begin by assuming that all things are subject to discussion? If, however, value depends upon relation to an interest, if it can arise only in an ego-centric situation, values that are achieved, accomplished, or arrived at depend upon a term that varies from moment to moment. The curious thing is not that people are so different, but that they are so much alike.

May not one circumstance that makes the subject of values difficult to discuss without confusion be this, that many values are such intimate things? Experience is shot through with values; they illuminate it with an iridescent subtlety; perhaps we know more about them than about anything else, more than we can easily put into words or more than we want to. It would not be surprising if the more elusive qualities of life did not lend themselves unreservedly to the method of definition.

Professor Dewey in his account of practical judgments is describing a cognitive activity, and he restricts the word cognitive in the way that is one of the characteristic features of instrumentalism. This sharper definition of cognition gives us, I believe, a really good and fruitful distinction, and the purpose of this paper is to insist upon it, noting, however, that it involves what a Hegelian might call "its Other," and that the total context, that instrumentalists so properly remind us of, is not irrelevant. The "Other" to which I chiefly attend, and to which acts of valuation refer, is not cognitive experience at all, in the sense (I think the right one) in which instrumentalists use the word. Also instrumentalism is more fairly and intelligibly stated in terms of verbs than in terms of nouns. One is reminded of James's metaphor, the

11. *Winds of Doctrine*, p. 163.

flights and perchings of a bird. The perchings are no less of the total context because instrumentalists are interested chiefly in the flights. Professor Dewey states candidly that his topic is the cognitive act of evaluation, and he would (rightly, I think) like to avoid the word value altogether. He is explicit in recognizing what I call immediate, intrinsic, or independent values. "Only a prior dogma to the effect that every conscious experience *is, ipso facto,* a form of cognition leads to any obscuration of the fact, and the burden of proof is upon those who uphold the dogma."[12] But though that part of the subject to which instrumentalism applies, *viz.*, the field of cognitive evaluations, is best described in terms of verbs, the points of repose, the non-cognitive "perchings" seem to have an affinity with the more static substantives. To ask a question about non-cognitive experience, expecting in the reply a statement of that experience's cognitive aspect, is just the *petitio* that Professor Dewey will not have.

In this whole matter I have done no more than expand upon a sentence or two in Santayana's *The Sense of Beauty*: "Evidently all values must be ultimately intrinsic. The useful is good because of the excellence of its consequences; but these must somewhere cease to be merely useful in their turn, or only excellent as means; somewhere we must reach the good in itself and for its own sake, else the whole process is futile, and the utility of our first object illusory" (pp. 28–29). Also: "Values spring from the immediate and inexplicable reaction of vital impulse, and from the irrational part of our nature" (p. 19). Readers of the same author's *Reason in Art* may have been surprised that what he says about intrinsic values in the above passage from the *Sense of Beauty* receives no emphasis in the later work. Its title, however, indicates the subject-matter of cognitive valuations, whereas the earlier book dealt with the non-cognitive aspect of experience. The *Life of Reason* is a work in ethics, while the *Sense of Beauty* is a work in esthetics. Such separations exist, of course, not in life, but in literature, and so an instrumentalist might protest that it is a distinction with an intellectual purpose. All I ask, however, is that experience recognized as non-cognitive should not be given instrumentalistic responsibilities.

Now Professor Dewey, whose pages on "Judgments of Value"

12. *Essays in Experimental Logic*, p. 351. [*Middle Works* 8:24.]

I have had particularly in mind, does not confuse what I have called dependent and independent values. He begins by warning us against that confusion. He observes "that contemporary discussion of values and valuation suffers from confusion of the two radically different attitudes—that of direct, active, non-cognitive experience of goods and bads, and that of valuation, . . . "[13] He points out that "'to value' means two radically different things; to prize and to appraise; to esteem and to estimate; to find good in the sense described above (independent value) and to judge it to be good, to *know* it as good,"[14] *i.e.*, to judge that it is good for reasons that can be adduced. Professor Dewey's account is complicated a little by its relation to a discussion in epistemology. He chooses, as any one has a right to do, to tie the word value up to a cognitive act called valuation, but he states explicitly what he is doing, and I see no excuse for misunderstanding. But by so doing, does not the word value become synonymous, in the instrumentalist presentation, with the word use. Now if this is true, if the instrumentalist means use when he says value, why not employ the simpler word, particularly if he (and I think he is right) feels that the word value has become infected with many artificial suggestions? When a word is thus compromised, it is well to drop it if possible, and find another. Let us try the experiment of substituting the word use for the word value in the instrumentalist account and see what we get. It seems to me that we get a statement of precisely what the instrumentalist means, but a statement with which no one would disagree. "My theme is that a judgment of value is simply a case of practical judgment, a judgment about the doing of something."[15] Value occurs when we face the question, What things or methods have the value of utility under the circumstances? That is, the exposition begins by limiting the values discussed to cases that are cases of judgment, in the instrumentalist's sense. I can not help feeling that when we say "use," as well as mean it, we say something equivalent to the proposition "utility is usefulness" which no instrumentalist would call a judgment at all.

In the above statement of my own, written for the most part three years ago, I attach value rather to what is not judged at all,

13. *Loc. cit.*, p. 354. [*Middle Works* 8:26.]
14. *Loc. cit.*, p. 354. [*Middle Works* 8:26.]
15. *Loc. cit.*, p. 358. [*Middle Works* 8:29.]

but is independently esteemed, appreciated, or endured. This is in agreement with Aristotle's notion of the good as that with reference to which instrumentalities are selected. It is, if you like, a verbal matter, but aside from purposes of moral edification, there is as much reason for characterizing value by irresponsibility as by specific responsibility. The upshot of it all is that the problems of value, wherever we attack them, take us quickly into a region of experience, to which instrumentalism was never intended to apply, and where instrumentalists can not, as such, easily follow the lead of the subject-matter. Nor does it follow from this that rival theories of value are any better than instrumentalists think they are.

The city of Syracuse (New York) has a very beautiful institution. The state fair is held there every autumn, and on the evening of the last day there is a parade of all the city's children. The people of Syracuse regard this parade with an almost passionate affection. They begin to take their places on the curb a long time before the procession begins. It seems quite natural to say they value it supremely; to ask a citizen of Syracuse, while the children were passing, what it was good for, wherein the value of the spectacle lay, would, I fancy, seem almost blasphemous. Does value attach really to things like this or to the means used to bring them about? Of course it is a verbal question, but it is a question that takes us to considerations where instrumentalism is no longer a sufficient point of view.

Appendix 4

THE LEGAL STATUS OF WAR
by Salmon O. Levinson

Suppose the world at peace. Abruptly Germany declares war upon France and invades her territories without even disguising the intention of annexation or even of reducing her neighbor to vassalage. What happens legally? What happens, that is as far as international law is concerned? Or, if this question seems to be framed on the basis of the present hatred of Germany, ask a similar question about an unjustified attack by the United States upon Mexico or Canada. The resulting legal situation is in no uncertainty. Immediately the war comes under the sanction of international law. It is henceforth a "legal war." Other nations are as much bound to neutrality and the observance of the rules laid down by international law as if the war were a benign enterprise.

Most discussions concerning war ignore this primary fact, namely, that the civilized world puts all wars, as soon as they are initiated, upon the same plane of legality, without any regard to their origin and objectives. The present legal situation is summed up in the definition given by Charles Sumner:

> War is a contest between nations under the *sanction of international law* for the establishment of justice between them.

It is this fact which ties the hands of those who desire a permanent improvement in international relations. If it is lawful to do a thing, why make such a cry about its being done? If war is legal, why object to militarism, which is a necessary effect of the legality of war rather than, as is popularly assumed, the cause of war? If war is legitimate it inevitably follows that those extensive and chronic preparations for war which constitute militarism are as practically sensible as they are legally justified. As long as international law continues to legalize war all nations are moral accessories before the fact to "collective murder." Conversely, outlaw war and militarism is out of a job.

[First published in *New Republic* 14 (1918): 171–73. For Dewey's reply, see this volume, pp. 122–26.]

It may be contended that although these statements have applied in the past they will not hold good if the League to Enforce Peace comes into existence. But however radical the plan for the formation of such a League may have seemed before the war, a fundamental defect is now obvious. It does not propose to declare war illegal; it proposes simply to refine those regulations under which war is legal: To increase the preliminary ceremonies which must be gone through in order that the benediction of legality may descend upon a war. So far so good. But as long as nations are educated to think of war as a legalized institution the distinction made by the League between "justiciable" and "non-justiciable" might utterly defeat the main purpose of the League. The distinction invites manipulation at the hands of astute statesmen with aggrandizing tendencies. What more could a Bismarck or a Disraeli desire than exclusion from the forceful jurisdiction of the supreme Tribunal of all causes involving "national honor" and "vital national interests"? The non-justiciable exception would be an open bid for skilled manoeuvering. Would not the assassination of the crown prince at Sarajevo have supplied a non-justiciable issue through which to usher in the present world war? The matters which reasonably constitute points of vital interest and honor to the respective nations are precisely the matters to be formulated and safeguarded in the proposed International Code. These large questions would then be fought out by experienced statesmen in the council chamber rather than by boys on the field of battle.

In the history of English law after the establishment of a right to trial and evidence before a court, private murderous brawls (though doubtless reduced in number) continued under the guise of "affairs of honor." From the time of Henry II down to the nineteenth century any private dispute might have two aspects: One a mundane, material aspect relating to property rights and as such justiciable—i.e., capable of determination upon evidence by a court; the other affecting the character, not the property, of the injured party, and hence non-justiciable, i.e., capable of settlement not by a court upon evidence, but only by a murderous conflict called a duel. Since either alternative was lawful, it was open to any skilled bully to emphasize the honor or prestige element in a dispute, turn his back upon the courts, and, in full exercise of his legal rights, insist upon a settlement on "the field of honor."

In fact, the whole history of the duel closely parallels the course of international law with respect to war. For centuries efforts were made in most countries to moderate and regulate dueling by "Codes," fixing the terms and conditions, weapons, distance, duties of seconds, etc., etc. The code became more and more elaborate; more and more "humane." Seconds were morally bound to act as a "council of conciliation." But the whole thing rested on the premise of the legality of dueling. It assumed affairs of honor in which it was the obligation as well as the right of a gentleman to resort to the shedding of blood. An interesting volume might be written comparing the code of honor between individuals with that called international law between nations, the Hague Conventions occupying the place of culminating futility in the latter. In one case as the other, we want not laws *of* war, but laws *against* war, just as we have laws *against* murder, not laws *of* murder.

Perhaps three-fourths of the contents of treatises on international law are devoted to rules and regulation of war. On this subject Woolsey says:

> International law assumes that there must be wars and fighting among nations and endeavors to lay down rules by which they shall be brought within the limit of justice and humanity. In fact, wars and the relations in which nations stand to one another, as belligerent or neutral, form the principal branch of international law, so much so, that in a state of assured and permanent peace there would be little need of this science.

The quotation enforces the similarity between international law and the old dueling codes. Both are intended simply to set certain limits within which a perfectly legal practice shall go on. The aim of both is simply to mitigate and humanize. Upon the whole the advantage is on the side of the dueling codes; for at least they were enforceable; while, as the present war shows, it is quite possible for any nation which is ruthlessly bent upon victory to ignore under the pleas of self-preservation, military necessity, or *lex talionis*, any provision which it finds in its way. As long as war is the lawful method of establishing justice between nations there seems indeed to be something incongruous in the notion of war plus rosewater, and much to be said for the logic, though not the morality, of a nation which, like Germany, carries the idea of war to its extreme conclusion as a legitimate science.

The outlawing of war is manifestly the primary condition under which the League to Enforce Peace can be made effective. If war is to remain lawful, its antecedent, military preparation, is legitimate and necessary; if war is made criminal international force is required for prevention and punishment. The power to enforce any law must always be adequate. A trial before an international court must not be an alternative to war; it must be made a substantial and complete substitute for war. We must not indulge in the absurdity of committing ourselves to the proposition that we may use force to compel a nation to submit its cause to arbitration, but shall not use force to execute the decision of the international court in such arbitration.

War, though made illegal, might still conceivably occur but it would be branded as a crime and the force of the world would be organized to deal with the criminal. Without these safeguards reduction of armaments would only too probably be a mere temporary expedient during economic convalescence, to be later evaded under one pretext or another when some nation thought that its interests would be furthered by resorting to war.

With these safeguards, reduction of armaments would occur as a matter of course to the point required to protect domestic tranquillity and other intra-national needs. In course of time the very existence of a tribunal where all international wrongs may be redressed would render the great force behind it protective and merely potential, like the force now behind our own national and state tribunals.

In closing I wish to say that I write from the standpoint of a lawyer, although not an international lawyer. My experience has been largely in dealing with problems arising from conflicts of interests due to industrial breakdowns and a consequent need for reorganization. It has convinced me that the problem of adjusting large conflicting corporate interests is not essentially different as a human problem from that of the adjustment of conflicting national interests. At present, however, the practical application of such a point of view to international affairs is hampered and at critical moments made impossible by the survival of the old tradition of the legality and necessity of war. When war is released from the embrace of international law, then and then only can sensible methods of adjustment be resorted to with adequate promise of success. Moreover, the elimination of war would automatically sweep away most of the present vexing international questions. The problems of contraband, blockade, in short the freedom of the seas, buffer states, the so-called balance of power, the sanctity of neutrality treaties, integrity of small nations, the "rectification of boundaries," are created by the existence of war and have no significance under peace conditions.

To sum up, two things are indispensable to the reorganization of the world: The specific outlawing of war by the code of nations and the ability by force to execute the decrees of the international tribunal.

NOTES

54.1 "Education and Social Direction"] Published in *Dial* on 11 April 1918, one year after the United States entered World War I, with three other essays dealing with education and the war: "The University and Democracy" by Charles A. Beard, "On Creating a Usable Past" by Van Wyck Brooks, and "The Creative and Efficiency Concepts of Education" by Helen Marot.

55.12 New York school administrator] John L. Tildsley, associate superintendent of schools in charge of high schools, whose investigation of classroom practices at the De Witt Clinton High School, New York City, resulted in the transfer of six teachers and the trial and suspension of Thomas Mufson, Samuel Schmalhauser, and A. Henry Schneer. For a report of an address by Tildsley, in which he explained his ideas on instinctive obedience, see *New York Times*, 10 December 1917, p. 10. For more concerning this case, see *Middle Works* 10:158–63, 173–77.

59.7 present minister of education] Herbert Albert Laurens Fisher.

60.15 Mr. Arthur Dean] Arthur Davis Dean, professor of vocational education at Teachers College, Columbia University, and former chief of the vocational school division of the New York State Education Department, who spoke at this convention about training for social service in the schools.

61.18–19 a recent school trouble in New York City] For the De Witt Clinton High School case, see note for p. 55.12.

64.6–7 Mrs. Talbot] Anna Hedges Talbot, specialist in the New York State Education Department on vocational training for girls, who spoke at this convention about educational values of Red Cross work.

73.23–24 Mr. Schwab] Charles M. Schwab, president and chairman of the board of directors, Bethlehem Steel Corporation, was appointed director general of the Emergency Fleet Corporation, U.S. Shipping Board, on 16 April 1918. For his statements, see *New York Times*, 25 January 1918, p. 11; 28 February 1918, p. 9.

73.24 Cardinal Bourne] For prediction by Francis Bourne, archbishop of Westminster, of social upheaval in Great Britain as a result of the war, see *New York Times*, 10 February 1918, sec. 1, p. 4.

79.21 today's paper] For Pennsylvania Railroad report, see *New York Times*, 5 March 1918, p. 17.

85.34–35 President Sanford] Edmund Clark Sanford, president of Clark College 1909–20.

87.6 Mr. Schwab] See note for p. 73.23–24.

94.36 lobby at Albany] Probably a reference to New York primary politics—the intense opposition among upstate Democrats to William Randolph Hearst as Democratic candidate for governor and attendant accusations against Tammany Hall.

98.1 "What Are We Fighting For?"] Published 22 June 1918 and prefaced with this note: "This is the second of a series of forward-looking articles on America's aims and ideals in the war, written for The Independent by the leaders of thoughtful America. The first article was written by President Lowell of Harvard University. . . ." Succeeding articles, all bearing the same title, were contributed by less well-known authors.

150.2 Mr. Creel's critics] George Creel was chairman of the controversial Committee on Public Information, created in April 1917, one week after American entry into World War I. The other committee members were Secretary of War Newton D. Baker, Secretary of the Navy Josephus Daniels, and Secretary of State Robert Lansing. Creel and the journalists who worked under him were accused of censorship and news management. See Creel's *How We Advertised America* (New York: Harper and Bros., 1920).

158.1 Baron Ishii] Kikujiro Ishii, designated baron in 1914 and viscount in 1916, frequently spoke on German propaganda while in the United States as head of the Imperial Japanese War Mission. The speech Dewey refers to was probably one delivered in New York City in September 1917.

175.21 some addresses of Baron Goto in America] Shimpei Goto, Japanese foreign minister immediately preceding Yasuya Uchida. For his addresses, discussing Japan's plans to aid China and American misunderstanding of Japan, see *New York Times*, 7 May 1919, p. 15; 20 May 1919, p. 5.

175.31–32 recent interview of Foreign Minister Uchida] This 17 May Tokyo interview, the same as that quoted on p. 177.34–38, in which Uchida deplored suspicion of Japan and promised full sovereignty to China, was reported in *New York Times*, 18 May 1919, sec. 1, p. 8, as well as the 20 May *Shanghai Times* cited in the Checklist of References.

175.32 Baron Ishii] For Ishii interview, promising a fair deal in China, see *New York Times*, 16 May 1919, p. 4. See also note for p. 158.1.

192.17–18 activities of Ota in Stockholm] A Japanese official, whose name was variously given as Ota, Oda, or Oka, was rumored to have attempted to negotiate during World War I secret treaties between Japan and Germany. Several reports of Japan's denial of such treaties appeared in newspapers of this period. "This morning the papers here reported the denial of Japan that she had made a secret treaty with Germany. The opinion here seems to be that they did not, but merely that preliminaries had begun with reference to such a treaty" (John Dewey and Alice Chipman Dewey, *Letters from China and Japan* [New York: E. P. Dutton and Co., 1920], p. 269, from an entry dated Peking, 8 July 1919, the dateline of "The International Duel in China").

231.10 Siems-Carey] A railway-building company.

231.36–37 Baron Shibusawa's proposal] Eiichi Shibusawa, Japanese financier and patron of art and science, who in 1915 headed a delegation to the United States. Eighty-three years old at this time, Shibusawa helped to underwrite Dewey's lectures in Japan.

249.22 K.O.N.] See p. 288.24 of text.

256.14 Mr. Wedda] Joseph Wedda, chairman of the Polish affairs section of the Committee on Public Information. See note for p. 150.2.

256.16 Mr. Smulski] John F. Smulski, Chicago banker and former treasurer of Illinois, was president of the Polish National Department and general chairman of the Detroit Convention, which is discussed on pp. 235–54, 300–306.

256.28 Polish army] Polish National Army, an independent army in France, authorized by the Allies, created 4 June 1917 under the control of the Polish National (Paris) Committee.

257.22 Class Five] The final draft classification, which included, in addition to several other groups, all resident aliens.

259.28 Mr. Albert C. Barnes] Barnes's articles on the Polish question are "Democracy, Watch Your Step!" *Dial* 65 (1918): 595–97; and "The Paderewski Adventure," *New Republic* 17 (1919): 367–69.

260.6 a letter written by Mr. Barnes] In a letter to Dewey of 20 April 1918, Barnes explained that the Polish study was suggested to him by *Democracy and Education*, that it would be an excellent opportunity to test some of the basic principles of that book to ascertain whether they were practical ideas or the mere ruminations of a college professor (Joseph Ratner/John Dewey Papers, Special Collections, Morris Library, Southern Illinois University at Carbondale; see Note on "Confidential Report of Conditions among the Poles in the United States," p. 399, footnote 2). Since in the same letter Barnes mentioned the use of scientific methods, to which Dewey refers in the sentence following the quotation, this was probably the letter Dewey was recalling.

260.20 Mr. Brand Blanshard] Blanshard's "The Church and the Polish Immigrant" (Philadelphia [?]: privately printed, 1920, 79 pp.) and Dewey's were the only printed reports resulting from the study.

260.22 Mrs. A. Levitas] Anzia Yezierska, short-story writer and novelist. For biographical details, see introduction to *The Poems of John Dewey*, ed. Jo Ann Boydston (Carbondale and Edwardsville: Southern Illinois University Press, 1977).

260.23 Mr. Irwin Edman] Edman's article "The Fourth Part of Poland" appeared in *Nation* 107 (1918): 342–43.

265.26–27 the platform adopted in 1892] Dewey presents an extracted version of the Polish Socialist Party platform.

283.18 *Posen Journal*] *Kuryer Poznanski.*

286.25 one Catholic bishop] Paul P. Rhode.

287.12–13 Penrose machine . . . Vare faction] Boies Penrose and the Vare brothers, Edwin H. and William S., were leaders of state and local Republican machines competing for control of Philadelphia.

288.20–21 Mr. Debski] Alexander H. Debski, editor of *Telegram Codzienny* (*Daily Telegram*), a K.O.N. newspaper in New York City.

289.4 Bishop Rhode] Paul P. Rhode, diocese of Green Bay, Wis., at this time the only Polish bishop in the United States.

294.1 New York City] In the 1917 mayoral election, John Purroy Mitchel, the Fusion candidate running for reelection, had introduced the Gary, Ind., school plan into the New York City public-school system. Morris Hillquit ran as the Socialist candidate on a pacifist platform.

294.9 Mr. Kulakowski] See pp. 400–401.

294.11 Mr. Sosnowski] George J. Sosnowski, who, on 14 June 1918, with Debski and Bronislaw D. Kulakowski, met with Capt. Henry A. Uterhart of the Military Intelligence Bureau "for the purpose of endeavoring, if possible, to prove that the K.O.N. was a patriotic Polish organization and not pro-German as has been frequently charged" (Uterhart to Gen. Marlborough Churchill, 17 June 1918, Military Intelligence Division of Record Group 165, Records of the War Department General and Special Staffs, National Archives, Washington, D.C.).

295.10 Mr. Stalinski] John Stalinski, of whom Dewey wrote, "Upon the whole he is the most intelligent and impartial of all the Poles I have talked to" (Dewey to Uterhart, 10 August 1918, MID, RG 165, DNA).

295.38 Syski] Rev. Alexander Syski, a Catholic priest of Boston. See William I. Thomas and Florian Znaniecki, *The Polish Peasant in Europe and America*, 5 vols. (Boston: R. G. Badger, 1920), 5:30. For Smulski, see note for p. 256.16.

301.29 Senator Hitchcock] See p. 401, footnote 9.

305.7 *New York Evening Post*] The correspondent was Irwin Edman. His articles appeared in that newspaper on 28, 29, 30 August, and 2 September 1918.

312.38 Sienkiewicz] Henryk Sienkiewicz, winner of the 1905 Nobel Prize in Literature.

312.38 Osuchowski] Anthony Osuchowski, philanthropic Warsaw lawyer.

322.11 Class Five] See note for p. 257.22.

324.18 Camp Niagara] Training place of recruits for the independent Polish National Army.

NOTE ON "CONFIDENTIAL REPORT OF CONDITIONS AMONG THE POLES IN THE UNITED STATES"

The "Confidential Report of Conditions among the Poles in the United States" (hereafter referred to as the "Report") resulted from the Philadelphia Polish study undertaken, at the suggestion of Albert C. Barnes, by John Dewey and several of Dewey's Columbia University graduate students in the spring and summer of 1918. Barnes, by 1918 a self-made millionaire and the owner of a large collection of postimpressionist French paintings, had been a student in Dewey's social philosophy seminar at Columbia during the previous academic year, a meeting which marked the beginning of a lifelong friendship cemented by a shared interest in education, sociology, philosophy, and particularly art.

Dewey stated in the "Report" that the

> main object of the inquiry was to ascertain forces and conditions which operate against the development of a free and democratic life among the members of this group, to discover the influences which kept them under external oppression and control. (260.2–6)

The following portion of the 18 May 1967 oral history interview (at the Center for Dewey Studies, Southern Illinois University at Carbondale) of Brand Blanshard, the Yale philosopher who was a study participant, sheds additional light on the study's origin:

> Barnes was an enthusiast about Dewey's social philosophy, and toward the end of the academic year, he asked Dewey whether he would like to come down to Philadelphia and attempt to put his social theory into practice. Dewey asked him what he meant, and Barnes explained that there was a large group of Polish immigrants who were forming a kind of cyst in Philadelphia society. They were retaining their old world language, customs, religious belief, educational ideas, to a certain extent even their native dress, and Barnes asked Dewey if this was the sort of phenomenon that he would be interested in investigating. Dewey said yes, he was very much interested.

In a letter of 1 August 1973, Blanshard clarified his use of a term:

I do not know whether Dewey used the word "cyst" in referring to the Polish community. It was used by me to describe the problem that I think we all conceived ourselves as facing, most of all perhaps Dr. Barnes. The Poles formed a distinct community, retaining to a surprising degree the language, the religion, and the social ideas they had brought with them from the old country, and showing a resistance that was worth studying to influences from the outside. The community was not a slum; many of its members were prosperous and respected men of business. But it was a society within a society, and it was this relative isolation that most of us were investigating. My impression is that Dewey too began with this notion of his work, but that his notion of what he could do most usefully changed as his knowledge of Polish political tensions developed.[1]

In part at least, the study was a natural outgrowth of Dewey's ideas, particularly of the concepts he expressed in 1916 in *Democracy and Education*. In a letter to Dewey of 20 April 1918, Barnes attributed the suggestion of the study to his reading of that book. Dewey remarked on 16 May, "Such a thing as this undertaking of the summer might well be a normal part of graduate instruction, a kind of field work to give experience and also to test a man."[2]

Barnes purchased the Richmond Street house in Philadelphia in which the graduate students and Dewey, while he was in town, lived during the study's duration. During this period, discussion of the Polish study and situation dominated the detailed correspondence between Barnes and Dewey. In addition to initiating the project and paying all expenses, including the eventual printing of the "Report," Barnes also seems to have entertained ambitious hopes for the project's impact. Dewey wrote to his wife, Alice, on 6 July, "Mr Barnes seems worried; his original expectations were extravagant"; and, one week later, "Mr Barnes will help keep my backbone stiff; working for him will be a good thing for me practically, as he expects action."[3] There is, however, in response to the urging, an occasional strong demurrer; to Barnes, Dewey wrote:

1. Blanshard to J. Christopher Eisele, 1 August 1973, Eisele private correspondence.
2. Dewey to Barnes, 16 May 1918, Joseph Ratner/John Dewey Papers, Special Collections, Morris Library, Southern Illinois University at Carbondale. The Dewey-Barnes correspondence is in the Barnes Foundation, Merion, Pa. Dewey authorized Joseph Ratner's copying of that material, which has not been available for research at the Barnes Foundation. All references here are to the copies in the Ratner/Dewey Papers.
3. Dewey to Alice Dewey, 6 and 13 July 1918, John Dewey Papers, Special Collections, Morris Library, Southern Illinois University at Carbondale.

My ambitions are high, but also highly specialized. Im going to do this job, and do it right, but what you call the big game doesn't stir a single pulse faster—There is an individual as well as a general psychology.[4]

How did it come about that what began, at least ostensibly, as a sociological study led to Dewey's writing a "Report" for a federal investigative agency? Blanshard offers this explanation:

Dewey found the Polish community itself rather sharply divided, and I think his chief concern was that the reactionary segments of Polish opinion should not have the exclusive ear of Washington. He was looking forward to the state of Poland after the war, and was anxious that the State Department should not throw its weight behind a conservative economy in Poland.[5]

It is clear that, as the study progressed, Dewey developed firm opinions of his own regarding the Polish situation. The evidence indicates that Dewey took the initiative in contacting government officials and, after unsuccessful attempts through other channels, succeeded in submitting his findings to the Military Intelligence Bureau of the War Department (M.I.B.).

Although Dewey's graduate students were doing preliminary research for the study by mid-May, 1918, Dewey was at that time delivering the West Memorial Lectures at Stanford (the lectures that formed the basis for *Human Nature and Conduct*, published in 1922) and did not take an active part until July. When he returned to the East, having taken an apartment in San Francisco for Alice and their daughter Jane, he spent the summer in New York City, Philadelphia, and at the family farm in Huntington, Long Island.

Dewey soon added to his original function as "adviser and general supervisor" (260.28) an assignment of his own:

I saw that it would be more interesting for me, as well as enable me to be of more use to the others if I took a subject myself, so I have been seeing some of the Poles to get their ideas about the international situation, and the future of Poland.[6]

Dewey was impressed by the leaders of the K.O.N., the Congress (or Committee) of National Defense, particularly by Bronislaw D. Kulakowski, the editor of its official journal *Wici*, with whom

4. Dewey to Barnes, 26 July 1918.
5. Blanshard to Eisele, 1 August 1973.
6. Dewey to family, 21 July 1918.

Dewey met several times in New York during the week of 18 July. "He knows European history and politics like an educated European which he is, and more American history than most Americans."[7] In mid-August, Dewey finally had a necessary but "dreaded" meeting with Ignace Jan Paderewski, official United States delegate of the Polish National (Paris) Committee, which stood in opposition to the K.O.N. Dewey had come to view Paderewski as "the cover behind which" operated the Paris Committee, "consisting of a small party of conservative reactionaries, who were tied with the Czar before the war."[8]

In July, Dewey presented his case to the Commission of Inquiry, which had been set up in September 1917, five months after America entered the war, by Col. Edward M. House, President Woodrow Wilson's political adviser, to collect and collate data for later use at the Peace Conference. The Inquiry, as it was popularly known, was under the direction of Sidney E. Mezes, president of the College of the City of New York. At Paris, the Inquiry was known as the territorial and economic section of the American Peace Commission.

On 19 July, Dewey sent a memorandum to Mezes:

> In consequence of reports turned in by the workers and then of a more extended personal inquiry undertaken by myself I ascertained certain facts and reached certain conclusions which have a definite and important bearing upon the American-Polish phase of our international policy. The matter is acute and urgent because of the proposition in the Bill introduced by Senator Hitchcock[9] to "recognize the Polish National

7. Dewey to family, 21 July 1918.
8. Dewey to Alice Dewey, 3 and 12 August 1918.
9. Gilbert M. Hitchcock, Democratic senator from Nebraska. Albert Barnes reported that "Hitchcock ignored a letter written to him at that time calling attention to the fact that a scientific study of Polish conditions in America was being made and that the organization and its data were at his disposal" (Barnes, "Democracy, Watch Your Step!" *Dial* 65 [1918]: 596). A month later, Dewey wrote that Irwin Edman "says the Pres asked Sen Hitchcock to postpone introducing his bill for a few weeks. So it appears it never was actually introduced" (Dewey to Barnes, 13 August 1918). The M.I.B.'s report of its 17–19 August interviews with Dewey included a discussion of this bill: "Prof. Dewey stated . . . that the introduction of the bill was delayed at the suggestion of the President of the United States. Mr.——— [name deleted; either Joseph Wedda of the Committee on Public Information, or James C. White of the Polish Associated Press] admitted that Senator Hitchcock was to introduce such a bill and that the action had been delayed at the request of high governmental authorities, just whom he did not know" (memorandum to Maj. Henry T. Hunt, 3 September 1918, Military Intelligence Division of Record Group 165, Records of the War Department General and Special Staffs, National Archives, Washington, D.C. [MID, RG 165, DNA]).

Committee, whose headquarters are in Paris, France, as the official representatives of the Polish people."[10]

In a letter accompanying the memorandum, Dewey explained, "Im afraid my memorandum is bald and will sound very dogmatic." Stressing that "the only thing is to get a postponement of action until an inquiry can be made by those in whose conclusions the President would have confidence," Dewey assured Mezes that he was "not bidding for any share in the inquiry" but "should like an opportunity to make some suggestions."[11]

Mezes replied that he was "not in a position to be of any assistance with regard to matters pending before Congress, either directly or indirectly"; in any case, it would not be advisable for him to do anything "until after a careful study of the whole situation."[12]

Dewey clarified his position: the Hitchcock bill "was the occasion of my writing rather than its subject matter or purpose. All I was interested in was precisely a careful study of the whole situation—precisely as you have phrased it."[13]

Mezes gave Dewey's memorandum for analysis to Robert H. Lord, Harvard history professor who was the Inquiry's regional specialist for Poland and Russia; at the Peace Conference he was chief of the Polish Division, American Peace Commission. In an undated comment on Dewey's memorandum, Lord acknowledged, "It is true that the Polish National Committee in Paris does not receive the support of the whole Polish public either in this country or in Poland," but explained that it

> on the other hand, represents those elements which have been unwaveringly pro-Ally since the beginning of the War. . . . If we have to work with one party or the other, there can be little doubt which one we shall have to select. And the crux of the situation is that we have to choose between them.

Listing the advantages of recognizing the Paris Committee "as being the best representation of the nation available," Lord

10. Dewey memorandum to Mezes, 19 July 1918, Record Group 256, Records of the American Commission to Negotiate Peace, National Archives, Washington, D.C. (RG 256, DNA).
11. Dewey letter to Mezes, 19 July 1918, RG 256, DNA.
12. Mezes to Dewey, 22 July 1918, RG 256, DNA.
13. Dewey to Mezes, 27 July 1918, RG 256, DNA.

"doubt[ed] whether there is great need for any such investigation as Professor Dewey suggests."[14]

Dewey wrote to Lord on 27 July, explaining:

> It was inevitable that the memorandum I presented should leave the impression that I was a somewhat ardent partisan of the K.O.N. Such is not the case, though at the present time I confess I am quite anti so far as the leaders of the Polish Alliance faction are concerned. I am interested that the K.O.N. should not be misrepresented. . . . Instead of taking a purely passive attitude in Polish affairs or of recognizing any single faction, the American policy should be to use its enormous power and prestige at the present time, first to have a show-down as to the facts, and eliminate petty gossip, purely personal animosity, and malicious misrepresentation, and then to harmonize the various groups and get in contact thereby with representatives of all factions.[15]

In a letter to Alice, Dewey expressed discouragement probably attributable to his failure with the Inquiry: "The enterprise in Phila isnt going so well . . . he [Barnes] will have the right to hold me responsible if nothing much comes out of it."[16]

Dewey next decided to approach Colonel House himself.[17] House had been Wilson's closest adviser since 1912, when he had helped him secure the Democratic nomination; he had become intimate with many European leaders during 1914–16 while serving as Wilson's personal representative abroad, and acted as the President's liaison with domestic as well as foreign figures. Dewey had indicated his awareness of House's function (and also a previous attempt to gain an official hearing on another issue) in a letter to Salmon O. Levinson six months earlier:

> In a conversation with one of the men who is doing some work in connection with post-war problems I had an occasion to present your idea, and he was so much interested that I took the liberty of giving him a copy of your paper. While I do not wish to be oversanguine, I am in some hopes that thru this channel it may get to House's and possibly Wilson's eyes.[18]

Among the influential leaders with whom House regularly

14. Lord report, RG 256, DNA.
15. Dewey to Lord, 27 July 1918, RG 256, DNA.
16. Dewey to Alice Dewey, 26 July 1918.
17. House's title dated from his earlier period as adviser to Texas governors, during which he was appointed to Governor James S. Hogg's staff with the title of "colonel."
18. Dewey to Levinson, 8 February 1918, Salmon O. Levinson Papers, Special Collections, The Joseph Regenstein Library, University of Chicago.

met to get a spectrum of views was Herbert Croly, editor of the *New Republic*, and it was to Croly that Dewey turned for an introduction to House. The *New Republic* had endorsed Wilson for reelection in 1916 and, until it later broke with him on the question of membership in the League of Nations, supported his position on most issues. Moreover, the *New Republic*—i.e., Croly—has been credited with influencing Wilson's thinking on issues concerned with the approaching peace.[19] On 2 August, Dewey telegraphed to Croly; the next day, "although no introduction on my part can be necessary," Croly wrote to House:

> I assume he wishes to see you in relation to the attitude of the government towards the two factions among the Poles and if such is the case all I can say is that I'm sure Prof. Dewey's preference for the K.O.N. is based on a thorough investigation. He has been conducting a survey among the Poles in Philadelphia for the last six weeks and has talked with large numbers of them. He feels strongly about the danger to the liberal cause in case our government allows its policy to be dictated by recognition of the Paderewski group and by a suspicion of the pro Germanism of their opponents. His investigation has been so thorough and he himself is a man of such eminent ability (he is certainly the greatest living American philosopher) that what he has to say is entitled to the most careful consideration.[20]

By this time, his sense of urgency increased by the approaching Detroit Convention (which is discussed in this volume in "Autocracy under Cover," the "Preliminary Confidential Memorandum," and the "Report"), Dewey wrote to his wife:

> What needs to be done practically is to get this convention postponed, get the Hitchcock bill changed to compel recognition of some organization which shall be really representative, and in connection with both of these things have the US gov employ its moral authority to make the Poles get together, and get them under the control of representative Americans, instead of under the manipulation via Paderewski and the priests of a little clique in Paris.[21]

On 5 August, Barnes accompanied Dewey to House's summer home in Manchester, Massachusetts, for an interview Dewey described in a letter to his family:

19. Arthur S. Link, *Woodrow Wilson and the Progressive Era, 1910–1917* (New York: Harper and Bros., 1954), pp. 264–65.
20. Croly to House, 3 August 1918, Edward M. House Papers, Yale University Library, New Haven, Conn.
21. Dewey to Alice Dewey, 3 August 1918.

After waiting all the afternoon, saw the Colonel for about twenty minutes. He is all his reputation makes him as an effective and affable listener—quick and responsive to points, but giving no more idea of any impression made on him than an oiled sphinx. I dont think I got anywhere with him, so it would have been discouraging if I had had any expectations in particular.[22]

House recorded in his diary that he advised Dewey and Barnes to visit Senator Hitchcock, but did not mention taking further action.[23]

Part of the reason for the cool reception Dewey had encountered up to this point probably stemmed from disparate perceptions of Paderewski, whose influence transcended his role as representative of the Paris Committee, which was headed by the less popular Roman Dmowski. Politically important as a unifying leader of the Polish community, Paderewski had in addition charismatic personal qualities. House wrote a few years later about the composer-pianist who

gave up his music and devoted his entire time and energies to work for the Allies and for Poland. . . . Before Paderewski came to the United States to devote himself to the Polish cause, the American Poles were divided by misunderstandings and suspicions and lacked a concrete and definite program. . . . He gave to the American Poles a single purpose.[24]

In 1916, Paderewski met House, who introduced him to Wilson.[25] House and Paderewski "pored over maps—his maps and mine—of Central and Eastern Europe, and together we traced what we thought should be a homogeneous Poland."[26]

In *What Really Happened at Paris*, Robert H. Lord, in response to a question about the Peace Conference, is reported to have assessed Paderewski's character and influence in these terms:

Mr. Paderewski is so obviously a thoroughly high-minded and disinterested patriot that he commands confidence. . . . I think he gained a great

22. Dewey to Alice and Jane Dewey, 9 August 1918.
23. Diary of Edward M. House, 5 August 1918, House Papers.
24. House, "Paderewski: The Paradox of Europe," *Harper's* 152 (1925–26): 30–31.
25. For an account of Paderewski's influence on the development of Wilson's statements on Poland, 22 January 1917 and 8 January 1918, see Rom Landau, *Ignace Paderewski* (New York: Thomas Y. Crowell Co., 1934), pp. 101–20.
26. House, "Paderewski," p. 31.

many things for Poland that a statesman who was less trusted could never have secured. . . . I think he did what no other Pole could have done.[27]

In the foreword to this account, House wrote:

He [Paderewski] came as the spokesman of an ancient people whose wrongs and sorrows had stirred the sympathies of an entire world. This artist, patriot, and statesman awakened the Congress to do justice to his native land, and sought its help to make a great dream true.[28]

How Dewey finally attracted the attention of the M.I.B. is not precisely known, though the likeliest link seems to have been through Carlton J. H. Hayes, history professor at Columbia during Dewey's years there and, during World War I, a captain in the M.I.B., acting as aide to its director, Gen. Marlborough Churchill. On 13 August, Capt. Henry A. Uterhart wrote to Dewey, "Professor Hayes is down here with us and I understand that he has written you suggesting that you come to Washington some time in the near future."[29] The telegram Churchill sent two days later requesting that Dewey come to Washington (259.5) bears at the top the name "Mr. Hayes."[30] A memorandum to Maj. Henry T. Hunt discussing Dewey's Washington M.I.B. interviews states: "Prof. John Dewey came from Philadelphia at the request of Mr. Hayes."[31] When the "Report" was nearly complete, Dewey received a letter "from Hayes indicating that our activities have been of some use."[32] It is reasonable to assume that the two men (who shared interests and association memberships, among them the League of Free Nations, in addition to being colleagues) had previously discussed international politics. Moreover, Hayes's official capacity at the M.I.B. undoubtedly led to his being aware of Dewey's activities in connection with the Polish study.

Through Hayes's intervention, Dewey had finally gained a receptive official audience. Interrupted by the M.I.B.'s 15 August telegram while visiting his daughters Lucy and Evelyn in New York, Dewey spent about a week in Washington; he met with the M.I.B. all of Saturday, 17 August, and part of Monday, and then

27. Edward M. House and Charles Seymour, eds., *What Really Happened at Paris* (New York: Charles Scribner's Sons, 1921), p. 451.
28. *Ibid*., p. viii.
29. Uterhart to Dewey, 13 August 1918, MID, RG 165, DNA.
30. Churchill to Dewey, 15 August 1918, MID, RG 165, DNA.
31. Memorandum to Hunt, 3 September 1918, MID, RG 165, DNA.
32. Dewey to Barnes, 19 September 1918.

prepared the two preliminary confidential memoranda, which are discussed in the Textual Commentary. On 23 August, Dewey wrote from Philadelphia to House:

I am to submit an extensive memorandum as soon as I can prepare it. When I shall have sent you a copy of that, I do not think I shall need to bother you any more, as the expedition is soon breaking up and we shall return to our ordinary occupations.[33]

"My interruption to go to Washington," Dewey informed his family, "tu[r]ned out to be not so much an interruption as a conclusion."[34]

Writing from Washington about the "Report," "which it is hoped will get to people high enough up to have some influence,"[35] Dewey commented on his venture:

So far as I can now see when I leave here, things will have practically come to a head one way or another and my activities in saving the nation—or nations—will have come to an end. The rest of my work will be merely the kind of intellectual study which is more in my line. I shall be glad and sorry; if this sort of thing could be strung out more instead of being so highly concentrated and intensified I should be mainly sorry.[36]

On 25 September, Dewey wrote to President Wilson, explaining that the completed "Report"

embodies some conditions which we unexpectedly encountered while making a sociological research in Philadelphia. . . . The object of the research, the report, and the article in the New Republic was to point out wherein the forces operative among Poles in the United States run counter to the American principles which you have so clearly set forth in your various public announcements.[37]

In response to Wilson's request to look over the "Report," his secretary, Joseph P. Tumulty, stressed the importance of the first two paragraphs of its "General Conclusions." On 4 October, referring to a newspaper clipping and the "Report," Wilson replied to Dewey, "I have examined them with real interest and am served by the information which they convey."[38]

33. Dewey to House, 23 August 1918.
34. Dewey to family, 28 August 1918.
35. Dewey to Alice and Jane Dewey, 18 August 1918.
36. Dewey to daughters, 20 August 1918.
37. Dewey to Wilson, 25 September 1918, Woodrow Wilson Papers, Library of Congress, Washington, D.C.
38. Wilson to Tumulty, 30 September 1918; Tumulty to Wilson, 3 October 1918; Wilson to Dewey, 4 October 1918.

While he was completing the "Report," Dewey forecast its effectiveness:

It is hard not to get rather discouraged about the whole situation. I imagine that in two or three months things may be back pretty nearly where they were, though I think we have given them permanently a slightly different turn, which, as the line approaches infinity, may reach quite a different spot than they would otherwise reach. But if the government really wants to be fooled, it will realise its desire, whether or no.[39]

Included in a group of documents "giving the K.O.N. side of the Controversy," Dewey's "Report" was described by Capt. A. V. Dalrymple as "particularly illuminating as an introduction to the whole controversy."[40]

The effect on Dewey of his involvement in the Polish study is reflected in a letter written three months after submitting the "Report"; returning to John Macrae's earlier suggestion of a book "on the American idea of world politics,"[41] Dewey replied:

When things have settled down again enough so that serious scientific studies can be made instead of propaganda, regarding our new foreign problems, I should think a conjoint book along that line would be useful—not confining it to[o] closely to the foreign problems of the U S but all the difficulties &c which will come up in national destinies affecting international relations. European political history and problems will now have a new meaning for the American reader.[42]

39. Dewey to Barnes, 10 September 1918.
40. Dalrymple to Churchill, 2 October 1918, MID, RG 165, DNA.
41. Macrae to Dewey, 15 March 1918, E. P. Dutton and Co. Archives, New York, N.Y.
42. Dewey to Macrae, 19 December 1918.

Textual Apparatus

Textual Commentary
Textual Notes
Emendations List
Line-end Hyphenation
Substantive Variants in Quotations
Checklist of Dewey's References

Index

TEXTUAL COMMENTARY

Although John Dewey spent much of 1918 and 1919 lecturing on philosophy and education at three American universities—Columbia, Stanford, and California—and in Japan and China, the written record of these years as preserved in this volume is predominantly social and political. For example, only two of the relatively few essays on philosophy are purely technical, and even the two essays on education spring directly from wartime issues. Because of the topical nature of the material, which contains many references obscured by time, a section of explanatory notes appears immediately following the text.

Of the forty items which appear here, two, "The Motivation of Hobbes's Political Philosophy" and the "Introductory Word" to F. Matthias Alexander's *Man's Supreme Inheritance*, were included in larger works; nine appeared in academic journals. Most, however, were published in periodicals aimed at a wider audience: one each in *Nation* and *Independent*, eight in *Dial*, and sixteen, nearly half, in the *New Republic*, a journal whose birth coincided with the outbreak of World War I.

The lengthy "Confidential Report of Conditions among the Poles in the United States," privately printed, has not until now been readily available. Two other items on the Polish question, "Preliminary Confidential Memorandum" and "Second Preliminary Confidential Memorandum," were never published by Dewey.[1] These three items are discussed in detail later.

Dewey's works of this period do not present the problems caused by multiple texts, as only the "Preliminary Confidential Memorandum" offers a choice of copy-text. Ten essays exist solely in their originally published form. Of the remaining articles, only one was republished in Dewey's name during his lifetime: "On the Two Sides of the Eastern Sea" first appeared in the *New Re-*

1. The two memoranda appeared in the appendix of Louis Gerson, *Woodrow Wilson and the Rebirth of Poland, 1914–1920* (New Haven: Yale University Press, 1953).

public in July 1919 and was republished in Dewey's collective volume *China, Japan and the U.S.A.* (1921) with minor editorial corrections.

All other republications of essays in this volume during Dewey's lifetime were in collections edited by Joseph Ratner: twenty in *Characters and Events* (New York: Henry Holt and Co., 1929); one in *Intelligence in the Modern World* (New York: Modern Library, 1939); and one in *Education Today* (New York: G. P. Putnam's Sons, 1940). These works are credited as the first appearance of several emendations that would have been made independently for the present volume. Most of the changes that Ratner introduced in these works involved substitution of the past for the present tense, alterations in spelling and punctuation, a few changes in wording, and some omissions. The only emendations accepted from those edited volumes were necessary corrections or desirable clarifications.

Dewey's "The Motivation of Hobbes's Political Philosophy" appeared in *Studies in the History of Ideas* with essays by other writers on Greek philosophy, philosophers of the seventeenth and eighteenth centuries, and modern logic. Although the volume as a whole met with mixed reviews, Dewey's contribution was favorably received. For example, Joseph A. Leighton wrote in *Philosophical Review* that the volume was misnamed. Outlining two historical approaches which might be followed, one focusing on the development of a philosopher's ideas and the other tracing the evolution of an idea, Leighton stated that few of the contributors conformed to either approach. He said that Dewey, however, did succeed in doing so and "makes out a good case for the view that Hobbes aimed at giving a rational and scientific foundation to morals and politics in order to free them from all subservience to divinity."[2] The volume as well as Dewey's contribution were praised in *Dial*:

> First, the book comes in a period of philosophic dearth, so far as publications are concerned; and second, it appears at a time when historical sanity is tremendously needed, an invigoration of the historical sense; while in a third place, the essays are uncommonly interesting.

Quoting the first half of the article's opening paragraph, the re-

2. Leighton, *Philosophical Review* 28 (1919): 214.

viewer commented that Dewey "goes on to correct, strikingly, some of the misconceptions associated with Hobbes."[3]

As the only previous appearance of "The Motivation of Hobbes's Political Philosophy," its publication in *Studies in the History of Ideas* has served as copy-text for the present edition. Except for the correction of accidentals, all emendations were made to correct errors in the intricate quotation and documentation, as in the altered edition number at 20.29 and altered page numbers at 23n.3 and 38n.4. The substitution of Vol. II for Vol. III, a punctuation change, and the addition of "and," all in footnote forty-six, were necessary to distinguish between references to two works by Thomas Hobbes. The "e" in "Hobbes" was deleted at 20.1 and 23.35, and *Law* changed to *Laws* at 28.33 for accurate reference to the book titles; and the wording changed at 38n.6 for correct reference to the chapter title. Three substantive errors in quotations at 24.19, 25.15, and 26.24, whether Dewey's or a compositor's, warranted restoration to the original. A misplaced quotation mark at 29.22 and two misplaced ellipses at 27.35 and 29.13 were also corrected.

Within a six-week period in early 1918, Dewey delivered at least four speeches, three of which appear here: "Vocational Education in the Light of the World War" on 25 January, "America in the World" on 22 February, and "Internal Social Reorganization after the War" on 5 March. The fourth address, however, "Education for Democracy," given on 3 February, at the Detroit Open Forum, was not published and no manuscript is extant. However, based on the following excerpt from the 4 February 1918 *Detroit News*, and the rest of the newspaper report, which included a discussion of military training, it is clear that Dewey elaborated on ideas in the essays on education published here.

> We must not accept the schemes of Europe, but must work out our own destiny along these as well as other lines. Our present systems are very bad, especially in vocational training, and we must devise a means of caring for the youth until he is at least 18 years old. Instead of following we should have the courage to provide a system that the rest of the world will copy.

"Vocational Education in the Light of the World War" was

3. *Dial* 65 (1918): 218. The volume was also reviewed in *Revue de métaphysique et de morale* 29 (Supp. to Jan.-Mar. 1922): 12–13.

Dewey's address to the fourth annual convention of the Vocational Education Association of the Middle West. In *Manual Training Magazine* 19 (1917–18): 240–43, Charles A. Bennett described that convention as "essentially a patriotic meeting. From beginning to end the atmosphere was tense with interest in the problems of education made vital by the present military conflict with Germany." Bennett, in his "mentally reconstructed program," recalled Dewey's talk as "universal military training to become universal training for social service: a prophetic vision by Dr. Arthur Dean, made vivid and reasonable by America's greatest educational philosopher, Professor John Dewey."

The only appearance of this address, in the Association's *Bulletin No. 4* (Chicago, 1918), has necessarily served as copy-text for this volume; it required numerous emendations to correct printing errors possibly caused by an unclear typescript or by a lack of editing. The errors probably attributable to composition include the reversed commas and semicolons at 59.26,27 and 64.36,38; the comma transposed from 65.32 to 65.33; and the repetition of "about" at 59.15. Omission of the dash at 60.25 may have been Dewey's or the printer's; it has been supplied here. Two substantive errors, also probably compositorial, were corrected: the word "morale" at 60.24 in the phrase "morale and civic training" was emended to "moral"; the word "or" at 67.22 in the phrase "young or human beings" was emended to "of." Two clarifications were required, the first involving a switch in subject at 58.19, where "he" was emended to "it." In the complex sentence at 65.15–24, Dewey may have initially intended to say, "Now unless these experiments rest upon a fundamental sub-structure, they are going to break down." As his ideas developed, however, he introduced another subject, "this change," at 65.21. Therefore, the misplacement of "unless" was corrected by moving it from the beginning of the sentence to 65.21; at 65.22, "must rest" was emended to "rests" to complete the clause "unless this change rests upon."

Immediately upon reading "America in the World" in the 14 March issue of *Nation*, John Macrae of E. P. Dutton wrote to Dewey:

> I feel that you could write a book of world-wide importance on this subject, more especially on the American idea of world politics. Won't you

> undertake such a book for us? I am convinced the book is needed and that you are the man to write it.[4]

Dewey replied, "I appreciate your suggestion about a book on American political ideals; it is very attractive. I don't see where the time is going to come from however. However I shan't forget the idea."[5] Four days later, Macrae, "trusting you will forgive my persistency," urged:

> I hope you will let this idea pass beyond the bounds of thought and bring it into action. The subject is of international importance, and the time is rapidly approaching when Americans should understand the significance and the importance of the American idea. I think the idea is of such great value, that it is worthy of your laying aside other work for this more important national need.[6]

As he had promised, Dewey did not "forget the idea"; he wrote to Macrae nine months later only to further postpone writing such a book. It was a project for which he apparently never found the time.

Copy-text for "Internal Social Reorganization after the War" is its original appearance, in *Journal of Race Development* 8 (1918): 385–400. Beyond the correction of accidentals, four substantive emendations were necessary: "chronic employment" was changed to "chronic unemployment" at 76.35, "product" changed to "production" at 80.2, "in" before "which" deleted at 84.40, and an unnecessary "that" after "seen" deleted at 86.9.

Dewey wrote "Morals and the Conduct of States," published 23 March 1918 in the *New Republic*, as an elaboration of the ideas put forth by Salmon O. Levinson in "The Legal Status of War" (Appendix 4 in this volume), published two weeks earlier in the *New Republic*. During February and March, Dewey's friend Levinson, a Chicago lawyer, corresponded frequently with Dewey about both articles. Eager to see "The Legal Status of War" in print, Levinson wrote and telegraphed to Dewey a staccato succession of questions regarding the status of proof and date of publication; Dewey, acting as mediary, responded quickly to Levinson's inquiries. Levinson also sent revisions and corrections to

4. Macrae to Dewey, 15 March 1918, E. P. Dutton and Co. Archives, New York, N.Y.
5. Dewey to Macrae, 25 March 1918.
6. Macrae to Dewey, 29 March 1918.

Dewey instead of to the *New Republic*; one change he requested which was not made, to begin a new paragraph on page 390 where the words "Perhaps three-fourths" appear,[7] has been made in Appendix 4. Eleven years later, writing about Levinson's campaign centered about the phrase the "Outlawry of War," Dewey described "The Legal Status of War" as the "first statement of his [Levinson's] idea."[8]

Their correspondence sheds light not only on these two essays but also on Dewey's writing processes and on his commonly misunderstood position on the *New Republic*. At one point, Dewey reminded Levinson, "But you overestimate, often, my connection & influence with the N.R. people. I haven't got any status which would enable me to affect the date of publication of any contribution."[9] In discussing another contributor with Levinson, Dewey cautioned, "I have no editorial relationship to the New Republic, and have to be rather careful about acting as a medium of transmission."[10]

In mid-February, Dewey reported that "The Legal Status of War" was in type (it was published 9 March), and that he had been asked by Herbert Croly, editor of the *New Republic*, to write a follow-up article. Levinson, "delighted" by this news, suggested that Dewey "take up that point we purposely left out because it would unduly expand the [Levinson's] article, namely—that outlawing war would by one stroke practically serve to harmonize the ethics of nations with those of individuals."[11] Two days before the publication of "Morals and the Conduct of States," Dewey wrote to Levinson:

> The follow-up article has been in Mr. Croly's hands for a week or so. I called it "Morals and the Conduct of the State." It did not cover the exact ground that you and I talked over, because I find as a rule that my articles when I come to write them do not come out as I plan, but I endeavored to link it up with yours.[12]

Dewey did have an official relationship with *Dial* unlike his

7. Levinson to Dewey, 16 February 1918, Salmon O. Levinson Papers, Special Collections, The Joseph Regenstein Library, University of Chicago.
8. Dewey, "Apostles of World Unity: Salmon O. Levinson," *World Unity Magazine* 4 (May 1929): 101.
9. Dewey to Levinson, 13 February 1918.
10. Dewey to Levinson, 27 February 1918.
11. Levinson to Dewey, 16 February 1918.
12. Dewey to Levinson, 21 March 1918.

informal status at the *New Republic*. In the issue of 6 June 1918, page 521, announcing *Dial*'s forthcoming move from Chicago to New York City on 1 July and the change from fortnightly to weekly publication on 3 October, the editors explained: "This step is taken in order to consider more comprehensively the shifting forces which are now making for a new social order." The editorial policy would be extended "to include, in addition to the present literary features, discussion of internationalism and a programme of reconstruction in industry and education." The announcement continued:

> The Editors will be John Dewey, Thorstein Veblen, Helen Marot, and George Donlin. . . . Dewey is known in America for his creative contributions to the problems of education. Abroad he is accepted as America's senior thinker and philosopher since the death of William James. Mr. Dewey will write for THE DIAL on educational subjects.

Problems arose at once, however. Dewey wrote to his wife, Alice, on 13 July:

> I found Randolph Bournes name down as one of the associate editors of the Dial; it was quite plain from the organization plan that the associate editors would be the real editors and I have written Mr Johnson [president of Dial Publishing Co.] withdrawing from the Dial.[13]

The painful rift between Dewey and his former disciple on the issue of pacifism, a rift mirroring the split in the intellectual community, had been deepened by their public exchange in May about F. Matthias Alexander's *Man's Supreme Inheritance* (see page 421). Adjustments were made:

> After I resigned from the Dial the publisher came around, and put Bourne off the editorial staff, and presented a scheme by which I should be put down simply as one of the editors of the special reconstruction numbers which will come once a month; with Bourne off, there seemed to be no reason for not doing it an[d] one thousand reasons for doing it, so I am going back on.[14]

Dewey's four articles on the League of Nations—"The Approach to a League of Nations," "The League of Nations and the New Diplomacy," "The Fourteen Points and the League of Na-

13. Dewey to Alice Dewey, 13 July 1918, John Dewey Papers, Special Collections, Morris Library, Southern Illinois University at Carbondale.
14. Dewey to family, 7 September 1918.

tions," and "A League of Nations and Economic Freedom"—were published by *Dial* in 1918 between 2 November and 14 December. Dewey wrote to Albert C. Barnes about this group of essays:

> I have been writing a series of short articles on The Approach to a League of Peace—nothing new in them but Ive tried to popularize and repeat the idea that the approach is primarily thru administrative commissions which will deal with economic needs and problems rather than thru tribunals and international lawsuits.[15]

To Levinson, Dewey wrote, "I have been writing some things for the Dial along the line of the need of a League on economic and industrial grounds."[16]

Dewey was contemplating a trip to Japan well before he began his sabbatical from Columbia at the University of California in late September, 1918. In July, he had written to Alice about an offer "to go to Japan to make a report on Japan as a factor in the future international situation," adding several days later, "If it is possible to go I should like the trip very much, and I suppose you would too. It is a pretty academic question, practically speaking."[17] Then, in late 1918, Dewey wrote to Levinson, "I have an invitation to give a few lectures at the Imperial Univ in Tokyo, which ought to be helpful in getting us into closer relations with things than might otherwise be the case."[18]

The eight lectures Dewey delivered at the Imperial University between 25 February and 21 March 1919, entitled "The Position of Philosophy at the Present:—Problems of Philosophic Reconstruction," were developed into *Reconstruction in Philosophy*, published in 1920 by Henry Holt and Co. His original outlines for those lectures are included in the present volume. From Kyoto, Dewey assessed his forthcoming book: "Incidentally I have a semi-popular book on Philosophic Reconstruction out of my lectures, and could send it to the press with a few [w]eeks leisure for corrections."[19]

The two articles in this volume that deal specifically with Ja-

15. Dewey to Barnes, 24 October 1918, Joseph Ratner/John Dewey Papers, Special Collections, Morris Library, Southern Illinois University at Carbondale. See Note on "Confidential Report of Conditions among the Poles in the United States," p. 399, footnote 2.
16. Dewey to Levinson, 9 December 1918.
17. Dewey to Alice Dewey, 13 and 26 July 1918.
18. Dewey to Levinson, 21 December 1918.
19. Dewey to Barnes, 23 April 1919.

pan were published in 1919 by *Dial*: "Japan and America" on 17 May, and the three-part "Liberalism in Japan" on 4 and 18 October and 1 November. Copy-text for "Liberalism in Japan" is this first appearance, in *Dial* 67 (1919): 283–85, 333–37, 369–71. Nearly half the emendations are corrections of typographical errors, such as the reversal of two letters at 159.13, which produced "slave" in a context clearly requiring "salve." It is possible that a compositor misread "police," as "policy" at 168.14, as it is clearly the police to whom Dewey referred. An unnecessary "the" before "three" at 166.18 may have been a false start for "three" and was deleted. Having consistently used the past tense in this article, Dewey undoubtedly intended to use the past tense at 166.29; "begin" was therefore emended to "began." The addition of closing dashes at 160.1 and at 168.9 was necessary to clarify the meaning of the two sentences.

After three months, having accepted a joint invitation from five educational organizations to lecture in several cities in China, Dewey left Japan on 28 April 1919. He spent most of May sightseeing and lecturing in Shanghai, Hangchow, and Nanking before settling down in Peking to deliver lectures at National University and Tsing Hua College.[20] By June, Dewey had been granted an extension of his leave from Columbia to remain in China another year. Dewey arrived in Shanghai three days before the May 4th Movement, which he described on 24 June in "The Student Revolt in China"; he later wrote to Wendell T. Bush that this article "couldnt give the color of the thing however nor what it meant to the boys and girls, or even to the people of China."[21]

By the time Dewey left for the East, he had worked out an arrangement with the *New Republic* to write an average of one article a month; he was also under contract to *Asia* for six articles. When, once again, John Macrae of E. P. Dutton wrote to urge him to do a book, Dewey responded that he was "not likely to write any special book on China" but that Macrae might "like to consider collecting these [articles] after publication into a book."[22] Macrae replied that he would "be delighted to publish a volume

20. Dewey's China lectures have been translated and edited by Robert W. Clopton and Tsuin-chen Ou in *John Dewey: Lectures in China, 1919–1920* (Honolulu: University Press of Hawaii, 1973).
21. Dewey to Bush, 1 August 1919, Wendell T. Bush Papers, Special Collections, Columbia University Library, New York, N.Y.
22. Dewey to Macrae, 20 September 1919.

of your essays, selected from the articles appearing in the New Republic, or any other magazine."[23] Although that volume never appeared, Dutton did publish in 1920 the Deweys' *Letters from China and Japan*, edited by Evelyn Dewey.

Of Dewey's eight articles about China, two were published in *Asia* and six in the *New Republic*. Copy-text for "Militarism in China" is its original publication, in *New Republic* 20 (1919): 167–69. The spellings of "Yuan Shi-Kai," "Tuan Chi-Jui," and "Tu-chun(s)" in that copy-text were emended to "Yuan Shih-kai," "Tuan Chi-jui," and "Tuchun(s)" because, although there was a good deal of variety in contemporary spelling and capitalization, particularly in "Yuan Shih-kai," the *New Republic* version was not among the acceptable ones. On the other hand, three versions of Tsingtao in three separate essays (Tsingtau as an adjective at 187.1, Tsing-tao at 225.25, and Tsingtao, the preferred form, at 238.25) were all common contemporary spellings, often within the same periodical article, both as noun and adjective, and have therefore not been emended here.

Two reviews Dewey wrote in 1918 are included in this volume. A few days before the first of these, his review of *Dial* editor Helen Marot's *Creative Impulse in Industry*, appeared in the *New Republic*, Dewey wrote to Albert Barnes:

> Where my self regarding sentiment comes in on Miss Marot is here—I have learned from experience enough so that it is really tickled only when I get back an idea with some new trimmings—with some of its implications which I hadnt thot of brought out. And that was [what] happened in the case of the idea of a school which should make a feature of the administrative control of industrial conditions. Something Ive written may sound as if I had had the idea, but language is a great thing [and] will go further than one's own consciousness has gone.[24]

It was at F. Matthias Alexander's request that Dewey wrote the introductory word, which appears in the present volume, to the 1918 E. P. Dutton and Co. edition of Alexander's *Man's Supreme Inheritance*, previously published in 1910 in England and the United States; this new edition would incorporate Alexander's *Conscious Control*, published in 1912 in England. British spellings of words such as "civilisation" and "favourable" in the introductory word have been silently regularized to Dewey's known

23. Macrae to Dewey, 28 October 1919.
24. Dewey to Barnes, 28 October 1918.

usage. In September 1917, John Macrae had sent to Dewey the manuscript for *Man's Supreme Inheritance*: "Mr. Alexander is very desirous that this new and revised edition should have a preface by you."[25] After publication of *Man's Supreme Inheritance* in 1918, Randolph Bourne's review, "Making Over the Body," appeared on 4 May; Dewey's "Reply to a Reviewer" appeared on 11 May; and Bourne continued the debate in "Other Messiahs," 25 May, all published in the *New Republic*. The first two articles appear in the present volume.

As a result of the Polish study in Philadelphia during the spring and summer of 1918, Dewey wrote four documents, all of which appear in this volume: "Autocracy under Cover," "Preliminary Confidential Memorandum," "Second Preliminary Confidential Memorandum," and "Confidential Report of Conditions among the Poles in the United States" (hereafter referred to as the "Report"). For detailed background, see Note on "Report," page 398.

Dewey completed "Autocracy under Cover" by 1 August 1918: "I have got an article written which I hope will come out in the N Rep. of Aug. 8., stating a side which has not got in to the American Press—"[26] On 12 August, writing to thank Col. Edward M. House, President Woodrow Wilson's adviser, for an interview the previous week, Dewey enclosed "an article written under my direction. It is intentionally ex parte. There is nothing in it which cannot be substantiated, but I do not sympathise with some of the practical policies of the K.O.N."[27] This "article written under Dewey's direction," possibly by Irwin Edman, was almost certainly "Autocracy under Cover." Revisions became necessary:

> I had rewritten the latter half of my article once & now have to rewrite it again. Have telephoned NR editors about delay & promised the article when I go up tomorrow— . . . Chief reason for second rewriting of latter part of article is however that we have positive proof [about] his [Ignace Jan Paderewski's] influence at Washington.[28]

During his interviews with the Military Intelligence Bureau

25. Macrae to Dewey, 14 September 1917.
26. Dewey to Alice Dewey, 1 August 1918.
27. Dewey to House, 12 August 1918, Edward M. House Papers, Yale University Library, New Haven, Conn.
28. Dewey to Barnes, 15 August 1918.

(M.I.B.) in Washington, 17–19 August, Dewey discussed "Autocracy under Cover"; the M.I.B.'s report stated that Dewey

> said that he had prepared an article which was to appear in the "New Republic" of August 24th, in which he had compared the methods of those calling the [Detroit] convention to that of Tammany Hall.[29]

This article elicited a strong reaction from *Wolna Polska*, a newspaper "popularly regarded as his [Paderewski's] personal organ" (309.6). On 25 September, when Dewey wrote to President Wilson about the completed "Report," he enclosed "a translation from the Wolna Polska of September 4, 1918, which resulted from an article entitled 'Autocracy under Cover' which I published in the New Republic for August 24, 1918."[30] The notation "The New Republic, J.D." [not in Dewey's hand] appeared in the margin beside this sentence: "They [opponents of the Polish National (Paris) Committee] have managed to break into a New York magazine, until recently known for its pacifism and before that openly pro-German, and now conducting curiously entangled editorial policies."

The only item in this volume offering a choice of copy-text is the "Preliminary Confidential Memorandum," for which two typescripts exist. One typescript (TS) is in the Military Intelligence Division of Record Group 165, Records of the War Department General and Special Staffs, National Archives; a duplicate of this TS is in the Edward M. House Papers, Yale University Library. They are identical except for four handwritten changes, discussed later. The second TS in the Woodrow Wilson Papers, Library of Congress, was apparently retyped from that in the House Papers; it is cleaner, more error-free, and less liberally hyphenated. As evidence exists that Dewey himself, after returning to Philadelphia from Washington, sent the memorandum to House,[31] and as it is clear that Dewey was not involved in the preparation of the Wilson TS, the House TS has been chosen as copy-text.

29. Memorandum to Maj. Henry T. Hunt, 3 September 1918, Military Intelligence Division of Record Group 165, Records of the War Department General and Special Staffs, National Archives, Washington, D.C. (MID, RG 165, DNA).
30. Dewey to Wilson, 25 September 1918, Woodrow Wilson Papers, Library of Congress, Washington, D.C.
31. "Growing out of my interviews, I was asked by Major Hunt to submit some memoranda. I enclose copies of two preliminary memoranda" (Dewey to House, 23 August 1918).

Four handwritten changes, which do not appear in the TS of the Military Intelligence Division, are superimposed on the typed word in the House TS: a change of "the resolution" to "a resolution" at 251.30, "purported" to "purports" at 251.30, "had" to "has" at 251.35, and "the policy" to "a policy" at 252.26. Only the change of "the policy" to "a policy" was incorporated by the retyped TS in the Wilson Papers. Since it cannot be established that Dewey would have changed these words and overlooked mistypings such as "Austiran" at 251.23, "Britian" at 251.26, and "hre" at 252.11, these four changes have not been accepted for the present edition. Completed and submitted while Dewey was in Washington during the week of 17 August 1918,[32] apparently prepared hurriedly, under pressure, and without time for correction, this document required more than the usual amount of emendation of accidentals. Its liberal hyphenation is a stylistic feature characteristic of the M.I.B. at that time as seen in some of its communications; the spelling of the words "dis-interested," "dis-satisfaction," "dis-satisfied," "over-ruled," "re-acts," and "re-organization" has been regularized therefore to Dewey's known usage. Editorial decisions were made to delete "is" before "ostensibly" at 248.19; to substitute words at 249.4, 253.20, and 253.39, the first two instances having textual notes; and, at 250.15, as to which phrase to delete. All these changes are noted in the Emendations List.

Only the House TS is extant for the "Second Preliminary Confidential Memorandum" and serves necessarily as copy-text for the present edition. Without the heavy hyphenation of the first memorandum and with fewer typographical errors, it required, beyond minor corrections, only two changes: a transposition of the phrases "among even educated Americans" and "of Polish questions" at 255.30, and the addition of "always" at 256.4.

Dewey prepared the "Report," and possibly the two memoranda just discussed, in a combination of ways. In Washington he had rented a typewriter; the M.I.B. had also provided him with a typewriter and stenographer, whose services apparently continued until the "Report" was completed. Although Dewey had written from Washington indicating that he preferred typing to dic-

32. The memorandum to Major Hunt, 3 September 1918, discussing Dewey's M.I.B. Washington interviews, stated: "Later Prof. Dewey submitted a written memorandum embodying his ideas."

tating,[33] he dictated at least part of the "Report" from an outline. On the other hand, the three misspellings of "Dmowski" indicate that some of the "Report" was prepared from a draft typed by Dewey, since he misspelled the name the same way, "Dmoski," in correspondence of this period. His daughter Lucy did library research, and his daughter Evelyn, with the help of the stenographer, completed the "Report" by mid-September, 1918.[34]

On 10 September, Dewey wrote to Albert Barnes, "I think that your idea about printing the report is a good one."[35] To his family, Dewey explained, "Barnes is going to have the report put in type on the theory that nobody would read such a long typwritten thing."[36] Writing to Colonel House about the completed "Report," Dewey noted, "It is so long that for ease of reading I had it printed."[37] Barnes, who lived in Merion, Pennsylvania, probably had the "Report" printed in Philadelphia; he paid for the printing and took complete charge of this phase. By 9 September, Dewey had sent part of the "Report" to Barnes;[38] between 14 and 19 September, Dewey sent the final pages and several insertions to Barnes and, to save time, left it to him to fit some of them in. See textual note for insertion on pp. 270.34–271.33 of the "Report."[39]

It is unclear how much proof for the "Report" Dewey saw. He wrote to Barnes on 19 September, "The galley sent was uncorrected for ordinary errors, and if my material came duly to hand there is no reason for going over the proof, assuming their proof readers will take care of errors."[40] The only appearance of the "Report," privately printed, Philadelphia (?), 1918, 80 pp., has necessarily served as copy-text for the present edition. The full range of variety in the capitalization of the published "Report" reflects the conditions of its preparation; capitalization emendations were restricted to eight corrections. Where the copy-text

33. Dewey to daughters, 20 August 1918.
34. Information in this paragraph is based on the following letters: Dewey to Barnes, 18 and 29 August, 10 September 1918. Dewey to Alice Dewey, 12 August 1918; Dewey to Alice and Jane Dewey, 18 August 1918; Dewey to daughters, 20 August 1918; Dewey to family, 28 August 1918; Evelyn Dewey to Mother and Jane Dewey, 14 August 1918; Lucy Dewey to family, 18 August, 13 and 17 September 1918.
35. Dewey to Barnes, 10 September 1918.
36. Dewey to family, 14 September 1918.
37. Dewey to House, 20 September 1918.
38. Barnes to Dewey, 9 September 1918.
39. Dewey to Barnes, 14, 15, 16, 17, 19 September 1918.
40. Dewey to Barnes, 19 September 1918.

spelling of proper names represented an acceptable variation, as in the case of "Dantzig," "Iswolsky," "Lenine," "Maklakoff," "Pittsburg," and "Roumania," no change was made. Six necessary emendations were made in the quotations, three to correct accidentals at 265.31, 276.1, and 279.34, and three involving substantives: "and" was changed to "of" at 265.34, "external" to "internal" at 270.27, and "so-called" deleted at 292.35. With regard to substantives in the rest of the text, five words probably mistyped or misheard by the stenographer were emended to similar words which made more sense or were more characteristic of Dewey: "out" to "our" at 261.4, "contracts" to "contrasts" at 263.2, "owing" to "owning" at 285.14, "effected" to "affected" at 320.27, and "secession" to "cessation" at 321.35. There were ten instances of the addition, deletion, or substitution of words required to clarify meaning, two corrections for number agreement, two transpositions, and one repetition deletion. All changes are recorded in the Emendations List.

Copies of the "Report" are located in the Woodrow Wilson Papers, Library of Congress, and at the University of California at Berkeley. On 10 September 1918, Dewey wrote to Barnes, "We shall need about half a dozen copies for the Intelligence Bureau alone, another for the State Department, and another for the War Department, one for the Colonel [House], one for the Justice, etc."[41] The number for the M.I.B. soon doubled.[42] Dewey sent the cover letters for the "Report" to Barnes and, in addition, wrote to the recipients himself.[43]

H. F. S.

41. Dewey to Barnes, 10 September 1918.
42. Dewey to Barnes, 17 September 1918.
43. On 20 September, Dewey wrote to Maj. Henry T. Hunt, "You will receive very shortly six copies of my somewhat belated report on Polish conditions. I am sending copies also to each member of the Military Intelligence Bureau with whom I came in contact when I was in Washington, namely, Captains Uterhart and Dalrymple, and Lieuts. Horgan and Montgomery" (MID, RG 165, DNA). On the same day, Dewey wrote to Capt. A. V. Dalrymple that he was sending three copies of the "Report" (MID, RG 165, DNA). Also on 20 September, Dewey wrote to Colonel House about the completed "Report" (House Papers); and, on 25 September, to President Wilson (Wilson Papers). On 28 September, the Justice Department wrote to Dewey acknowledging his letter of 25 September, but explained that they had not received the "Report" and requested a second copy (Ratner/Dewey Papers). On 4 October, Wilson wrote to Dewey acknowledging receipt of the "Report" (Wilson Papers).

TEXTUAL NOTES

20.29 (1671)] The page numbers Dewey cites at 20.32 and 20.38 match the 1671, not the 1670, edition of Thomas Tenison's *The Creed of Mr. Hobbes Examined.*

25.15 equally] In both David G. Ritchie's *Natural Rights*, page 9, and C. H. Firth's introduction to *The Clarke Papers*, page lxi, from which Ritchie quotes, the word "free" does not appear. The word "freedom" in *Natural Rights* on the line above and just to the right of "equally" may account for the word insertion.

26.24 sometimes the Barons] The appearance of the word "Counties" on page 134 of George Lawson's *An Examination of the Political Part of Mr. Hobbs*, from which Dewey was quoting, might account for the word substitution.

135.15 VI] Since Dewey includes article VI in discussing this category, and since this article also deals with territorial issues, it is apparent that he intended to include it within the original grouping.

166.31–32 Yokohama] "Yokahama" is Dewey's usual misspelling.

204.15 ten] Using the numbers Dewey gives in the third paragraph of this article, the answer arrived at is one hundred and ten.

249.4 the hands] The word "thousands" was apparently an erroneous transcription of "the hands." The phrase reappears on page 304.12–13: "The actual business of the convention was put in the hands of seven sectional meetings."

253.20 entrust the] The typescript has at this point what looks like a typed-over "entthet."

270.34–271.33 "The following quotations from the official protest . . . them play."] On 16 September 1918, Dewey wrote to Albert C. Barnes: "Since sending the telegram it has occurred to me that I could save time by sending you the material to be inserted. The first two passages about the Regency I cant tell where they should go, not having any carbon of the first part, but you can find a place for them. They have got after Sosnowsky in N Y on acct of the regency and they will stand more education on that point than I had put in" (Joseph Ratner/John Dewey Papers, Special Collections, Morris Library, Southern Illinois University at Carbondale; see Note on "Confidential Report of Conditions among the Poles in the United States," p.

399, footnote 2). Dewey probably intended these passages to be inserted in the section "The German Occupation, The Council of State and the Regency"; Barnes, however, placed them in the section dealing with the Russian Revolution following the clause "the cession of the province of Chelm to Ukrainia" because it was this aspect of the treaty of Brest-Litovsk that the Regency protested.

277.29–30 Leroy-Beaulieu, . . . *Tsars*,] Dewey is apparently quoting Stanislas Posner, who was, in turn, quoting Leroy-Beaulieu. The material could not have appeared in *Empire of the Tsars*, Leroy-Beaulieu's best-known work, which was written before the occurrence of the events discussed in the quotation.

292.35 attempts] The adjective "so-called" was obviously picked up from its appearance a few words later in the quotation to describe "Polish governments abroad." It is clear that Dewey did not intend to say that the attempts themselves were "so-called."

314.12 brother-in-law] Zofia Naimska's sister Mary was married to Edward H. Lewinski-Corwin.

EMENDATIONS LIST

All emendations in both substantives and accidentals introduced into the copy-text are recorded in the list that follows, with the exception of the changes in formal matters described below. The copy-text for each item is identified at the beginning of the list of emendations in that item; for those items in which republications are cited as the first appearance of emendations, relevant publication information and symbols are supplied. The page-line number at left is from the present edition; all lines of print except running heads are counted. The reading to the left of the square bracket is from the present edition; the bracket is followed by an abbreviation for the source of the emendation's first appearance. W means Works—the present edition—and is used for emendations made here for the first time. For emendations restricted to punctuation, the curved dash ~ means the same word(s) as before the bracket; the inferior caret ‸ indicates the absence of a punctuation mark.

The abbreviation [*rom.*] means roman type and is used to signal the omission of italics. The asterisk before an emendation page-line number indicates that the reading is discussed in the Textual Notes.

A number of formal, or mechanical, changes have been made throughout:

1. Book and periodical titles are in italic type, and have been supplied and expanded where necessary. Articles and sections of books are in quotation marks.

2. The form of Dewey's documentation has been made consistent: *op. cit.* has been eliminated; volume numbers are upper-case roman with the following periods removed; section and chapter numbers are arabic; abbreviations have been regularized.

3. Single quotation marks have been changed to double when not inside quoted material; however, opening or closing quotation marks have been supplied where necessary and recorded.

4. The following spellings have been editorially regularized to the characteristic Dewey usage, given to the left of the bracket:

centre(s)] center 129.13, 137.12, 137.17, 160.27, 180.5, 211.32, 211.33, 262.22, 269.38, 278.16, 281.37, 285.4, 303.13, 306.34, 325.31
cooperate (all forms)] coöperate 48.35, 51.4, 74.27, 82.34, 82.40, 104.35, 105.25, 105.37, 273.23–24, 276.29, 300.12
cooperate (all forms)] co-operate 60.33, 64.25, 64.27, 64.28, 65.23, 69.15
coordinate (all forms)] co-ordinate 350.25, 353.29
coordination] coördination 291.6, 311.19, 312.27–28
disinterested] dis-interested 252.11
dissatisfaction] dis-satisfaction 249.24
dissatisfied] dis-satisfied 250.3
enterprise(s)] enterprize 98.3, 102.16, 102.26, 103.18
fantasies] phantasies 96.31
guarantees] guaranties 108.20, 110.20
meagre (all forms)] meager 309.26, 323.29, 337.10
moreover] more-over 249.6
naïve] naive 113.29, 196.4
overruled] over-ruled 251.25
Partisans] Partizans 104.4–5
practice (all forms)] practise 99.32, 145.8, 347.6
program] programme 43.14, 91.23
reacts] re-acts 250.29, 250.37
reestablishment] reëstablishment 280.39–281.1, 326.16
reorganization] re-organization 252.32
self-respect] self respect 64.3
so-called] socalled 256.8
so-called] so called 303.6
through] thru 98.17, 98.19, 98.29, 101.36, 105.10, 256.4, 257.6
valuation-judgments] valuation judgments 4.25–26
wartime] war time 112.18

"The Objects of Valuation"

Copy-text is the only previous publication of the article, in *Journal of Philosophy, Psychology and Scientific Methods* 15 (1918): 253–58.

3n.6 Value] W; Valued
5.5 it] W; it it
5.24 follows:] W; follows:[4]
5n.3 committal] W; commital
5n.10 with which] W; which

6.7 view."[4]] W; view."

"The Motivation of Hobbes's Political Philosophy"

Copy-text is the only previous publication of the article, in *Studies in the History of Ideas*, edited by the Department of Philosophy (New York: Columbia University Press, 1918), 1:88–115.

19.21 the name] W; the the name
20.1 *Hobbs*] W; *Hobbes*
20.24 Government";—] W; ~;"—
*20.29 (1671)] W; (1670)
22.23 Con-Covenanters] W; Con-Coventanters
23.35 *Hobbs's*] W; *Hobbes's*
23n.3 432] W; 429
24.19 not] W; not that,
*25.15 equally] W; equally free
*26.24 sometimes the Barons] W; Counties, and Barons
26n.4 Auguste] W; August
27.34–35 Law, which, . . . possesses] W; law . . . which possesses
28.33 *Laws*] W; *Law*
29.13 equity which . . . is] W; equity . . . which is
29.22 ‸on account of "the] W; "~ ‸~
31.20 booke] W; books
34.9 right] W; rights
38n.4 162] W; 164
38n.5 30; and Vol. II] W; 30. Vol. III
38n.6 Who Bear] W; that

"Philosophy and Democracy"

Copy-text for this essay is its first appearance, in *University* [of California] *Chronicle* 21 (1919): 39–54. Its republication in *Characters and Events*, ed. Joseph Ratner (New York: Henry Holt and Co., 1929), 2:841–55 (CE), is cited as the first appearance of one emendation.

43.30 incompatibilities] W; incompatabilities
44.10 economic] CE; economics

"Vocational Education in the Light of the World War"

Copy-text for this article is its only previous appearance, in *Bulletin No. 4*, Vocational Education Association of the Middle West (Chicago, 1918), 9 pp.

58.19 it] W; he
59.15 an average] W; about an average
59.26 war,] W; ~;
59.27 factories;] W; ~,
60.24 moral] W; morale
60.25 thing—] W; ~‸
64.1 goes] W; go
64.36 led,] W; ~;
64.38 goods;] W; ~,
65.15 Now] W; Now unless
65.21 unless this] W; this
65.22 rests] W; must rest
65.32 present,] W; ~‸
65.33 recreation‸] W; ~,
67.22 young of] W; young or

"America in the World"

Copy-text for this article is its original publication, in *Nation* 106 (1918): 287. Its republication in *Characters and Events*, ed. Joseph Ratner (New York: Henry Holt and Co., 1929), 2:642–44 (CE), with the title "America and the World," is cited as the first appearance of one emendation.

71.21–22 Old World] W; old world
71.38 Old World] CE; old world

"Internal Social Reorganization after the War"

Copy-text for this article is its first publication, in *Journal of Race Development* 8 (1918): 385–400. Its republication in *Characters and Events*, ed. Joseph Ratner (New York: Henry Holt and Co., 1929), 2:745–59 (CE), with the title "Elements of Social Reorganization," is cited as the first appearance of three emendations.

73.4 Labor] W; labor
74.9 past,] W; ~;
76.35 chronic unemployment] W; chronic employment
77.13 symptom‸] W; ~,
77.35 population,] W; ~‸
78.34 distribution] CE; distribuion
80.2 production] CE; product
83.34 comfortable] CE; confortable
84.40 which] W; in which
86.9 seen,] W; seen that,
86.9 dimly,] W; ~‸
86.9 today,] W; ~‸
86.15 together;] W; ~,

"A New Social Science"

Copy-text for this essay is its first appearance, in *New Republic* 14 (1918): 292–94.

88.23 Constitution] W; constitution
90.37 They have] W; It has
91.10 it has] W; has

"Political Science as a Recluse"

Copy-text for this article is its original publication, in *New Republic* 14 (1918): 383–84. Its republication in *Characters and Events*, ed. Joseph Ratner (New York: Henry Holt and Co., 1929), 2:728–32 (CE), is cited as the first appearance of one emendation.

93.10 causal] CE; casual
95.2 either,] W; ~‸
95.25–26 ill-considered] W; ~‸~

"What Are We Fighting For?"

Copy-text for this article is its first appearance, in *Independent* 94 (1918): 474, 480–83. Its republication in *Characters and Events*, ed. Joseph Ratner (New York: Henry Holt and Co., 1929),

2:551–60 (CE), with the title "The Social Possibilities of War," is cited as the first appearance of four emendations.

98.11–12 arrangements] CE; arrangement
99.20 obliterating] CE; obliberating
104.8 of such] CE; such
104.9 Fundamental] CE; fundamental
105.31 effected] W; affected
110.22 which] W; in which
110.23 against in] W; against

"The Post-War Mind"

Copy-text for this article is its first publication, in *New Republic* 17 (1918): 157–59.

115.32 then,] W; ~‸

"The New Paternalism"

Copy-text for this essay is its first appearance, in *New Republic* 17 (1918): 216–17. Its republication in *Characters and Events*, ed. Joseph Ratner (New York: Henry Holt and Co., 1929), 2:517–21 (CE), with the title "Propaganda," is cited as the first appearance of the emendation.

118.10 Act] CE; act

"Morals and the Conduct of States"

Copy-text for this essay is its original publication, in *New Republic* 14 (1918): 232–34.

124.4 recognized,] W; ~‸

"The Fourteen Points and the League of Nations"

Copy-text for this article is its only previous appearance, in *Dial* 65 (1918): 463–64.

*135.15 VI] W; VII

"A League of Nations and Economic Freedom"

Copy-text for this article is its first appearance, in *Dial* 65 (1918): 537–39.

141.31–32 laissez-faire] W; ~‸~

"Japan and America"

Copy-text for this essay is its only previous appearance, in *Dial* 66 (1919): 501–3.

153.6 immigration] W; immigraton

"Liberalism in Japan"

Copy-text for this essay is its first appearance, in *Dial* 67 (1919): 283–85, 333–37, 369–71. Its republication in *Characters and Events*, ed. Joseph Ratner (New York: Henry Holt and Co., 1929), 1:149–69 (CE), is cited as the first appearance of twelve emendations.

159.13 salve] W; slave
160.1 Russia—] CE; ~‸
160.1–2 who constantly clamor] CE; that constantly clamors
160.16 reasonable,] W; ~‸
161.15 discussed] W; discusssed
161.20–21 Marxians,] W; ~‸
162.4 population] CE; populaton
162.12 factories] CE; factores
165.24 would] CE; would not
165.38 lèse majesté] W; lese majeste
166.18 three] CE; the three
166.29 began] CE; begin
*166.31–32 Yokohama] CE; Yokahama
168.9 Statesmen—] CE; ~,
168.14 police,] W; policy‸
169.33 divisive] CE; devisive
170.29 with] CE; will

171.40 notion] CE; motion

"On the Two Sides of the Eastern Sea"

Copy-text for this article is its first appearance, in *New Republic* 19 (1919): 346–48. Its republication in *China, Japan and the U.S.A.* (New York: Republic Publishing Co., 1921), pp. 3–9 (CJ), is cited as the first appearance of two emendations; republication in *Characters and Events*, ed. Joseph Ratner (New York: Henry Holt and Co., 1929), 1:170–76 (CE), is cited as the first appearance of one emendation.

174.2 days'] CJ; ~‸
175.34 East] CJ; east
177.38 deprecated.)] W; ~).
179.16 the two] CE; they two

"The Discrediting of Idealism"

Copy-text for this article is its original publication, in *New Republic* 20 (1919): 285–87.

181.19 à outrance] W; a l'outrance
183.15 à la improvvisatore] W; a la improvisatore

"The International Duel in China"

Copy-text for this article is its only previous appearance, in *New Republic* 20 (1919): 110–12.

193.12 Doctrine] W; doctrine
198.22 illustration,] W; ~‸

"Militarism in China"

Copy-text for this article is its original publication, in *New Republic* 20 (1919): 167–69.

199.22 China‸] W; ~,

200.16, 202.31 Shih-kai] W; Shi-Kai
201.34, 202.26 Chi-jui] W; Chi-Jui
203.31–32 Tuchuns, military governors,] W; Tu-chuns‸ military governors‸
204.5 Tuchun] W; Tu-chun
*204.15 ten] W; twenty

"Transforming the Mind of China"

Copy-text for this essay is its first appearance, in *Asia* 19 (1919): 1103–8. Its republication in *Characters and Events*, ed. Joseph Ratner (New York: Henry Holt and Co., 1929), 1:285–95 (CE), is cited as the first appearance of three emendations.

206.14 island] CE; Island
207.7 achievement] W; achievements
210.22 as] CE; in
210.22 norm] W; norms
214.21 romantic] CE; romatic

"Chinese National Sentiment"

Copy-text for this article is its original appearance, in *Asia* 19 (1919): 1237–42.

216.31–32 mobility] W; nobility
217.15 Emperor] W; emperor

"The American Opportunity in China"

Copy-text for this essay is its first appearance, in *New Republic* 21 (1919): 14–17. Its republication in *Characters and Events*, ed. Joseph Ratner (New York: Henry Holt and Co., 1929), 1:296–303 (CE), as the first part of "America and China," is cited as the first appearance of one emendation.

228.10 Burlingame] W; Burlinghame
231.21 mentioned,] W; ~‸
232.8 Doctrine] CE; doctrine

234.26 unparalleled] W; unparallelled

"*Our Share in Drugging China*"

Copy-text for this article is its only previous publication, in *New Republic* 21 (1919): 114–17.

236.10–11 Opium-smoking] W; ~‸~
237.36 this time] W; this,
238.17 government] W; Government
238.24,27 Dairen] W; Darien
240.2–4 it . . . present‸,] W; it (as we do not do at the present) that our post-office at Shanghai cannot be employed for sending narcotics into China by parcel-post,
240.6 people).] W; ~‸.

"*Preliminary Confidential Memorandum*"

Copy-text for this memorandum is the typescript in the Edward M. House Papers, Yale University Library, New Haven, Conn.

248.2–4 MEMORANDUM/ . . . /RE] W; Memorandum/Re
248.18 then] W; them
248.19 convention, ostensibly] W; convention‸ is ostensibly
*249.4 the hands] W; thousands
249.9 beyond] W; beyound
249.26 recrimination] W; recrimmination
250.2 withheld] W; witheld
250.7 attack Americans] W; attact Americans
250.11 Cross."] W; ~",
250.13 Cross"] W; ~‸
250.15 with the] W; with the under the
250.18 offices] W; officea
250.20 efficiency] W; eficiency
250.37 prestige] W; presitge
251.3 hesitation] W; hesitiation
251.9 constituted] W; constitued
251.16 commissions] W; commisions
251.23 Austrian socialists] W; Austiran socialists
251.26 Britain] W; Britian
251.36 is,] W; ~‸

252.5 facts:] W; ~;
252.11 here] W; hre
252.18 "plenipotentiary,"] W; "~",
252.32 unification] W; unfication
253.17 weighty] W; wieghty
*253.20 entrust the] W; entthet
253.36 them;] W; ~‸
254.1 affairs of] W; affairs to
254.4 their] W; thier

"Second Preliminary Confidential Memorandum"

Copy-text for this memorandum is the typescript in the Edward M. House Papers, Yale University Library, New Haven, Conn.

255.1–2 CONFIDENTIAL MEMORANDUM] W; *Memorandum - Confidential*
255.29–256.1 ignorance . . . and] W; ignorence among even educated Americans of Polish questions, and
256.3 Czecho-Slovaks] W; Checko-Slovaks
256.4 almost always] W; almost
256.9,26,33 ignorance] W; ignorence
257.2 already] W; alread
257.3 un-American] W; unAmerican
257.19 publicity] W; publisity
258.9 methods] W; metjods

"Confidential Report of Conditions among the Poles in the United States"

Copy-text for this report is its only previous publication (privately printed: Philadelphia [?], 1918), 80 pp.

260.20 Blanshard] W; Blanchard
260.30 above,] W; ~‸
261.4 our] W; out
261.31 takes up local] W; takes local
263.2 contrasts] W; contracts
263.39 Miliukov] W; Miliokov
264.36 relations] W; relation
265.24 securing] W; securing first

265.31 equality] W; equalty
265.33–34 prohibition of] W; prohibition and
268.10 oppressed] W; opppressed
269.16 Kosciusko] W; Kosciusco
269.34 State] W; state
270.27 internal] W; external
271.26, 297.4, 321.18 Dmowski] W; Dmoski
271.33 have them] W; have
272.36, 273.22, 282.8 Daszynski] W; Dascynski
274.9 von Beseler] W; Von Besseler
276.1 ‸saying that "it] W; "~ ‸~
276.36 vacillating] W; vaccilating
277.4 Kingdom] W; Kingdon
277.6 archduke] W; archbishop
*277.29–30 Leroy-Beaulieu, . . . *Tsars*,] W; Leroy-Beaulieu's *Empire of the Tsars*‸
277.35 Björnson] W; Bjorson
278.29–30 anti-Semitic] W; anti-semitic
279.14 counteracted] W; conteracted
279.25 says:] W; ~‸
279.34 Paderewski] W; Paderwski
281.3 Skirmunt] W; Skermunt
281.8 Europe.] W; ~,
281.8 Kozicki] W; Kozciski
281.9 Rozwadowski] W; Rozwadowska
281.11 Fronczak] W; Franczek
282.4 (*a*) that] W; that (*a*)
282.20–21 persists] W; perasists
282.32 naturally] W; it naturally
283.19 chief British] W; British chief
283.31 imperialistic] W; imperalistic
285.14 owning] W; owing
287.9–10,15–16 Republican] W; republican
288.25 initials] W; intitials
288.33 Zakopane] W; Zachopane
290.6 press] W; presss
290.37 Victims'] W; Victim's
292.4 The] W; 1. The
*292.35 attempts] W; so-called attempts
292.37 The] W; [¶] The
293.4–5 including] W; includ-/
293.23 forgo] W; forego
294.2 Mitchel] W; Mitchell
294.2 Hillquit] W; Hilquit
295.11 dragoman] W; dragomam
295.20 replied,] W; ~‸
295.25–26 Poland and Russia] W; Poland Russia

296.23 Allies] W; allies
298.12 are:] W; ~,
298.18 Allies;] W; ~,
299.5 accuracy;] W; ~,
300.32, 303.12 Citizens'] W; ~‸
301.2 Rhode] W; Rohde
303.40 Philadelphia] W; Philadephia
304.12 The] W; That the
305.19 branches:] W; ~,
306.31 and] W; to
310.39 Wronski] W; Vronski
311.8 Paderewskis] W; Paderewski
312.3 devoted] W; devotes
312.11 regarding] W; in connection with the funds regarding
314.1 Sembrich] W; Sembich
*314.12 brother-in-law] W; brother
314.12 (2) Lewinski-Corwin] W; Corwin Lewinski
314.14 *The Political*] W; "A Political
315.8,13,15,30,31 Turczynowicz] W; Turchynowicz
315.14 sanitariums] W; sanatariums
318.14 are, to] W; is, to
320.27 affected] W; effected
321.23 Dowbor-Musnicki] W; Dowber-Musnicki
321.28 First] W; first
321.35 cessation] W; secession
322.24–25 of dissatisfaction] W; to dissatisfaction
323.13 Army] W; army
324.5 maintenance] W; maintainence
325.4 control] W; Control
325.28 in securing] W; of securing
327.19 which] W; and which
327.22 learning,] W; ~‸

"Syllabus of Eight Lectures on 'Problems of Philosophic Reconstruction'"

Copy-text for the syllabus is its only previous appearance, in *Journal of Philosophy, Psychology and Scientific Methods* 16 (1919): 357–64.

346.15 Modern] W; 1. Modern

"Introductory Word"

Copy-text for this introduction is its only previous appearance, in F. Matthias Alexander's *Man's Supreme Inheritance* (New York: E. P. Dutton and Co., 1918), xiii–xvii.

352.20 spasmodic] W; spasdomic

LINE-END HYPHENATION

I. Copy-text list.

The following are the editorially established forms of possible compounds which were hyphenated at the ends of lines in the copy-text:

7.12	subject-matter
15.7	non-laboratory
46.12	highway
72.1	peace-loving
93.10	supernatural
99.11	airplane
101.19	realignments
121.7	safeguard
122.10–11	supernational
127.22	outgrowth
129.17	commonplace
145.4	subconscious
163.23	newspapers
166.33	newspaper
167.33	semi-official
168.15	newspapers
177.20	counterbalance
189.4	widespread
194.22	semi-promise
201.35	outbreak
208.38	onlooker
211.17	railways
211.18	retelling
211.28	standpoint
213.23	short-cut
215.17	preconceptions
231.10	railway
232.17–18	standpoint
235.16	cooperation
235.29	cooperate
240.2	post-office
240.30	wholesale
248.12–13	headquarters
249.30–31	presswork
284.15	ultra-conservative
285.17	ship-building
308.24	countercharge
310.15	so-called
346.8	pseudo-science
351.9	subconscious
353.16–17	subconscious
353.22	neuro-muscular
353.26	override
354.18–19	re-education

II. Critical-text list.

In transcriptions from the present edition, no line-end hyphens in ambiguously broken possible compounds are to be retained except the following:

15.18	subject-matter	145.34	gum-shoe
46.36	semi-magical	163.8	over-lords
68.4	over-technical	163.17	world-power
71.4	spread-eagleism	174.19	all-pervading
72.21	fruit-bearing	197.28	self-glorification
75.27	self-respect	205.5	self-sufficiency
81.3	one-sided	230.12	re-alignment
100.33	post-war	297.15	cut-throat
107.5	non-rational	304.1	self-elected
107.11	non-rational	325.32	tittle-tattle
124.32	well-wishing	344.9	break-down
144.36	candle-dip	349.4	ready-made

SUBSTANTIVE VARIANTS IN QUOTATIONS

Dewey represented source material in varying ways, from memorial paraphrase to verbatim copy, in some places citing his source fully, in others mentioning only authors' names, and, in still others, omitting documentation altogether.

Dewey's substantive variations in quotations have been considered important enough to warrant this special list. All material inside quotation marks, except that obviously being emphasized or restated, has been searched out; Dewey's citations have been verified and, when necessary, emended.

Except for required corrections noted in the Emendations List, all quotations have been retained as they appear in the copy-text; in cases of possible compositorial or typographical errors, changes in substantives or accidentals that restore original readings are noted as *Works* (W) emendations. Although Dewey, like many scholars of the period, was unconcerned about precision in matters of form, many of the changes in quotations may well have occurred in the printing process. For example, comparing Dewey's quotations with the originals reveals that some editors and compositors house-styled the quoted materials as well as Dewey's own. Therefore, in the present edition, the spelling and capitalization of the source have been reproduced.

Dewey frequently changed or omitted punctuation in quoted material. When such changes or omissions have substantive implications, the punctuation of the original reading has been restored; those changes are recorded in the Emendations List. Dewey often did not indicate that he had omitted material from his source. Omitted short phrases appear in the following list; omissions of more than one line are noted by a bracketed ellipsis [. . .]. Italics in source material have been treated as substantives. Both Dewey's omitted and added italics are noted here.

Differences between Dewey's quotations and the source attributable to the context in which the quotation appears, such as changes in number or tense, are not recorded.

The sources of Dewey's quotations from Cicero, Cumberland, Milton, and the letter from Hobbes to Mersenne as presented by Tönnies in "Siebzehn Briefe des Thomas Hobbes an Samuel Sorbière" (all references in "The Motivation of Hobbes's Political Philosophy) appear in the Checklist of Dewey's References, but no correction of these quotations is included here because Dewey translated this material himself directly from Latin. Since the fourth edition, 1696, of John Eachard's *Mr. Hobbs's State of Nature Considered*, cited by Dewey in the same essay, was unobtainable, the fifth edition, 1705, has been used.

References for "Confidential Report of Conditions among the Poles in the United States" present a more complex problem. Dewey does not identify his sources for quotations in this document and mentions few sources in correspondence of the period. Some of the periodicals he probably used are no longer available or obtainable. Many of the documents quoted were apparently translated by Dewey from French or possibly German, or from Polish by a translator; there are discussions in Dewey's correspondence about the translation of Polish documents. An English version was cited if it closely matched the quotation; if the source was translated, the reference appears in the Checklist of Dewey's References, but no correction of the quotation is included here.

The form used in this section is designed to assist the reader in determining whether Dewey had the source before him or was relying on memory. Notations in this section follow the formula: page-line numbers from the present edition, followed by the lemma, then a bracket. After the bracket, the original form appears, followed by the author's surname, shortened source-title from the Checklist of Dewey's References, and the page-line reference to the source, all in parentheses.

"The Objects of Valuation"

4.5 case] case so far as I can see (Perry, "Dewey and Urban," 174.6) [*Middle Works* 11:366.30–31]

5.24–25 Syracuse] Syracuse (New York) (Bush, "Value and Causality," 95.36) [*Middle Works* 11:387.13]

6.2 affection. It] affection. They begin to take their places on the curb a long time before the procession begins. It (Bush, "Value and Causality," 95.40–41) [*Middle Works* 11:387.17–18]

6.2 natural] quite natural (Bush, "Value and Causality," 95.41) [*Middle Works* 11:387.18]
6.3 that they] they (Bush, "Value and Causality," 95.41) [*Middle Works* 11:387.18]
6.3 supremely. Does] supremely; [. . .]. Does (Bush, "Value and Causality," 95.42–96.1) [*Middle Works* 11:387.19–21]
6.3 really attach] attach really (Bush, "Value and Causality," 96.2) [*Middle Works* 11:387.22]

"Concerning Alleged Immediate Knowledge of Mind"

10.11 puzzling] most puzzling (Taylor, *Problem of Conduct*, 98.14)
10.27 emotion being] emotion would be (Taylor, *Problem of Conduct*, 99.13)
10.28 came] came in (Taylor, *Problem of Conduct*, 99.14)
12.14 an emotion] the emotion (Taylor, *Problem of Conduct*, 99.14)
12.15 origin] production (Taylor, *Problem of Conduct*, 99.16)
12.34 what] just what (Taylor, *Problem of Conduct*, 98.21)
13.9 a fact] an immediate fact (Singer, "Consciousness and Behavior," 16.25–26)
13.10 in the world] of all the world (Singer, "Consciousness and Behavior," 17.18)
13.17 be still] still be (Watson, *Behavior*, 8.19)
14.27 absence] the absence (Watson, *Behavior*, 4.36)
14.29 one jot] by one jot (Watson, *Behavior*, 4.38)

"The Motivation of Hobbes's Political Philosophy"

19.4 Until] Until towards (Figgis, *Divine Right*, 11.21)
20.4 Magna Charta] [*ital.*] (Lawson, *Hobbs*, 67.22–23)
20.5 It is] Its (Lawson, *Hobbs*, 67.23)
20.8 Aristotle] *Aristotle* & *Cicero* (Lawson, *Hobbs*, 68.7–8)
20.31 Policy] [*ital.*] (Tenison, *Hobbes*, 156.29)
20.32 blaze] a blaze (Tenison, *Hobbes*, 156.30)
20.33 on earth] upon earth (Tenison, *Hobbes*, 170.28–29)
21.5 as the] for the (Figgis, *Divine Right*, 219.14)
21.6 some] some one (Figgis, *Divine Right*, 219.16)
21.17 King] K. (Tönnies, "Siebzehn Briefe," 223.17)
21.17 last] length (Tönnies, "Siebzehn Briefe," 223.18)
21.19 Duke] D. (Tönnies, "Siebzehn Briefe," 223.20)
21.25–26 *unless . . . Church*] [*rom.*] (Hobbes, *Seven Problems*, 5.11)
21.26 *depend wholly*] wholly (Hobbes, *Seven Problems*, 5.12)
21.26 *upon . . . power*] [*rom.*] (Hobbes, *Seven Problems*, 5.12)
22.22 *De Cive*,] *De Cive*, in Latin, (Hobbes, *Considerations*, 415.4)

22.27 depends] depend (Tönnies, "Hobbes-Analekten," 302.21)
22.29 may] may perhaps (Tönnies, "Hobbes-Analekten," 302.23)
22.29 this] this opinion (Tönnies, "Hobbes-Analekten," 302.23)
23.9 taught] contained (Hobbes, *Six Lessons*, 333.21)
23.10 the clergy] those of the clergy (Hobbes, *Six Lessons*, 333.22)
23.14 popish] the venom of popish (Hobbes, *Considerations*, 432.18–19)
23.14–15 division and distinction] *distinction* and *division* (Hobbes, *Considerations*, 432.19–20)
23.15 spiritual] [*ital.*] (Hobbes, *Considerations*, 432.20)
23.15 civil] [*ital.*] (Hobbes, *Considerations*, 432.21)
23.17–18 position] positions (Hobbes, *Rudiments*, xxii.26)
23.18 in those points] those (Hobbes, *Rudiments*, xxii.27)
23.21 made] had made (Hobbes, *Rudiments*, xxiii.8)
23.23 the princes] princes (Hobbes, *Rudiments*, xxiii.11)
23.24 laws] civil laws (Hobbes, *Rudiments*, xxiii.12)
24.2 Book] [*ital.*] (Eachard, *Hobbs*, 8.25)
24.4 thousands of] thousand (Eachard, *Hobbs*, 8.27)
24.4 easily be] be easily (Eachard, *Hobbs*, 11.3)
24.5 much] much of it (Eachard, *Hobbs*, 11.4)
24.6 Dunstable stuff] [*ital.*] (Eachard, *Hobbs*, 11.5)
24.6 which] that (Eachard, *Hobbs*, 11.5)
24.6 who] that have (Eachard, *Hobbs*, 11.6)
24.7 Policy] [*ital.*] (Eachard, *Hobbs*, 11.7)
24.7 Morality] [*ital.*] (Eachard, *Hobbs*, 11.7)
24.16 dignitaries] dignities (Hobbes, *Rudiments*, 79n.13)
24.18 besides] beside (Hobbes, *Rudiments*, 79n.15)
24n.4 believe] firmly believe that (Harrington, *Prerogative*, 259.27)
24n.4 and . . . be] and will in future Ages be (Harrington, *Prerogative*, 259.28)
24n.5 in this] at this (Harrington, *Prerogative*, 259.28)
25.13 have] have legitimately (Ritchie, *Natural Rights*, 9.29)
25.14 property] *i.e.* property (Ritchie, *Natural Rights*, 9.30)
26.1 Judgements,] Judgement, Peace, War (Lawson, *Hobbs*, 116.12)
26.6–7 whether they are] whether (Lawson, *Hobbs*, 123.20)
26.7 only] but only (Lawson, *Hobbs*, 123.21)
26.8 even to] to (Lawson, *Hobbs*, 123.22)
26.9 do. Romans] do. [. . .] *Rom.* (Lawson, *Hobbs*, 123.24–125.13)
26.10 Nor] Neither (Lawson, *Hobbs*, 127.27)
26.12 the civil Laws] civil Laws (Lawson, *Hobbs*, 127.29)
26.16 God] his God (Lawson, *Hobbs*, 127.34)
26.20 agree neither] neither agree (Lawson, *Hobbs*, 133.19–20)
26.20 with one] one with (Lawson, *Hobbs*, 133.20)
26.23 as] unto us (Lawson, *Hobbs*, 134.20)
26.25 predominant and ascendant] ascendant and predominant (Lawson, *Hobbs*, 134.22)
27.27 you] you upon the like occasions (Harrington, *Oceana*, 59.48)
27.27 Governments] Government (Harrington, *Oceana*, 59.49)

28.2 deepest] the deepest (Figgis, *Divine Right*, 228.30)

28.24 once been] been once (Hobbes, *De Corpore Politico*, 227.14)

28.27 like] the like (Hobbes, *De Corpore Politico*, 227.25)

28.28 the opinions] that is to say, the opinions (Hobbes, *De Corpore Politico*, 227.27)

29.14 the law of] or ever was law in (Hobbes, *Dialogue*, 15.20)

29.23 lawyers] lawyers themselves (Hobbes, *Dialogue*, 45.12)

29.25 former judgments] former judges (Hobbes, *Dialogue*, 45.14)

30.14 connected] connected in the one case (Robertson, *Hobbes*, 57.23)

30.15 nature, it] nature, and in the other referred to such a basis to be afterwards supplied, it (Robertson, *Hobbes*, 57.24–25)

30.16 an observer] a mere observer (Robertson, *Hobbes*, 57.26–27)

30.16 nature] manners (Robertson, *Hobbes*, 57.27)

30.19 sympathy with all] all sympathy with (Robertson, *Hobbes*, 57.30)

30.32 mind's] mind (Hobbes, *Rudiments*, xix.27)

30.34 had thought] thought (Hobbes, *Rudiments*, xix.30)

30.35 body] [*ital.*] (Hobbes, *Rudiments*, xx.1)

30.35 man] [*ital.*] (Hobbes, *Rudiments*, xx.2)

30.36 civil government] [*ital.*] (Hobbes, *Rudiments*, xx.3–4)

31.1 war] wars (Hobbes, *Rudiments*, xx.17)

31.1–2 regarding] concerning (Hobbes, *Rudiments*, xx.18–19)

31.2–3 subjects; and] subjects, the true forerunners of an approaching war; and (Hobbes, *Rudiments*, xx.20–21)

31.17 to bee true] true (Hobbes, *Letters*, 471.2)

31.17 doctrine,] doctrine, (though yett it wanteth polishing), (Hobbes, *Letters*, 471.2–3)

31.19 the] y^{t} (Hobbes, *Letters*, 471.5)

32.9 do] do notwithstanding (Hobbes, *Rudiments*, iv.5–6)

32.9–10 the ocean] [*ital.*] (Hobbes, *Rudiments*, iv.6)

33.6 a dissolute] dissolute (Hobbes, *Answer to Bramhall*, 287.12)

33.22 the doctrine] this doctrine (Hobbes, *Human Nature*, xvii.18)

36.5–6 which . . . good] the present good (to which, by strict consequence, many unforseen evils do adhere) (Hobbes, *Rudiments*, 48.20–21)

36.28–29 true and peculiar] peculiar and true (Hobbes, *Rudiments*, 16n.3)

36.30 may] may either (Hobbes, *Rudiments*, 16n.4)

36n.2 with] of (Hobbes, *Leviathan*, 170.25)

37.12 man] a man (Hobbes, *De Corpore Politico*, 116.14)

37.15 peregrinations] peregrination (Hobbes, *De Corpore Politico*, 116.18)

38.17 the subject] subject (Hobbes, *De Corpore Politico*, 162.24)

38n.8–9 That . . . people] [*ital.*] (Hobbes, *De Corpore Politico*, 214.10–12)

39.19 that is] is (Hobbes, *Rudiments*, 178.27)

"Philosophy and Democracy"

45.22 distinct] abrupt (Dewey, *Democracy and Education*, 382.27) [*Middle Works* 9:337.30]

"The League of Nations and the New Diplomacy"

133.17 who] which (Barclay, *New Methods*, xi.9)
133.19 likely] likely, however, (Barclay, *New Methods*, xi.11–12)

"The Fourteen Points and the League of Nations"

136.24–25 assistance] assistance also (*President Wilson's Addresses*, 469.4–5)
138.19 in time be likely] be likely in time (*President Wilson's Addresses*, 478.14)

"The Discrediting of Idealism"

181.36 uttermost] utmost (*President Wilson's Addresses*, 484.22)

"The International Duel in China"

196.30 develop] help develop (*Shanghai Times*, 5 July 1919, 7.3.133)
196.30 railways] railroads (*Shanghai Times*, 5 July 1919, 7.3.134)
196.31 to join] by joining (*Shanghai Times*, 5 July 1919, 7.3.135)

"Militarism in China"

201.40 consideration] importance (Harding, "China," 103.2.54)

"Chinese National Sentiment"

217.20 with] by (Huc, *Journey*, 117.15)
217.22 then earn their money] earn their money, then (Huc, *Journey*, 117.17–18)
217.22–23 But . . . to] But don't let us (Huc, *Journey*, 117.18)

217.26 company. Whereupon] company; and thereupon (Huc, *Journey*, 117.22)

"Confidential Report of Conditions among the Poles in the United States"

267.14 object] object alone (Tadema, *Poland*, 19.14)
267.14 the unification] the overthrow of Germany's sinister power, the unification (Tadema, *Poland*, 19.14–15)
267.15 Monarchy] Monarch (Tadema, *Poland*, 19.16)
267.15–16 concentrates itself] concentrated herself (Tadema, *Poland*, 19.17)
267.16 toward] towards (Tadema, *Poland*, 19.18)
267.16 turn all its] turned all her (Tadema, *Poland*, 19.18)
270.27 interferences] interference ("Text of Treaty," 54.1.54)
270.27 those] these ("Text of Treaty," 54.2.1)
270.28 and . . . determine] and to let Germany and Austria determine ("Text of Treaty," 54.2.2)
270.28–29 their future fate] the future fate of these territories ("Text of Treaty," 54.2.3–4)
272.18 who is] and at the time ("Addresses," 397.1.19)
272.18 that] that in his opinion ("Addresses," 397.1.21)
272.19–20 question] problem ("Addresses," 397.1.22)
272.21 suggestion] conception of the rights of the Polish Nation ("Addresses," 397.1.25–26)
272.21 the nucleus] a nucleus ("Addresses," 397.1.27)
272.22 a State . . . brings] the resurrecting State, brings ("Addresses," 397.1.27)
272.23 expression] the expressions ("Addresses," 397.1.29)
272.23 its most] most ("Addresses," 397.1.29)
278.2 Poles. Almost] polonais, mais loyalistes et catholiques, [. . .]. Presque (Posner, "La Vie politique," 621.19–24)
292.34 struggle] its struggle ("Resolution," 2.2.63)
292.34–35 Polish independence] the Political independence ("Resolution," 2.2.65)
292.35 and . . . attempts] or attempts ("Resolution," 2.2.65–66)
305.32 priests. The main] priests. The loyalists declare this domination is intolerable and un-American. Their main (*Christian Science Monitor*, 5.6.1–3)
305.33 Legions] Legion (*Christian Science Monitor*, 5.6.5)

"Creative Industry"

333.12 Schools] The schools (Marot, *Creative Industry*, xiv.1)
333.15 to play] for play (Marot, *Creative Industry*, 10.14)
333.18 time] of another time (Marot, *Creative Industry*, 21.5)

"Reply to a Reviewer"

354.29 till] until (Bourne, "Making Over the Body," 28.41) [*Middle Works* 11:360.6]

CHECKLIST OF DEWEY'S REFERENCES

Titles and authors' names in Dewey references have been corrected and expanded to conform accurately and consistently to the original works; all corrections appear in the Emendations List.

This section gives full publication information for each work cited by Dewey. When Dewey gave page numbers for a reference, the edition he used was identified exactly by locating the citation. Similarly, the books in Dewey's personal library have been used to verify his use of a particular edition. For other references, the edition listed here is the one from among the various editions possibly available to him that was his most likely source by reason of place or date of publication, or on the evidence from correspondence and other materials, and its general accessibility during the period.

"Addresses Forwarded to President Wilson." *Wici* 4 (24 April 1917): 397–98.

Alexander, F. Matthias. *Man's Supreme Inheritance*. New York: E. P. Dutton and Co., 1918.

Bagehot, Walter. *Physics and Politics*. Rev. ed. New York: Colonial Press, 1900.

Barclay, Thomas. *New Methods of Adjusting International Disputes and the Future*. London: Constable and Co., 1917.

Bode, Boyd H. "Consciousness and Psychology." In *Creative Intelligence: Essays in the Pragmatic Attitude*. New York: Henry Holt and Co., 1917.

Bourne, Randolph. "Making Over the Body." *New Republic* 15 (1918): 28–29. [*The Middle Works of John Dewey, 1899–1924*, edited by Jo Ann Boydston, 11:359–60. Carbondale: Southern Illinois University Press, 1982.]

Bush, Wendell T. "Value and Causality." *Journal of Philosophy, Psychology and Scientific Methods* 15 (1918): 85–96. [*Middle Works* 11:378–87.]

Christian Science Monitor, 31 August 1918, p. 5.

Cicero, Marcus Tullius. *De Re Publica*. In *Scripta Quae Manserunt Omnia*, edited by Reinholdus Klotz, vol. 2. Leipzig: B. G. Teubneri, 1874.

The Clarke Papers: Selections from the Papers of William Clarke. Vol. 1. Edited by C. H. Firth. Westminster: Camden Society, 1891.

"The Convention of Polish Immigrants." *Wici* 5 (September 1918): 1–14.

Corwin, Edward H. Lewinski. *The Political History of Poland*. New York: Polish Book Importing Co., 1917.

Cram, Ralph Adams. *The Nemesis of Mediocrity*. Boston: Marshall Jones Co., 1917.

Cumberland, Richard. *De Legibus Naturae*. London: E. Flesher, 1672.

Dewey, John. *Democracy and Education*. New York: Macmillan Co., 1916. [*Middle Works* 9.]

———. *John Dewey: Lectures in China, 1919–1920*. Translated and edited by Robert W. Clopton and Tsuin-chen Ou. Honolulu: University Press of Hawaii, 1973.

———. "The Logic of Judgments of Practise." *Journal of Philosophy, Psychology and Scientific Methods* 12 (1915): 505–23, 533–43. Republished in *Essays in Experimental Logic*. Chicago: University of Chicago Press, 1916. [*Middle Works* 8:14–82.]

Eachard, John. *Mr. Hobbs's State of Nature Considered, in a Dialogue between Philautus and Timothy*. 5th ed. In *Dr. Eachard's Works*, 11th ed. London: J. Phillips, 1705.

Figgis, John Neville. *The Divine Right of Kings*. 2d ed. Cambridge: At the University Press, 1914.

———. *Studies of Political Thought from Gerson to Grotius, 1414–1625*. Cambridge: At the University Press, 1907.

Free Poland 4 (16 June 1918): 226.

Harding, Gardner L. "China and the World War." *Current History* 6 (1917): 100–104.

Harrington, James. *The Oceana and Other Works*, edited by John Toland. 3d ed. London: A. Millar, 1747. [*The Commonwealth of Oceana*; *The Prerogative of Popular Government*.]

Hobbes, Thomas. *Behemoth; or, The Long Parliament*. Edited by Ferdinand Tönnies. London: Simpkin, Marshall, and Co., 1889.

———. *The Elements of Law, Natural and Politic*. Edited by Ferdinand Tönnies. London: Simpkin, Marshall, and Co., 1889.

———. *The English Works of Thomas Hobbes*. Edited by William Molesworth. 11 vols. London: John Bohn, 1839–45. [*An Answer to a Book Published by Dr. Bramhall Called "The Catching of the Leviathan,"* vol. 4; *Behemoth*, vol. 6; *Considerations upon the Reputation, Loyalty, Manners, and Religion of Thomas Hobbes*, vol. 4; *De Corpore Politico: or, The Elements of Law*, vol. 4; *A Dialogue between a Philosopher and a Student of the Common Laws of England*, vol. 6; *Elements of Philosophy*, vol. 1; *An Historical Narration concerning Heresy*, vol. 4; *Human Nature*, vol. 4; *Leviathan*, vol. 3; *Philosophical Rudiments*, vol. 2.]

———. *The English Works of Thomas Hobbes*. Edited by William Molesworth. Vol. 7. London: Longman, Brown, Green, and Longmans, 1845. [*Letters and Other Pieces*; *Seven Philosophical Problems*; *Six Lessons to the Savilian Professors of the Mathematics*.]

Hobson, John Atkinson. *Democracy after the War*. London: George Allen and Unwin, 1917.

Holcombe, Chester. "A Sketch of the Relations between China and the Western World." In *China and the Far East*, edited by George H. Blakeslee. New York: Thomas Y. Crowell and Co., 1910.

Huc, Évariste R. *A Journey through the Chinese Empire*. Vol. 1. New York: Harper and Bros., 1855.

James, William. *Pragmatism: A New Name for Some Old Ways of Thinking*. New York: Longmans, Green, and Co., 1907.

Japan Weekly Chronicle, 17 July 1919, pp. 81–82.

Kerner, Robert J. Review of *The Political History of Poland* by Edward H. Lewinski-Corwin. *American Historical Review* 23 (1918): 846–47.

Kuryer Polski (Milwaukee, Wis.), 9 June 1918, p. 3.

"Labor and the New Social Order: A Report on Reconstruction by the Sub-Committee of the British Labor Party." *New Republic*, 16 February 1918, part 2, pp. 1–12.

Lawson, George. *An Examination of the Political Part of Mr. Hobbs, His "Leviathan."* London: Francis Tyton, 1657.

Levinson, Salmon O. "The Legal Status of War." *New Republic* 14 (1918): 171–73. [*Middle Works* 11:388–92.]

Locke, John. *The Philosophy of Locke*. Edited by John E. Russell. New York: Henry Holt and Co., 1891.

Marot, Helen. *Creative Impulse in Industry*. New York: E. P. Dutton and Co., 1918.

Milton, John. *Angli pro populo Anglicano defensio*. London: Du Gardianis, 1650.

"Mr. Dmowski's Instructions Sent from the Lausanne Agency to the Interparty Circle in Warsaw, May 1917." *Wici* 4 (31 December 1917): 1076–89.

New York Times, 8 September 1918, sec. 2, p. 2.

Perry, Ralph Barton. "Dewey and Urban on Value Judgments." *Journal of Philosophy, Psychology and Scientific Methods* 14 (1917): 169–81. [*Middle Works* 11:361–74.]

———. "The Truth-Problem. II." *Journal of Philosophy, Psychology and Scientific Methods* 13 (1916): 561–73.

Plato. *Theaetetus*. In *The Dialogues of Plato*, edited by Benjamin Jowett, vol. 2. 3d ed. New York: Macmillan Co., 1892.

Polska Partia Socjalistyczna (Pamphlets). London: 1898–1904.

Posner, Stanislas. "La Vie politique en Pologne avant la guerre." *Mercure de France* 114 (1916): 603–27.

President Wilson's State Papers and Addresses. Edited by Albert Shaw. New York: George H. Doran Co., 1918.

"Resolution Passed by the Polish National Defense Committee." *Wici* 5 (14 May 1918): 2.

Ritchie, David G. *Natural Rights*. London: Swan Sonnenschein and Co., 1895.

Robertson, George Croom. *Hobbes*. London: William Blackwood and Sons, 1886.
Shanghai Times, 20 May 1919, p. 7.
Shanghai Times, 5 July 1919, p. 7.
Shibusawa, Eiichi. "America and Japan." *Century* 91 (1916): 541–44.
Singer, Edgar A., Jr. "Consciousness and Behavior: A Reply." *Journal of Philosophy, Psychology and Scientific Methods* 9 (1912): 15–19.
Tadema, Laurence Alma. *Poland, Russia and the War*. London: St. Catherine Press, 1915.
Taylor, Alfred Edward. *The Problem of Conduct*. New York: Macmillan Co., 1901.
Telegram Codzienny (New York, N.Y.), 11 September 1918, p. 2.
Tenison, Thomas. *The Creed of Mr. Hobbes Examined*. 2d ed. London: Francis Tyton, 1671.
"Text of Treaty Signed by Russia." *Current History* 8 (1918): 54–56.
Tönnies, Ferdinand. "Hobbes-Analekten." *Archiv für Geschichte der Philosophie* 17 (1904): 291–317.
———. "Siebzehn Briefe des Thomas Hobbes an Samuel Sorbière." *Archiv für Geschichte der Philosophie* 3 (1890): 58–71, 192–232.
Turczynowicz, Laura de Gozdawa. *When the Prussians Came to Poland*. New York: G. P. Putnam's Sons, 1916.
Veblen, Thorstein. *Imperial Germany and the Industrial Revolution*. New York: Macmillan Co., 1915.
Watson, John B. *Behavior: An Introduction to Comparative Psychology*. New York: Henry Holt and Co., 1914.
Wells, H. G. "The Liberal Fear of Russia." *Harper's Weekly* 59 (1914): 268–70.
Wenley, Robert Mark. *The Life and Work of George Sylvester Morris*. New York: Macmillan Co., 1917.

INDEX

The Collected Works of John Dewey, 1882–1953

Index to The Collected Works of John Dewey, 1882–1953

The Early Works, 1882–1898

Volume 1: 1882–1888, Early Essays and *Leibniz's New Essays*
Volume 2: 1887, *Psychology*
Volume 3: 1889–1892, Essays and *Outlines of a Critical Theory of Ethics*
Volume 4: 1893–1894, Early Essays and *The Study of Ethics: A Syllabus*
Volume 5: 1895–1898, Early Essays

The Middle Works, 1899–1924

Volume 1: 1899–1901, Journal Articles, Book Reviews, and Miscellany Published in the 1899–1901 Period, and *The School and Society,* and *The Educational Situation*
Volume 2: 1902–1903, Journal Articles, Book Reviews, and Miscellany in the 1902–1903 Period, and *Studies in Logical Theory* and *The Child and the Curriculum*
Volume 3: 1903–1906, Journal Articles, Book Reviews, and Miscellany in the 1903–1906 Period
Volume 4: 1907–1909, Journal Articles and Book Reviews in the 1907–1909 Period, and *The Pragmatic Movement of Contemporary Thought* and *Moral Principles in Education*
Volume 5: 1908, *Ethics*
Volume 6: 1910–1911, Journal Articles, Book Reviews, Miscellany in the 1910–1911 Period, and *How We Think*
Volume 7: 1912–1914, Essays, Books Reviews, Encyclopedia Articles in the 1912–1914 Period, and *Interest and Effort in Education*
Volume 8: 1915, Essays and Miscellany in the 1915 Period and *German Philosophy and Politics* and *Schools of To-Morrow*
Volume 9: 1916, *Democracy and Education*
Volume 10: 1916–1917, Journal Articles, Essays, and Miscellany Published in the 1916–1917 Period
Volume 11: 1918–1919, Journal Articles, Essays, and Miscellany Published in the 1918–1919 Period
Volume 12: 1920, Essays, Miscellany, and *Reconstruction in Philosophy* Published during 1920
Volume 13: 1921–1922, Journal Articles, Essays, and Miscellany Published in the 1921–1922 Period
Volume 14: 1922, *Human Nature and Conduct*
Volume 15: 1923–1924, Journal Articles, Essays, and Miscellany Published in the 1923–1924 Period

The Later Works, 1925–1953

Volume 1: 1925, *Experience and Nature*
Volume 2: 1925–1927, Essays, Reviews, Miscellany, and *The Public and Its Problems*
Volume 3: 1927–1928, Essays, Reviews, Miscellany, and "Impressions of Soviet Russia"
Volume 4: 1929, *The Quest for Certainty*
Volume 5: 1929–1930, Essays, *The Sources of a Science of Education*, *Individualism, Old and New*, and *Construction and Criticism*
Volume 6: 1931–1932, Essays, Reviews, and Miscellany
Volume 7: 1932, *Ethics*
Volume 8: 1933, Essays and *How We Think*, Revised Edition
Volume 9: 1933–1934, Essays, Reviews, Miscellany, and *A Common Faith*
Volume 10: 1934, *Art as Experience*
Volume 11: 1935–1937, Essays, Reviews, Trotsky Inquiry, Miscellany, and *Liberalism and Social Action*
Volume 12: 1938, *Logic: The Theory of Inquiry*
Volume 13: 1938–1939, *Experience and Education*, *Freedom and Culture*, *Theory of Valuation*, and Essays
Volume 14: 1939–1941, Essays, Reviews, and Miscellany
Volume 15: 1942–1948, Essays, Reviews, and Miscellany
Volume 16: 1949–1952, Essays, Typescripts, and *Knowing and the Known*
Volume 17: 1885–1953, Miscellaneous Writings